antitrust issues in intellectual property law

Bradford P. Lyerla
Editor-in-Chief

Section of Intellectual Property Law
AMERICAN BAR ASSOCIATION

Cover Design: Amy Mandel, ABA Section of Intellectual Property Law;
Best Design Chicago, Inc.

Printed in the United States of America

20 19 18 17 16   5 4 3 2 1

Library of Congress Cataloging-in-Publication Data

Names: Lyerla, Bradford P., author. | Roney, Edward M., author. | Newman, David L., author. | Noonan, Kevin E., author. | Van Horn, Shawn M., author.
Title: Antitrust issues in intellectual property law / by Bradford P. Lyerla, Edward M. Roney, David L. Newman, Kevin E. Noonan, and Shawn M. Van Horn.
Description: First edition. | Chicago : American Bar Association, 2016. | Includes bibliographical references and index.
Identifiers: LCCN 2016018449 | ISBN 9781634254458 (print : alk. paper)
Subjects: LCSH: Antitrust law—United States. | Intellectual property—United States.
Classification: LCC KF3116 .L94 2016 | DDC 346.7304/8—dc23
LC record available at https://lccn.loc.gov/2016018449

Contents

Preface

Antitrust Issues in Intellectual Property Law (2015 Edition) is a concise, handy reference that collects case law dealing with every aspect of antitrust issues with intellectual property law. This book presents the cases decided in the past year on each point, as well as relevant earlier cases, and is a resource for anyone who has to know or give an opinion on antitrust issues in intellectual property law, including:

- new lawyers and seasoned litigators
- jurists
- federal judges
- intellectual property attorneys
- antitrust attorneys
- patent attorneys
- in-house counsel

This publication was created to provide you with accurate and authoritative information concerning the subject matter covered; however, this publication was not necessarily prepared by persons licensed to practice law in a particular jurisdiction.

Acknowledgments

The authors would like to acknowledge and thank the partners of their respective law firms. Writing a book like this is a big commitment. It takes a lot of time, and some of that time unavoidably takes away from other matters. We want to thank our partners for supporting our effort. That support took many forms, but an important one is that other deadlines have been extended and an occasional tardy deadline has been forgiven. This book would not have been possible without such forbearance from our colleagues. We believe that an effort such as ours in writing this book is for the greater good and, in the end, when the scores are tallied, the benefit from our time and effort in writing this book will more than outweigh the costs of the occasional distraction that writing has caused us. Happily, those we practice law with seem to see it in the same way that we do. So a sincere "thank you" to our partners and colleagues.

Also, Kevin wishes to thank Andrea Orth, Nicole Grimm, and Daniel Organ for legal research supporting Chapter 4, and Nicole Grimm and Daniel Organ for legal research supporting Chapter 5. For myself, I want to thank Shaun Van Horn for his cheerful acceptance of a number of thankless tasks relating to all of the chapters in material ways. He has been a joy to work with. And finally, for all of us, we want to thank Ed Roney, our managing editor. This book was Ed's idea, and his organizational skills and tireless efforts made it happen.

BPL

About the Authors

Bradford P. Lyerla, Editor-in-Chief, co-chair of Jenner & Block's Patent Litigation and Counselling Practice, is a nationally recognized trial lawyer who focuses on patent and trade secret litigation. Recognized as a leader in his field by numerous organizations, he is highly regarded by peers and clients alike for his trial skills, litigation wisdom, and strategic thinking. He has tried dozens of high-stakes trials and argued numerous appeals representing a who's who of prominent corporations involved in technologies ranging from pharmaceuticals and medical devices to food and chemical manufacturing to communications and computing.

Edward M. Roney, Managing Editor, is an attorney with Coats and Bennett PLLC. His practice is focused in the areas of patent litigation and post-grant reviews, trade secret and unfair competition litigation, and intellectual property licensing. He represents a diverse range of clients from emerging growth to Fortune 500 companies across many industries and technologies. He has negotiated and drafted numerous technology and software licenses and has represented leading consumer electronics companies with the patenting of their technology. Mr. Roney is a former technology executive, having co-founded a fabless semiconductor manufacturer, which provided highly integrated chipsets, software, and licensed intellectual property to the world's top cellular handset manufacturers. Further, *Inc.* magazine recognized him for having one of the fastest-growing companies in the United States, and the *Wall Street Journal* honored him for his leadership in wireless communications.

David L. Newman is a partner and chair of the Intellectual Property Group at Gould & Ratner, LLP. Mr. Newman focuses his practice on intellectual property law, including patents, trademarks, copyrights, and trade secrets. His experience includes handling litigation involving intellectual property, preparing and prosecuting applications for obtaining various types of intellectual properties, and opinion work involving business methods, computers, consumer goods, electronic commerce, mechanical devices, medical devices, pharmaceuticals, and telecommunications. Mr. Newman has handled numerous litigations involving U.S. and foreign patents, unfair trade practices, copyrights, trade dress, trademarks, trade secrets, antitrust, and breach of contract throughout the country. He has been involved in all aspects of practice before the U.S. Patent and Trademark Office, including patent appeals, reissues, and reexamination proceedings. Mr. Newman has taught courses involving claim drafting for patent applications and is a periodic guest lecturer on intellectual property topics at the DePaul University Kellstadt Graduate School of Business.

Kevin E. Noonan, Ph.D., is a partner with McDonnell Boehnen Hulbert & Berghoff LLP. An experienced biotechnology patent lawyer, Dr. Noonan brings more than ten years of extensive work as a molecular biologist studying high-technology problems to serving the unique needs of his clients. His practice involves all aspects of patent prosecution, interferences, and litigation. He represents pharmaceutical companies both large and small on a myriad of issues, as well as several universities in both patenting and licensing to outside investors. He has also filed amicus briefs to district courts, the Federal Circuit, and the Supreme Court involving patenting issues relevant to biotechnology. Dr. Noonan is a frequent speaker, commentator, and author on a variety of intellectual property law topics. He is a founding author of the Patent Docs weblog, a site focusing on biotechnology and pharmaceutical patent law. In 2010, he was interviewed for a segment that aired on the television program *60 Minutes* that addressed the issue of gene patenting.

Shaun M. Van Horn is a partner with Jenner & Block LLP. Mr. Van Horn litigates matters and counsels clients in competition law, intellectual property, and technology disputes. He counsels clients on a range of antitrust topics and across numerous industries, including healthcare, pharmaceuticals, industrial chemicals, construction, textiles, medical equipment, municipal airports, automotive, social media, dairy products, egg products, and intermodal shipping services. Mr. Van Horn focuses his practice on competition law matters, particularly concerning the intersection of competition law and intellectual property. He represents clients in connection with antitrust issues at the Department of Justice and in premerger review by the Federal Trade Commission. Mr. Van Horn contributes regularly to the ABA Antitrust IP Committee's e-Bulletin.

chapter 1

Introduction

I. Overview of Intellectual Property and Antitrust Law

This book is about the intersection of intellectual property law and antitrust law. It is a busy intersection and there is no reason to think that the heavy traffic will abate anytime soon. In the past year alone, Congress, regulators, and courts have all made significant statements affecting the historical balance between the competing policies underlying intellectual property and antitrust law. It may be that we now are in the midst of restriking that balance. Time will tell.

This book is a snapshot. This, the inaugural edition, focuses on developments in intellectual property and antitrust law that have occurred in the past 24 months. It is expected that this book will be followed by biannual editions that will focus on new developments in intellectual property and antitrust law. There is every reason to believe that the law in these areas will continue to develop rapidly, and this book is intended to help the intellectual property practitioner remain informed on recent developments and the numerous ways in which antitrust law limits, disciplines, and counterbalances intellectual property law and vice versa.

This is not a treatise. This book is aimed at intellectual property lawyers and it is not encyclopedic. There are numerous issues in antitrust law that are not addressed here. Just as there are many important intellectual property topics that are not addressed here. The subject matter of this book is limited to where the two overlap, and outcomes for clients will be directly affected by the interplay between intellectual property and antitrust law.

This book is organized into five chapters. Chapters 2, 3, and 4 examine IP-antitrust issues broadly, from procurement and acquisition to licensing and enforcement. Chapter 5 discusses the unique antitrust issues that arise under the Hatch-Waxman Act regarding disputes between brand-name and generic drug companies, while Chapter 6 focuses on antitrust issues affecting the enforcement of IP adopted by a standard-setting organization.

Chapter 2 discusses the antitrust concerns that arise in the acquisition, procurement, and ownership of IP. The FTC and DOJ have, in recent years, indicated that they will focus on the competition risks associated with the acquisition of IP by companies already holding related IP. For example, in 2013, the DOJ reviewed multiple sizeable patent portfolio purchases, particularly Google's acquisition of Motorola Mobility's wireless device patents, which included many standard-essential patents. Likewise, the FTC has entered into numerous consent decrees across a range of industries to require the acquiring party to enter into long-term licenses or to divest certain IP assets for the sake of competition.

IP procurement faces similar antitrust scrutiny, but in the context of private litigation and usually many years after the IP has been procured. In particular, IP holders continue to face *Walker Process* claims from competitors, who argue that they procured their IP by fraud and therefore do not benefit from the limited antitrust immunity conferred by the patent. Of course, the competitor in a *Walker Process* claim must prove that the IP holder committed an antitrust violation, independent of the fraud, in order to succeed on the claim. This can be a difficult challenge. In *In re Lipitor Antitrust Litigation*, for example, direct purchasers of Lipitor identified substantial evidence that Pfizer had improperly hidden information from the USPTO to acquire a follow-on patent to its blockbuster anticholesterol pharmaceutical, but the court concluded in light of prior litigation between Pfizer and others that the fraud claim was not plausible under *Twombly*.

Even when a company legitimately procures or otherwise acquires its IP, antitrust issues may arise from its mere ownership of the IP. Private litigation in this area focuses on both unilateral and group action by IP owners who refuse to provide third-party access to their IP. One recent high-profile example of this class of cases is *Novell, Inc. v. Microsoft Corp.*, in which the Tenth Circuit affirmed Microsoft's right to refuse to share its Windows-related IP with software developers, including Novell, the maker of WordPerfect, even though Microsoft's decision to stop sharing its IP was arguably made for the specific purpose of enabling Microsoft's competing software products to overtake its direct competitors.

Chapter 3 addresses the antitrust issues that arise from the licensing arrangements entered into by the IP holder. Although antitrust issues sometimes arise from licensing arrangements under unilateral action (i.e., refusing to license) and during mergers and acquisitions (i.e., collaterally impacting existing license arrangements), the majority of antitrust cases in the licensing area involve an antitrust claim based upon the relationship between the licensor and licensee. Chapter 3 lays out the analytical framework that the agencies and courts use to evaluate competition concerns with licensing. That analytical framework, which is embodied in the FTC/DOJ *Guidelines for the Licensing of Intellectual Property*, starts from the premise that IP shall be treated like other types of property. The agencies recognize that licensing arrangements tend to be pro-competitive and they explicitly reject an outdated presumption that an IP right automatically confers market power.

Against the backdrop of this analytical framework for evaluating IP licensing, Chapter 3 explores more than fifteen different types of licensing arrangements into which parties enter and the antitrust issues relevant to each. The licensing types range from basic price, output, and field-of-use restricted licenses to licenses involving exclusivity, modified royalty structures, grantback clauses, and cross-licensing provisions. Some of the licensing types, especially exclusive cross-licenses and exclusive grantback clauses, can raise substantial antitrust concerns. Some arrangements may also invoke IP doctrines related to antitrust, such as patent exhaustion, patent misuse, or coercive reciprocity.

Chapter 4 details how antitrust-IP issues arise during different stages of the litigation process. The chapter begins by examining *MiniFrame v. Microsoft* and a series of suits involving SanDisk. These examples highlight the tension between IP and antitrust where the owner of certain IP implements complex, though ultimately legal, restrictions on the use of its IP. These cases are meant to give the reader an understanding of the common legal issues, such as market power and modes of analysis, that drive the outcomes in IP-antitrust litigation.

The chapter then marches through the various stages of litigation, noting some of the most prevalent IP-antitrust issues. There are procedural questions, such as which court has jurisdiction over the antitrust claims and which law shall apply to those claims. A review of recent cases highlights some of the core elements upon which a plaintiff's antitrust claim will rise or fall, such as whether the plaintiff has "antitrust standing," the complaint adequately defines the relevant market, or the plaintiff sufficiently details the alleged anticompetitive conduct.

Some recent litigations raise unique factual issues, such *Cascades v. RPX*, which concerns whether a defensive patent pooling entity qualifies as a monopsony under the Sherman Act where its members refuse to negotiate licenses except through the collective patent pool, and a lawsuit between Capital One and Intellectual Ventures, in which Capital One counterclaimed that the plaintiff patent troll violates antitrust laws by using the threat of serial litigation to coerce patent settlements.

Finally, Chapter 4 examines *Walker Process* claims, the sham litigation exception to the *Noerr-Pennington* defense, and the patent misuse defense.

Chapter 5 digs into the tide of litigation over the past decade regarding pay-for-delay settlements arising under the Hatch-Waxman Act. By virtue of the unique framework created by Congress to facilitate generic drug companies' entry into the market, brand-name pharmaceutical companies are incentivized to pay their generic rivals a sum of money (or other benefits) to not enter into competition with the name-brand product. The chapter discusses the number, types, and trends of reverse payment settlements to date, as well as the pros and cons of such settlements.

The chapter also details the federal appellate history of antitrust challenges to reverse payment settlements, which began with the Sixth Circuit's decision to strike down one such settlement in *In re Cardizem*. Following that decision, however, at least four other federal appellate courts came to the opposite conclusion, casting doubt upon the Sixth Circuit's holding and distinguishing the Sixth Circuit's case on its facts. These appellate decisions culminated in the Supreme Court's 2012 decision in *FTC v. Actavis*, which held that reverse payment settlements would not be immune from antitrust scrutiny but would instead be evaluated under the rule of reason test. The chapter carefully analyzes the *Actavis* holding, and its dissent, and considers how that holding may impact subsequent reverse payment antitrust claims.

Chapter 6 is devoted to the antitrust concerns that exist when certain IP is incorporated into a standard set by a standard-setting organization (SSO). Over time, it has become customary for SSOs to demand that if a party's IP is incorporated into one of the SSO's standards, then the party must agree to license its IP on fair, reasonable, and nondiscriminatory terms (FRAND). The chapter evaluates the case law and agency guidance that has built up on this topic. Courts now routinely hold that a FRAND commitment is enforceable by third parties as beneficiaries of the commitment to the SSO. A corollary to this rule is that parties working with an SSO to set a standard must disclose to the SSO any IP that the party believes would be infringed by compliance with the standard.

A particularly salient SSO issue in the past few years has been whether the owner of a patent that has been incorporated into a standard, called a "standard-essential patent" or SEP, has the right to pursue injunctive relief notwithstanding a prior commitment to abide by FRAND. It appears now that the Federal Circuit and the agencies believe that injunctive relief may sometimes be available even to a patent holder who has agreed to license under FRAND. The courts and agencies are seeking to strike the proper balance between providing aggressive protection for IP so as to encourage innovation and incentivize participation in pro-competitive standard setting and, on the other hand, to avoid the risk that holders of SEPs will extract unwarranted licensing fees based purely upon the lock-in effect of standard setting. European antitrust authorities are in the process of confronting the same issues and seek to strike a similar balance.

chapter 2

Antitrust Issues in the Acquisition, Procurement, and Ownership of Intellectual Property

I. Introduction

Parties considering mergers, acquisitions, joint ventures, or joint development agreements should consider whether these collaborations will limit or appear to limit competition. They must be careful to properly procure their intellectual property to avoid later antitrust disputes. In managing their intellectual property portfolios, intellectual property holders also should be aware of potential antitrust issues associated with their refusal to sell or license their property, especially if such refusal is done in concert with others. FTC and DOJ officials recently reaffirmed that they will continue to focus on competition concerns in the patent area, including portfolio acquisitions.[1] This chapter will address antitrust issues associated with acquiring, procuring, and owning intellectual property.

II. Acquisition

The acquisition of intellectual property presents three antitrust questions: (1) what markets may be affected, (2) how will the acquisition affect market power in those markets, and (3) what are permissible methods of intellectual property acquisition?

1. ABA, Intellectual Prop. Comm., *DOJ and FTC Will Continue to Focus on Competition Concerns in the Patent Area,* TIDBITS, Mar. 15, 2013.

Sections 2.1, 2.2, and 2.3 discuss three kinds of relevant markets that may be implicated: goods, technology, and innovation markets. Sections 2.4 and 2.5 discuss important principles for assessing whether market power may exist: monopolization and barriers to entry. Sections 2.6, 2.7, 2.8, and 2.9 discuss antitrust issues that arise when acquiring intellectual property in various ways: exclusive versus non-exclusive licenses, joint ventures, cross-licensing and pooling arrangements, and grantbacks.

§ 2.1 Goods Markets

Related markets of goods can be relevant to evaluating the competitive effects of an acquisition or licensing arrangement. For example, "[a] restraint in a licensing arrangement may have competitive effects in markets for final or intermediate goods made using the intellectual property, or it may have effects upstream, in markets for goods that are used as inputs, along with the intellectual property, to the production of other goods."[2] When reviewing a transfer of intellectual property through an acquisition or license, federal agencies evaluate the delineation of the goods market as detailed in Section 1 of the U.S. Department of Justice and Federal Trade Commission's *Horizontal Merger Guidelines*.[3]

In the context of a proposed acquisition of intellectual property, antitrust authorities analyze the relevant product market to determine whether the acquisition will have anticompetitive effects in that market. For example, the DOJ closely examined the product market for wireless device operating systems in connection with three separate proposed acquisitions.[4] At the end of 2011, Google's Android accounted for approximately 46 percent of the U.S. smartphone operating system platform subscribers, while Apple, Research In Motion, and Microsoft held 30, 15, and 6 percent of subscribers, respectively.[5] The DOJ scrutinized three patent portfolio acquisitions: (1) Google's acquisition of 17,000 issued patents and 6,800 applications from Motorola Mobility, including hundreds of Standard Essential Patents (SEPs) relevant to wireless devices; (2) the

2. U.S. Dep't of Justice & Fed. Trade Comm'n, Antitrust Guidelines for the Licensing of Intellectual Property § 3.2 (Apr. 6, 1995) [hereinafter Antitrust-IP Licensing Guidelines], *available at* http://www.justice.gov/atr/public/guidelines/0558.htm.

3. U.S. Dep't of Justice & Fed. Trade Comm'n, Horizontal Merger Guidelines § 5.2 (Aug. 19, 2010) [hereinafter Horizontal Merger Guidelines] ("The Agencies normally calculate market shares for all firms that currently produce products in the relevant market, subject to the availability of data.").

4. Dep't of Justice, Statement of the Department of Justice's Antitrust Division on Its Decision to Close Its Investigations of Google Inc.'s Acquisition of Motorola Mobility Holdings Inc. and the Acquisitions of Certain Patents by Apple Inc., Microsoft Corp. and Research In Motion Ltd. (Feb. 13, 2012).

5. *Id.*

acquisition by Rockstar Bidco, a partnership including RIM, Microsoft, and Apple, of 6,000 patents and patent applications, including many SEPs relevant to wireless devices, from Nortel; and (3) Apple's acquisition of patents held by CPTN Holdings LLC, formerly owned by Novell.[6] After carefully analyzing the product market and relying on assurances from the acquiring companies about their intended licensing practices with respect to the newly acquired patents, the DOJ determined that the acquisitions were unlikely to substantially lessen competition.[7]

The FTC and the lawyers for Integrated Device Technologies, Inc. and PLX Technology, Inc. disputed the relevant market to consider when analyzing the proposed purchase of PLX.[8] The FTC contended that the relevant market was PCIe switches.[9] In contrast, PLX contended that PCIe switches were not a relevant market because PCIe switches were part of a wider "systems interconnect solutions" market, in which PCIe competes with various data transfer protocols including Ethernet and InfiniBand.[10] FTC Commissioner Julie Brill's public comments about the case suggest that the FTC believed, after interviews with IDT and PLX customers, that customers would most likely pay the increased price and not switch to the alleged substitutes for PCIe switches if faced with a price increase following the merger.[11]

Other product markets involving patents that have been the subject of recent antitrust inquiry include over-the-counter motion sickness medication;[12] generic pharmaceuticals to supplement fluoride;[13] the market for air-conditioning recycling, recovery, and recharge services;[14] and magnesium plates for photoengraving applications.[15]

§ 2.2 Technology Markets

Technology markets "consist of the intellectual property that is licensed . . . and its close substitutes—that is, the technologies or goods that are close enough substitutes significantly to constrain the exercise of market power

6. *Id.*

7. *Id.*

8. Julie Brill, Comm'r, Speech on Merger Enforcement in High-Tech Markets (Jan. 28, 2013).

9. *Id.*

10. *Id.*

11. *Id.*

12. Complaint, *In re Prestige Brands Holdings, Inc. & Insight Pharm. Corp.*, No. C-4487 (F.T.C. Aug. 27, 2014).

13. Complaint, *In re Endo Health Solutions, Inc. et al.*, No. C-4430 (F.T.C. Jan. 29, 2014).

14. Press Release, FTC, FTC Order Restores Competition in U.S. Market for Equipment Used to Recharge Vehicle Air Conditioning Systems (Nov. 26, 2012).

15. Press Release, FTC, FTC Order Restores Competition in Market for Magnesium Plates for Photoengraving (Oct. 12, 2012).

with respect to the intellectual property that is licensed."[16] The federal agencies rely upon technology markets to analyze the competitive effects of a licensing arrangement when "intellectual property are marketed separately from the products in which they are used."[17] For example, when a patented product is sold with an implied license permitting its use, there is no need for a separate analysis of the technology market.[18] When technology markets are relevant, courts and agencies consider whether other technologies are alternatives.[19]

Magnesium Elektron's acquisition of Revere Graphics Worldwide, Inc. in September 2007 resulted in a single company possessing the intellectual property used to manufacture magnesium plates for photoengraving applications.[20] In 2012, the FTC compelled Magnesium Elektron to provide licenses to its intellectual property and transfer technical know-how to a potential competitor, Universal Engineering, to enable competition in the technology market for the manufacture of magnesium plates for photoengraving applications.[21]

The FTC had a similar dispute with Honeywell International, Inc. regarding Honeywell's proposed acquisition of Intermec, Inc.[22] According to the FTC, Honeywell, Intermec, and Motorola are the only 2D scan engine firms in the United States that "have deep and broad portfolios of relevant IP that insulate them and their customers from infringement suits."[23] A key issue in the complaint, however, involved identifying the relevant market for 2D scan engines. "2D scan engines are hardware components that include a two-dimensional ("2D") image sensor and translate a barcode into a digital format that computer processors can interpret and analyze."[24] The FTC took the position that so-called "1D" scan engines and scanning functions found on smartphones and other consumer devices are not substitutes for 2D scan engines because 1D scan engines are unable to read most types of 2D images and therefore do not constrain prices of 2D scan engines. Ultimately, to obtain FTC approval, Honeywell agreed to

16. ANTITRUST-IP LICENSING GUIDELINES, *supra* note 2, § 3.2.2.

17. *Id.*

18. *Id.* at 8 n.19.

19. *See, e.g.*, *DSM Desotech, Inc. v. 3D Sys. Corp.*, 2013 WL 389003, at *11 (N.D. Ill. Jan. 31, 2013) (granting summary judgment to defendant where court found there was no genuine dispute that other technologies were alternatives to stereolithography).

20. Press Release, FTC, FTC Order Restores Competition in Market for Magnesium Plates for Photoengraving (Oct. 12, 2012).

21. *Id.*

22. Complaint, *In re Honeywell Int'l, Inc.*, No. C-4418 (Nov. 22, 2013).

23. *Id.* at 3.

24. *Id.* at 1.

provide 12-year licenses for both Honeywell and Intermec's patent portfolios to some of the major consumers of 2D scan engines.[25]

The FTC also challenges transactions that may limit the availability of licenses for intellectual property. In 2015, Eli Lilly and Co. proposed to acquire Novartis Animal Health for $5.4 billion. Both companies engaged in development and licensing of canine heartworm parasiticides.[26] The proposed transaction would result in one firm, Eli Lilly, controlling more than 43 percent of the relevant market.[27] The FTC alleged that this combination would allow Eli Lilly to increase the pricing for canine heartworm parasiticides.[28] The FTC approved the merger, subject to Eli Lilly's agreement to divest its canine heartworm parasiticide business, to ensure availability to parasiticide licenses.[29]

§ 2.3 Innovation Markets

Sometimes a "licensing arrangement may have competitive effects on innovation that cannot be adequately addressed through the analysis of goods or technology markets."[30] In these cases, the federal agencies analyze the competitive effect of the licensing arrangement in a separate innovation market.[31] An innovation market concerns the development of goods that do not yet exist or the development of new or improved goods or processes in geographic markets where there is no actual or likely potential competition in the relevant goods."[32]

Concerns regarding innovation markets often animate agency action during a merger. For example, the FTC filed a complaint against Houghton International, Inc. for its purchase of D.A. Stuart GmbH because as a result of that acquisition, Houghton would have control of almost 75 percent of the North American market for aluminum hot rolling oil.[33] The agency was concerned that "the acquisition could decrease innovation for this vital input into aluminum manufacturing."[34] Similarly, in Nielsen's

---

25. Press Release, FTC, FTC Approves Final Order Settling Charges That Honeywell's Acquisition of Intermec Was Anticompetitive in U.S. Market for Two Dimensional Bar Code Scanners (Nov. 27, 2013).

26. Complaint, *In re Eli Lilly & Co. & Novartis AG*, No. C-4500, ¶ 5 (Dec. 19, 2014).

27. *Id.* ¶ 7.

28. *Id.* ¶ 9.

29. Press Release, FTC, FTC Approves Final Order Preserving Competition in Market for Treating Heartworm Disease in Dogs (Mar. 4, 2015).

30. Antitrust-IP Licensing Guidelines, *supra* note 2, § 3.2.3.

31. *Id.*

32. *Id.*

33. Press Release, FTC, Houghton International Agrees to Sell Aluminum Production Assets to Settle Charges That 2008 Acquisition of Stuart Was Anticompetitive (July 14, 2010).

34. *Id.*

proposed acquisition of Arbitron, Inc., the FTC filed a complaint based upon its apparent concern that the merger would negatively affect innovation "by eliminating future competition between Nielson and Arbitron for the provision of national syndicated cross-platform audience measurement services."[35]

The risk of reduced product development motivated, in part, the FTC's opposition to the proposed merger between Medtronic, Inc. and Covidien PLC.[36] Medtronic proposed to merge with Covidien in exchange for cash and stock valued at $42.9 billion. However, Medtronic and Covidien were the only two companies developing drug-coated balloon catheters indicated for the fem-pop artery, which are used to treat peripheral artery disease in the fem-pop artery. In the United States, only one company, C.R. Bard, Inc., supplied such catheters. Covidien and Medtronic were in clinical-stage trials to enter the U.S. market with competing products.[37] The FTC complaint alleged that the merger would eliminate competition between Covidien and Medtronic, increase the likelihood that the combined entity would delay a product launch, and would reduce research and development for drug-coated balloon catheters.[38] To garner agency support for the deal, the parties agreed that Covidien would divest its drug-coated balloon catheter business to a third party, helping to ensure continued research and development in this area.[39]

The FTC's consent agreement with Google in 2013 reflected agency concerns with respect to two innovation markets—innovation in the wireless devices market and innovation in the online advertising market. Google's acquisition of Motorola's patent portfolio in 2012 permitted Google to threaten to seek injunctions against other mobile device companies for alleged infringement of former Motorola standard essential patents.[40] Following the FTC's investigation, Google agreed to make changes to ensure competition "in the online marketplace and in the market for innovative wireless devices."[41] In addition to Google committing to license its SEPs on FRAND terms, Google "promised to provide all websites the option to keep their content out of Google's vertical search offerings, while still

35. Complaint, *In re Nielsen Holdings N.V. & Arbitron, Inc.*, No. C-4439 (Feb. 24, 2014).

36. Complaint, *In re Medtronic, Inc. & Covidien PLC*, No. C-4503 (Jan. 13, 2015).

37. *Id.* ¶ 7.

38. *Id.* ¶ 9.

39. Press Release, FTC, FTC Approves Final Order Preserving Future Competition in the Market for Drug-Coated Balloon Catheters Used to Treat Peripheral Artery Disease (Jan. 21, 2015).

40. Press Release, FTC, Google Agrees to Change Its Business Practices to Resolve FTC Competition Concerns in the Markets for Devices Like Smart Phones, Games and Tablets, and in Online Research (Jan. 3, 2013).

41. *Id.*

having them appear in Google's general or 'organic' web search results."[42] This action was in response to allegations that "Google misappropriated content, such as user reviews and start ratings, from competing websites in order to improve its own vertical offerings, such as Google Local and Google Shopping."[43] The agency had raised concerns that this practice "might chill firms' incentives to innovate on the Internet."[44]

Where the government determines, however, that a proposed merger will not chill innovation, no corrective action is necessary. The FTC investigated Zillow, Inc.'s proposed acquisition of Trulia, Inc. in 2014. Zillow and Trulia operated the largest and second-largest consumer-facing web portals for home buying that sell advertising space to real estate agents seeking to attract customers buying and selling homes.[45] The FTC opened an investigation due to evidence that the two companies competed closely with each other for consumer traffic and for real estate advertising dollars. A focus of the investigation was "whether the merger would reduce competition on the consumer-facing side of the platforms, *i.e.*, whether the merger would substantially lessen competition for consumers interested in researching home buying or selling online." The investigation concluded that "the combined entity will continue to have strong incentives to develop new features in order to grow its consumer audience."[46] The FTC found no other competition risks and closed the investigation.

§ 2.4 Monopolization

Though the grant of a patent confers a limited right of monopoly on the patent holder, antitrust law applies when a party seeks to monopolize a market through the acquisition of patents. Federal agencies will thus analyze certain transfers of intellectual property rights using the standards typically used to review mergers.[47] Section 7 of the Clayton Act prohibits merger if "in any line of commerce or in any activity affecting commerce in any section of the country, the effect of such acquisition may be substantially to lessen competition, or to tend to create a monopoly."[48] It has long been accepted that a party's action to acquire patents, even though not in and of itself unlawful, violates the antitrust laws when the patents are acquired as part of an overall monopolization scheme.[49]

42. *Id.*

43. *Id.*

44. *Id.*

45. Statement of Commissioner Ohlhausen, Commissioner Wright, and Commissioner McSweeny Concerning Zillow, Inc./Trulia, Inc., FTC File No. 141-0214 (Feb. 19, 2015).

46. *Id.*

47. Antitrust-IP Licensing Guidelines, *supra* note 2, § 5.7.

48. Horizontal Merger Guidelines, *supra* note 3, § 1

49. *See Kobe, Inc. v. Dempsey Pump Co.*, 198 F.2d 416 (10th Cir. 1952).

Where a proposed merger threatens to create a monopoly in a given market, the regulatory agencies may block the merger or seek to compel licensing of key intellectual property as a condition to approve the merger. For example, the FTC conditioned Robert Bosch GmbH's acquisition of SPX Service Solutions U.S. LLC on an agreement to grant manufacturers of equipment used to recharge vehicle air-conditioning systems licenses to key patents that they need to compete in the market for such equipment.[50] According to the FTC, Bosch's acquisition of SPX would give it a "virtual monopoly" in the market for air-conditioning recycling, recovery, and recharge (ACRRR) devices. Moreover, SPX held various ACRRR standard-essential patents based on the industry standards set by SAE International. The FTC obligated Bosch not to "pursue any actions for injunctive relief on these patents and to make them available on a royalty free basis to implementers of the relevant SAE standards in the ACRRR market." The FTC further required that Bosch deliver to SAE "a letter of assurance that going forward it will license any additional SEPs it may acquire or develop for the two relevant industry standards on FRAND terms to any third party that wants to use the technologies covered by the patents to make ACRRR devices in the United States." The FTC had contended that SPX's decision to seek injunctive relief against willing licensees of their FRAND-encumbered SEPs violated section 5 of the FTC Act.[51]

Similarly, where a proposed transaction would remove one party, or one of few parties, from the relevant market that has an incentive to oppose the other party's intellectual property claims, the agency may challenge the transaction. The FTC challenged the proposed acquisition of EagleView Technology Corp. by Verisk Analytics, Inc.[52] The companies competed in the market for rooftop aerial measurement services and reports for insurance purposes, and their combination would have resulted in a single company with more than 90 percent of the market share. Moreover, Verisk "owns the dominant software platform through which insurers use Rooftop Aerial Measurement Products to estimate property damage claims" and, therefore, "has a strong incentive to withstand the threat of patent litigation from EagleView (which already has forced others from the market)."[53] The FTC further contended that the risk of patent litigation from EagleView, combined with a lack of revenue incentive, created a substantial barrier to entry. In support, the FTC pointed to

50. Press Release, FTC, FTC Order Restores Competition in U.S. Market for Equipment Used to Recharge Vehicle Air Conditioning Systems (Nov. 26, 2012).

51. *See also infra* p. 16 discussing merger in context of SEP patents.

52. Complaint, *In re Verisk Analytics, Inc., Ins. Servs. Office, Inc., & EagleView Tech. Corp.*, No. 9363 (F.T.C. Dec. 16, 2014).

53. *Id.* at 2.

numerous cases in which EagleView has "aggressively asserted its patent rights," eliminating most competitors from the market through threats of litigation.[54] Shortly after the FTC filed its challenge, Verisk abandoned the transaction.[55]

Where a merger results in a monopoly in a particular product or technology market, the FTC may take action to restore competition. The FTC compelled Magnesium Elektron to sell necessary intellectual property to a newly created competitor to permit some competition in the manufacture of magnesium plates for photoengraving applications.[56] According to the FTC, Magnesium Elektron's acquisition of Revere Graphics Worldwide, Inc. in 2007 combined the "only two manufacturers and sellers of magnesium plates for photoengraving in the world at that time."[57] The FTC alleged that this combination violated the FTC Act and section 7 of the Clayton Act.[58]

The acquisition of patents may also result in civil litigation based upon monopolization. For example, in *Clean Conversion v. CleanTech Biofuels*,[59] Clean Conversion Technologies, Inc. (CCT), a licensee of patents for pressurized steam classification (PSC) conversion, brought suit against its licensor, CleanTech Biofuels, Inc., in response to CleanTech's efforts to terminate CCT's license through litigation and, simultaneously, to purchase all known patents related to PSC technology. The suit claimed that CleanTech's acquisition strategy constituted a scheme to monopolize the PSC market in violation of sections 1 and 2 of the Sherman Act. The plaintiff alleged that the patent holder acquired the patents with the intent to monopolize the market. As evidence, it referenced the above-market value premium that the purchaser paid to the prior patent holder and to the patent holder's securities filings, in which it stated the company's "intention to consolidate the ownership of the intellectual property rights to PSC technology to corner the PSC market."

The court rejected CleanTech's motion to dismiss the monopolization suit. The court found that CCT had antitrust standing because CleanTech's alleged actions, if true, reflected harm to competition, not just to CCT. The court distinguished CCT's action by pointing out that CCT did not allege that "it suffered antitrust injury from CleanTech's enforcement of its patent rights" but that it "suffered an injury to competition as a result

54. *Id.* at 10.

55. Press Release, Verisk Analytics, Verisk Analytics Ends Effort to Acquire EagleView Technology Corporation (Dec. 16, 2014).

56. Press Release, FTC, FTC Order Restores Competition in Market for Magnesium Plates for Photoengraving (Oct. 12, 2012).

57. *Id.*

58. *Id.*

59. *Clean Conversion Techs., Inc. v. CleanTech Biofuels, Inc.*, No. 12-cv-239, 2012 WL 3585171 (S.D. Cal. Aug. 20, 2012).

of CleanTech's effort to conspire to consolidate the market and monopolize the market power into one entity."[60] CCT adequately pleaded market power by CleanTech in the PSC conversion market because it pled facts showing the exclusionary effect of CleanTech's refusal to license its acquired patents and the otherwise high barriers to entry.[61] Finally, the court rejected CleanTech's *Noerr-Pennington* defense because the infringement litigation commenced by CleanTech was only implicated to the extent that it supported a broader scheme to violate the antitrust laws, and, in any event, CleanTech failed to identify any petitioning activity subject to protection.[62]

§ 2.5 Barriers to Entry

Harm to competition from a transfer of intellectual property "depends in part on the degree of concentration in, the difficulty of entry into, and responsiveness of supply and demand to changes in price in the relevant markets."[63] In particular, "[t]he risk of anticompetitive coordination is increased when the relevant markets are concentrated and difficult to enter" because new participants cannot readily enter the market to offset a super-competitive price.[64]

In 2012, the existence of barriers to entry played a role in the FTC's decision to challenge a high-tech market merger, which resulted in the abandonment of the merger. Electronics component manufacturer Integrated Device Technologies, Inc. proposed to purchase competitor PLX Technology, Inc. for $330 million.[65] According to the FTC, the deal would give the combined firm a near-monopoly in the market for a type of integrated computer circuits called PCIe switches, which perform critical connectivity functions in computers and other electronic devices widely used by American consumers and businesses.[66] The FTC complaint alleged that "IDT and PLX are the only firms offering 3rd generation PCIe switches today, and this head-to-head competition would be eliminated by the proposed acquisition."[67] Shortly after the FTC filed its complaint, the parties decided to abandon the proposed merger.

In comments the following month, FTC Commissioner Julie Brill commented on some of the lessons learned from the proposed IDT-PLX

60. *Id.* at *4.

61. *Id.* at *5.

62. *Id.* at *7; *see also infra* p. 131 further discussing application of *Noerr-Pennington* doctrine in this case.

63. Antitrust-IP Licensing Guidelines, *supra* note 2, § 4.1.1 (citing the 1992 Merger Guidelines).

64. *Id.*

65. Press Release, FTC, FTC Issues Complaint Seeking to Block Integrated Device Technology, Inc.'s Proposed $330 Million Acquisition of PLX Technology, Inc. (Dec. 18, 2012).

66. *Id.*

67. *Id.*

merger. One of the lessons Commissioner Brill cited related to how the FTC should analyze claims about market entry. She noted that a key question is: "[W]hat was the past evidence regarding entry and repositioning telling us about the likelihood of either happening in the post-merger world? If, as was argued, the market truly was at an inflection point or was threatened by technological leapfrogging, then I could think of no better yardstick than natural experiments that have already occurred to test these arguments."[68]

§ 2.6 *Exclusive versus Non-exclusive Licensing*

A critical issue for assessing the antitrust impact of the acquisition of intellectual property is whether the acquisition will be exclusive or non-exclusive. Exclusive arrangements raise greater antitrust concerns because they prevent competitors from accessing intellectual property. There are two kinds of exclusivity that occur in licensing arrangements and each poses distinct antitrust concerns. First, the licensor may engage in "exclusive dealing" by restricting the licensee from selling, distributing, or using technologies by competitors of the licensor. Second, a license can be exclusive to the licensee where the terms of the license prevent the licensor from licensing to others or even from using the technology itself. Sections 2.7, 2.8, and 2.9 will discuss specific arrangements that should be scrutinized.

In *United States v. United Technologies* (UTC),[69] the DOJ was concerned that UTC's acquisition of Goodrich would lessen competition in the development, manufacture, and sale of large main engine generators, aircraft turbine engines, and engine control systems for larger aircraft turbine engines. The proposed final judgment issued on August 2, 2012, requires UTC to divest Goodrich assets used to design, develop, and manufacture engine control products. Part of the divestiture is an exclusive, irrevocable, royalty-free license for Goodrich intellectual property that is used exclusively for engine control products and a similar, but non-exclusive, license for intellectual property that is used primarily for engine control products.[70] The proposed judgment explains: "These licenses will further ensure that the acquirer [of the divestiture assets] has the assets it needs to be a viable competitor in the engine controls systems business."[71]

68. Julie Brill, Comm'r, Speech on Merger Enforcement in High-Tech Markets (Jan. 28, 2013).

69. *See* Mem. Op., *United States v. United Techs. Corp. & Goodrich Corp.*, 1:12-cv-01230 (D.C. Dist. May 29, 2013).

70. Competitive Impact Statement, *United Techs. Corp.*, 1:12-cv-01230, at 24 (July 26, 2012).

71. *Id.*

The FTC orders issued in 2012 suggest the divestiture of non-exclusive licenses may be more common. In *In re Carpenter Technology*,[72] Carpenter Technology Corp. planned to acquire Latrobe Specialty Metals. The April 12, 2012, FTC order required respondents to divest specialty metal products and related intellectual property. The divested license for intellectual property was "a perpetual, non-exclusive, fully paid-up and royalty-free license(s) with rights to sublicense."[73] Similarly, in *In re Teva Pharmaceutical*,[74] a July 2, 2012, FTC order required respondents to divest the generic fentanyl and cyclobenzaprine and related intellectual property. The licenses were also perpetual, non-exclusive, fully paid-up, royalty-free, and with rights to sublicense.[75]

The FTC's investigation of Google in 2012 resulted in two changes to Google's exclusive practices. Although the FTC approved Google's acquisition of Motorola's patent portfolio in 2012, the FTC entered into a consent decree with Google in 2013, under which Google agreed to commit to provide FRAND licenses to the wireless market for all of Google SEPs. Google had been seeking or threatening injunctions against other wireless companies that allegedly infringed the Motorola patents. In addition, Google agreed to change its AdWords contracts, so as to allow advertisers to more easily use competing online advertising products. Some FTC commissioners believed that Google's terms of use for its API were making it difficult for advertisers to use competing online advertising products. However, at least one FTC commissioner has suggested that the recent Google/Motorola and Bosch cases touch the outer boundary of FTC enforcement power and have limited import. Commissioner Maureen Ohlhausen recommended that "any agency or party interested in relying on those decisions proceed with caution and consider all of the Commissioner statements that were issued in connection with those decisions."[76] Commissioner Ohlhausen issued dissenting statements in both decisions on the grounds that both

72. *In re Carpenter Tech. Corp. & Latrobe Specialty Metals, Inc.*, 2012 F.T.C. Lexis 72.

73. *Id.* at *33–34.

74. *In re Teva Pharm. Indus. Ltd.*, 2012 F.T.C. Lexis 117.

75. *Id.* at *18, *23; *see also In re Novartis AG*, 2012 F.T.C. Lexis 148, at *9–10 (Sept. 4, 2012) (requiring divestiture of all products related to three ANDAs—calcipotriene topical solution, lidocaine/prilocaine cream, and metronidazole topical gel—including perpetual, non-exclusive licenses under that patent); *In re Watson Pharm., Inc.*, 2012 F.T.C. Lexis 195, at *18 (Dec. 13, 2012) (requiring divestiture of Irsradipine and Loxapine Products and Morphine Sulphate Naltrexone Extended Release Products including perpetual, non-exclusive licenses to related intellectual property).

76. Maureen K. Ohlhausen, Comm'r, Speech, The Never-Ending yet Vital Pursuit of Greater Cooperation, Convergence, and Transparency (Mar. 22, 2013), *available at* https://www.ftc.gov/sites/default/files/documents/public_statements/never-ending-yet-vital-pursuit-greater-cooperation-convergence-and-transparency/130322chinainstitute.pdf.

decisions lacked transparency, failed to provide adequate guidance, created conflicts between the FTC and other U.S. governmental institutions, and risked sending a message to foreign counterparties that the United States does not place a very high value on intellectual property rights.

Industry participants have also weighed in on the FTC's consent decree in the Google/Motorola case. On one side, Microsoft and Apple applauded the FTC's decision to require Google/Motorola to license their SEPs on FRAND terms.[77] On the other side, other industry participants have filed comments with the FTC arguing that the FTC's consent decree should be limited to the Google/Motorola case. For example, Ericsson commented that, although it agrees with the Commission that, in general, injunctive relief should be available against an unwilling licensee who refuses to accept a license on FRAND terms, "the specific procedures described in the order, if widely adopted, may cause unintended and undesirable consequences, particularly within the telecommunications industry."[78]

Another criticism of the FTC's Google/Motorola decision is that the FTC improperly relied on FTC Act section 5 as a basis to challenge Google/Motorola's post-merger patent licensing. For example, the Intellectual Property Owners Association (IPO), a trade association with over 200 company-members, submitted a comment, in which it stated that it "opposes the unrestricted use of Section 5 of the Federal Trade Commission Act, . . . as a standalone basis for intervention by the Commission in situations where the agency cannot rely on a violation of the antitrust laws as the basis for exercising governmental power to restore or preserve competition."[79] As the IPO argued, "the use of 'unfair' as a legal standard for prohibiting certain types of conduct must necessarily be accompanied by well-defined limits that apprise market participants as to what is permitted and what is not."[80] IPO expressed concern that "[n]o such limiting principles or definitions are discernible from the Complaint and the Statement of the Commission in this matter."[81]

§ 2.7 *Joint Ventures*

Joint collaboration with other entities can be a mutually beneficial way to develop new intellectual property. However, joint ventures will be

77. *#463: In re Motorola Mobility LLC & Google Inc.*, F.T.C. No. 121-0120, *available at* https://www.ftc.gov/policy/public-comments/initiative-463 (providing comments by Apple Inc. and Microsoft Corporation on Feb. 22, 2013).

78. *Id* (providing comments of Ericsson Inc. on Feb. 22, 2013).

79. *Id* (providing comments of Intellectual Property Owners Associations on Jan. 31, 2013).

80. *Id.*

81. *Id.*

scrutinized to ensure that they do not impose illegal competitive restraints or otherwise have the effect of foreclosing competitors from a vital resource.

In 2012, a complaint filed by the DOJ challenged a set of agreements among Verizon, Time Warner Cable, Cox Communications, and Bright House Networks to sell each other's services, create a joint entity to develop new products and services, and create a future option for members to operate a virtual wireless network using Verizon's fiber-based network (FiOS).[82] Three key provisions regarding the joint venture in the proposed final judgment demonstrate that (1) the DOJ was concerned with the duration of the venture, so it required government approval for participants to continue in the venture after December 2016; (2) the DOJ was concerned that the agreement prohibited members from independently developing technologies regarding the integration of wire-line and wireless services, so it required the agreement to be amended to allow Time Warner Cable and Bright House Networks to independently develop any technology they present to the joint entity for development but which the joint entity declined to pursue; and (3) the DOJ required that when members exit the joint entity they be granted a perpetual, royalty-free, non-exclusive license to intellectual property then owned by the joint entity so that members could sublicense venture-developed technology to other wireless carriers if they choose after leaving.[83]

In a recent joint venture outside the United States, two Swedish companies Tele2 and Telenor transferred mobile-frequency licenses to a network joint venture.[84] The putative basis for the joint venture, called Net4Mobility, was to pool limited resources such as frequency licenses.[85] A third Swedish company lodged a complaint with the Swedish competition authority Konkurrensverket, alleging that this transfer of licenses to a joint venture violates the antitrust laws because it gives the Net4Mobility venture an unfair advantage over operators with fewer frequencies.[86]

The Chinese antitrust authority, Ministry of Commerce, approved a joint venture between three technology and security companies. As a condition of approval, China required an eight-year commitment from the parties to make licenses, programming code, and standards for its technology available to other companies and to refrain from certain intellectual

82. *United States v. Verizon Commc'ns, Inc.*, 77 Fed. Reg. 51,048 (Aug. 23, 2012).

83. *Id.*

84. ABA Antitrust Section Intellectual Property Committee, *Swedish Mobile Operator Files Antitrust Complaint Against Rivals for Transferring Mobile-Frequency Licenses to a Joint Venture*· TIDBITS, Jan. 11, 2013, at 5, *available at* http://www.americanbar.org/content/dam/aba/publications/antitrust_law/at315000_tidbits_20130111.authcheckdam.pdf.

85. *Id.*

86. *Id.*

property development paths that could restrict competition. These conditions mirror the conditions imposed by the European Commission when it approved the transaction in November 2012.[87]

In 2015, the European Commission opened an investigation to "assess whether the proposed creation of a joint venture between three collective rights management organizations (CMOs) in the online licensing of musical works is in line with the EU Merger Regulation."[88] The CMOs manage the copyrights of authors, performers and writers of musical works, and grant licenses on their behalf and redistribute the royalties collected.[89] The initial investigation revealed that the proposed joint venture between the CMOs would result in each CMO ceasing its offer of multinational licenses for its own repertoire, and instead requiring prospective licensees to bargain with the joint venture for a multinational license for all of the CMOs' repertoires. This new bargaining power for multinational licenses could adversely affect digital service providers in the European Economic Area because the operation of digital music relies upon multinational licenses. The net effect could be higher prices for consumers and less choice for digital music.[90]

§ 2.8 Cross-Licensing and Pooling Arrangements

While joint ventures are a common way to develop new intellectual property with others, competitors can also acquire rights to existing intellectual property through cross-licensing and pooling agreements. Non-exclusive cross-licensing is generally pro-competitive—it decreases litigation and permits additional development.

In the context of patent transfers, cross-licensing is an important tool that can help prevent unexpected patent litigation, especially litigation brought by patent assertion entities. In March 2013, Google launched a website to encourage private companies to cooperate to reduce patent litigation by entering into cross-licensing agreements.[91] The website includes four sample agreements, titled (1) License on Transfer Agreement, (2) Non-sticky Defensive Patent License, (3) Sticky Defensive Patent License, and

---

87. ABA Antitrust Section Intellectual Property Committee, *MOFCOM Approves Electronic Security Joint Venture with Licensing and Disclosure Requirements*, TIDBITS, Dec. 14, 2012, at 5, *available at* http://www.americanbar.org/content/dam/aba/publications/antitrust_law/at315000_tidbits_20121214.authcheckdam.pdf.

88. Press Release, European Union, Mergers: Commission Opens In-Depth Investigation into a Joint Venture for Online Music Licensing Between Collecting Societies PRSfM, STIM and GEMA (Jan. 14, 2015).

89. *Id.*

90. *Id.*

91. ABA Antitrust Section Intellectual Property Committee, *Google Launches New Website to Encourage Companies to Cooperate to Reduce Patent Litigation, Especially by PAEs*, TIDBITS, Mar. 15, 2013, at 3, *available at* http://www.americanbar.org/content/dam/aba/publications/antitrust_law/at315000_tidbits_20130315.authcheckdam.pdf.

(4) Field-of-Use Agreement.[92] Under the terms of the License on Transfer Agreement, every company that participates agrees that when it transfers a patent (other than as part of a legitimate spin-out), the transferred patent automatically becomes licensed to the other companies that are participants at the time of the transfer.

Another example of a recent cross-licensing arrangement in a patent portfolio sale is the Kodak case. Pursuant to bankruptcy court approval, Eastman Kodak Co. sold $525 million of its digital imaging patents portfolio.[93] Under the terms of the sale, Kodak agreed to license its patents to a consortium of twelve companies organized by Intellectual Ventures Management LLC and RPX Corp.[94] The sale was accompanied by an agreement between Kodak and other participants in the deal, including Apple, FlashPoint Technologies, and Fujifilm Corp., to resolve ongoing patent litigation.[95] RPX is among the leading patent licensing consortiums with the purpose of acquiring pools of patents for defensive purposes.[96]

§ 2.9 *Grantbacks*

Grantbacks are another method of acquiring intellectual property. Under a grantback license, a licensee permits the licensor to use any improvements the licensee makes to the licensed technology.

Grantbacks can be pro-competitive, "especially if they are nonexclusive," because they promote innovation and subsequent licensing of the results of innovation.[97] The federal agencies analyze grantbacks under the rule of reason.[98] "An important factor in the Agencies' analysis of a grantback will be whether the licensor has market power in a relevant technology or innovation market. If the Agencies determine that a particular grantback provision is likely to reduce significantly licensees' incentives to invest in improving the licensed technology, the Agencies will consider the extent to which the grantback provision has offsetting procompetitive effects, such as (1) promoting dissemination of licensees' improvements to the licensed technology, (2) increasing the licensors' incentives to disseminate the

---

92. *Id.*

93. ABA Antitrust Section Intellectual Property Committee, *Bankruptcy Court Approves Kodak's $525M Sale of Its Digital Imaging Patent Portfolio*, TIDBITS, Jan. 11, 2013, at 3, *available at* http://www.americanbar.org/content/dam/aba/publications/antitrust_law/at315000_tidbits_20130111.authcheckdam.pdf.

94. *Id.*

95. *Id.*

96. *Id.* See *supra* § 2.2 for further discussion of recent litigation involving patent licensing consortiums.

97. U.S. DEP'T OF JUSTICE & FED. TRADE COMM'N, INTELLECTUAL PROPERTY: PROMOTING INNOVATION AND COMPETITION § 5.6 (Apr. 2007).

98. *Id.*

licensed technology, or (3) otherwise increasing competition and output in a relevant technology or innovation market. In addition, the Agencies will consider the extent to which grantback provisions in the relevant markets generally increase licensors' incentives to innovate in the first place."[99]

In *PNY v. SanDisk*,[100] the court dismissed with leave to amend various section 2 monopolization claims made by PNY Technologies regarding SanDisk's use of its patent portfolio regarding the flash memory market. SanDisk claims to own more than 1,400 U.S. patents relating to flash memory technology that cover 100 percent of the flash memory technologies that are or can be used to manufacture or assemble flash memory devices, flash memory systems, or flash memory products for sale in the United States.[101] PNY alleged that there are "no closely suitable substitute technologies to which a manufacturer or aggregator of flash memory devices, systems, or products can switch to avoid using SanDisk's memory patented technology."[102] Among other antitrust claims, PNY asserted that SanDisk's licensing of its patent portfolio violated the antitrust laws because it required that licensees grant back to SanDisk a worldwide, royalty-free cross-license to all future flash-memory-related innovations developed by the licensee, inhibiting efforts to design around SanDisk's patents and stifling licensees' incentives to innovate.[103]

The court found the complaint deficient in its allegation of facts and dismissed with leave to amend PNY's claims regarding illegal licensing tactics by SanDisk. Following a brief background description of the "tension between patent rights and antitrust claims," the court marched through each of PNY's specific licensing claims. The court also noted that "[t]here is nothing inherently illegal or anticompetitive about a grant-back provision in a patent license."[104] PNY does not allege that "facts to show that the grant-back provision is anticompetitive," such as that the grant-back has stifled competition.[105]

III. Procurement

The means by which intellectual property is procured may raise antitrust concerns. With respect to patents, the courts have developed the *Walker*

99. *Id.*

100. *PNY Techs., Inc. v. SanDisk Corp.*, No. 11-04689, 2012 WL 1380271 (N.D. Cal. Apr. 20, 2012).

101. *Id.* at *2.

102. *Id.*

103. *Id.*

104. *Id.* at *12.

105. *Id.*; *see infra* p. 88 discussing all of the antitrust claims at issue in this case.

Process doctrine, under which proof that a patent holder knowingly and willfully misrepresented material facts to the PTO will deny the patent holder exemption from the antitrust laws ordinarily provided by that patent.[106] In addition to statutory prohibitions of fraud in the procurement of trademarks,[107] there is also case law suggesting that *Walker Process* will apply to trademark claims as well.[108]

§ 2.10 Securing Patents

If a patent is secured from the PTO improperly, then enforcement of that patent by the patent owner may subject the patent owner to potential antitrust liability. The relevant doctrine is called the *Walker Process* doctrine. *Walker Process* antitrust claims are often brought as counterclaims. They arise as follows: A patent owner accuses a defendant of infringing a patent. The defendant responds with a counterclaim alleging that the attempted enforcement of the patent is an antitrust violation and further alleging the traditional elements of an antitrust claim (standing, relevant market, market power, and damages). The patent owner responds that its lawsuit to enforce its patent cannot violate the antitrust laws because the prosecution of a lawsuit is immune to antitrust liability under the *Noerr-Pennington* doctrine.[109] The defendant/counterclaimant responds that its antitrust counterclaim pierces the immunity under *Noerr-Pennington* because its antitrust counterclaim is a *Walker Process* antitrust claim. To overcome the qualified immunity of *Noerr-Pennington*, the *Walker Process* claim must adequately plead fraud in the procurement of the patent.[110]

In *Arctic Cat, Inc. v. Polaris Industries, Inc.*,[111] the court provided a useful summary of the *Walker Process* doctrine:

---

106. *Walker Process Equip. Inc. v. Food Mach. & Chem. Corp.*, 382 U.S. 172, 176–80 (1965); *see Noblepharma AB v. Implant Innov., Inc.*, 141 F.3d 1059 (Fed. Cir. 1998) (detailing elements of *Walker Process* claim); *infra* § 4.10 (describing *Walker Process*).

107. Lanham Act § 38, 15 U.S.C. § 1120 ("Any person who shall procure registration in the Patent and Trademark Office of a mark by a false or fraudulent declaration or representation, oral or in writing, or by any false means, shall be liable in a civil action by any person injured thereby for any damages sustained in consequence thereof.").

108. *Vendo Co. v. LektroVend Corp.*, 433 U.S. 623, 652 (1977) (Blackmun, J., concurring) ("[T]he enforcement of restrictive provisions in a license to use . . . a trademark may violate the Sherman Act.").

109. *E. R.R. President's Conference v. Noerr Motor Freight, Inc.*, 365 U.S. 127, 135 (1961); *United Mine Workers v. Pennington*, 381 U.S. 657, 670 (1965).

110. *Walker Process* should not be confused with the "sham litigation" exception, which also overcomes *Noerr-Pennington* immunity. *See generally Cal. Motor Transp. Co. v. Trucking Unlimited*, 404 U.S. 508 (1972); *Prof'l Real Estate Investors, Inc. v. Columbia Pictures, Inc.*, 508 U.S. 49 (1993). The "sham litigation" exception is discussed at p. 126 and may be raised without regard to how the patent was procured. However, *Walker Process* and "sham litigation" claims are often plead together.

111. 2014 WL 5325361, slip op. at *25 (D. Minn. 2014).

> Because a patent is a monopoly, a patent-holder can generally enforce its rights under a patent without fear of antitrust liability. Simpson v. Union Oil Co., 377 U.S. 13, 24, 84 S.Ct. 1051, 12 L.Ed.2d 98 (1964). But under the Walker Process doctrine "[a] patentee who brings an infringement suit may be subject to antitrust liability for the anticompetitive effects of that suit if the alleged infringer (the antitrust plaintiff) proves . . . that the asserted patent was obtained through knowing and willful fraud." Nobelpharma AB v. Implaint Innovations, Inc., 141 Fed. 1059, 1068 (Fed. Cir. 1998)(citing Walker Process Equip., Inc. v. Food Mach. &Chem. Corp., 383 U.S. 172, 177, 86 S.Ct. 347,15 L.Ed.2d 247 (1965)). To establish fraud on the PTO, a party may assert "either a fraudulent misrepresentation or a fraudulent omission." *Id.* at 1070. The misrepresentation or omission alleged "must evidence a clear intent to deceive the examiner and thereby cause the PTO to grant an invalid patent." *Id.* With regard to allegations based on fraudulent omissions, "there must be evidence of intent separable from the simple fact of omission." Dippin' Dots, Inc. v. Mosey, 476 F.3d 1337, 1347 (Fed.Cir. 2007).[112]

Applying those principles, the court concluded that Arctic Cat's claim for *Walker Process* fraud was deficient. It was based on the same omissions of fact that Arctic Cat relied on in its inequitable conduct claims, which the court previously had concluded did not adequately allege materiality and intent. "Because these allegations do not support a claim for inequitable conduct, they are also insufficient to allege *Walker Process* fraud."[113]

In *Tyco Healthcare Group LP v. Mutual Pharmaceutical Co.*,[114] the Federal Circuit affirmed the trial court that had granted summary judgment dismissing Mutual's *Walker Process* claim.[115] Mutual argued that Sandoz, from which Tyco acquired the patents-in-suit, had obtained the patents from the PTO fraudulently. Mutual contended that Tyco constructively knew of the fraud when it asserted the patents against Mutual and that knowledge stripped Tyco's lawsuit of its antitrust immunity. Mutual identified two pieces of evidence to support its *Walker Process* claim: (1) Tyco had read the patents' prosecution histories when it acquired the

112. *Id.*

113. *Id.*

114. Order, *Tyco Healthcare Grp. LP v. Mut. Pharm. Co.*, No. 07-cv-01299, 2015 WL 3460790 (D.N.J. May 29, 2015) (No. 501).

115. The Federal Circuit also considered, and remanded for further fact finding, Mutual's argument that there was "a disputed issue of fact concerning whether Tyco's infringement suit was 'objectively baseless' so as to fall within the sham-litigation exception to *Noerr-Pennington* immunity." *Id.* at 1343-45.

patents from Sandoz, and (2) Tyco knew of the "Memo for the Record," a Sandoz document that contained some support for an invalidity argument. The trial court had rejected both pieces of evidence, and the Federal Circuit agreed. In the Federal Circuit's view, although the evidence supported an inference that Tyco knew that an invalidity challenge was likely, a reasonable finder of fact could not find that Mutual had carried its burden to show "no less than clear, convincing proof of intentional fraud involving affirmative dishonesty."[116]

In *In re Lipitor Antitrust Litigation*,[117] a class of direct purchaser plaintiffs of Pfizer's pharmaceutical product Lipitor, a drug used to limit cholesterol levels in human blood, brought antitrust claims against Pfizer and others based upon sections 1 and 2 of the Sherman Act. Among other claims, the plaintiffs argued that one of Pfizer's Lipitor-related patents, the '995 patent, should be invalidated under *Walker Process* because Pfizer engaged in fraud in the procurement of that patent at the USPTO. The initial patent Pfizer obtained regarding Lipitor was the '893 patent. The '995 patent claimed the enantiomer of the '893 patent. While an enantiomer of a patented molecule would ordinarily be considered obvious to a person of ordinary skill, Pfizer presented evidence to the USPTO that the enantiomer of the '893 patent had "surprising" and "unexpected" properties in that it was tenfold as active as the originally patented molecule. Plaintiffs, in short, claimed that Pfizer fabricated or massaged the evidence of the tenfold activity increase and manufactured the story that the enantiomer's properties were surprising.[118]

The court dismissed the class plaintiffs' *Walker Process* claim against Pfizer under *Bell Atlantic Corp. v. Twombly*[119] because it did not find the allegations plausible in light of the litigation and prosecution history of the '995 patent. First, a generic company, Ranbaxy, had challenged Pfizer's '995 patent in litigation by raising all of the same facts underlying the *Walker Process* claim. Judge Farnan of the Delaware District Court considered the identical facts under the more lenient standard used to determine whether a patent holder engaged in inequitable conduct.[120] The court believed it was implausible that plaintiffs could meet the higher standard of *Walker Process* if Ranbaxy had failed to meet the lower standard on the same facts.[121]

---

116. *Id.* at 1350 (quoting *C.R. Brad, Inc. v. M3 Sys. Inc.*, 157 F.3d 1340, 1364 (Fed. Cir. 1998)).

117. Order, *In re Lipitor Antitrust Litig.*, No. 12-cv-2389, 2013 WL 4780496 (D.N.J. Sept. 5, 2013) (MDL No. 2332).

118. *Id.* at *3–5.

119. *Bell Atl. Corp. v. Twombly*, 550 U.S. 544 (2007).

120. *See Therasense, Inc. v. Becton, Dickinson & Co.*, 649 F.3d 1276 (Fed. Cir. 2011).

121. 2013 WL 4780496, at *19.

Second, the court found it persuasive that parallel litigation in Canada and Australia had rejected similar claims against Pfizer. In fact, the Australian court "specifically held that Pfizer did not intentionally misrepresent anything to the relevant patent office."[122] Third, the court found instructive "[t]he PTO's reissuance of the '995 patent despite its aware[ness] of all of the foregoing" allegations of fraud.[123] As the court summarized, "[p]laintiffs' *Walker Process* claim rests on a glimmer of hope that a factfinder will somehow be convinced that Pfizer intentionally lied to the PTO, when a District Court has already found after a trial that Pfizer did not misrepresent anything to the PTO, let alone that Pfizer lied intentionally."[124]

The court also addressed whether direct purchaser plaintiffs have standing to pursue a *Walker Process* claim.[125] Pfizer argued that the court should follow other courts that have denied standing to purchasers to pursue *Walker Process* claims because granting standing would conflict with the Declaratory Judgment Act and the Hatch-Waxman Act, would "upset the delicate balance between the patent and antitrust laws," and "purchasers' claims are derivative of generic manufacturers' claims, such that purchasers have not suffered the sort of 'direct' injury necessary for antitrust standing."[126] Although the court recognized the need to be "cautious about exposing patent holders to ancillary attacks, including antitrust attacks, because the threat of vexatious litigation would 'disturb the incentives for innovation,'" the court relied upon the Federal Circuit decision in *Ritz Camera v. SanDisk*,[127] which held that direct purchasers have standing to pursue *Walker Process* claims. Unlike other cases, the Federal Circuit did not limit its holding to cases in which the patents have already been "tarnished" in another proceeding. The court nevertheless suggested that the situation in Lipitor might call for a different result because *Ritz Camera* "did not speak to patents whose validity has been confirmed after repeated scrutiny, and where repeated challenges failed to result in findings of intentional misconduct."[128]

In *FTC v. Cephalon, Inc.*,[129] the court found that Cephalon was precluded from relying on "litigation uncertainty" to defend against a *Walker Process* antitrust claim challenging a pay for delay settlement. In an earlier trial involving Cephalon and Apotex, the court had found that Cephalon

122. *Id.*

123. *Id.* at *20.

124. *Id.*

125. As a technical matter, the court sidestepped the standing issue by pointing out that it would resolve the *Walker Process* claim on its merits anyway. *Id.* at *17.

126. *Id.* at *15.

127. *Ritz Camera & Image, LLC v. SanDisk Corp.*, 700 F.3d 503 (Fed. Cir. 2012).

128. 2013 WL 4780496, at *17.

129. 36 F. Supp. 3d 527 (E.D. Pa. 2014)

obtained the patent-in-suit by intentionally failing to disclose to the Patent Office that another company had invented the drug formulation for which it sought a patent. That ruling was affirmed by the Federal Circuit.[130]

In the instant suit, the FTC argued that Cephalon should be barred from introducing evidence relating to the merits of its patent for any one of three reasons. First, *Actavis*[131] directs that perceived merits of the underlying suit are irrelevant to antirust liability. Second, principles of collateral estoppel preclude relitigation of the inequitable conduct issue. Third, the undisputed facts establish as a matter of summary judgment that the patent is invalid.

Cephalon argued in contrast that what matters for antitrust purposes is whether there was legitimate uncertainty for both sides at the time the accused settlement was negotiated. Because the court's finding of inequitable conduct did not occur until five years later, that finding is not probative to whether Cephalon had acted anticompetitively.

The court accepted the FTC's collateral estoppel argument. The earlier finding that the patent had been procured by fraud stripped the patent of antitrust immunity and Cephalon would not be permitted to rely on "litigation uncertainty" relating to the merits of such a patent to defend against the FTC's antitrust claim.[132]

Kimberly-Clark v. First Quality Baby Products[133] illustrates how patent prosecution conduct and strategy can provide a factual basis, at least in part, for an antitrust claim. There, after years of patent litigation between the parties involving disposable training pants, Kimberly-Clark filed a new infringement complaint based on a newly issued continuation patent whose parent had been invalidated in a prior case by the same judge who had the new case. First Quality took the position that the court's opinion invaliding the parent patent and the Federal Circuit's opinion affirming the trial court together made clear that the continuation patent must be invalid too. First Quality filed an antitrust counterclaim asserting a "sham litigation" claim and Kimberly-Clark moved to dismiss.

The court denied the motion to dismiss, citing Kimberly-Clark's assertion of the continuation patent even after the Federal Circuit affirmed the invalidity of the parent patent. This, the court reasoned, distinguished the case from others in which *Noerr-Pennington* immunity was applied.[134]

---

130. *Apotex, Inc. v. Cephalon, Inc.*, 500 F. App'x 959 (Fed. Cir. 2013).

131. *FTC v. Actavis, Inc.*, 133 S. Ct. 2223 (2013).

132. *See also infra* p. 138.

133. *Kimberly-Clark Worldwide, Inc. v. First Quality Baby Prods. LLC*, No. 14-cv-1466, slip op. (E.D. Wis. Apr. 9, 2015).

134. *Id.* at 11.

The court also found it pertinent—at least at the pleading stage—that Kimberly-Clark had a practice of filing continuation patents so that it could add new claims to protect its monopoly. In particular, the court seemed concerned that Kimberly-Clark wrote new claims to read on a redesign provided by First Quality in confidential settlement negotiations, while allowing First Quality to believe that Kimberly-Clark concurred that the redesign would not infringe.[135] Based on those allegations, the court could not conclude at the pleading stage that Kimberly-Clark had not lost its immunity to antitrust liability.[136]

§ 2.11 Securing Copyrights and Trademarks

In *Southern Snow Manufacturing v. SnoWizard Holdings*,[137] Southern Snow alleged that SnoWizard procured various patents and trademarks relating to ice-shaving machines and flavors of snowballs produced by those machines were invalid because they were procured from the USPTO by fraud. The court was called upon to decide on a pretrial order regarding legal issues only whether SnoWizard's trademarks had to be registered in order for Southern Snow to bring a claim under Lanham Act section 1120 and whether the *Walker Process* doctrine could apply to trademarks, as opposed to patents, alleged to have been procured by fraud.

The court held that Southern Snow did not have a Lanham Act section 1120 claim because, by its plain language, the provision applies only to registered marks and SnoWizard's marks were not yet registered. The statute applies to "[a]ny person who shall procure registration in the Patent and Trademark Office . . . ." The court identified no controlling precedent on the issue of whether actual registration—as opposed to a mere application for registration—could be challenged under section 1120. But the court relied upon numerous cases in other jurisdictions that limit the application of section 1120 to actually registered marks.[138]

However, the court permitted Southern Snow to proceed to trial on its *Walker Process* claim against SnoWizard's trademarks. The court readily agreed that Southern Snow could pursue a *Walker Process* claim against SnoWizard's patents, subject to meeting all of the elements of such a claim. The court noted that although there is no controlling authority that such a claim can be pursued against procured trademarks, "the attempted enforcement of a trademark registration may constitute an antitrust

135. *Id.*

136. *See also infra* p. 139.

137. Nos. 06-9170, 09-3394, 10-0791, 11-1499, 2013 WL 620266 (E.D. La. Feb. 19, 2013).

138. Citing *Country Mut. Ins. Co. v. Am. Farm Bureau Fed'n*, 876 F.2d 599 (7th Cir. 1989) (Easterbrook, J.).

violation if Plaintiffs establish the elements of an antitrust violation under Section 2 of the Sherman Act."[139] The court agreed with defendants, however, that "it is equally clear that the nature of a trademark, which does not in any way represent a monopoly conferred upon a particular product, will make it particularly difficult to establish that 'the plaintiffs' actions have led to or resulted in a dangerous probability that it will gain a monopoly over the product in issue.'"[140]

IV. Ownership

Despite the FTC's recent decisions in the *Bosch* and *Google/Motorola* cases to require FRAND licensing of SEPs, the general rule is that a patent holder has no obligation to license its patent and may unilaterally refuse to deal with potential licensees. This conclusion flows from the Supreme Court's view that "the mere possession of monopoly power, and the concomitant charging of monopoly prices, is not only not unlawful; it is an important element of the free-market system. . . . [T]o safeguard the incentive to innovate, the possession of monopoly power will not be found unlawful unless it is accompanied by an element of anticompetitive *conduct*."[141] There are, however, a number of exceptions to this general rule and jilted licensees often raise these arguments against patent holders.

§ 2.12 Refusal to Sell or License

Even before *Trinko*, however, courts have held that a patent holder has the right to refuse to license its patent, except under very limited circumstances. Two of the leading cases for this proposition are *Image Technical v. Kodak*[142] and *In re Independent Service Organizations.*[143] In 2007, the FTC and DOJ jointly published the results of an extensive workshop regarding antitrust enforcement and intellectual property rights, which included an extensive debate about the holdings in both the *Image Technical v. Kodak* and *In re Independent Service Organizations* cases. On the one hand, many commentators criticized the Ninth Circuit's holding in *Image Technical v. Kodak*, which upheld liability under Sherman Act section 2 for a patent holder's refusal to license based on a subjective test. The Ninth Circuit had held that a "reluctance to sell . . . patented or copyrighted parts was a presumptively legitimate business justification,"

139. 2013 WL 620266, at *4.
140. *Id.*
141. *Verizon Commc'ns Inc. v. Trinko*, 540 U.S. 398, 407 (2004).
142. *Image Technical Servs., Inc. v. Eastman Kodak Co.*, 125 F.3d 1195 (9th Cir. 1997).
143. *In re Indep. Serv. Orgs. Antitrust Litig.*, 203 F.3d 1322 (Fed. Cir. 2000).

but in *Kodak*, the presumption was rebutted by evidence that the patent holder had denied licensing as a pretext for harming competition. By contrast, in *In re Independent Service Organizations*, the Federal Circuit rejected the Ninth Circuit's subjective test and held that a "patent holder may enforce the statutory right to exclude others . . . free from liability under the antitrust laws" in the "absence of any indication of illegal tying, fraud in the Patent and Trademark Office, or sham litigation." Some panelists expressed concern that the *Independent Service Organizations* holding could be stretched too far and immunize conduct detrimental to markets and innovation.

Recent cases faithfully adhere to the main proposition that a patent holder may refuse to license its patents, but courts have continued to closely examine the boundaries of that right especially where markets are adversely affected and antitrust laws may be implicated.

In *Novell, Inc. v. Microsoft Corp.*,[144] the Tenth Circuit affirmed the trial court's post-trial entry of judgment in favor of Microsoft on claims arising under section 2. Novell proceeded to trial on the argument that Microsoft had unlawfully sought to maintain its monopoly in operating systems by unilaterally refusing to deal with Novell, which produced word-processing software (WordPerfect) in direct competition with the word-processing software produced by Microsoft (Word). The jury failed to return a verdict at trial in 2011, but the trial court entered judgment for Microsoft, and Novell appealed to overturn the judgment.[145]

The dispute between Novell and Microsoft arose out of Microsoft's actions in the mid-1990s in the run-up to its release of the operating system Windows 95. Novell, an independent software vendor, relied upon Microsoft providing access to its intellectual property behind Windows 95—application programming interfaces (APIs) and namespace extensions (NSEs)—in order to develop its word-processing software. Microsoft initially agreed to share its intellectual property with Novell in June 1994. But Microsoft reversed course in October, informing all of its software vendors that they would not be able to rely upon Microsoft's earlier-released APIs. An internal e-mail by Microsoft CEO Bill Gates on October 3, 1994, stated, "I have decided that we should not publish these [NSEs]. We should wait until we have a way to do a high level of integration [which] will be harder for the likes of Notes, WordPerfect to achieve, and which will give [Microsoft] Office a real advantage." Although Novell was ultimately able to develop a Windows-compatible WordPerfect product, it took until almost nine months after the release of Windows 95 and,

144. *Novell, Inc. v. Microsoft Corp.*, 731 F.3d 1064 (10th Cir. 2013).
145. *Id.* at 1066.

according to Novell, caused irreparable damage to WordPerfect's position in the market.[146]

The crux of Novell's case against Microsoft was that Microsoft had maintained its monopoly by unilaterally refusing to share its intellectual property with Novell so that Novell could program its updated version of WordPerfect. To prove this claim, Novell relied upon the *Aspen Skiing* doctrine. The Tenth Circuit identified two elements necessary to make out an *Aspen Skiing* claim: (1) there must be a preexisting voluntary and presumably profitable course of dealing between the monopolist and rival, and (2) the monopolist's discontinuation of the preexisting course of dealing must suggest a willingness to forsake short-term profits to achieve an anticompetitive end.[147] Microsoft conceded the first element, but Novell's case foundered on the second.

The Tenth Circuit explored and expounded upon the short-term profit element of an *Aspen Skiing* claim: "[T]he animating concern here is that a dominant firm may be able to forgo short-term profits longer than smaller rivals, and it may have an incentive to take on those losses to drive rivals form the market."[148] The court was concerned, however, that merely looking at whether the monopolist forgoes short-term profit might ignore other legitimate reasons for forsaking profit, such as promotional discounts. So the court determined that "we also require a showing that the monopolist's refusal to deal was part of a larger anticompetitive enterprise . . . . Put simply, the monopolist's conduct must be irrational but for its anticompetitive effect."[149] Turning back to the case at hand, the court held that "Novell has presented no evidence from which a reasonable jury could infer that Microsoft's discontinuation of this arrangement suggested a willingness to sacrifice short-term profits, let alone in a manner that was irrational but for its tendency to harm competition."[150] The court easily concluded that Microsoft's strategy was a profit-maximizing one, because even if cutting off software developers from the Windows 95 API might have marginally decreased operating system sales, it surely benefits Microsoft's own software sales.

Although the *Novell* court did not dwell upon the fact that Microsoft's monopoly power hinged upon its intellectual property, the court did highlight its concern about protecting the incentive to create such intellectual property: "the antitrust laws rarely impose on firms—even dominant

146. *Id.* at 1068–69.
147. *Id.* at 1075.
148. *Id.*
149. *Id.*
150. *Id.* at 1076.

firms—a duty to [license intellectual property] with their rivals."[151] Moreover, "[i]f the law were to make a habit of forcing monopolists to help competitors by keeping prices high, sharing their property, or declining to expand their own operations, courts would paradoxically risk encouraging collusion between rivals . . . [and] [t]he monopolist might be deterred from investing, innovating, or expanding . . . with the knowledge that anything it creates it could be forced to share; the smaller company might be deterred, too, knowing it could just demand the right to piggyback on its larger rival."[152]

In *Apple iPod iTunes*,[153] the court granted summary judgment in favor of Apple on one Sherman Act section 2 claim but denied summary judgment on another. Plaintiffs brought a class action alleging that Apple intentionally modified its anti-piracy system, called FairPlay, so as to prevent RealNetworks, a company that offered an online music store in direct competition with Apple's iTunes, from being able to download its music onto Apple's iPods. In July 2004, RealNetworks launched Harmony, which allowed consumers of RealNetworks's online music store to download music onto their Apple iPods. But in October 2004, Apple updated its iTunes software with a new program called iTunes 4.7, which employed a new version of FairPlay that was incompatible with Harmony. Apple also refused to license FairPlay to RealNetworks. And in September 2006, Apple released an update to its iTunes software called iTunes 7.0, which further modified FairPlay such that only music downloaded from iTunes could function on an iPod.[154] Plaintiffs alleged that both the July 2004 and the September 2006 modifications to FairPlay violated section 2 of the Sherman Act's prohibition on monopolization.

The court in *Apple iPod* recognized the broad rights of Apple to refuse to license its intellectual property, but concluded that with respect to the September 2006 software upgrade, it could not conclude that the upgrade was a genuine product improvement. "In general, under antitrust law, 'there is no duty to aid competitors.'"[155] "If a design change is a product improvement, that design change does not violation Section 2, even if it is performed by a monopolist and harms competitors as a result. . . . [C]ourts may not balance the benefits or worth of the product improvement against its anticompetitive effects."[156] If the court concludes that the design change is a product improvement, then the plaintiff must show that the change

151. *Id.* at 1066.
152. *Id.* at 1073.
153. *Apple iPod iTunes Antitrust Litig.*, 796 F. Supp. 2d 1137 (N.D. Cal. 2011).
154. *Id.* at 1140.
155. *Id.* at 1145 (citing *Trinko*).
156. *Id.* at 1143 (citations omitted).

"constitutes an anticompetitive abuse or leverage of monopoly power, or a predatory or exclusionary means of attempting to monopolize the relevant market."[157] The court concluded that the 2004 improvement constituted a "genuine improvement" because Apple upgraded FairPlay in response to increased hacking efforts and the software upgrade made hacking more difficult.[158] The court also held that Apple's refusal to license FairPlay to RealNetworks in 2004 did not constitute an anticompetitive abuse or leverage of monopoly power because although "[l]iability under Section 2 . . . can arise when a defendant voluntarily alters a course of dealing," RealNetworks presented "no evidence" of a prior course of dealing.[159] In contrast, the court held there was a material factual dispute as to whether the 2006 modification was a genuine improvement. The plaintiffs' expert provided evidence that the 2006 change did not improve the iPod because "[a]dding foreign files to the iPod's internal database would not corrupt the iPod" and because "[t]he new code included in iTunes 7.0 did not guard against the risk of corruption, but actually made the software worse, because it transformed small errors in the database . . . into enormous errors."[160]

In *MiniFrame v. Microsoft*,[161] the court dismissed Sherman Act section 2 antitrust claims brought by MiniFrame against Microsoft based on Microsoft's decision to change its Windows operating system license from a per computer license to per user license. Prior to 2007, Microsoft did not include a restriction on its licenses on the number of users who could simultaneously access a single Windows client operating system.[162] MiniFrame, an Israeli corporation, developed a product called "SoftXpand" that allowed multiple users to simultaneously access and use a single Windows client operating system on a single PC.[163] When Microsoft changed its licensing agreements for its client operating systems to include a single-user restriction, the SoftXpand product became essentially worthless because SoftXpand's customers were required to purchase licenses for each user regardless of how many PCs were employed.[164]

The *MiniFrame* court dismissed all of the monopolization theories advanced by MiniFrame against Microsoft. The court rested its decision principally on Microsoft's patent rights. "Patent holders possess broad

157. *Id.*

158. *Id.* at 1144.

159. *Id.* at 1145.

160. *Id.* at 1146–57. Apple ultimately prevailed against the plaintiffs in a jury trial. *Apple Wins iPod Antitrust Trial*, Wall St. J., Dec. 16, 2014.

161. *Miniframe Ltd. v. Microsoft Corp.*, No. 11-cv-7419, 2013 WL 1385704 (S.D.N.Y. Mar. 28, 2013).

162. *Id.* at *1.

163. *Id.*

164. *Id.*

authority to enforce their intellectual property rights without violating the antitrust laws."[165] Attendant to this authority, "patent holders may freely impose conditions or limitations on the use of their technology."[166] "[C]ourts 'will not inquire into [a patent holder's] subjective motivation for exerting [its] statutory rights, even though [its] refusal to sell or license [its] patented invention may have an anticompetitive effect, so long as that anticompetitive effect is not illegally extended beyond the statutory patent grant.'"[167]

In *Bookhouse of Stuyvesant Plaza v. Amazon.com, Inc.*,[168] self-proclaimed "brick-and-mortar" bookstores brought a putative class action against the major online retailer of e-books and six of the largest book publishers in the United States. The plaintiffs asserted claims against all defendants under section 1 of the Sherman Act and against Amazon under section 2 of the Sherman Act. The defendants sought to dismiss, and the court granted, dismissal of all claims.[169]

Plaintiffs' claims stem from Amazon's "closed ecosystem" for its e-books reader, called the Kindle, on which a user can view e-books. Plaintiffs allege that the Kindle has approximately 60 percent of the "dedicated e-reader market."[170] In order to view an e-book on the Kindle, however, the publishers require Amazon to use "digital rights management" (DRM) access control technology on the e-books. DRM prevents unauthorized use, sharing, or copying of the content on the e-books. And, although not required by the publisher contracts, Amazon takes the DRM one step further. Amazon's DRM technology restricts the devices on which e-books distributed by Amazon can be read to Kindle devices or non-Kindle devices that have been enabled with a Kindle app.[171] According to plaintiffs, Amazon's decision to operate its e-books platform as a closed ecosystem was done intentionally to leverage Amazon's "domination of the dedicated e-reader market and lacks a pro-competitive justification."[172]

The court dismissed plaintiffs' monopoly claims against Amazon on multiple grounds. First, the court concluded that the allegations of Amazon's monopoly power in the "dedicated e-reader market" and "small media tablet market" were inadequate because the complaint mentioned, but failed to take account of, numerous substitute products that are capable

165. *Id.* at *3.
166. *Id.*
167. *Id.*; *see also infra* p. 86 discussing licensing aspects of case and appeal.
168. *Bookhouse of Stuyvesant Plaza v. Amazon.com, Inc.*, 2013 WL 6311202 (S.D.N.Y. Dec. 5, 2013).
169. *Id.* at *1.
170. *Id.*
171. *Id.* at *2.
172. *Id.*

of displaying e-books, such as the iPhone, iPad, Android devices, the BlackBerry, Mac computers, and PC computers.[173] Second, even assuming a properly defined market, the court rejected plaintiffs' theories of anticompetitive conduct. The plaintiffs pointed to the allegedly unlawful agreements between the publishers and Amazon. The court concluded that the allegations did not show that an unlawful agreement was plausible because "plaintiffs allege only that the Publishers were aware that Amazon was using device-specific DRM and operating its e-book platform as a closed ecosystem, and did nothing to stop it. That simply is not enough."[174] The plaintiffs also complained that Amazon has not allowed them to sell e-books on Amazon's devices and apps. "But no business has a 'duty' to aid competitors."[175] The court emphasized that it was not equipped to act as a central planner or to set the price or other terms of dealing for private parties. The court noted that plaintiffs could not proceed under the *Aspen Skiing* doctrine, because plaintiffs had not alleged any prior voluntary course of dealing that would give rise to such a claim.[176]

A recent declaratory judgment action, *Actelion Pharmaceuticals Ltd. v. Apotex, Inc.*,[177] seeks a court order to put an end to a third party's demand for an alleged monopolist to share its patented product.[178] Actelion, a brand-name drugmaker, holds a patent for Tracleer, a drug designed to treat pulmonary arterial hypertension. Because Tracleer can have severe side effects on its users, the FDA required Actelion to adopt a Risk Evaluation and Mitigation Strategy (REMS) whereby Tracleer is made available only through specialized clinics that carefully monitor and control the risk of side effects.[179] In 2011, Apotex, Inc., a generic drug company, informed Actelion of its desire to file an Abbreviated New Drug Application (ANDA) seeking FDA approval to market a generic version of Tracleer and sought samples of Tracleer from Actelion so that it could perform bioequivalency testing.[180] Actelion refused to provide Tracleer samples, and Apotex threatened to file suit to compel Actelion to comply with the request. Actelion filed a declaratory judgment action to resolve the issue.[181]

173. *Id.* at *7.

174. *Id.* at *3.

175. *Id.* at *7.

176. *Id.*

177. *Actelion Pharm., Ltd. v. Apotex Inc.*, No. 12-cv-05743, 2013 U.S. Dist. LEXIS 135524 (D.N.J. Sept. 6, 2013).

178. Complaint, *Actelion Pharm., Ltd. v. Apotex Inc.*, No. 12-cv-05743, 2013 U.S. Dist. LEXIS 135524 (Sept. 14, 2012) (No. 1).

179. *Id.* at 5–7.

180. *Id.* at 7.

181. *Id.* at 7–9.

According to Actelion, Apotex has identified three species of monopoly claims against it. Actelion claims none has merit. First, Apotex claims that Actelion cannot refuse to deal with Apotex. Actelion relies upon *Trinko* for the proposition that it has "an independent right to choose with whom it deals."[182] It further argues that it "has the right not to deal with or assist a rival."[183] Second, Actelion admits that *Aspen Skiing* could theoretically provide an exception to the general right of Actelion to refuse to deal, but pleads that "Actelion does not have a history of providing samples of Tracleer to Apotex," so the exception is inapplicable.[184] Third, Actelion says a potential exception also could arise under the "essential facilities" doctrine. But, in addition to the fact that the Supreme Court has cast doubt upon the existence of this doctrine, Actelion argues that it is inapplicable here because the doctrine cannot compel the sharing of a patent and Apotex has feasible alternatives to obtaining Tracleer from Actelion.[185]

The Actelion dispute with Apotex raises, however, various statutory rights that may trump the antitrust rules. Actelion acknowledges that Apotex is requesting the Tracleer samples pursuant to the FDA's bioequivalency requirement for filing an ANDA.[186] Actelion devotes a portion of its complaint to arguing that the REMS program did not create an obligation for brand-name companies to provide samples to their generic rivals.[187] Thus, in resolving this dispute, a court may not be required to address the antitrust issues if the FDA statutory framework imposes a requirement on Actelion.

The same antitrust principles driving the analysis in the patent context are applied in cases involving copyright licensing. The court refused to dismiss certain antitrust claims brought by Radio Music License Committee, Inc. (RMLC) against SESAC, Inc. based on SESAC's licensing practices.[188] SESAC is one of the three major performing rights organizations (PROs) operating in the United States, alongside the American Society of Composers, Authors and Publishers (ASCAP) and Broadcast Music, Inc. (BMI). These PROs "serve an important role in the music industry by

182. *Id.* at 10.

183. *Id.*

184. *Id.* at 12.

185. *Id.* at 12–13.

186. *Id.* at 8–9.

187. *Id.* at 10–11.

188. *Radio Music License Comm., Inc. v. SESAC, Inc.*, 29 F. Supp. 3d 487 (E.D. Pa. 2014). In parallel, the organization representing local television stations filed suit against SESAC, arguing that SESAC's blanket licensing practices with television stations violated the Sherman Act. The court denied summary judgment to SESAC in that case. *Meredith Corp. v. SESAC, Inc.*, 1 F. Supp. 3d 180 (S.D.N.Y. 2014). This case is detailed in *infra* § 3.9.

'acting as intermediaries between customers and [the holders of copyrights to musical works] and offering "one-stop-shop" licenses for the public performance of works.'"[189] Notably, SESAC is the only PRO not subject to a DOJ consent decree regarding its licensing practices. The consent decrees regarding ASCAP and BMI mandate that those PROs "(i) must accept all qualified music composers and producers as affiliates; (ii) must not enter into exclusive contracts with their affiliates; (iii) must not insist that consumers take a blanket license," among other restrictions.[190]

The gravamen of RMLC's complaint against SESAC was that SESAC had increased its licensing fees to supra-competitive levels by four wrongful actions: offering only a blanket license to its repertory (and refusing to offer any other licensing options), procuring a "critical mass of must-have works," creating de facto exclusive dealing contracts with its affiliates, and refusing to provide transparency as to the works in its repertory.[191] RMLC alleged that through these actions SESAC managed to increase its blanket license fee by 8 percent to 20 percent per annum since 2009 for analog and website broadcasting, and 5 percent per annum for digital radio broadcasting. RMLC alleges that none of these increases in license fees are related to "growth in size or popularity" of SESAC's repertory, and have forced radio stations to devote more of their revenues to the SESAC license.[192]

RMLC brought three antitrust claims against SESAC: horizontal price fixing, group boycott or concerted refusal to deal, and monopolization. SESAC moved to dismiss the first two counts based on insufficient pleading of an agreement between SESAC and its affiliates; SESAC moved to dismiss the third count based on a failure to allege exclusionary conduct.[193]

The court dismissed the first two counts because it agreed with SESAC that the complaint failed to allege a plausible hub-and-spoke conspiracy. RMLC argued that SESAC orchestrated a hub-and-spoke conspiracy with its affiliates by having each affiliate agree to exclusively license through SESAC. Because RMLC had no direct evidence of such agreement other than the parallel exclusive dealing of each affiliate, it had to demonstrate the existence of "plus factors" that would suggest an illicit agreement. RMLC argued that it was against the affiliates' self-interest to license exclusively through SESAC because "the affiliates' self-interest should be to maintain maximum flexibility to negotiate the best possible license fee

189. *Id.* at 491.
190. *Id.* at 492.
191. *Id.* at 495.
192. *Id.* at 494.
193. *Id.* at 494–95.

for their work, including the ability to negotiate direct licenses with individual" radio stations.[194] The court rejected RMLC's plus-factor analysis because exclusive licensing through the PRO was not against the affiliates' self-interest, and because SESAC's licenses with the affiliates did not preclude direct licensing, but rather required an affiliate who elected to license directly with buyers to forgo royalties from SESAC.[195]

The court refused to dismiss the monopolization count, however, because it concluded that RMLC had adequately pleaded monopoly power and exclusionary conduct. Although the court could not resolve whether the market should be defined as only including SESAC's repertory or also including other works, the court relied upon the allegations of supra-competitive prices to conclude that SESAC "possesses monopoly power."[196] The court determined that SESAC adequately alleged exclusionary conduct because "[t]he complaint cogently portrays how SESAC allegedly obtained and preserves its monopoly power . . . . Plaintiff alleges that SESAC excludes competitors by obtaining a critical mass of must-have works, selling them exclusively in the blanket license format, discouraging direct licensing by refusing to offer carve-out rights and obscuring the works in its repertory." The court acknowledged that SESAC does not expressly forbid direct licensing, but concluded that the complaint contained sufficient allegations that the practical reality is that SESAC, as the only PRO not subject to a consent decree, pays a portion of its supra-competitive profits to its affiliates to ensure exclusivity.[197]

§ 2.13 Group Boycotts

While a refusal to deal claim arises under section 2 of the Sherman Act, group boycott claims arise under section 1 of the Sherman Act and relate to an agreement between parties, although not necessarily competitors. Boycotts are best described as "joint efforts by a firm or firms to disadvantage competitors by either directly denying or persuading or coercing suppliers or customers to deny relationships the competitors need in the competitive struggle."[198] For example, in one of the seminal boycott cases, *Klor's, Inc. v. Broadway-Hale Stores, Inc.*,[199] the Court held that an agreement between

194. *Id.* at 497.
195. *Id.* at 498.
196. *Id.* at 500.
197. *Id.* at 502.
198. *Nw. Wholesale Stationers, Inc. v. Pac. Stationery & Printing Co.*, 472 U.S. 284, 294 (1985).
199. 359 U.S. 207, 212 (1959).

an appliance manufacturer and one of its retailers that the manufacturer would refuse to supply a competitor retailer was per se illegal.[200]

A recent case involving patent pooling for the purpose of defending against patent suits brought by non-practicing entities (NPEs, also described as "trolls") highlights the antitrust risk created by entering into patent pools. In *Cascades Computer Innovation v. RPX Corp.*,[201] the plaintiff Cascades controls a portfolio of patents, one of which allegedly optimizes the operation of Android, an operating system for smartphones and tablet computers. The defendants—HTC Corporation, Motorola Mobility Holdings, Inc., and Samsung Electronics Co. Ltd.—manufacture a high percentage of all Android-compatible devices sold in the United States. Cascades alleges that defendants agreed to negotiate licenses for Cascades-controlled patents only through a third party "defensive patent aggregator" called RPX. Cascades alleges that this conduct constitutes a conspiracy to monopsonize the market to buy Cascades' patent licenses, in violation of sections 1 and 2 of the Sherman Act.[202]

Following the dismissal of Cascades' initial complaint, the court denied the defendants' motion to dismiss Cascades' amended complaint, finding that the amended complaint "alleges specific facts raising a reasonable inference that the [defendants] engaged in a so-called 'hub-and-spoke' conspiracy to force sub-competitive pricing for Cascades' patent licenses by monopsonizing the market."[203] Under this theory, RPX forms the hub of the conspiracy and each of the manufacturers operates as spokes of the conspiracy. The rim connecting the spokes represents the horizontal conspiracy.[204]

By contrast, in *Sky Angel U.S., L.L.C. v. National Cable Satellite Corp.*,[205] the court dismissed without prejudice the plaintiff's group boycott claim for failure to state a claim where the plaintiff failed to identify a plurality of actors who participated in the alleged boycott. Sky Angel operates FAVE-TV, a subscription service that distributes the content of television networks in real time using a closed and encrypted fiber-optic transmission path to carry the video programs to central locations, then distributes the programming from those central locations to television-connected

200. *Fashion Originators' Guild of Am., Inc. v. FTC*, 312 U.S. 457 (1941) (per se rule applied to group boycott by clothing designers, manufacturers, suppliers, and retailers who refused to sell clothes to retailers who bought clothes from competing manufacturers and suppliers).

201. Order, *Cascades Computer Innovation v. RPX Corp.*, No. 12-cv-01143, 2013 WL 316023 (N.D. Cal. Jan. 24, 2013) (No. 113).

202. *Id.* at 1.

203. *Id.* at 2.

204. *See also infra* p. 100 discussing both dismissal rulings in detail.

205. 947 F. Supp. 2d 88 (D.D.C. 2013).

set-top boxes via high-speed Internet connections.[206] The defendant, National Cable Satellite Corp. (d/b/a C-SPAN) is a D.C.-based nonprofit corporation created by the cable industry and distributes video of legislative proceedings and other programming via three networks. C-SPAN's board consists of many high-ranking executives and board members from U.S. telecommunications companies.[207]

Sky Angel's suit arose out of a contract entered with C-SPAN in 2009, under which C-SPAN granted to Sky Angel a non-exclusive right to carry the C-SPAN network "by means of an internet-protocol based stream which shall be secure and capable of being accessed only in a manner which would not allow any form of subsequent distribution . . . including without limitation, distribution over public internet."[208] Although C-SPAN and C-SPAN2 went "live" on FAVE-TV on July 10, 2009, C-SPAN instructed Sky Angel to cease carrying C-SPAN's networks on FAVE-TV on July 13, 2009, so that C-SPAN could review Sky Angel's "distribution technology" and develop a "precise legal framework."[209]

In November 2012, Sky Angel filed its complaint against C-SPAN, alleging claims under sections 1 and 2 of the Sherman Act. The section 1 claim alleged that C-SPAN's termination of the contract with Sky Angel "constitutes an agreement among C-SPAN's cable MVPD [multichannel video programming distributors] board members unreasonably restraining trade with Sky Angel—a group boycott and per se violation."[210]

The court dismissed Sky Angel's group boycott claim for failure to state a claim because the complaint identified only one party and not a plurality of conspiring parties, which is an essential ingredient of a group boycott claim. As the court noted, "[w]hen determining whether a single entity is capable of engaging in concerted action for purposes of Section 1, 'the relevant inquiry . . . is whether there is a contract, combination, or conspiracy amongst separate economic actors pursuing separate economic interests such that the agreement deprives the market place of independent centers of decisionmaking and therefore of diversity of entrepreneurial interests."[211] Although there is a presumption that agreements within a single firm constitute independent action, "[a]greements made within a firm can constitute concerted action . . . when the parties to the agreement act on interests separate from those of the firm itself."[212]

206. *Id.* at 94.
207. *Id.*
208. *Id.* at 95.
209. *Id.*
210. *Id.* at 96.
211. *Id.* at 100 (citing *Am. Needle, Inc. v. Nat'l Football League*, 560 U.S. 183 (2010)).
212. *Id.*

The court concluded that it would be plausible for the board members of C-SPAN to take concerted action because they engage in competitive pricing for real-time multi-channel video programming distribution subscription packages and thus have the requisite "diversity of entrepreneurial interests." However, the court found Sky Angel's allegations as to the formation of an agreement were insufficient because Sky Angel identified the actions of only one person on the board, the director who communicated the termination to Sky Angel, as evidence of the agreement. "'Concerted action' between multiple persons remains a fact that must be pleaded," and the court dismissed Sky Angel's group boycott for failure to adequately plead action between multiple persons.[213]

More recently, in *SD3, LLC v. Black & Decker (U.S.), Inc.*, the court rejected a group boycott claim somewhat similar to the allegations in the *RPX* case.[214] Plaintiffs, SD3, LLC and its parent, SD3 SawStop, (collectively, SD3), owners of intellectual property related to Active Injury Mitigation Technology (AIMT) for table saws, alleged that numerous manufacturers of table saws, such as Black & Decker and Robert Bosch, engaged in a group boycott to refuse to license plaintiffs' AIMT because the adoption of the new technology would raise the minimum safety standard under applicable product liability laws and thereby adversely affect the defendants' businesses.[215] The plaintiffs alleged two means by which defendants conspired to exclude "SawStop," the name of SD3's AIMT, from the market in violation of Sherman Act section 1: first, by agreeing among themselves not to license the technology, and second, by agreeing to reject the plaintiffs' proposal as proposed to a relevant standard-setting organization to adopt SawStop as the industry standard for table saws.

The court found lacking SD3's allegations of a group boycott based on an agreement to not license the SawStop technology. In explaining the motion to dismiss standard in antitrust cases, the court noted that the pleading "must allege that each individual defendant joined the conspiracy and played some role in it because, at the heart of any antitrust conspiracy is an agreement and a conscious decision by each defendant to join it."[216] Here, the court concluded that "Plaintiffs' conspiracy allegations are belied by their negotiating history with varying Defendants. . . . Plaintiffs allege that they negotiated with Defendants Emerson, Ryobi, and Black & Decker, respectively, well after the alleged group boycott began in October

213. *Id.* at 101.

214. *SD3, LLC v. Black & Decker (U.S.), Inc.*, No. 1:14-cv-00191, 2014 U.S. Dist. LEXIS 96256 (E.D. Va. July 15, 2014).

215. *Id.* at *4–5.

216. *Id.* at *8 (citing *In re Elec. Carbon Prods. Antitrust Litig.*, 333 F. Supp. 2d 303, 311–12 (D.N.J. 2004)).

2001."[217] Indeed, the complaint disclosed that one of the Defendants, Ryobi, had agreed to license the SawStop technology for a 3 percent royalty that could be escalated to 8 percent, SD3's opening royalty demand, if it proved profitable.[218] In the eyes of the court, the fact that three of the defendants extensively negotiated licenses with plaintiffs after the alleged boycott began substantially undercut the claim, and failed to "explain why the failure of some Defendants to reach a licensing agreement with them is not simply the natural, unilateral reaction to a technology with uncertain commercial viability and safety."[219]

The court similarly rejected plaintiffs' argument that defendants had engaged in illicit conduct by voting at a standard-setting organization to block SawStop from becoming an industry-standard technology, thus requiring all defendants to adopt it (SD3 calls this the "standards conspiracy"). The court noted that many of the defendants had no role at all in the standard setting, even though the complaint "lumps their allegations together."[220] Even as to the defendants that did vote against adopting SawStop as the industry standard, however, the court found the allegations lacking because the standard-setting organization did not preclude SawStop from participating in the market, such as by selling its technology directly or to third parties; it simply refused to impose SawStop as a required technology.[221] The court concluded by noting that, in this case, and without further specific allegations about a conspiracy, "'the [Defendants] had agreed among themselves to do what was only natural anyway,' which was to find a more economically-appealing alternative technology."[222]

A group boycott argument also arose in the context of a standard-setting organization in *TruePosition, Inc. v. Ericsson Telephone Company*.[223] The plaintiff, a developer of positioning technology used to locate mobile handsets, brought a claim under section 1 of the Sherman Act against mobile phone manufacturers as well as the manufacturers' standard-setting organization (3GPP) for acting in concert to exclude TruePosition's technology called Uplink Technology (UTDOA) from the newest and most advanced 4th generation (4G) global standard for mobile telecommunications technologies.[224] TruePosition claimed that "inclusion in the 3GPP

217. *Id.* at *9.
218. *Id.* at *11.
219. *Id.* at *15.
220. *Id.* at *17.
221. *Id.* at *20.
222. *Id.*
223. 899 F. Supp. 2d 356 (E.D. Pa. 2012).
224. *Id.* at 358.

standard is vital to commercial success" and the exclusion of its UTDOA from the 3GPP standard was detrimental to its business.[225]

The standard-setting organization, 3GPP, moved to dismiss the lawsuit for failure to state a claim. The court had previously denied a similar motion filed by the manufacturer defendants whose employees served on the committees of the organization.[226] The claim against 3GPP relied upon the theory that 3GPP had given the employees of TruePosition's competitors apparent authority to act on behalf of the organization in setting the standards that excluded TruePosition's technology: "the Corporate Defendants openly and repeatedly manipulated their power as Chairmen of multiple 3GPP committees, and thereby invoked the standard-setting authority of 3GPP to exclude UTDOA from two releases of the 3GPP standards."[227]

To evaluate TruePosition's claim, the court relied upon the Supreme Court's decision in *American Society of Mechanical Engineers, Inc. v. Hydrolevel Corp.*[228] In that case, Hydrolevel, a producer of a low-water fuel cutoff device for use in heating boilers, sued its competitors who sat on the relevant American Society of Mechanical Engineers (ASME) committees as well as ASME itself. Hydrolevel settled with the corporate defendants but proceeded to trial against ASME on its antitrust claim. ASME argued on appeal that it should not be held responsible for the actions of other companies' employees who violated the antitrust laws while serving on ASME's committee. The Supreme Court disagreed. It concluded that ASME's liability under a theory of apparent authority is consistent with the intent behind the antitrust laws, especially in light of the power wielded by ASME's influence in engineering matters.[229] The Court further held that ASME could be held liable whether or not ASME ratified the committees' decisions and whether or not the committee members acted solely to benefit their own companies.[230]

The TruePosition court concluded that TruePosition's complaint fell squarely within the holding of Hydrolevel and rejected 3GPP's efforts to distinguish its situation. 3GPP argued that the chairpersons who excluded TruePosition's technology could only achieve their alleged unlawful conspiracy by violating 3GPP's rules, rendering *Hydrolevel* inapposite. The court decided, however, that it was "because of, and not in spite of, their apparent authority as Chairmen of pertinent 3GPP subcommittees that

225. *Id.*
226. *Id.*
227. *Id.* at 360.
228. 456 U.S. 556 (1982).
229. *Id.* at 571.
230. *Id.* at 573–74.

the Corporate Defendants were supposedly able to abuse 3GPP's standardization process, including their rules and regulations, for their own benefit."[231] 3GPP also argued that *Hydrolevel* does not relieve TruePosition of the requirement to allege concerted action by 3GPP in connection with the alleged conspiracy. The court concluded that "[t]his is not a case involving mere membership in a standard-setting organization."[232] TruePosition alleged concerted activity in this case because it alleged facts to demonstrate the apparent authority provided by 3GPP and facts to demonstrate concerted action by those individuals exercising apparent authority.[233]

In *In re Credit Default Swap Antitrust Litigation*, a refusal to license intellectual property necessary for electronic trading of credit default swaps (CDS) resulted in civil litigation against numerous investment banks accused of orchestrating the refusal to license in order to charge supra-competitive bid/ask prices for their CDS products.[234] Plaintiffs, a class of purchasers of CDS, alleged that numerous investment banks who operated as broker-dealers of CDS ("Dealer-Defendants"), as well as International Swaps and Derivatives Association (ISDA), and both Markit Group Holdings Limited and its subsidiary Markit Group Ltd. (collectively, "Markit") conspired, through numerous secret meetings in 2008, to prevent third-party exchanges from licensing the intellectual property held by Markit and ISDA in order to allow Dealer-Defendants to control the CDS market and maintain inflated prices for CDS products. Plaintiffs brought claims under sections 1 and 2 of the Sherman Act, as well as state unjust enrichment law.[235]

The court found that the plaintiffs adequately pleaded a section 1 claim. "The Complaint alleges facts to support that a conspiracy existed . . . that representatives of all Dealer-Defendants secretly met and communicated during certain time periods at certain places and agreed to block [third party exchanges] from entering the CDS market. . . . Dealer-Defendants accomplished this task by, among other things, securing agreements from Markit and ISDA not to license necessary information."[236] The court highlighted numerous "plus factors" identified in the complaint. There was a common motive to conspire because no single Dealer-Defendant could prevent exchanges from emerging, but all Dealer-Defendants would profit from such prevention. The evidence showed that the parallel acts were

231. 899 F. Supp. 2d at 363.

232. *Id.* at 364.

233. *Id.* at 365.

234. *In re Credit Default Swap Antitrust Litig.*, No. 13-md-2476, 2014 WL 4379112 (S.D.N.Y. Sept. 4, 2014).

235. *Id.* at *1.

236. *Id.* at *10.

against the apparent individual economic self-interest of the alleged conspirators because "Markit and ISA had incentives to facilitate exchange trading, and [third-party exchanges] offered sizeable first-mover advantages to Dealer-Defendants that joined the venture. There was evidence of frequent inter-firm communications because, for example, representatives of Dealer-Defendants were strategically placed in other relevant entities—such as Markit, ISDA, [and others]."[237] The court rejected the defendants' argument that the allegations were "equally consistent with a non-collusive explanation" based on responding to the global financial crisis in 2008 because such explanation "hardly explains the alleged secret meetings and coordinated actions."[238]

The court concluded, however, that plaintiffs had not adequately pleaded a section 2 claim. Plaintiffs alleged that defendants conspired to monopolize the CDS market. The court found it significant that plaintiffs alleged that "Dealer-Defendants *collectively* sought to monopolize the CDS market; plaintiffs do not allege that Dealer-Defendants sought to confer monopoly power on any single entity." Upon reviewing the relevant case law, the court held that "[i]t is settled that such a 'shared monopoly' theory cannot support a Section 2 attempt-to-monopolize claim."[239] "There is no binding authority, however, on whether a conspiracy-to-monopolize claim can be based on a 'shared monopoly.'"[240] A judge sitting in the same district had recently noted in another case that a "shared monopoly" theory may be viable "in the context of a claim for conspiracy to monopolize if the aim of the conspiracy is to form a single entity to possess the illegal market power, or where two or more competitors seek to allocate a market and exclude competitors, even if they do not form a single corporate entity."[241] Although the court appeared open to adopting its sister court's ruling regarding "shared monopoly," it held that the theory would not apply in this case because "the Complaint does not allege that the aim of the defendants' conspiracy was to form a single entity to possess monopoly power . . . [a]nd . . . plaintiffs do not contend that Dealer-Defendants sought to allocate the CDS market."[242]

Finally, the court rejected various standing objections raised by the defendants. Under antitrust standing doctrine, "[a] plaintiff must

---

237. *Id.*

238. *Id.* at *11.

239. *Id.* at *13 (citing *H.L. Hayden Co. of N.Y., Inc. v. Siemens Med. Sys., Inc.*, 879 F.2d 1005, 1018 (2d Cir. 1989)).

240. *Id.* (citing non-binding cases).

241. *Id.* at *14 (citing *Arista Records LLC v. Line Grp. LLC*, 532 F. Supp. 2d 556, 580 (S.D.N.Y. 2007)).

242. *Id.*

plausibly plead both that it suffered an antitrust injury and that it is an efficient enforcer of the antitrust laws."[243] Markit argued that plaintiffs failed to show injury from any alleged anticompetitive conduct because "it sounds like plaintiffs would have liked Markit to increase, not reduce, its collaboration by working with [third-party exchanges]."[244] The court rejected Markit's characterization of the complaint. "The attempt to recast the Complaint allegations is unavailing. The charge is that Markit's withholding of licensure—far from reflecting insufficient collaboration—directly resulted from Markit's anticompetitive collusion with Dealer-Defendants. . . . [B]ecause of a secret agreement with Dealer-Defendants secured to prevent competition, Markit acted against its own interests and withheld licenses."[245] The court further evaluated standing under the "efficient enforcer" standard set out by the Supreme Court and concluded that plaintiffs met the requirements to efficiently enforce the antitrust laws. In doing so, the court rejected the defendants' argument that the third-party exchanges that were denied the licenses were the only entities with sufficient enforcement interest. "Both the plaintiffs and the [third-party exchanges] are naturally motivated to enforce the antitrust laws due to their distinct injuries. [Third-party exchanges] lost profits on their venture, whereas plaintiffs paid supracompetitive prices on their CDS transactions."[246]

Group boycott arguments also may arise in the context of copyright licensing, as they did in *Regional Multiple Listing Service of Minnesota v. American Home Realty Network*.[247] The plaintiff, Regional Multiple Listing Service of Minnesota, Inc. (RMLS) initiated copyright infringement action against defendant American Home Realty Network, Inc. (AHRN) based on allegations that AHRN "uses photographs and other copyrighted materials from RMLS's real estate listing service without permission."[248] AHRN, in turn, brought counterclaims against RMLS, alleging that it violated federal and state antitrust laws by conspiring with its brokers to refuse to license the information on its listing service to AHRN and by initiating sham copyright litigation against AHRN to deter AHRN from competing against RMLS's current brokers.[249] The theory of AHRN's antitrust claims was that RMLS did not want to allow AHRN access to its listings

243. *Id.* at *7 (citing *Gatt Commc'ns, Inc. v. PMC Assoc., LLC*, 711 F.3d 68, 76 (2d Cir. 2013)).

244. *Id.*

245. *Id.*

246. *Id.* at *9.

247. *Reg'l Multiple Listing Serv. of Minn., Inc. v. Am. Home Realty Network, Inc.*, 9 F. Supp. 3d 1032 (D. Minn. Mar. 31, 2014).

248. *Id.* at 1034.

249. *Id.*

information because AHRN does not ensure that buyer-side referrals will go to RMLS brokers, while the other participants in RMLS exclusively refer buyer-side queries to RMLS-affiliated brokers.[250] AHRN alleged that there was no alternative source of the listing information than RMLS. In an earlier decision, the court held that these allegations "sufficed to state a claim against RMLS for violation of § 1 of the Sherman Act. After concluding that the *Noerr-Pennington* doctrine did not immunize RMLS because AHRN adequately pleaded that the sham exception applied, the Court found that AHRN adequately pleaded a plausible conspiracy, both between RMLS and other listing services across the country . . . and between RMLS and its member-brokers."[251]

In the most recent decision in the case, the court refused to grant dismissal of the antitrust claims against two newly added counterclaim defendants, Edina Realty, one of the RMLS members, and its parent HomeServices. AHRN alleged that Edina and HomeServices participated in the conspiracy orchestrated by RMLS.

The court held that cease and desist letters sent by Edina and HomeServices sufficed to show that they had participated in the sham litigation efforts against AHRN. AHRN alleged that HomeService sent it a letter on behalf of Edina and others demanding that AHRN cease all "infringement of copyrights." The letter did not describe any particular infringing activity by AHRN. AHRN also identified a letter sent by Edina stating that it was "rescinding any agreement that its agents or brokers had entered into with AHRN, and that Edina Realty had no interest in entering any future agreements with AHRN."[252] Edina and HomeServices argued that merely sending cease and desist letters, without any follow-through action to initiate litigation, undermined AHRN's sham litigation claim against them. The court disagreed. Relying on prior case law, the court held that even the mere threat of infringement litigation can violate the sham litigation doctrine under *Noerr-Pennington*.[253]

The court also held that the group boycott allegations that had been deemed sufficient to make out a claim against RMLS also made out a claim against Edina and HomeServices. The actions of Edina and HomeServices were part and parcel of the same effort to cut off a competitor, AHRN, of an input necessary to compete—namely, the listings held by RMLS. The court rejected Edina's argument that AHRN never sought a license from Edina because Edina had sought "referral agreements" from Edina, which

250. *Id.* at 1036.
251. *Id.* at 1037.
252. *Id.* at 1039.
253. *Id.* at 1042.

would have provided the listing information indirectly, and because Edina refused to even discuss a license agreement with AHRN.[254] The court also rejected counterclaim defendants' argument that "competitors cannot be forced to cooperate with each other . . . [such as] to compel one company to license its intellectual property to its competitors."[255] The court dismissed this argument as a mischaracterization of the claim. The unlawful conduct of RMLS, Edina, and HomeService is that they are participating "in a conspiracy with other brokers and with RMLS to collectively restrict all access to the listing data, which is essential for AHRN to operate its business in the relevant market."[256]

§ 2.14 Tying

One type of unlawful monopoly practice recognized by courts is the tying of products by a monopolist. Illegal tying arrangements can include the tying of an intellectual property license to a product in which a company has a monopoly. In a recent case, the court refused to dismiss defendants' antitrust counterclaim that Oracle had unlawfully tied its software support service contracts to the sale of its Solaris operating system.[257] The dispute grew out of Oracle's acquisition of Sun Microsystems, Inc., the original maker of the Solaris operating system. Defendants alleged that Sun had "routinely permitted its customers, as well as third-party support suppliers servicing them, the ability to obtain Solaris updates and firmware promptly upon release for free or a reasonable and fair cost."[258] According to defendants, Oracle changed the terms when it took over from Sun: "Now customers who want updates and firmware must sign an annual contract for technical support services to be performed by Oracle for those hardware systems. No customer may purchase updates or firmware without software services."[259]

The court rejected Oracle's motion to dismiss the defendants' antitrust claims. The court recounted the holding in *Eastman Kodak v. Image Tech. Servs., Inc.*: a company "by tying its services to its parts—might 'profitably . . . maintain supracompetitive prices in the [service] aftermarket [where] switching costs were high relative to the increase in service prices, and the number of locked-in customers were high relative to the number of

254. *Id.* at 1042–43.
255. *Id.* at 1044.
256. *Id.* at 1044.
257. Order, *Oracle Am., Inc. v. Terix Computer Co.*, No. 5:13-cv-03385 (N.D. Cal. Nov. 7, 2014).
258. *Id.* at 5.
259. *Id.*

new purchases.'"[260] The court noted that many courts and commentators have questioned the economic rationale of *Eastman Kodak*, but conceded that "Kodak remains the law of the land and this court is bound to follow it."[261] The court considered, however, Ninth Circuit precedent interpreting *Eastman Kodak*. "Since Kodak, the Ninth Circuit has made clear that the presentation of contract terms that give notice to the consumer of any potential supracompetitive prices in an aftermarket can save otherwise impermissible activity from violating Section 1."[262] To determine whether a party's tying claim is viable, "the law permits an inquiry into whether a consumer's selection of a particular brand in the competitive market is the functional equivalent of a contractual commitment, giving that brand an agreed-upon right to monopolize its consumers in an aftermarket."[263]

Turning to the facts presented against Oracle, the court concluded that the defendants' antitrust claims met the requirements under Kodak to state a claim. "Defendants have pleaded a relevant aftermarket in Solaris updates and firmware that is distinct from the initial market for serves in which Oracle is not alleged to have substantial market power."[264] With respect to the Ninth Circuit's contractual limits on aftermarket claims, the court stated, "Defendants are not resting on any market power that arises solely from contractual rights that customers knowingly and voluntarily gave, at least to those customers who purchase their server before Oracle implemented its new policy." The court noted that "Sun's customers might ultimately be shown to have consented to a future restrictive aftermarket in Solaris updates," but found that issue to hinge of factual issues.[265] The court rejected Oracle's argument that defendants' market definition was facially implausible because Oracle contended "'it has always been the only legitimate source of updates' and 'never ran an updates business' separate from its services. "Defendants' allegations are that this is exactly what Sun did before the acquisition."[266]

---

260. *Id.* at 9.
261. *Id.* at 9.
262. *Id.*
263. *Id.* at 10.
264. *Id.* at 11.
265. *Id.* at 12.
266. *Id.*; *see also infra* p. 148 (discussing case in context of licensing and copyright misuse, respectively).

chapter 3

Antitrust Issues in Licensing Intellectual Property

I. Introduction

Intellectual property holders typically exploit their intellectual property by forming licensing agreements with third parties. If performed appropriately, licensing intellectual property can foster pro-competitive behavior between parties. However, if not performed appropriately, licensing intellectual property may be perceived as anticompetitive, which may result in increased exposure to antitrust liability. This chapter focuses on antitrust issues associated with the licensing of intellectual property and explores the boundary between forming pro-competitive and anticompetitive licensing agreements.

II. Analyzing Antitrust Issues in Licensing Agreements

There are generally two types of conduct by an intellectual property holder that give rise to antitrust liability in intellectual property licensing. First, there are multilateral actions between an intellectual property holder and a third party such as a licensee that result in a restraint of trade. Multilateral action cases are generally analyzed under section 1 of the Sherman Act,[1] which states that "[e]very contract, combination in the form of trust or otherwise, or conspiracy, in restraint of trade or commerce among the several States, or with foreign nations, is declared to be illegal."[2] A violation of section 1 of the Sherman Act has three elements: (1) an agreement,

1. 15 U.S.C. § 1.
2. *Id.*

(2) which unreasonably restrains competition, and (3) which affects interstate commerce.[3] The overwhelming majority of antitrust issues in intellectual property licensing are associated with multilateral action cases such as an intellectual property holder imposing a restraint on the licensee's use of intellectual property in a licensing agreement.

Second, there are unilateral actions by the intellectual property holder resulting in or expanding monopoly power. Unilateral action cases are analyzed under section 2 of the Sherman Act.[4] This chapter primarily focuses on the multilateral actions of intellectual property holders and provides an analytical framework for determining whether an intellectual property licensing agreement may create antitrust liability under section 1 of the Sherman Act.

§ 3.1 The DOJ and FTC Licensing Guidelines

The U.S. Department of Justice and the U.S. Federal Trade Commission jointly released in 1995 antitrust guidelines for the licensing of intellectual property,[5] hereinafter the *Licensing Guidelines* or *Guidelines*. The *Licensing Guidelines* provide the antitrust enforcement policy of the DOJ and the FTC, hereinafter in this chapter collectively referred to as the *Agencies*. The *Licensing Guidelines* describe the analytical framework used by the *Agencies* in examining potential anticompetitive practices associated with the licensing of patents, copyrights, trade secrets, and know-how. In contrast to previous position statements by the *Agencies*, it is important to recognize that the *Agencies* state in the introduction of the *Licensing Guidelines* that "[t]he intellectual property laws and the antitrust laws share the common purpose of promoting innovation and enhancing consumer welfare."[6] Therefore, these guidelines provide an excellent starting point for analyzing and evaluating the antitrust implications of intellectual property licensing agreements. Although the *Licensing Guidelines* are now twenty years old, they remain a frequently cited source when analyzing licensing and competition issues. Because of their continuing influence and the likelihood that IP practitioners have limited experience

---

3. *See Richter Concrete Corp. v. Hilltop Basic Res., Inc.*, 547 F. Supp. 893, 917 (S.D. Ohio 1981), *aff'd*, 691 F.2d 818 (6th Cir. 1982); *Consol. Farmers Mut. Ins. Co. v. Anchor Sav. Ass'n*, 480 F. Supp. 640, 648 (D. Kan. 1979); *Mardirosian v. Am. Inst. of Architects*, 474 F. Supp. 628, 636 (D.D.C. 1979).

4. 15 U.S.C. § 2.

5. U.S. Dep't of Justice & Fed. Trade Comm'n, Antitrust Guidelines for the Licensing of Intellectual Property (Apr. 6, 1995) [hereinafter Licensing Guidelines], *available at* http://www.justice.gov/atr/public/guidelines/0558.htm.

6. *Id.* § 1.

with the *Guidelines*, this chapter will discuss the *Licensing Guidelines* in detail. It should be noted that the *Agencies* did not address antitrust enforcement policy for trademarks in the *Licensing Guidelines*; however, the *Agencies* mention that the same general principles may also be applied to trademarks.[7]

§ 3.1.1 General Principles

The *Licensing Guidelines* provide guiding principles used by the *Agencies* in shaping their antitrust enforcement policy. First, the *Agencies* apply the same general antitrust principles to the use of intellectual property as to the use of any other form of property. The *Agencies* describe that "[i]ntellectual property has important characteristics, such as ease of misappropriation, that distinguishes it from many other forms of property . . . and *[does] not require the application of fundamentally different principles.*"[8] The *Agencies* further comment that "[i]ntellectual property is thus neither particularly free from scrutiny under the antitrust laws, nor particularly suspect under them."[9] In addition, the *Agencies* recognize that the *Licensing Guidelines* "apply equally to domestic and international licensing arrangements."[10]

Second, the *Agencies* do not presume that intellectual property creates market power. The *Agencies* define market power as "the ability to profitably maintain prices above, or output below, competitive levels, for a significant period of time."[11] The *Agencies* comment that "market power (or even a monopoly) that is solely 'a consequence of a superior product, business acumen, or historic accident' does not violate the antitrust laws."[12] The *Agencies* further note that market power does not "impose on the intellectual property owner an obligation to license the use of the property to others."[13]

Third, the *Agencies* recognize that licensing intellectual property is generally pro-competitive. The *Agencies* observe that licensing intellectual property "can facilitate integration of the licensed property with complementary factors of production" such as other intellectual property, manufacturing and distribution facilities, and workforces.[14] The *Agencies*

7. *Id.* § 1.0 n.1.
8. *Id.* § 2.1 (emphasis added).
9. *Id.*
10. *Id.*
11. *Id.* § 2.2.
12. *Id.*; *see also United States v. Grinnell Corp.*, 384 U.S. 563, 571 (1966).
13. Licensing Guidelines, *supra* note 5.
14. *Id.* § 2.3.

further comment that "licensing also can increase the incentive for its creation and thus promote greater investment in research and development . . . and may promote the coordinated development of technologies that are in a blocking relationship," where an item of intellectual property cannot be practiced without using another item of intellectual property.[15] In addition, the *Agencies* note that "[f]ield-of-use, territorial, and other limitations on intellectual property licenses may serve pro[-]competitive ends by allowing the licensor to exploit its property . . . and [by giving] a licensee an incentive to invest in the commercialization and distribution of products . . . and to develop additional applications for the licensed property."[16]

§ 3.1.2 Analytical Framework

In the *Licensing Guidelines*, the *Agencies* state that they "will focus on the actual effects of the agreement, not on its formal terms . . . [and] will not require the owner of intellectual property to create competition in its own technology."[17] Any licensing restraints of an intellectual property agreement that adversely affect "the prices, quantities, qualities or varieties of goods either currently or potentially available"[18] should be analyzed for anticompetitive effects. The *Licensing Guidelines* provide a framework by which to analyze anticompetitive effects in determining whether a restraint in an intellectual property licensing agreement may create antitrust liability under section 1 of the Sherman Act. This analytical framework includes the steps of:

1. determining any relevant markets affected by the agreement;[19]
2. determining whether the licensee or the licensor has market power within the relevant market;[20]
3. determining whether the type of relationship between the parties is horizontal or vertical;[21]
4. determining whether the licensing restraint should be analyzed using the rule of reason or the per se legal standard of review;[22] and
5. performing an analysis of the licensing restraint using the selected legal standard of review.

---

15. *Id.*
16. *Id.*
17. *Id.* § 3.1.
18. *Id.* § 3.2.
19. *Id.* § 3.2.
20. *Id.*
21. *Id.* § 3.3.
22. *Id.* § 3.4.

§ 3.1.2.1 Determining Any Relevant Markets

In the *Licensing Guidelines*, the *Agencies* define three markets as relevant to antitrust analysis: goods markets, technology markets, and innovation markets. Goods markets are markets for goods incorporating the intellectual property and include markets for goods used as inputs, along with the intellectual property, for the production of other goods.[23] Technology markets are markets for licensed intellectual property and "technologies or goods that are close enough substitutes to significantly constrain the exercise of market power with respect to the intellectual property licensed."[24] The *Agencies* note that they may rely on technology markets to analyze a licensing agreement when the rights to intellectual property are marketed separately from the goods in which they are used.[25] Innovation markets are associated with "research and development directed to particular new or improved goods or processes, and . . . research and development efforts, technologies and goods that significantly constrain the exercise of market power with respect to the relevant research and development."[26] The *Agencies* recognize that innovation markets may be used to analyze licensing agreements that "may affect the development of goods that do not yet exist . . . [or] may affect the development of goods or processes in geographic markets where there is no actual or likely potential competition in the relevant goods."[27] It is important to recognize that the *Agencies* will identify an innovation market "only when the capabilities to engage in the relevant research and development can be associated with specialized assets or characteristics of specific firms."[28]

§ 3.1.2.2 Determining Market Power within a Relevant Market

The *Agencies* define market power as "the ability profitably to maintain prices above, or output below, competitive levels for a significant period of time."[29] Further, the *Agencies* "will not presume that a patent, copyright, or trade secret necessarily confers market power upon its owner."[30] In *Illinois Tool Works v. Independent Ink*,[31] the Supreme Court reached the same conclusion that "Congress, the antitrust enforcement agencies, and most

23. *Id.* § 3.2.1.
24. *Id.* § 3.2.2.
25. *Id.*
26. *Id.* § 3.2.3.
27. *Id.*
28. *Id.*
29. *Id.* § 2.2.
30. *Id.*
31. *Ill. Tools Works v. Indep. Ink*, 547 U.S. 28 (2006).

economists have all reached . . . that a patent does not necessarily confer market power upon the patentee."[32]

For goods markets affected by a licensing agreement, the *Agencies* delineate the relevant market and determine market share as described in Section 1 of the *Horizontal Merger Guidelines*.[33] If the goods market is unlikely to be significant, then the *Agencies* delineate a technology market in which to evaluate likely competitive effects of the licensing agreement.[34] The *Agencies* will identify other technologies having comparable qualities and cost. Further, the *Agencies* will consider the extent to which competition from other technologies that are substitutes may limit the ability of a hypothetical monopolist to raise prices.[35] The *Agencies* assess the market share of each related technology using all relevant evidence including market share data that "accurately reflects the competitive significance of market participants" as well as "buyers' and market participants' assessments of the competitive significance of technology market participants."[36] However, if market share data is not available, then the *Agencies* "assign each technology the same market share" or, if new technology, "use the best available information to estimate market acceptance over a two-year period, beginning with commercial introduction."[37]

If the goods market and the technology market are unlikely to be significant, then the *Agencies* perform a similar assessment as with the technology markets by assessing the market share of each related innovation using all relevant evidence including market share data that "accurately reflect[s] the competitive significance of market participants" as well as "buyers' and market participants' assessments of the competitive significance of innovation market participants."[38] The *Agencies* may use "shares of identifiable assets or characteristics upon which innovation depends," "shares of research and development expenditures," and shares of "other products" to determine the market share of innovation market

32. *Id.* at 45–46.

33. LICENSING GUIDELINES, *supra* note 5, § 3.2.1 ("In general, for goods markets affected by a licensing arrangement, the Agencies will approach the delineation of relevant market and the measurement of market share in the intellectual property area as in Section 1 of the U.S. Department of Justice and the Federal Trade Commission Horizontal Merger Guidelines.").

34. *Id.* § 3.2.2.

35. *Id.* ("To identify a technology's close substitutes and thus to delineate the relevant technology market, the Agencies will, if the data permit, identify the smallest group of technologies and goods over which a hypothetical monopolist of those technologies and goods likely would exercise market power.").

36. *Id.*

37. *Id.*

38. *Id.* § 3.2.3.

participants.[39] However, if market share data is not available and "the competing innovations are comparably efficient,"[40] then the *Agencies* will "assign each innovation the same market share."[41]

§ 3.1.2.3 Horizontal versus Vertical Relationship

The analytical framework for antitrust analysis of licensing agreements includes determining whether the relationship between a licensor and a licensee is horizontal or vertical. A vertical relationship exists between a licensor and a licensee when "it affects activities that are in a complementary relationship, as is typically the case in a licensing arrangement."[42] Examples of a vertical relationship include a manufacturer acquiring the rights to use technology developed by a research and development business, a component manufacturer licensing rights in a component to a product manufacturer that combines multiple components in manufacturing a product, or a product manufacturer licensing rights to a distributor that sells and markets the product.[43]

In addition to a vertical relationship, a licensor and a licensee may have a horizontal relationship when "they would have been actual or likely potential competitors in a relevant market in the absence of the license."[44] The *Agencies* comment that "[t]he existence of a horizontal relationship between a licensor and its licensees does not, in itself, indicate that the arrangement is anticompetitive . . . [and] [i]dentification of such relationships is merely an aid in determining whether there may be anticompetitive effects arising from a licensing arrangement."[45] Examples of a horizontal relationship include a manufacturer acquiring the rights to use technology developed by another manufacturer selling similar products, or component manufacturers cross-licensing each other's technology that is substitutable at comparable costs.

---

39. *Id.*

40. *E.g.*, *Sensormatic*, FTC Inv. No. 941-0126, 60 Fed. Reg. 5428 (accepted for comment Dec. 28, 1994); *Wright Med. Tech., Inc.*, FTC Inv. No. 951-0015, 60 Fed. Reg. 460 (accepted for comment Dec. 8, 1994); *Am. Home Prods.*, FTC Inv. No. 941-0116, 59 Fed. Reg. 60,807 (accepted for comment Nov. 28, 1994); *Roche Holdings Ltd.*, 113 F.T.C. 1086 (1990); *United States v. Auto. Mfrs. Ass'n*, 307 F. Supp. 617 (C.D. Cal. 1969), *appeal dismissed sub nom. City of New York v. United States*, 397 U.S. 248 (1970), *modified sub nom. United States v. Motor Vehicles Mfrs. Ass'n*, 1982–83 Trade Cas. (CCH) ¶ 65,088 (C.D. Cal. 1982).

41. LICENSING GUIDELINES, *supra* note 5, § 3.2.3.

42. *Id.* § 3.3.

43. *Id.*

44. *Id.*

45. *Id.*

§ 3.1.2.4 Determining the Legal Standard

There are two main legal standards of review used for antitrust analysis of licensing agreements. First, the rule-of-reason legal standard of review is used in the vast majority of cases and provides the most deference.[46] The *Agencies*' general approach for antitrust analysis of licensing agreements under the rule of reason is to "inquire whether the restraint is likely to have anticompetitive effects, and if so, whether the restraint is reasonably necessary to achieve pro[-]competitive benefits that outweigh those anti-competitive effects."[47]

Second, the per se legal standard of review is used where a licensing restraint's "'nature and necessary effect are so plainly anticompetitive' that it should be treated as unlawful per se, without an elaborate inquiry into the restraint's likely competitive effects."[48] Further, the *Agencies* will assess which standard of review to use by determining whether "the restraint in question can be expected to contribute to an efficiency-enhancing integration of economic activity."[49] The *Agencies* note that "if there is no efficiency-enhancing integration of economic activity and if the type of restraint is one that has been accorded per se treatment, the Agencies will challenge the restraint under the per se rule."[50] The Supreme Court has held that the following licensing restraints are per se illegal:

- naked price fixing between competitors[51]
- output restraints[52]
- market division among horizontal competitors[53]
- certain group boycotts[54]

---

46. *Id.* § 3.4.

47. *Id.* § 3.4; *see FTC v. Ind. Fed'n of Dentists*, 476 U.S. 447 (1986); *NCAA v. Bd. of Regents of the Univ. of Okla.*, 468 U.S. 85 (1984); *Broad. Music, Inc. v. Columbia Broad. Sys., Inc.*, 441 U.S. 1 (1979); PHILLIP E. AREEDA, ANTITRUST LAW § 1502 (1986).

48. *Id.*; *see FTC v. Superior Court Trial Lawyers Ass'n*, 493 U.S. 411, 433 (1990); *Nat'l Soc'y of Prof'l Eng'rs v. United States*, 435 U.S. 679, 692 (1978).

49. *Id.* § 3.4; *see Broad. Music*, 441 U.S. at 16–24.

50. *Id.* § 3.4.

51. *See Superior Court Trial Lawyers Ass'n*, 493 U.S. at 421–23; *Albrecht v. Herald Co.*, 390 U.S. 145, 152 (1968).

52. *See Palmer v. BRG of Ga., Inc.*, 498 U.S. 46 (1990).

53. *Id.*

54. *See Fashion Originators' Guild of Am. v. FTC*, 312 U.S. 457, 465 (1941).

III. Licensing Restraints

§ 3.2 Price Restraints

A price restraint restricts the price at which a licensee may sell its products or licensed technologies to one or more customers. Price restraints consist of horizontal and vertical price restraints based on the relationship between the parties. An agreement having either a maximum or minimum vertical price restraint should be analyzed under a rule of reason analysis.[55] However, an agreement having a horizontal price restraint is subject to per se analysis and may create antitrust liability.[56]

§ 3.3 Output Restraints

An output restraint limits the amount of output a licensee can produce. An agreement having an output restraint between parties in a vertical relationship is generally analyzed under a rule of reason analysis.[57] However, an agreement having an output restraint between parties in a horizontal relationship may be subject to a per se analysis.[58]

§ 3.4 Customer Restraints

A customer restraint limits a licensee from selling its products or licensed technologies to one or more customers. Similar to territorial restraints, an agreement having a customer restraint between parties in a vertical relationship is generally analyzed under a rule of reason analysis.[59] However, an agreement having a customer restraint between parties in a horizontal relationship may be subject to a per se analysis.[60]

---

55. *Leegin Creative Leather Prods., Inc. v. PSKS, Inc.*, 127 S. Ct. 2705, 2713 (2007) (a nearly century-old precedent that a licensor and a licensee agreeing to set a minimum price that the licensee may charge for the licensor's goods is illegal under a per se standard of review was overturned by the Supreme Court, replacing it with the rule of reason standard of review).

56. Licensing Guidelines, *supra* note 5, § 3.4; *see United States v. Line Material Co.*, 333 U.S. 287, 314 (1948) ("[W]hen patentees join in an agreement as here to maintain prices on their several products, that agreement, however advantageous it may be to stimulate the broader use of patents, is unlawful per se under the Sherman Act.").

57. *Atari Games v. Nintendo of Am., Inc.*, 897 F.2d 1572, 1578 (Fed. Cir. 1990).

58. *Hartford-Empire Co. v. United States*, 323 U.S. 386 (1945).

59. Licensing Guidelines, *supra* note 5, § 2.3; *see In re Yarn Processing Patent Validity Litig.*, 541 F.2d 1127, 1135 (5th Cir. 1976); *Westinghouse Elec. & Mfg. Co. v. Cutting & Wash. Radio Corp.*, 294 F. 671 (2d Cir. 1923).

60. *United States v. Topco Assocs.*, 405 U.S. 596, 611–12 (1972).

Recent cases demonstrate that customer restraints may be challenged under the patent exhaustion doctrine.[61] In *Bowman v. Monsanto*,[62] Bowman purchased genetically altered seeds from a third party who was under an agreement with Monsanto that allowed the purchased seeds to be planted for only a single season but prohibited the use or sale for use of any re-created seeds for replanting.[63] Thus, the terms of the agreement forces farmers to purchase the genetically altered seeds from Monsanto each season.[64] After learning that Bowman was using re-created seeds for replanting, Monsanto sued Bowman for patent infringement.[65] Bowman raised patent exhaustion as a defense, arguing that Monsanto could not prohibit the use of the re-created seeds since they were the subject of a prior authorized sale.[66] The Supreme Court agreed with Monsanto and held that patent exhaustion extends to the actual article sold and not to subsequent re-creations of it.[67]

In *Lexmark v. Ink Technology*,[68] Lexmark brought suit against the defendants alleging that the defendants sold remanufactured patented inkjet cartridges in the United States, which were originally sold by Lexmark outside the United States, thereby infringing Lexmark's patents.[69] Lexmark offered its customers either (1) a single-use patent and contract license with a discount on the purchase price, which allowed customers use of the cartridges only once with a return program for the empty cartridges, or (2) a regular cartridge at the purchase price without any use restrictions.[70] The district court granted defendants motion to dismiss Lexmark's claims finding that the return program under Lexmark's single-use license was a post-sale use restriction invalid under the doctrine of patent exhaustion.[71] The court noted that the Supreme Court under *Quanta*[72] recognized that, even though consumers had notice of the conditions of the sale, "the patent rights of [the licensor] had been exhausted after the first unrestricted authorized sale by its licensee []."[73] Lexmark alleged that "the Return Program cartridges contained notices of a license restriction

61. See discussion of post-sale royalties and patent exhaustion, *infra*, pp. 75–79.
62. *Bowman v. Monsanto Co.*, 133 S. Ct. 1761 (2013).
63. *Id.* at 1765.
64. *Id.*
65. *Id.*
66. *Id.*
67. *Id.* at 1766–67.
68. *Lexmark Int'l, Inc. v. Ink Tech. Printer Supplies, LLC*, 2014 WL 1276133 (S.D. Ohio 2014).
69. *Id.* at *1.
70. *Id.*
71. *Id.* at *7.
72. *Quanta Computer, Inc. v. LG Elecs., Inc.*, 553 U.S. 617 (2008).
73. *Lexmark*, 2014 WL 1276133, at *6.

which bound the ultimate purchaser."[74] However, the court recognized that under *Quanta* "those post sale use restrictions do not prevent patent rights from being exhausted given that the initial sales were authorized and unrestricted."[75]

§ 3.5 Territorial Restraints

The Patent Act[76] provides that an "applicant, patent holder, or his assigns or legal representatives may in like manner grant and convey an exclusive right under his application for patent, or patents, *to the whole or any specified part of the United States*."[77] A territorial restraint limits the licensee's ability to make, use, or sell a product in a certain geographical area. Further, an agreement having a territorial restriction is generally analyzed under a rule of reason analysis and is commonly found to be lawful.[78] However, an agreement having a territorial restraint that partitions customers may be subject to a per se analysis.[79]

§ 3.6 Field-of-Use Restraints

A field-of-use restraint limits a licensee's use of its products or licensed technologies to a particular market or application. An agreement having a field-of-use restraint is analyzed under a rule of reason analysis and is commonly found lawful.[80] However, an agreement having a field-of-use restraint associated with unpatented products produced by patented manufacturing machines or processes may be found unlawful.[81]

In *SanDisk v. Kingston*,[82] Kingston filed counterclaims for injunctive relief including claiming that SanDisk had violated various antitrust laws.[83] One of Kingston's counterclaims under section 1 of the Sherman Act alleged that SanDisk's licensing agreements unreasonably restrain trade in the U.S. flash drive market, including by using a system-level field of use that produced double royalties on the same patents for the same products.[84] Because Kingston did not allege that SanDisk's licensing

74. *Id.*
75. *Id.*
76. 35 U.S.C.
77. 35 U.S.C. § 261 (emphasis added).
78. Licensing Guidelines, *supra* note 5, § 2.3; *see Ethyl Gasoline Corp. v. United States*, 309 U.S. 436, 456 (1940) ("may grant licenses to make, use or vend, restricted in point of space or time").
79. *Timken Roller Bearing Co. v. United States*, 341 U.S. 593, 598–99 (1951); *United States v. Crown Zellerbach Corp.*, 141 F. Supp. 118, 126 (N.D. Ill. 1956).
80. Licensing Guidelines, *supra* note 5, § 2.3; *Gen. Talking Pictures Corp. v. W. Elec. Co.*, 305 U.S. 124, 127 (1938).
81. *United States v. Studiengesellschaft Kohle, mbH*, 670 F.2d 1122 (D.C. Cir. 1981).
82. *SanDisk Corp. v. Kingston Tech. Co.*, 863 F. Supp. 2d 815 (W.D. Wis. 2012).
83. *Id.* at 823.
84. *Id.*

agreements were per se unreasonable, the court determined that SanDisk's licensing agreements would be evaluated under the rule of reason.[85] Under the rule of reason, the court recognized that Kingston first must prove that the alleged licensing restraints including the system-level field of use term in SanDisk's licensing agreements exceeded the scope of its patents.[86] Further, the court recognized that Kingston, second, must show that imposing these alleged restraints on SanDisk's competitors was likely to increase price or decrease output in the USB flash drive market.[87] Since the court determined that Kingston was unable to prove the second prerequisite by failing to show anticompetitive effects, the court did not address the first prerequisite associated with the alleged restraints in SanDisk's licensing agreements.[88]

§ 3.7 Exclusivity Restraints

The Patent Act expressly provides that the patent owner may "grant and convey an exclusive right under his application for patent, or patents, to the whole or any specified part of the United States."[89] Further, the courts have long held that a patent holder may grant a patent license to a licensee by agreeing not to assert the patent holder's exclusive rights against the licensee in exchange for consideration such as royalties.[90] Patent licenses may be non-exclusive or exclusive licenses of one or more rights in a patent. An exclusive license of all rights in a patent "amounts to an assignment—that is, a transfer of title in the patent—which confers constitutional standing on the assignee to sue another for patent infringement in its own name."[91] A non-exclusive patent license is "a covenant by the patent owner not to sue the licensee for making, using, or selling the patented invention and under which the patent owner reserves the right to grant similar licenses to other entities."[92] There are two types of exclusivity restraints that may raise antitrust concerns in licensing agreements: an exclusive grant restraint and an exclusive dealing restraint.

85. *Id.* at 824.

86. *Id.* at 824–25.

87. *Id.*

88. *Id.* 825–26; *see also infra* pp. 72–73 discussing rule of reason application to licenses based on global patent base in this case and pp. 88–91 (discussing case background).

89. 35 U.S.C. § 261.

90. *Genentech, Inc. V. Eli Lilly & Co.*, 998 F.2d 931, 949 (Fed. Cir. 1993) ("[T]he grant of an exclusive license is a lawful incident of the right to exclude provided by the Patent Act.").

91. *Intellectual Prop. Dev. v. TCI Cablevision*, 248 F.3d 1333, 1345 (Fed. Cir. 2001).

92. *Id.*

§ 3.7.1 Exclusive Grant Restraint

An exclusive grant restraint is one in which a licensor grants a licensee an exclusive license to certain intellectual property, which restricts the right of the licensor to license the intellectual property to a third party. An exclusive license is not only the licensor's waiver of one or more of the licensor's rights to exclude the licensee from making, using, or selling the intellectual property but also the licensor's agreement not to license a third party for the same rights and possibly may include limiting the licensor's rights.[93] The *Agencies* have commented that "[g]enerally, an exclusive license may raise antitrust concerns only if the licensees themselves, or the licensor and its licensees, are in a horizontal relationship."[94] A patent holder may also grant exclusive licenses to a licensee for a specific territory or field of use. Further, a patent holder may provide a limited exclusive license to a licensee by retaining the patent holder's right to practice the invention while waiving the patent holder's rights to license others.

In *American Needle v. New Orleans Louisiana Saints*,[95] American Needle was one of multiple companies licensed to make hats bearing the logos of National Football League (NFL) teams but lost the license after NFL Properties, the NFL's licensing entity, entered into an exclusive license with one of its competitors.[96] American Needle alleged that the NFL's grant of an exclusive license to make such hats violated the Sherman Act.[97] The district court denied American Needle's motion for summary judgment requesting a "quick look" analysis of the anticompetitive effects of the exclusive license, determining that the defendants' claims of pro-competitive effects precluded the "quick look" analysis.[98]

In addition, the district court denied the defendants' motion for summary judgment alleging that American Needle had failed to provide evidence of a proper product market.[99] American Needle presented evidence that, after the execution of the exclusive license, wholesale prices of the NFL hats had significantly increased while their output decreased, never returning to their pre-exclusivity levels.[100] Defendants contended that this evidence obviated the need for market definition in only horizontal action

93. *E. Bement & Sons v. Nat'l Harrow Co.*, 186 U.S. 70, 94 (1902).
94. Licensing Guidelines, *supra* note 5, § 4.1.2.
95. *Am. Needle, Inc. v. New Orleans La. Saints*, 2014 WL 1364022 (N.D. Ill. 2014).
96. *Id.* at *1.
97. *Id.*
98. *Id.*
99. *Id.* at *2.
100. *Id.*

cases; however, this was a vertical action case.[101] The court determined that the NFL teams' grant of an exclusive license was a horizontal action, relying on the Supreme Court's holding that despite the NFL teams' use of NFL Properties as a licensing agent and the longevity of the arrangement, the decision by the NFL teams to grant an exclusive license to their separately owned intellectual property was a concerted action.[102] Further, the defendants' argued that American Needle's suggested market, the wholesale market for NFL trademarked hats, was improperly narrow.[103] However, the district court determined that the wholesale market for NFL trademarked hats was a submarket distinct from a broader market of other apparel and non-apparel items.[104]

Furthermore, the court denied the defendant's motion for summary judgment alleging that American Needle had failed to show a causal connection between the exclusive license and any damages that it suffered.[105] The district court determined that there was sufficient evidence to permit a jury to find a causal link in that American Needle could have continued as a non-exclusive licensee and that its prospects were ended by the concerted actions of the defendants in providing the exclusive license.[106]

In *Pharmaceutical Research and Manufacturers of America v. FTC*,[107] the district court granted summary judgment dismissing a case brought by a trade organization representing the country's leading pharmaceutical researchers and companies to set aside a Final Rule issued by the FTC that required the pharmaceutical industry to report certain transfers of exclusive patent rights under the Hart-Scott-Rodino Antitrust Improvements Act (the "HSR Act").[108] The Final Rule clarifies the HSR Act's premerger notification requirements to include that transfers of patent rights within the pharmaceutical industry constitute an asset acquisition if "all commercially significant rights" in a patent are transferred even if the patent holder retains limited manufacturing rights or co-rights.[109] Further, the Final Rule expands the previous regulation under the HSR Act that transfers of exclusive licenses to "make, use, and sell" patents must be reported.[110]

---

101. *Id.*

102. *Id.*; *see Am. Needle, Inc. v. Nat'l Football League*, 580 U.S. 183, 201 (2010).

103. *Id.*

104. *Id.* at *2–3.

105. *Id.* at *4.

106. *Id.*

107. *Pharm. Research & Mfrs. of Am. v. FTC*, 44 F. Supp. 3d 95 (D.D.C. 2014).

108. *Id.* at 98; *see also* Reporting and Waiting Period Requirements, 78 Fed. Reg. 68,705 (Nov. 15, 2013) (the "Final Rule").

109. *Id.* at 101–02.

110. *Id.*

§ 3.7.2 Exclusive Dealing Restraint

The exclusive dealing restraint occurs when "a license prevents or restrains the licensee from licensing, selling, distributing, or using competing technologies."[111] The exclusive dealing restraint is analyzed under the rule of reason.[112] The *Agencies* commented that this analysis should consider "the extent to which the arrangement (1) promotes the exploitation and development of the licensor's technology and (2) anticompetitively forecloses the exploitation and development of, or otherwise constrains competition among, competing technologies."[113] Further, the *Agencies* noted that "[t]he likelihood that exclusive dealing may have anticompetitive effects is related, *inter alia*, to the degree of foreclosure in the relevant market, the duration of the exclusive dealing arrangement, and other characteristics of the input and output markets, such as concentration, difficulty of entry, and the responsiveness of supply and demand to changes in price in the relevant markets."[114]

§ 3.8 Tying Restraints

A tying restraint requires a licensee to sell a product to a buyer on the condition that the buyer also purchases a different product and may violate antitrust laws under some circumstances.[115] A licensing agreement having a tying restraint is typically analyzed under a rule of reason analysis.[116] The *Agencies* commented that a tying restraint is problematic where "(1) the seller has market power in the tying product, (2) the arrangement has an adverse effect on competition in the relevant market for the tied product, and (3) efficiency justifications for the arrangement do not outweigh the anticompetitive effects."[117]

In *Oracle v. TERiX*,[118] after being sued by Oracle for scheming to misappropriate updates and firmware to the Solaris operating system in violation of its licenses, the defendants countered with antitrust and competition law claims directed at Oracle's new technical support policy.[119] After acquiring Sun Microsystems, Oracle changed Sun's technical support policy of providing free updates and firmware to requiring customers

111. Licensing Guidelines, *supra* note, § 4.1.2; *see Tampa Elec. Co. v. Nashville Coal Co.*, 365 U.S. 320 (1961); *Beltone Elecs. Corp.*, 100 F.T.C. 68 (1982).

112. Licensing Guidelines, *supra* note 5, § 5.4.

113. *Id.*

114. *Id.*

115. Licensing Guidelines, *supra* note 5, § 5.3; *Eastman Kodak Co. v. Image Technical Servs., Inc.*, 504 U.S. 451, 461 (1992).

116. *Id.*

117. *Id.*

118. *Oracle Am., Inc. v. Terix Computer Co.*, 2014 WL 31344 (N.D. Cal. 2014).

119. *Id.* at *1.

to either buy Solaris support services from Oracle or be excluded from any updates and firmware.[120] The defendants identified four distinct tying charges: (Tie 1) "patches, bug fixes and updates" for Solaris tied to firmware to "support packages for hardware and software running on Oracle/Sun systems;" (Tie 2) "Solaris Updates" tied to "Solaris Support Services"; (Tie 3) "Sun/Oracle Firmware" tied to "Sun/Oracle Hardware Support Services'" and (Tie 4) "Critical Server Solaris Support Services" tied to "Non-Critical Server Solaris Support Services."[121]

The district court recognized three overarching principles set by the Ninth Circuit in evaluating tying cases.[122] First, the law permits the defendants "to restrict the relevant market to a single brand of the product at issue."[123] Second, the law prohibits the defendants from "resting on market power that arises solely from contractual rights that consumers knowingly and voluntarily gave to the defendant[s]."[124] Third, in determining whether the defendants' market power falls under the first or second principle, the law permits "an inquiry into whether a consumer's selection of a particular brand in the competitive market is the functional equivalent of a contractual commitment, giving that brand an agreed-upon right to monopolize its consumers in an aftermarket."[125]

Applying these principles, the court denied in part Oracle's motion to dismiss the defendants' tying-related counterclaims by allowing defendants' section 1 of the Sherman Act and Cartwright Act claims related to Ties 1–3 to proceed.[126] The court determined that defendants had pleaded "a relevant aftermarket in Solaris updates and firmware that is distinct from the initial market for servers in which Oracle is not alleged to have substantial market power."[127] Based on this relevant aftermarket, the court recognized that Oracle's alleged unique position could permit it to exercise market power.[128] The court also determined that the defendants were not resting on "any market power that [arose] solely from contractual rights that customers knowingly and voluntarily gave, at least to those

120. *Id.*

121. *Id.* at *3.

122. *Id.* at *5.

123. *Id.* (recognizing the Supreme Court's decision in *Eastman Kodak Co. v. Image Technical Servs., Inc.*, 504 U.S. 451, 464–78 (1992).

124. *Id.* (recognizing the Ninth Circuit's decision in *Forsyth v. Humana, Inc.*, 114 F.3d 1467 (9th Cir. 1997) (citing *Queen City Pizza, Inc. v. Domino's Pizza, Inc.*, 124 F.3d 430, 438–40 (3d Cir. 1997))).

125. *Id.*

126. *Id.*

127. *Id.*

128. *Id.*

customers who purchased their server before Oracle implemented its new policy."[129] Finally, the court recognized that nothing in the defendants' allegations resolved in Oracle's favor whether Sun's customers had consented to a future restrictive aftermarket in Solaris updates and firmware.[130]

In *Cablevision v. Viacom*,[131] the plaintiffs brought an antitrust action against Viacom alleging that Viacom forced the plaintiffs to license less popular programming networks in order to gain license rights to commercially critical programming networks.[132] The district court denied Viacom's motion to dismiss plaintiffs' per se tying claim under section 1 recognizing that plaintiffs had pled facts sufficient to support an inference of anticompetitive effects.[133] The court recognized that a particular tying arrangement is per se illegal if there exists "(1) a tying and tied product; (2) evidence of actual coercion by the seller that forced the buyer to accept the tied product; (3) sufficient economic power in the tying product market to coerce purchaser acceptance of the tied product; and (4) the involvement of a 'not insubstantial' amount of interstate commerce in the tied market."[134]

The court rejected Viacom's argument that the plaintiff must also plead and prove anticompetitive harm—in effect arguing to add a fifth requirement.[135] The court found that a per se theory of tying has no such requirement, but that, in any event, Cablevision had pled facts sufficient to support an inference of anticompetitive effects. The court also rejected Viacom's argument that the per se tying claim was insufficient because the plaintiffs had failed to identify distinct tying and tied product markets.[136] The court recognized that the plaintiffs had "proffered subscription, demographic and other statistical information, as well as factual allegations regarding cross-elasticity of demand and barriers to entry, that suffice at the pleading stage to make plausible its market definition allegations."[137]

In *Intellectual Ventures v. Symantec*,[138] the district court denied plaintiff's motion to strike Symantec's affirmative defenses of patent misuse, including allegations that the plaintiffs violated sections 1 and 2 of the Sherman Act by tying the patents-in-suit with other irrelevant and

129. *Id.* at *6.
130. *Id.*
131. *Cablevision Sys. Corp. v. Viacom Int'l Inc.*, 2014 WL 2805256 (S.D.N.Y. 2014).
132. *Id.* at *1.
133. *Id.*
134. *Id.*
135. *Id.* at *2.
136. *Id.* at *3.
137. *Id.* It should be noted that the rule of reason applies to tying arrangements more often than the per se rule that the court applied here.
138. *Intellectual Ventures LLC et al. v. Symantec Corp.*, 2014 WL 4773954 (D. Del. 2014).

unwanted patents in a package license and created and maintained an unlawful monopoly.[139] The court recognized the Federal Circuit's decision in *Philips*[140] that "package licenses are not *per se* patent misuse, because a 'package license is thus not anticompetitive in the way that a compelled purchase of a tied product would be.'" Further, the court noted that the Federal Circuit's analysis of Philips' package license under the rule of reason failed to support a finding of anticompetitive effects by Philips because the evidence failed to show that (1) "including [unwanted] patents in the patent packages had a negative effect on commercially available technology," (2) "there are 'problems with licensing patents individually,' including transaction and monitoring costs," (3) "changes in technology might render certain essential patents non-essential and vice-versa," and (4) "package licensing with royalties based on production output rather than patent input may be more efficient and avoid unnecessary litigation."[141] Unlike in *Philips*, the defendants argued that "at least some portion of the licensing cost is allegedly attributable to the unwanted patents.[142] Hence, the court determined that "a rule of reason analysis could result in a finding of patent misuse in this case."[143]

§ 3.9 Packaging/Bundling Restraints

A packaging restraint, also referred to as a bundling restraint, requires a licensee to license more than one patent or copyright from the patent holder. The consensual licensing of packaged or bundled patents or copyrights is lawful and does not result in misuse.[144] Further, the licensing of packaged or bundled patents is lawful where the use of one patent may not be performed without infringing other patents of the package or bundle.[145] However, an agreement having a packaging restraint may be found unlawful and may be subject to misuse when the licensee has been forced to license the package as a condition for licensing a desired patent or copyright.[146]

In 2013, the DOJ issued a Business Review Letter, entitled "Intellectual Property Exchange International, Inc. Business Review Request" on March 26, 2013, declining to state its present enforcement intentions

139. *Id.* at *1.
140. *U.S. Philips Corp. v. Int'l Trade Comm'n*, 424 F.3d 1179 (Fed. Cir. 2005).
141. *Id.* at *2.
142. *Id.*
143. *Id.*
144. *Automatic Radio Mfg. Co. v. Hazeltine Research*, 339 U.S. 827 (1950).
145. *Int'l Mfg. Co. v. Landon*, 336 F.2d 723 (9th Cir. 1964).
146. *MCA Television Ltd. v. Pub. Interest Corp.*, 171 F.3d 1265, 1277–79 (11th Cir. 1999).

regarding IPXI's novel business model.[147] IPXI's business model consists of converting patent licenses into tradeable instruments called "unit license rights" (ULRs) and providing a financial exchange for purchase and sale of such ULRs.[148] The DOJ recognized the potential pro-competitive benefits of IPXI's business model, such as increased licensing efficiency, sublicense transferability, and greater transparency.[149] However, the DOJ is concerned with potential anticompetitive harm such as pooling of patents from multiple patent holders, listing of competing ULRs, and sharing of competitively confidential information.[150]

In 2014, the DOJ opened review of the American Society of Composers, Authors and Publishers (ASCAP) and Broadcast Music, Inc. (BMI) consent decrees.[151] The consent decrees are the product of lawsuits brought by the United States against ASCAP[152] and BMI[153] for violation of section 1 of the Sherman Act.[154] The Antitrust Division of the DOJ is responsible for overseeing the enforcement of the consent decrees and periodically reviews the effectiveness of such decrees.[155] Since the consent decrees were originally entered in 1941, each of them has been amended with the BMI consent decree last amended in 1994 and the ASCAP consent decree last amended in 2001.[156]

The DOJ performed a review to examine the operation and effectiveness of the consent decrees, including determining whether the consent decrees should be modified to account for changes in how music is delivered and experienced by listeners.[157] As part of its review, the DOJ specifically requested public comments on any modifications to the consent decrees that would enhance competition and efficiency.[158] Further, the DOJ requested public comments as to whether the consent decrees should be modified to allow rights holders to permit ASCAP or BMI to license

147. Letter from William J. Baer, Ass't Att'y Gen., U.S. Dep't of Justice Antitrust Div., to Garrard R. Beeney, Sullivan & Cromwell LLP, Intellectual Property Exchange Int'l, Inc. Business Review Request (Mar. 26, 2013), *available at* http://www.justice.gov/atr/public/busreview/295151.pdf.

148. *Id.* at *1–6.

149. *Id.* at *6–7.

150. *Id.* at *8–12.

151. Antitrust Consent Decree Review, Am. Soc'y of Composers, Authors & Publishers/Broad. Music, Inc., (2014) [hereinafter Antitrust Consent Decree Review], *available at* http://www.justice.gov/atr/cases/ascap-bmi-decree-review.html.

152. *United States v. ASCAP*, 41-1395 (S.D.N.Y.).

153. *United States v. BMI*, 64-3787 (S.D.N.Y.).

154. Antitrust Consent Decree Review, *supra* note 150.

155. *Id.*

156. *Id.*

157. *Id.*

158. *Id.*

their performance rights to some music users but not others and whether the structure of such grants should be limited.[159] After the comment period ended on August 6, 2014, the DOJ had received comments from over fifty organizations and many more individuals.[160] The organizations that submitted comments included ASCAP, BMI, and various music and entertainment-related guilds, companies, and associations, such as the Screen Actors Guild–American Federation of Television and Radio Artists, National Association of Broadcasters, Consumer Electronics Association, Sony/ATV Music Publishing, Netflix, and Pandora Media.[161]

In *Meredith v. SESAC*,[162] groups of local television stations brought an action against the third and smallest performing rights organization (PRO), the Society of European Stage Authors and Composers (SESAC), claiming that its practices of issuing blanket licenses to the rights to perform the copyrighted music of its members violated sections 1 and 2 of the Sherman Act.[163] Unlike ASCAP and BMI, SESAC has never been subject to a consent decree and has instead been free to unilaterally set the license terms to perform the music of its more than twenty thousand affiliated composers.[164]

As background, most television programs contain music such as theme music, which is copyrighted under federal copyright law.[165] Hence, as a practical matter, local television stations typically obtain from each PRO a blanket license to the music performances of its members, since there are far too many music performances contained in these programs to realistically negotiate individual licenses.[166] Under a blanket license, a station is authorized to perform all compositions of a PRO's members an unlimited number of times for a fee.[167]

SESAC had executed a standard affiliation agreement with a vast majority of its members, which does not restrict direct licensing by the member and is silent to the terms of any licenses offered by SESAC.[168] For the remaining 0.3 percent to 0.5 percent of its members, with content typically in higher demand, SESAC had executed a supplemental affiliation agreement, which included (1) providing an advance or guaranteed mone-

---

159. *Id.*

160. ASCAP and BMI Consent Decree Review Public Comments (2014), *available at* http://www.justice.gov/atr/cases/ascapbmi.

161. *Id.*

162. *Meredith Corp. v. SESAC LLC*, 1 F. Supp. 3d 180 (S.D.N.Y. 2014).

163. *Id.* at 185–86.

164. *Id.* at 185.

165. *Id.* at 187.

166. *Id.* at 187–88.

167. *Id.* at 190.

168. *Id.* at 193.

tary amount to the member, (2) large monetary penalties for the member issuing a direct license, (3) referring any request for a direct license to SESAC, and (4) allowing the member to provide a direct license only if SESAC did not reach agreement and only at a rate no less than SESAC's current licensing rates.[169]

The district court for the most part rejected SESAC's motion for summary judgment except on two theories of the plaintiffs' section 1 claim.[170] First, the court held that the plaintiffs' theory that SESAC's blanket license is per se anticompetitive is contrary to the Supreme Court's decision in *BMI v. CBS*,[171] and instead should be assessed under a rule of reason analysis.[172] The court noted that the Supreme Court in *BMI v. CBS* recognized the pro-competitive features of a blanket license and that such license is a practical solution to a market shortcoming and is "designed to increase economic efficiency and render markets more, rather than less, competitive."[173] Further, the court recognized that the Supreme Court's statements in *BMI v. CBS* regarding a blanket license equally applied to the blanket license offered by SESAC.[174] Also, in response to a SESAC observation that "the very purpose of deeming a practice unlawful *per se* is that it must be unlawful *regardless of case-specific circumstances*,"[175] the court stated that "[p]laintiff's bid to apply *per se* analysis based on case-specific facts, to condemn a practice that, on other facts, has been upheld as lawful, would defeat the purpose such a rule serves—isolating, at the threshold, practices that are always anti-competitive."[176]

Second, the court dismissed the plaintiff's theory that the more than twenty thousand SESAC members who were party to the standard affiliation agreement conspired to restrain trade by expecting SESAC to act illegally and knowing of or agreeing to the steps SESAC purportedly took to impede alternative forms of licensing.[177] However, the court allowed the plaintiffs to advance a narrower theory that SESAC's members who were party to the supplemental affiliation agreement recognized that provisions of such agreement that penalized members for direct licensing served to insulate SESAC's blanket license from competition.[178]

169. *Id.* at 193.
170. *Id.* at 195–96.
171. *Broad. Music, Inc. v. CBS, Inc.*, 441 U.S. 1 (1979).
172. *Meredith*, 1 F. Supp. 3d at 203.
173. *Id.* at 204.
174. *Id.*
175. *Id.* at 205 (emphasis in original).
176. *Id.*
177. *Id.* at 209–10.
178. *Id.* at 211–13.

In considering SESAC's motion for summary judgment as to the rule-of-reason review under section 1 and its possession of monopoly power under section 2, the court determined that the facts in the summary judgment record offered strong support for the plaintiff's proposed relevant market of "the market for television-performance rights to works within SESAC's repertory," as proposed by the plaintiff.[179] Specifically, the court recognized such facts to support the propositions that (1) "virtually all composers affiliated with only one of the three PROs," (2) "almost all local stations have licenses from all three PROs," and (3) "local stations have not responded to SESAC's price increases by replacing SESAC licenses with alternative licenses."[180]

Similar to *Meredith v. SESAC*, in *RMLC v. SESAC*,[181] a nonprofit organization negotiating public-performance-right licenses on behalf of radio stations brought an action against SESAC for violating sections 1 and 2 of the Sherman Act.[182] The district court determined that RMLC's section 1 and 2 claims were based on "the confluence of four of SESAC's licensing practices."[183] These four licensing practices are (1) "SESAC's blanket license (and its refusal to offer other licensing options)," (2) "its procurement of a critical mass of must-have works," (3) "its *de facto* exclusive dealing contracts with its affiliates," and (4) "its lack of transparency as to the works in its repertory."[184]

The court dismissed RMLC's section 1 claims on the grounds that RMLC failed to prove that SESAC orchestrated a hub-and-spoke conspiracy.[185] A hub-and-spoke conspiracy is "a form of agreement in which one party—the hub—facilitates agreement among a number of other parties—the spokes—which are usually organizations in the hub's supply chain."[186] Further, a hub-and-spoke conspiracy "requires agreements between each spoke and the hub and between and among each of the spokes themselves."[187] The court concluded that RMLC had failed to allege sufficient facts to show agreements among SESAC's members, as modeled by the rim of the hub-and-spoke conspiracy that represents agreements between and among each of the spokes.[188]

179. *Id.* at 217–18.
180. *Id.*
181. *Radio Music License Comm., Inc. (RMLC) v. SESAC, Inc.*, 29 F. Supp. 3d 487 (E.D. Pa. 2014).
182. *Id.* at 490–91.
183. *Id.* at 495.
184. *Id.*
185. *Id.* at 496–97.
186. *Id.* at 497.
187. *Id.*
188. *Id.*

As to RMLC's section 2 claim that SESAC possessed monopoly power, the court held that RMLC had alleged a plausible claim based on RMLC's allegations that "SESAC's anticompetitive conduct has driven up the price of copyright licenses and deteriorated the quality of service insofar as customers only have the option of purchasing a blanket license."[189] The court rejected both of SESAC's arguments that RMLC's exclusionary conduct allegations were without merit.[190] First, the court dismissed SESAC's argument that the excluded parties are its affiliates that are suppliers and not direct competitors by observing that SESAC's members are both actual suppliers and potential competitors.[191] Second, the court dismissed SESAC's argument that it contractually forces its members "to utilize its services or threatens with legal sanctions those who contemplate taking their business elsewhere" by noting that SESAC uses "a carrot rather than a stick approach to retaining affiliates."[192] Finally, the court dismissed SESAC's argument that "copyright law, by definition, establishes a legal monopoly to artistic works" by recognizing that RMLC is not alleging "SESAC violated the Sherman Act merely by obtaining rights to copyrighted works."[193]

§ 3.10 Royalty Restraints

Royalty restraints are generally lawful unless the court or enforcement agency determines that the royalty restraint violates public policy.[194] See Chapter 6 for royalty restraints associated with reasonable and nondiscriminatory-encumbered patents.

§ 3.10.1 Royalty Rate

An intellectual property holder has a right to exploit its intellectual property by charging as high a royalty rate as it can obtain.[195] The royalty rate should be related to the licensee's utilization of the intellectual property.[196] If the royalty rate is not related to the utilization of the intellectual property, then the royalty rate and associated royalty provisions in the licensing agreement may be found invalid. In one example, a patent license agreement that "condition[s] the grant of a patent license upon payment of royalties on products which do not use the teachings of the patent" is

189. *Id.* at 502.
190. *Id.* at 500–01.
191. *Id.*
192. *Id.* at 501.
193. *Id.*
194. *Verizon Commc'ns v. Law Offices of Curtis V. Trinko, LLP*, 540 U.S. 398, 407 (2004).
195. *Standard Oil Co. v. United States*, 283 U.S. 163, 172 (1931).
196. *Zenith Radio Corp. v. Hazeltine Research*, 395 U.S. 100 (1969); *Trading Techs v. Refco Grp.*, 2006 U.S. Dist. LEXIS 14068 (N.D. Ill. 2006).

unlawful.[197] In another example, a patent license agreement that requires the payment of royalties for a product that may but does not utilize the intellectual property is unlawful.[198]

In *SanDisk v. Kingston*,[199] Kingston filed counterclaims for injunctive relief, including claiming that SanDisk had violated various antitrust laws.[200] One of Kingston's section 1 counterclaims alleged that SanDisk's licensing agreements unreasonably restrained trade in the U.S. flash drive market by requiring a worldwide royalty base, including in nations where SanDisk did not have any patents.[201] Because Kingston did not allege that SanDisk's licensing agreements were per se unreasonable, the court determined that SanDisk's licensing agreements would be evaluated under the rule of reason.[202] Under the rule of reason, the court determined that Kingston first must prove that the alleged restraints including the worldwide royalty base term in SanDisk's licensing agreements exceeded the scope of its patents, and second must show that imposing these alleged restraints on SanDisk's competitors was likely to increase price or decrease output in the USB flash drive market.[203] Since the court determined that Kingston was unable to prove the second prerequisite by failing to show anticompetitive effects, the court did not address the first prerequisite associated with the alleged restraints in SanDisk's licensing agreements.[204]

In *MPEG v. GXI*,[205] GXI licensed patents in MPEG's patent pool in exchange for royalty payments to MPEG.[206] MPEG commenced this action for GXI's breach of the licensing agreement including for GXI's failure to pay sufficient royalties.[207] GXI filed counterclaims based on MPEG's violations of New York's antitrust laws, which are based on the Sherman Act.[208] In its counterclaims, GXI alleged that MPEG violated the antitrust laws of New York, including by unreasonably charging royalties and by not adjusting the royalty rate as retail prices changed.[209] The court deter-

197. *Zenith*, 395 U.S. at 135.

198. *United States v. Microsoft Corp.*, 1995 U.S. Dist. LEXIS 20533, at *12 (D.D.C. 1995).

199. *SanDisk Corp. v. Kingston Tech. Co.*, 863 F. Supp. 2d 815 (W.D. Wis. 2012).

200. *Id.* at 817.

201. *Id.* at 824.

202. *Id.*

203. *Id.* at 824–25.

204. *Id.*; *see also supra* pp. 59–60 discussing rule of reason application to field of use restriction in this case) and *infra* pp. 88–91 discussing case background.

205. *MPEG LA, L.L.C. v GXI Int'l, LLC*, 2013 N.Y. Misc. LEXIS 2498 (N.Y. Sup. Ct. June 10, 2013).

206. *Id.* at *1.

207. *Id.*

208. *Id.*

209. *Id.* at *4–5.

mined that GXI did not allege any facts to support its contention that MPEG unreasonably charged royalties and that "the amount of the royalty cannot, by itself, serve as a basis to find an antitrust violation."[210] The court noted that "there is no requirement that royalties be 'reasonable,' so long as they do not adversely affect competition."[211] Regarding GXI's counterclaim that MPEG did not adjust the royalty rates as retail prices changed, the court commented that "there was nothing in the Licensing Agreement that provided for such an adjustment."[212]

§ 3.10.2 Discriminatory Royalties

An intellectual property holder is permitted to apply a different royalty rate for each licensee.[213] However, other factors may limit the ability of an intellectual property holder to discriminate amongst its licensees if it causes an adverse effect on competition.

§ 3.10.3 Patent Pre-issuance Royalties

A patent license agreement requiring a royalty payment for a pre-issuance patent may not be patent misuse in some circumstances.[214] For instance, a hybrid license that includes a patent license and a trade secret license may not be patent misuse.[215]

§ 3.10.4 Patent Post-Expiration Royalties

A patent license agreement requiring a royalty payment beyond the expiration of a patent is unenforceable and may be subject to patent misuse.[216] Further, a patent holder collecting royalties from a patent licensee beyond the expiration of the patent may be subject to a claim of patent misuse.[217]

In *Kimble v. Marvel*,[218] the Ninth Circuit construed the Supreme Court's decision in *Brulotte v. Thys*[219] that "a patent licensing agreement requiring a licensee to make royalty payments beyond the expiration date of the underlying patent was unenforceable because it represented an

210. *Id.* at *9.
211. *Id.* at *8.
212. *Id.* at *9.
213. *Standard Oil*, 283 U.S. at 179.
214. *Painton & Co. v. Bourns, Inc.*, 442 F.2d 216, 223 (2d Cir. 1971).
215. *Aronson v. Quick Point Pencil Co.*, 440 U.S. 257 (1979).
216. *Brulotte v. Thys Co.*, 379 U.S. 29 (1964).
217. *Zila, Inc. v. Tinnell*, 502 F.3d 1014 (9th Cir. 2007); *Scheiber v. Dolby Labs*, 293 F.3d 1014 (7th Cir. 2002); *Boggild v. Kenner Prods.*, 776 F.2d 1315 (6th Cir. 1985); *Pitney-Bowes, Inc. v. Mestre*, 701 F.2d 1365 (11th Cir. 1983); *Modrey v. Am. Gage & Mach.*, 478 F.2d 470, 474–75 (2d Cir. 1973).
218. *Kimble v. Marvel Enters. Inc.*, 727 F.3d 856 (9th Cir. 2013).
219. *Brulotte v. Thys Co.*, 379 U.S. 29 (1964).

improper attempt to extend the patent monopoly."[220] While recognizing the Seventh Circuit's criticism of the *Brulotte* rule, the Ninth Circuit held that "a so-called 'hybrid' licensing agreement encompassing inseparable patent and non-patent rights is unenforceable beyond the expiration date of the underlying patent, unless the agreement provides a discounted rate for the non-patent rights or some other clear indication that the royalty at issue was in no way subject to patent leverage."[221]

In *Kimble v. Marvel*,[222] relying heavily on *stare decisis*, the Supreme Court declined to overrule the *Brulotte* rule that a patentee cannot continue to receive royalties for sales made after the expiration of the patent.[223] In the majority opinion by Justice Kagan, with a dissenting opinion filed by Justice Alito joined by Chief Justice Roberts and Justice Thomas, Justice Kagan wrote:

> Patents endow their holders with certain superpowers, but only for a limited time. In crafting the patent laws, Congress struck a balance between fostering innovation and ensuring public access to discoveries. While a patent lasts, the patentee possesses exclusive rights to the patented article—rights he may sell or license for royalty payments if he so chooses. But a patent typically expires 20 years from the day the application for it was filed. And when the patent expires, the patentee's prerogatives expire too, and the right to make or use the article, free from all restriction, passes to the public. This Court has carefully guarded that cut-off date, just as it has the patent laws' subject-matter limits: In case after case, the Court has construed those laws to preclude measures that restrict free access to formerly patented, as well as unpatentable, inventions.[224]

However, the majority opinion provided examples of circumventing the *Brulotte* rule in licensing patents.[225] In one example, the opinion stated that the *Brulotte* rule "allows a licensee to defer payments for pre-expiration use of a patent into the post-expiration period; all the decision bars are royalties for using an invention after it has moved in the public domain."[226] In another example, the opinion described that "[a] licensee could agree,

220. *Id.* at 857.
221. *Id.*
222. *Kimble v. Marvel Enters., LLC*, 135 S. Ct. 2401 (June 22, 2015).
223. *Id.* at *3.
224. *Id.* at *4.
225. *Id.* at *5.
226. *Id.*

for example, to pay the licensor a sum equal to 10% of sales during the 20-year patent term, but to amortize that amount over 40 years."[227] For a license agreement covering multiple patents, the majority condones royalties running until the latest-running patent under the licensing agreement expires.[228] Also, Justice Kagan wrote that "post-expiration royalties are allowable so long as tied to a non-patent right—even when closely related to a patent."[229] In one example, the opinion stated that "a license involving both a patent and a trade secret can set a 5% royalty during the patent period (as compensation for the two combined) and a 4% royalty afterward (as payment for the trade secret alone)."[230] Finally, the opinion described that "*Brulotte* poses no bar to business arrangements other than royalties—all kinds of joint ventures, for example—that enable parties to share the risks and rewards of commercializing an invention."[231]

§ 3.10.5 Sharing Royalties

A licensee may be required to share royalties from its sublicensee with the patent holder.[232]

§ 3.10.6 Fixing Royalties

A patent holder may agree with a licensee to fix a royalty rate to charge a sublicensee.[233]

§ 3.10.7 Post-Sale Royalties

Once a patent holder sells a patented product to a buyer, any subsequent buyers of the patented product from the buyer may not be liable for patent infringement and may not be required to pay any royalties.[234] This scenario is covered by the doctrine of patent exhaustion, which may also be referred to as the first sale doctrine. The doctrine of patent exhaustion is a common-law doctrine that limits the extent to which a patent holder may control a patented product after a first sale to a buyer. A patent holder may place restrictions on a patent's use by any subsequent buyers as long as the restrictions are consistent within the patent grant.[235] It is

---

227. *Id.*
228. *Id.*
229. *Id.*
230. *Id.*
231. *Id.*
232. *Standard Oil*, 283 U.S. at 170–71.
233. *Miller Insituform, Inc. v. Insituform of N. Am., Inc.*, 605 F. Supp. 1125, 1133 (M.D. Tenn. 1985).
234. *Adams v. Burke*, 84 U.S. 453, 457 (1873).
235. *Monsanto Co. v. McFarling*, 363 F.3d 1336, 1340 (Fed. Cir. 2004).

also important to recognize that a patent holder may license a right to use separate from licensing the right to sell or make.[236]

In *Tessera v. ITC*,[237] the Federal Circuit, in an opinion by Judge Linn, held that patent exhaustion is not affected by a licensee's failure to pay royalties.[238] Tessera appealed a final determination by the ITC that the importers did not violate Tessera's patents through importation of semiconductor chips.[239] Tessera argued that the ITC improperly found patent exhaustion without an authorized sale, contending that under the terms of its licenses, sales by its licensees are unauthorized sales until royalties are paid.[240] However, the court determined under a similar fact pattern as in *Quanta*[241] that Tessera's licensees were authorized to sell its products since nothing in the license limited the licensee's ability to sell the accused products.[242] The court noted:

> Tessera authorizes its licensees to sell the licensed products on credit and pay later. That some licensees subsequently renege or fall behind on their royalty payments does not convert a once authorized sale into a non-authorized sale.[243]

The court also recognized that "there is nothing in any of the license agreements to even remotely suggest that the existence of a condition subsequent, namely, the payment of royalties, operates to convert initial authorized sales into unauthorized sales for purposes of patent exhaustion."[244]

In *Ninestar v. ITC*,[245] the Federal Circuit sitting en banc recognized that patent exhaustion under *Quanta* is not applicable where the first sale of patented products occurred outside the United States.[246] As background, the ITC brought an enforcement proceeding pursuant to the Tariff Act after Ninestar and its subsidiaries continued to import and sell printer cartridges in the United States in violation of exclusion and cease-and-desist orders based on a finding of unfair trade practices due to infringement of U.S. patents.[247] The court noted that "[t]he patents, products, and

236. *Extractol Process, Ltd. v. Hiram Walker & Sons*, 153 F.2d 264, 268 (7th Cir. 1946).
237. *Tessera, Inc. v. Int'l Trade Comm'n*, 646 F.3d 1357 (Fed. Cir. 2011).
238. *Id.* at 1369.
239. *Id.* at 1360.
240. *Id.* at 1369.
241. *Quanta Computer, Inc. v. LG Elecs., Inc.*, 553 U.S. 617 (2008).
242. *Id.* at 1369–70.
243. *Id.* at 1370.
244. *Id.*
245. *Ninestar Tech. Co. v. ITC*, 667 F.3d 1373 (Fed. Cir. 2012).
246. *Id.* at 1378.
247. *Id.* at 1377; *see Certain Ink Cartridges & Components Thereof*, Inv. No. 337-TA-565, USITC Pub. 4196 (Apr. 17, 2009).

methods in *Quanta Computer* all concerned products manufactured and first sold in the United States, and the Court held that method patents as well as product patents are subject to exhaustion upon sale of products or components in the United States."[248] Since the vast majority of cartridges sold by Ninestar and its subsidiaries were in Europe and Asia, the court recognized that such sales were not subject to patent exhaustion.[249]

In *Keurig v. Sturm Foods*,[250] the Federal Circuit determined that sales of patented machines exhausted method claims even though the machines had non-infringing uses.[251] As background, Keurig brought an action against Sturm Foods alleging that Sturm Foods' cartridges used in Keurig's brewers directly infringed its patents.[252] The district court held that the substantial embodiment test articulated by the Supreme Court in *Quanta* did not apply to the facts of the case.[253] The court noted that the substantial embodiment test, also referred to as the *Quanta* test, provides that "method claims are exhausted by sale of an unpatented component article if that article includes all the inventive aspects of the patented method and has no reasonable noninfringing use."[254] The court concluded that "the exhaustion of Keurig's patent rights had been triggered by Keurig's initial authorized sale of a patented item that completely practiced the claimed invention, *viz.*, the brewer." Further, the court noted that "Keurig's method claims were not saved from exhaustion merely because a consumer could potentially use non-Keurig cartridges in a Keurig brewer in a noninfringing way."[255]

On appeal, Keurig argued that the district court erred by declining to apply the substantial embodiment test.[256] Further, Keurig maintained that "under the Quanta test, its rights were not exhausted because its brewers are capable of many uses that do not infringe the asserted method claims, specifically when used with reusable cartridges that have premade holes and therefore are not pierced during brewing."[257] Sturm rebutted that "the Quanta test was formulated to address an exhaustion issue based on the sale of unpatented items and therefore is not applicable here."[258] Further, Sturm argued that the "use of Keurig's brewers with a non-Keurig

248. *Id.*
249. *Id.*
250. *Keurig, Inc. v. Sturm Foods, Inc.*, 732 F.3d 1370 (Fed. Cir. 2013).
251. *Id.* at 1372.
252. *Id.*
253. *Id.*
254. *Id.*
255. *Id.*
256. *Id.*
257. *Id.*
258. *Id.*

cartridge cannot constitute infringement because Keurig's authorized sale of those brewers, which are covered by the asserted patents, exhausted Keurig's rights."[259] The court agreed with Sturm that Keurig's method claims were exhausted relying on the Supreme Court's decisions in *Quanta* and *Univis*.[260] The court recognized that the Supreme Court in these decisions had "established that method claims are exhausted by an authorized sale of an item that substantially embodies the method if the item (1) has no reasonable noninfringing use and (2) includes all inventive aspects of the claimed method."[261] Keurig also alleged that "purchasers of its brewers infringe its brewer patents by using Sturm cartridges to practice the claimed methods and therefore that Sturm is liable for induced infringement."[262] However, the court disagreed, finding that Keurig sold its brewers without conditions and therefore under *Quanta* "obtained unfettered right to use them in any way they chose, at least as against a challenge from Keurig."[263]

In *LifeScan v. Shasta*,[264] the Federal Circuit determined that the transfer, whether by sale or gift, of unpatented devices used to perform steps of a method patent exhausted the patent.[265] Shasta argued that under *Quanta* the transfer of glucose detection devices exhausted LifeScan's patent rights.[266] LifeScan disagreed and contended that *Quanta* did not apply since the devices have reasonable non-infringing uses.[267] However, the court rejected this argument concluding that there is no suggestion that users can put the glucose detection device to non-infringing uses.[268] The court noted that "alternative uses are relevant to the exhaustion inquiry under *Quanta* only if they are both 'reasonable *and intended*' by the patentee or its authorized licensees."[269]

Furthermore, LifeScan argued that patent exhaustion did not apply because the devices do not embody the essential features of its patent.[270] However, the court determined that the glucose detection device alone performs the key steps of the method claim—hence, substantially embodies the method claims.[271] LifeScan also argued that its glucose detection device

259. *Id.* at 1372–73.
260. *United States v. Univis Lens Co.*, 316 U.S. 241 (1942).
261. *Id.*
262. *Id.* at 1374.
263. *Id.*
264. *LifeScan Scotland, Ltd. v. Shasta Tech., LLC*, 734 F.3d 1361 (Fed. Cir. 2013).
265. *Id.* at 1368.
266. *Id.*
267. *Id.*
268. *Id.* at 1369.
269. *Id.* (emphasis in original) (citing *Quanta*, 553 U.S. at 631).
270. *Id.*
271. *Id.* at 1370.

does not embody the method claims because its test strips are inventive and could have been separately patented.[272] Again, the court rejected LifeScan's argument recognizing that "barring the use of the meter with strips manufactured by the accused infringer would bar the use of the meters for their contemplated function and extend the patent monopoly improperly as we recently held in *Keurig*."[273] The court noted that the Supreme Court in tying and patent exhaustion cases has "expressed particular concern with extension of the patent monopoly to items that must be renewed periodically and that are not themselves patentable."[274]

Finally, LifeScan argued that even if its devices substantially embody the method claims, patent exhaustion does not apply to those devices distributed for free.[275] In a matter of first impression, the Federal Circuit held that "in the case of an authorized and unconditional transfer of title, the absence of consideration is no barrier to the application of patent exhaustion principles."[276] The court noted that the Supreme Court has "more fundamentally described exhaustion as occurring when the patented product 'passes to the hands' of a transferee and when he 'legally acquires a title' to it."[277]

In *Lexmark v. Impression*,[278] the Federal Circuit ordered that this appeal be heard en banc, including to determine (1) whether the court should overrule *Kirtsaeng*[279] that held that "a sale of a patented item outside the United States never gives rise to United States patent exhaustion" and (2) whether the court in light of *Quanta* should overrule *Mallinckrodt*[280] that held that "a sale of a patented article, when the sale is made under a restriction that is otherwise lawful and within the scope of the patent grant, does not give rise to patent exhaustion."[281]

§ 3.11 Grantback Restraints

A grantback restraint requires a patent licensee to license back to the patent holder any improvements or technology associated with the patent.[282] An agreement having a grantback restraint that provides a non exclusive

272. *Id.* at 1371.
273. *Id.* at 1372–73.
274. *Id.* at 1373; *see Motion Picture Patents Co. v. Universal Film Mfg. Co.*, 243 U.S. 502 (1917); *Carbice Corp. of Am. v. Am. Patents Dev. Corp.*, 283 U.S. 27 (1931).
275. *Id.* at 1374.
276. *Id.*
277. *Id.*
278. *Lexmark Int'l, Inc. v. Impression Prods., Inc.*, 785 F.3d 565 (Fed. Cir. 2015).
279. *Kirtsaeng v. John Wiley & Sons, Inc.*, 133 S. Ct. 1351 (2013).
280. *Mallinckrodt, Inc. v. Medipart, Inc.*, 976 F.2d 700 (Fed. Cir. 1992).
281. *Lexmark*, 785 F.3d at 566.
282. Licensing Guidelines, *supra* note 5, at § 5.6; *Transparent-Wrap Match v. Stokes & Smith Co.*, 329 U.S. 637, 646 (1947).

license back to the patent holder is analyzed under a rule-of-reason analysis, since it encourages further dissemination of technology.[283] However, an agreement having a grantback restraint that provides an exclusive license back to the patent holder may be analyzed under a per se analysis.[284]

§ 3.12 Non-assertion Restraints

A licensor may request that a licensee refrain from asserting certain intellectual property rights against the licensor as a condition for obtaining a license.

In *In re Intel*,[285] the FTC alleged that Intel had monopoly power over general-purpose microprocessors and used such power to prevent others from enforcing their own intellectual property rights.[286] In settling the FTC proceedings, Intel agreed to provide its confidential product information to any microprocessor customer even upon the existence of an intellectual property dispute between the parties.[287] However, Intel has the right to stop providing its confidential product information to a microprocessor customer if such customer seeks an injunction to limit Intel's rights to its microprocessors.[288]

In *Intergraph v. Intel*,[289] the Federal Circuit reversed a district court's ruling regarding "coercive reciprocity," which is defined by the court as "the practice of using economic leverage in one market coercively to secure competitive advantage in another."[290] The district court referred to Intel's tying of a supply of Intel CPUs and technical information in exchange for Intergraph's relinquishment of certain patents without cost to Intel.[291] The Federal Circuit noted that Intergraph was interested in selling or licensing its patents and that Intel did not demand that Intergraph buy its products.[292] Further, the Federal Circuit commented that "[c]ommercial negotiations to trade patent property rights for other consideration in order to settle a patent dispute is neither tying nor coercive reciprocity in violation of the Sherman Act."[293]

283. *Id.*
284. *Hartford-Empire Co. v. United States*, 323 U.S. 386 (1945).
285. *In re Intel Corp.*, No. 9288 (F.T.C. Aug. 6, 1999) (complaint filed June 8, 1998).
286. *Id.* at *3–8.
287. *Id.* at *2.
288. *Id.* at *2–3.
289. *Intergraph Corp. v. Intel Corp.*, 195 F.3d 1346 (Fed. Cir. 1999).
290. *Id.* at 1360–61.
291. *Id.*
292. *Id.*
293. *Id.* at 1362.

§ 3.13 No Challenge Restraints

A no challenge restraint may restrict a licensee from challenging the validity of licensed intellectual property. In the seminal case of *Lear v. Adkins*,[294] the Supreme Court reviewed the history of its prior decisions relating to the doctrine of licensee estoppel and held that a license alone does not bar the licensee from challenging the validity of a patent.[295] However, the *Lear* doctrine "does not grant every licensee in every circumstance the right to challenge the validity of the licensed patent."[296] Since *Lear*, the courts have reached different conclusions as to whether licensee estoppel applies to license agreements associated with the settlement of litigation.

In *RTI v. Speakeasy*,[297] the court found determinative that a no challenge clause was executed prior to any litigation between the parties. After Speakeasy filed suit seeking a declaration that RTI's patents are invalid, RTI filed suit alleging Speakeasy's breach of a no challenge agreement between the parties made prior to any litigation.[298] The court noted that "*Lear* makes clear that courts should weigh the federal policy embodied in the law of intellectual property against even explicit contractual provisions and render unenforceable those provisions that would undermine the public interest."[299] Further, the court stated that it "believe[s] that enforcing no challenge clauses in pre-litigation settlements would significantly undermine the 'public interest in discovering invalid patents.'"[300]

In *Industrial Engineering v. Static*,[301] the court found determinative whether a no challenge clause was agreed to in the settlement of a prior litigation. Industrial Engineering filed suit against Static for its alleged failure to pay royalties under the parties' settlement and cross-licensing agreement, which the parties allegedly entered into to resolve previously pending lawsuits.[302] Further, the settlement and cross-licensing agreement included provisions expressly prohibiting the parties from challenging the validity of each other's patents.[303] Static filed counterclaims seeking to invalidate Industrial Engineering's patents.[304] While the court

294. *Lear, Inc. v. Adkins*, 395 U.S. 653 (1969).
295. *Id.* at 671.
296. *Gen-Probe, Inc. v. Vysis, Inc.*, 359 F.3d 1376, 1381 (Fed. Cir. 2004).
297. *Rates Tech., Inc. (RTI) v. Speakeasy, Inc.*, 685 F.3d 163 (2d Cir. 2012).
298. *Id.* at 166.
299. *Id.* at 171.
300. *Id.* at 172.
301. *Indus. Eng'g & Dev., Inc. v. Static Control Components, Inc.*, 2013 U.S. Dist. LEXIS 8999 (M.D. Fla. Jan. 23, 2013).
302. *Id.* at *2.
303. *Id.*
304. *Id.*

noted the exception to the *Lear* doctrine, when a no challenge clause is part of a settlement agreement reached during litigation, the court recognized that neither Industrial Engineering nor Static refer to the settlement and cross-licensing agreement in its pleadings.[305] Thus, the court's ability to determine whether the settlement and cross-licensing agreement was reached in the settlement of prior litigation between the parties is a factual determination best resolved at the summary judgment stage or at trial.[306]

In *Peparlet v. Shepherd*,[307] the court used "contractual estoppel" to affirm the no challenge clause in a prior settlement agreement. Peparlet filed suit against Shepherd for its alleged breach of a settlement agreement reached during prior litigation requiring Shepherd not to infringe the claims of a Peparlet patent.[308] Further, the settlement agreement included a provision expressly prohibiting Shepherd from challenging the validity of the Peparlet patent.[309] Shepherd filed counterclaims requesting that the court enter a declaratory judgment finding the associated patent invalid.[310] The court relying on "contractual estoppel" determined that the provision prohibiting Shepherd from challenging the validity of the Peparlet patent was clear and unambiguous—thus, enforceable.[311] Further, the court noted that "[u]pholding the terms of settlement agreements encourages patent owners to agree to settlements and promotes judicial economy."[312]

§ 3.14 Noncompete Restraints

A noncompete restraint limits the ability of the licensee to compete against the intellectual property holder. A patent license agreement having a noncompete restraint may be analyzed under a rule-of-reason analysis.[313]

§ 3.15 Licensee Veto Restraints

A licensee veto restraint provides that the intellectual property holder and its licensee must mutually consent to additional licenses or sublicenses of the intellectual property. An agreement between competitors having a licensee veto restraint may raise antitrust concerns.[314] In one example, a

---

305. *Id.* at *7.
306. *Id.* at *7–8.
307. *Peparlet Co. v. Shepherd Specialty Papers, Inc.*, 2013 U.S. Dist. LEXIS 69738 (N.D. Ohio May 16, 2013).
308. *Id.* at *2.
309. *Id.* at *2–3.
310. *Id.*
311. *Id.* at *6–7.
312. *Id.* at *8.
313. *Perceptron, Inc. v. Sensor Adaptive Machs., Inc.*, 221 F.3d 913, 919 (6th Cir. 2000).
314. *United States v. Krasnov*, 143 F. Supp. 184 (E.D. Pa. 1956), *aff'd*, 355 U.S. 5 (1957).

license agreement between competitors associated with a key patent and having a veto right restraint may be analyzed under the per se rule.[315] In another example, an agreement by a patent holder that provides a non-exclusive licensee with a licensee veto restraint may be analyzed under the per se rule.[316]

IV. Cross-License Agreements and Patent Pools

§ 3.16 General

A cross-licensing agreement is an agreement between two or more holders of different intellectual property to license the intellectual property to each other or to a third party.[317] A patent pool is a consortium of two or more companies agreeing to cross-license patents relating to a particular technology. The *Agencies* commented that cross-licensing agreements and patent pools may "provide procompetitive benefits by integrating complementary technologies, reducing transaction costs, clearing blocking [patents], and avoiding costly infringement litigation."[318] Further, the *Agencies* noted that a patent pool may be the only reasonable method for making the technology available to the marketplace by, for instance, mitigating any blocking patents.[319] A cross-licensing agreement and a patent pool will generally be analyzed under a rule of reason analysis.[320]

§ 3.17 Price and Output Restraints

Cross-licensing agreements and patent pools may have anticompetitive effects such as those associated with "collective price or output restraints in pooling arrangements . . . if they do not contribute to an efficiency-enhancing integration of economic activity among the participants."[321] Cross-licensing or patent pool arrangements that fix prices or allocate market share may be analyzed under the per se rule.[322]

315. *United States v. Besser Mfg. Co.*, 96 F. Supp. 304 (E.D. Mich. 1951).

316. *Mason City Tent & Awning Co. v. Clapper*, 144 F. Supp. 754 (W.D. Mo. 1956).

317. Licensing Guidelines, *supra* note 5, § 5.5.

318. *Id.*

319. A blocking patent is a patent associated with a particular technology area that may prevent another patent from being used, since the other patent relies on technology covered by the blocking patent.

320. *Standard Oil*, 283 U.S. at 171.

321. Licensing Guidelines, *supra* note 5, § 5.5; *compare NCAA v. Bd. of Regents of the Univ. of Okla.*, 468 U.S. 85 (1984), *with Broad. Music*, 441 U.S. 1 (1979).

322. *Id.*; *see United States v. Singer Mfg. Co.*, 374 U.S. 174 (1963); *United States v. New Wrinkle, Inc.*, 342 U.S. 371 (1952).

§ 3.18 Exclusionary Restraints

Cross-licensing agreements and patent pools may harm competition when parties that have collective market power exclude others from these arrangements.[323] The *Agencies* commented that cross-licensing agreements or patent pools among competing technologies may be anticompetitive when "(1) excluded firms cannot effectively compete in the relevant market for the good incorporating the licensed technologies and (2) the pool participants collectively possess market power in the relevant market."[324] The *Agencies* noted that these arrangements are analyzed to determine whether the exclusionary restraint is "reasonably related to the efficient development and exploitation of the pooled technologies and will assess the net effect of those limitations in the relevant market."[325]

§ 3.19 R&D Restraints on Patent Pools

Patent pools may harm competition when they discourage participants from engaging in research and development.[326] However, these arrangements may benefit competition by "exploiting economies of scale and integrating complementary capabilities of the pool members, (including the clearing of blocking [patents]), and is likely to cause competitive problems only when the arrangement includes a large fraction of the potential research and development in an innovation market."[327]

§ 3.20 Settlements Involving Cross-Licensing Agreements

The *Agencies* commented that settlements involving cross-licensing agreements between horizontal competitors should be analyzed to consider whether "the effect of the settlement is to diminish competition among entities that would have been actual or likely potential competitors in a relevant market in the absence of the cross-license.[328] Further, the *Agencies* stated that "[i]n the absence of offsetting efficiencies, such settlement agreements may be challenged as unlawful restraints of trade."[329]

---

323. *Id.*; *see Nw. Wholesale Stationers, Inc. v. Pac. Stationery & Printing Co.*, 472 U.S. 284 (1985).

324. *Id.*

325. *Id.*

326. *Id. See generally United States v. Mfrs. Aircraft Ass'n, Inc.*, 1976-1 Trade Cas. (CCH) ¶ 60,810 (S.D.N.Y. 1975); 1982–83 Trade Cas. (CCH) ¶ 65,088 (C.D. Cal. 1982); *United States v. Auto. Mfrs. Ass'n*, 307 F. Supp. 617 (C.D. Cal 1969), *appeal dismissed sub nom. City of New York v. United States*, 397 U.S. 248 (1970), *modified sub nom. United States v. Motor Vehicle Mfrs. Ass'n*, 1982–83 Trade Cas. (CCH) ¶ 65,088 (C.D. Cal. 1982).

327. *Id.*

328. *Id.*; *see Singer*, 374 U.S. 174.

329. *Id.*

chapter 4

Antitrust Issues in Litigating Intellectual Property

I. Introduction

There is a tension between patent law and antitrust law that courts must apply to the specific circumstances brought before them. On the one hand, a patent holder has a legally sanctioned right to exclude others from making, using, selling, offering to sell, or importing a patented article.[1] The policy basis for this right is the public good served by "bring[ing] new designs and technologies into the public domain through disclosure."[2] This right permits a patent holder to "exact royalties as high as he can negotiate" from the patent grant,[3] and even refuse to license an invention entirely.[4] On the other hand, the patent right is not unlimited, and one of the limits is antitrust, the laws of which were enacted to promote competition.[5] While there may be actions permissible under the patent grant that would otherwise raise antitrust concerns, the existence of a patent alone does not provide an absolute shield to antitrust liability.[6]

The agencies have provided some guidance to help parties understand and manage potential conflicts between the patent and antitrust laws. The FTC and DOJ jointly prepared the 1995 *Antitrust Guidelines*

---

1. 35 U.S.C. § 271(a); *Zenith Radio Corp. v. Hazeltine Research, Inc.*, 395 U.S. 100, 135 (1969).

2. *Bonito Boats, Inc. v. Thunder Craft Boats, Inc.*, 489 U.S. 141, 151 (1989).

3. *Brulotte v. Thys Co.*, 379 U.S. 29, 33 (1964).

4. *Image Technical Servs., Inc. v. Eastman Kodak Co.*, 125 F.3d 1195, 1215 (9th Cir. 1997).

5. *Loctite Corp. v. Ultraseal Ltd.*, 781 F.2d 861, 876–77 (Fed. Cir. 1985).

6. *Atari Games Corp. v. Nintendo of Am., Inc.*, 897 F.2d 1572, 1576 (Fed. Cir. 1990).

for the Licensing of Intellectual Property.[7] The 1995 *Licensing Guidelines* address many of the most common antitrust concerns with licensing as well as provide an overview of the legal framework agencies will use to review competition concerns involving intellectual property. In addition, in 2007, the FTC and DOJ prepared an extensive review of antitrust concerns arising from intellectual property.[8] This publication addresses topics such as unilateral refusals to license intellectual property, competition concerns arising from collaborative ventures and standard-setting organizations, antitrust review of cross-licensing and patent pools, and a renewed analysis of antitrust violations in the licensing and exploitation of patents. These agency guidelines provide a logical starting point when a party is confronted with an antitrust concern involving certain intellectual property.

The tension between patent and intellectual property law is illustrated in *MiniFrame v. Microsoft*.[9] Plaintiff MiniFrame brought suit against Microsoft under section 2 of the Sherman Act, based on a change in Microsoft's policy regarding its Windows operating system, wherein licenses for the system were granted on a per-user rather than a per-computer basis. MiniFrame sold software that permitted several users to access Windows from a single computer, and thus the change in Microsoft's policy significantly reduced demand for MiniFrame's product. The basis for MiniFrame's antitrust complaint was that Microsoft, which allegedly had market power in the relevant market for computer operating systems, by its behavior refused to deal with MiniFrame, or its customers, on "commercially reasonable and non-discriminatory terms."[10]

The district court granted Microsoft's motion to dismiss. While the existence of monopoly power is a necessary component of an antitrust assessment, it is not by itself enough, according to the court. Rather, there must be anticompetitive conduct coupled with market power in order for a plaintiff to make out an antitrust violation.[11] Such conduct is defined as "willful acquisition or maintenance of that power as distinguished from growth or development as a consequence of a superior product, business

7. U.S. Dep't of Justice & Fed. Trade Comm'n, Antitrust Guidelines for the Licensing of Intellectual Property § 3.2 (Apr. 6, 1995), *available at* http://www.justice.gov/atr/public/guidelines/0558.htm.

8. U.S. Dep't of Justice & Fed. Trade Comm'n, Antitrust Enforcement and Intellectual Property Rights: Promoting Innovation and Competition (Apr. 2007), *available at* http://www.justice.gov/atr/public/hearings/ip/222655.htm.

9. *MiniFrame Ltd. v. Microsoft Corp.*, No.11 CIV. 7419 RJS, 2013 WL 1385704 (S.D.N.Y. Mar. 28, 2013), *aff'd*, 551 F. App'x 1 (2d Cir.).

10. *Id.* at *1.

11. *Verizon Commc'ns Inc. v. Law Offices of Curtis v. Trinko LLP*, 540 U.S. 398, 407 (2004).

acumen, or historic accident."[12] And attempted monopolization under section 2 of the Sherman Act requires "(1) that the defendant has engaged in predatory or anticompetitive conduct with (2) a specific intent to monopolize and (3) a dangerous probability of achieving monopoly power."[13]

The district court rejected MiniFrame's contention that either the change in licensing scheme (from single computer to single user) or Microsoft's pricing of its own multiuser server software (which directly competed with MiniFrame's product) constituted anticompetitive conduct. The basis for this determination was the existence of Microsoft's patents: the court characterized the patent grant as providing "broad authority to enforce . . . intellectual property rights without violating the antitrust laws,"[14] and indeed has a statutory exemption from such liability for refusing to license its patent to others.[15] The court characterized Microsoft's behavior as being for "a wholly justifiable business purpose," analogous to circumstances where other intellectual property rights holders have limited distribution of their products.[16]

Even in the absence of IP rights, the court found no affirmative obligation to deal that could be imposed on Microsoft. Generally, a corporation has "no duty to aid competitors."[17] And the few exceptions to this general rule (such as a refusal to deal with rivals after previous cooperation, with concomitant loss of short-term profits) require a showing of predatory rather than merely competitive behavior, such as selling a product at a loss in order to force rivals from the marketplace.[18] None of these circumstances being adequately pled, the court dismissed MiniFrame's complaint.

On appeal, the Second Circuit affirmed the trial court's decision dismissing MiniFrame's suit. However, the Second Circuit rested its decision only upon MiniFrame's failure to "allege that Microsoft had any prior dealing" with Microsoft, upon which its refusal to deal or *Aspen Skiing* claim could be based.[19] The appellate court declined to address the trial court's "alternative rationale that Microsoft's conduct is immune from antitrust liability based on intellectual property law."[20]

12. *United States v. Grinnell Corp.*, 384 U.S. 563, 570–71 (1966).
13. *Spectrum Sports, Inc. v. McQuillan*, 506 U.S. 447, 456 (1993).
14. *MiniFrame Ltd. v. Microsoft Corp.*, No. 11 CIV. 7419 RJS, 2013 WL 1385704, at *3 (S.D.N.Y. Mar. 28, 2013) *aff'd*, 551 F. App'x 1 (2d Cir. 2013).
15. 35 U.S.C. § 271(d)(4).
16. *MiniFrame Ltd.*, 2013 WL 1385704, at *3 (citing *Metro-Goldwyn-Mayer Studios Inc. v. Grokster, Ltd.*, 545 U.S. 913, 941 (2005)).
17. *Trinko*, 540 U.S. at 411.
18. *Aspen Skiing Co. v. Aspen Highlands Skiing Corp.*, 472 U.S. 585, 600 (1985).
19. *MiniFrame Ltd. v. Microsoft Corp.*, 551 F. App'x 1, 2 (2d Cir. 2013).
20. *Id.*

II. The SanDisk Cases

Assertion of a large portfolio of patents involving technology relating to flash memory devices by patent holder SanDisk has been the source of several antitrust claims and counterclaims in patent litigation in the 2012–2013 time period.

In *PNY v. SanDisk*,[21] the district court granted SanDisk's motion to dismiss for failure to satisfy Federal Rule of Civil Procedure 8 regarding sufficiency of allegations of antitrust injury plead in PNY's complaint. The case involved SanDisk's "extensive patent portfolio" (more than 1,400 patents) relating to flash memory technology and specifically targeted SanDisk's alleged practice of requiring "multitiered licensing and royalties in the downstream market."[22] These practices included a "uniform, nonnegotiable license" giving SanDisk control over pricing for flash memory devices. Specific acts alleged by PNY as the basis for its antitrust allegations, on grounds sounding in sections 1 and 2 of the Sherman Act, included payment of multiple royalties from flash memory manufacturers and upon sale of the final product; payment of royalties worldwide that include sales from countries where SanDisk has no patent protection; requiring licensing of SanDisk's entire patent portfolio, rather than the specific patents that cover alleged infringing devices; and a grantback cross-license to later-developed technologies (which PNY alleged inhibited efforts to design around SanDisk's patents). In addition, PNY complained that SanDisk's practices forced competitors to pay royalties directly to SanDisk or indirectly (and in some instances at higher rates) whether buying from licensed vendors or manufacturing flash memory independently. PNY also alleged a conspiracy between SanDisk and other "vertically integrated" manufacturers (including Toshiba and Samsung) directed to aggregator companies, like PNY, who did not independently manufacture flash memory themselves.[23]

The court based its decision to grant SanDisk's motion to dismiss on specific deficiencies in PNY's complaint and informed by the Supreme Court's decision in *Twombly*.[24] The court first set forth the relevant markets, specifically an "upstream" market in flash memory and a "downstream" market for "devices, systems and products" having flash memory.

---

21. *PNY Techs., Inc. v. SanDisk Corp.*, No. 11-04689, 2012 WL 1380271 (N.D. Cal. Apr. 20, 2012).

22. *Id.* at *1.

23. *Id.* at *3.

24. *Id.* at *5; *see also Bell Atl. Corp. v. Twombly*, 550 U.S. 544, 557 (2007).

The question it then considered was whether SanDisk had "monopoly power" in either or both of these markets, such power comprising one of the requirements of a well-pled complaint for Sherman Act violations. PNY satisfied this aspect as to the upstream market, because SanDisk purportedly controls 100 percent of that market. PNY failed, however, to establish market power as to the downstream market, because its allegations are merely "conclusory," and the court discredited the complaint's equation of the power to collect royalties and the power the control prices. Nor was the court satisfied with PNY's allegations that SanDisk had the power to exclude competition based on allegations of exclusion regarding one particular competitor: "The allegation that SanDisk contracted with a small number of competitors to exit 'one or more of the Relevant Markets' does not support the conclusion that SanDisk has sufficient power to exclude all competition *generally* from any of the downstream markets."[25] Turning to the question of whether SanDisk's market share in the downstream market is sufficient to establish market power, the court found the allegations substantively deficient, insofar as SanDisk's share (about 40 percent) was less than the generally accepted proportion (a 65 percent market share) needed to show market power. Nor did PNY provide sufficient specific allegations to establish that SanDisk has erected anticompetitive barriers to entry to the downstream markets.

Regarding the second prong of the test for antitrust violations under sections 1 and 2 of the Sherman Act, the court found that PNY did not allege sufficient evidence to support its allegations that SanDisk had engaged in anticompetitive behavior—that is, had "use[d] that monopoly power to foreclose competition, to gain a competitive advantage, or to destroy a competitor."[26] For example, the court stated that while PNY alleged SanDisk charges a "double royalty" on goods sold under its licenses, it was just as likely that SanDisk collects different royalties on different patents from its portfolio, relevant to the sales at each level of the production chain, and the court further held that PNY had not supported its pleadings with facts to the contrary. Similarly, the court noted that there is nothing inherently illegal about a grantback clause in a license for later-developed technology[27] and that PNY had not alleged facts showing that these provisions were being abused. Finally, the court found PNY's

25. *PNY Techs.*, 2012 WL 1380271, at *8 (emphasis in original).

26. *Id.* at *10 (quoting *Eastman Kodak Co. v. Image Technical Servs., Inc.*, 504 U.S. 451, 482 (1992)).

27. *Id.* at *12 (citing *Transparent-Wrap Mach. Corp. v. Stokes & Smith Co.*, 329 U.S. 637, 647 (1947)).

allegations of anticompetitive behavior stemming from the "portfolio" nature of the license agreement to be unsatisfactory because PNY had not alleged facts demonstrating anticompetitive conduct that, in fact, created or maintained an illegal monopoly.[28]

The court also faulted PNY for failing to properly allege antitrust injury, a requirement for a private action under the statute.[29] The "injury" alleged by PNY stemmed directly from the terms of the SanDisk license. The court found that PNY did not plead adequately, however, the consequence of SanDisk's anticompetitive conduct. Thus, the allegations did not support PNY's private complaint for antitrust violations under the Sherman Act.

The court dismissed PNY's allegations of a conspiracy under section 1 of the Sherman Act for failure to allege sufficient facts supporting the allegations, but granted PNY leave to amend.

Similarly, the district court found that the defendant failed to prove its antitrust counterclaim in *SanDisk v. Kingston*[30] based on its failure to establish that SanDisk's licensing practices had an anticompetitive effect on the domestic USB flash drive market. In this case, defendant Kingston refused to enter into SanDisk's license for patented flash memory technology and SanDisk sued for patent infringement, prompting Kingston to assert Sherman Act violations as counterclaims. On summary judgment, the district court found in Kingston's favor on SanDisk's infringement claims and in SanDisk's favor on Kingston's section 2 allegations, leaving Kingston's section 1 counterclaims for trial. Following trial, applying a "rule of reason" analysis, the district court found that SanDisk's licensing agreements exceeded the scope of its patents (1,700 by this court's count), based on license terms requiring royalties on sales made in countries where it did not have patent protection. However, the court found that Kingston had not established that SanDisk's alleged anticompetitive behavior had "adversely affect[ed] the USB flash drive market *in the United States*."[31] The court found that Kingston did not establish that raising costs to aggregators (companies that assembled USB flash drive components and sold them under their own brand) by compelling such aggregators to pay royalties to SanDisk raised the overall market price to consumers or forced aggregators out of the domestic USB flash drive market. In addition, the

---

28. *See supra* p. 21 discussing dismissal of the grantback-related claim in this case.
29. *Id.* at *13; *see also Cargill, Inc. v. Monfort of Colo., Inc.*, 479 U.S. 104, 113 (1986).
30. *SanDisk Corp. v. Kingston Tech. Co.*, 863 F. Supp. 2d 815 (W.D. Wis. 2012).
31. *Id.* at 824 (emphasis added).

court found that Kingston's evidence did not take into account legitimate royalties from other SanDisk patents.[32]

In *Ritz Camera and Image v. SanDisk*,[33] the Federal Circuit affirmed the district court's grant of SanDisk's motion to dismiss. In particular, the Federal Circuit agreed with the district court that Ritz failed to prove that SanDisk had obtained certain of the patents in its flash memory portfolio through fraud and thus should incur antitrust liability under *Walker Process*.[34] In proceedings below, declaratory judgment plaintiff Ritz Camera, a "direct purchaser of goods protected by [a] patent[,]" asserted an antitrust count under the *Walker Process* doctrine regarding two of SanDisk's patents (U.S. Patent Nos. 5,172,338 and 5,991,517), and SanDisk moved to dismiss on the grounds that Ritz as a purchaser "faced no threat of an infringement action."[35] The district court found that such a purchaser was not "categorically precluded" from bringing an action under section 2 of the Sherman Act.[36] In an interlocutory appeal on the certified standing question, the Federal Circuit affirmed, in an opinion by Judge Bryson joined by Judges Dyk and Moore. Citing its own and Supreme Court precedent, the opinion found that there is nothing in the *Walker Process* doctrine that would preclude a plaintiff that can allege antitrust injury and satisfy the other requirements of an antitrust claim (market power and abuse of that power to monopolize or attempt to monopolize the relevant market) from bringing the action. Indeed, the panel found support in *Big Bear Lodging Association v. Snow Summit, Inc.*[37] that direct purchasers may be "preferred" antitrust plaintiffs.

III. Procedural Issues

Courts face multiple procedural issues in antitrust cases associated with intellectual property. Since antitrust claims typically use the same facts as their corresponding patent claims, courts often must determine whether an antitrust counterclaim is compulsory under the Federal Rules of Civil

32. *See also supra* pp. 59–60 discussing rule of reason application to field of use restriction in this case and p. 72 discussing rule of reason application to field of use restrictions.

33. *Ritz Camera & Image, LLC v. SanDisk Corp.*, 700 F.3d 503 (Fed. Cir. 2012).

34. *Id.* at 508; *see also Walker Process Equip., Inc. v. Food Mach. & Chem. Corp.*, 382 U.S. 172 (1965).

35. 700 F.3d at 505.

36. *Id.*

37. *Id.* at 506 (citing *Big Bear Lodging Ass'n v. Snow Summit, Inc.*, 182 F.3d 1096, 1102 n. 4 (9th Cir.1999)).

Procedure. Further, courts must determine whether to bifurcate antitrust claims from their associated patent claims at the discovery or trial phases.

§ 4.1 Jurisdiction

The U.S. Court of Appeals for the Federal Circuit was established in 1982 primarily to bring conformity to patent jurisprudence. While the Federal Circuit has exclusive appellate jurisdiction over patent claims, the Federal Circuit also has exclusive appellate jurisdiction over non-patent claims based "in whole or in part" on 28 U.S.C. § 1338(a). Section 1338(a) provides district courts original jurisdiction for cases "arising under any Act of Congress relating to patents, plant variety protection, copyrights and trademarks."[38] Otherwise, other circuit courts have exclusive appellate jurisdiction. Since the Federal Circuit and the other circuit courts split jurisdiction over non-patent claims, the Federal Circuit often must decide whether it or another circuit court has jurisdiction.

A non-patent claim "arise[s] under" patent law only if "a well-pleaded complaint establishes either that federal patent law creates the cause of action or that the plaintiff's right to relief necessarily depends on resolution of a substantial question of federal patent law, in that patent law is a necessary element of one of the well-pleaded claims."[39] Antitrust claims do not "arise[] under" patent law "[s]ince there are 'reasons completely unrelated to the provisions and purposes' of federal patent law why petitioners 'may or may not be entitled to the relief they seek' under their monopolization claim."[40]

Federal Circuit jurisdiction over a non-patent claim may "depend[] on the nature of the case brought in the district court, not the nature of the issues raised by the appeal."[41] The Federal Circuit commented that "[t]he criteria for jurisdiction of the district court over a case are determined at the complaint stage, and a subsequent event such as the present separation order entered solely to direct appeals, *that does not alter those criteria*, cannot oust the appellate court of its potential jurisdiction over appeals from final decision in that case."[42]

In *Lotes v. Hon Hai*,[43] the Second Circuit reviewed questions regarding the extraterritorial reach of U.S. antitrust law, including "whether

38. 28 U.S.C. § 1338(a).

39. *Christianson v. Colt Indus. Operating Corp.*, 486 U.S. 800, 809 (1988).

40. *Id.* at 812 (quoting *Franchise Tax Bd. of Cal. v. Constr. Laborers Vacation Trust*, 463 U.S. 1, 26 (1983)).

41. 15A Charles Alan Wright, Arthur R. Miller & Edward H. Cooper, Federal Practice and Procedure § 3903.1 (2d ed. 1992); *see also Atari, Inc. v. JS&A Grp., Inc.*, 747 F.2d 1422 (Fed. Cir. 1984) (en banc).

42. *Atari, Inc.*, 747 F.2d at 1431–32 (emphasis in original).

43. *Lotes Co. v. Hon Hai Precision Indus. Co.*, 753 F.3d 395 (2d Cir. 2014).

the restrictions Congress has imposed on antitrust claims based on foreign conduct under the Foreign Trade Antitrust Improvements Act ("FTAIA") . . . are jurisdictional in nature."[44] The Second Circuit held that "the requirements of the FTAIA are substantive and nonjurisdictional" relying on a line of recent Supreme Court cases[45] and overruling the Second Circuit's prior decision in *Filetech v. France Telecom*.[46] Further, the court concluded that since Congress had not "clearly stated" that the requirements of the FTAIA are jurisdictional, such requirements "go to the merits of the claim rather than the adjudicative power of the court."[47] Also, the court held that "foreign anticompetitive conduct can have a statutorily required 'direct, substantial, and reasonably foreseeable effect' on U.S. domestic or import commerce even if the effect does not follow as an immediate consequence of the defendant's conduct, so long as there is a reasonably proximate causal nexus between the conduct and the effect," rejecting the Ninth Circuit's "direct . . . effect" interpretation in *United States v. LSL Biotechnologies*.[48]

In *MPHJ Technology Investments v. FTC*,[49] the district court determined that it lacked jurisdiction over MPHJ's claim alleging that the FTC's unfair practices investigation into MPHJ's use of patent demand letters and subsequent attempt at a settlement violated its First Amendment right to petition the government.[50] The FTC contended that the court lacked jurisdiction because MPHJ's claims were not ripe since there was no final agency action and because MPHJ had failed to exhaust its administrative remedies.[51] The court determined that MPHJ's claims were not ripe because there was no threat of prosecution by the FTC since no FTC action was beyond the investigative stage.[52] Also, the court determined that MPHJ had failed to exhaust its administrative remedies as required by the FTC Act because the FTC was still in the investigative stage with the outcome yet determined.[53]

44. *Id.* at 398.

45. *See Arbaugh v. Y & H Corp.*, 546 U.S. 500 (2006); *Sebelius v. Auburn Reg'l Med. Ctr.*, 133 S. Ct. 1235 (2006).

46. *Lotes*, 753 F.3d at 398; *see Filetech S.A. v. France Telecom S.A.*, 157 F.3d 922 (2d Cir. 1998).

47. *Lotes*, 753 F.3d 395.

48. *Id.* at 398; *see United States v. LSL Biotechnologies*, 379 F.3d 672, 680 (9th Cir. 2004).

49. *MPHJ Tech. Invs., LLC v. FTC*, 2014 WL 4724558 (W.D. Tex. 2014).

50. *Id.*

51. *Id.*

52. *Id.*

53. *Id.*

§ 4.2 Choice of Law

The Federal Circuit routinely exercises appellate jurisdiction over non-patent claims such as antitrust claims. However, the Federal Circuit's exercise of these non-patent claims presents a choice of law problem as to whether the Federal Circuit should apply the law from another circuit court or review the claim independently of other circuit courts.

In *Engineering and Inspection Services v. IntPar*,[54] the district court applied Federal Circuit law to determine personal jurisdiction in an action where the plaintiff brought multiple causes of action including a declaratory judgment of non-infringement of IntPar's patents and relief for violation of various antitrust statutes. The court noted that "[i]n an action where a plaintiff seeks a declaratory judgment of patent non-infringement, the issue of personal jurisdiction is 'intimately related' to patent law and thus governed by Federal Circuit law regarding due process."[55]

Further, the court in *In re Lipitor Antitrust Litigation*[56] commented that "[a]n antitrust claim only gives rise to Federal Circuit jurisdiction and only necessitates the application of Federal Circuit law, if 'patent law is essential to each of the theories' of liability under the antitrust claims alleged in the complaint."[57]

In *In re Lipitor Antitrust Litigation*, the district court applied Third Circuit law when analyzing antitrust claims brought by the plaintiffs. The court stated that "[i]f a plaintiff presents a claim 'supported by alternative theories in the complaint,' *i.e.*, theories other than patent law theories, that claim does not depend on patent law and accordingly the Federal Circuit lacks jurisdiction."[58] The court determined that the plaintiff's reverse payment theory of antitrust liability was independent of patent law.[59] Thus, the court determined that Third Circuit law applied to plaintiff's antitrust claims.[60]

Recent exemplary decisions relating to choice of law include *IGT v. Alliance Gaming*,[61] where the Federal Circuit applied the law of the Ninth Circuit when reviewing a district court's summary judgment ruling associated

---

54. *Eng'g & Insp. Servs., LLC v. IntPar, LLC*, No. CIV.A. 13-0801, 2013 WL 5589737 (E.D. La. Oct. 10, 2013).

55. *Id.* at *3.

56. *In re Lipitor Antitrust Litig.*, No. 3:12-cv-2389, 2013 WL 4780496 (D.N.J. Sept. 5, 2013).

57. *Id.* at *14 (quoting *Christianson v. Colt Indus. Operating Corp.*, 486 U.S. 800, 810 (1988)).

58. *Id.*

59. *Id.*

60. *Id.*

61. *IGT v. Alliance Gaming Corp.*, 702 F.3d 1338 (Fed. Cir. 2012).

with an antitrust claim, and *Cornucopia v. Dyson*,[62] where a district court applied Federal Circuit law when deciding a *Walker Process* claim.

§ 4.3 Bifurcation

Under Federal Rule of Civil Procedure 42(b), a case involving patent claims and antitrust claims may be bifurcated into a patent case and an antitrust case; alternatively, a court may stay the antitrust claims pending resolution of the patent claims.

In *Apotex v. Senju Pharmaceutical*,[63] a district court granted a motion to stay antitrust claims pending the outcome of a related patent infringement proceeding but denied a parallel motion to stay the same antitrust claims pending the outcome of a second related patent infringement proceeding. In granting the motion to stay, the district court determined that "resolution of the [first related patent infringement proceeding] could eliminate or narrow some of the antitrust claims and prevent unnecessary expenditure of time and resources . . . ."[64] Further, the district court noted that "the procedural posture of the instant litigation also favors a stay; there has not yet been any discovery, scheduling conferences, or filing of an answer."[65] In denying the parallel motion to stay, the district court determined that resolution of the second related patent infringement proceeding would not clarify any of the antitrust claims.[66]

In *Cascades Computer Innovation v. RPX*,[67] a district court ordered the plaintiff to show cause as to why the current antitrust proceeding should not be stayed pending the outcome of a related patent infringement proceeding.

In *P&G v. Cao Group*,[68] a district court denied a plaintiff's motion to bifurcate the plaintiff's patent infringement claims from the defendant's antitrust counterclaims. In deciding whether to bifurcate the claims, the district court considered "whether bifurcation would be conducive to expedition of litigation and to efficient judicial administration," "whether bifurcation would prejudice the parties," and "whether the issues sought to be tried separately are significantly different."[69] The district court rejected the plaintiff's motion to bifurcate because "there is a substantial overlap

62. *Cornucopia Prods. v. Dyson, Inc.*, 881 F. Supp. 2d 1086 (D. Ariz. 2012).
63. *Apotex Inc. v. Senju Pharm. Co.*, 921 F. Supp. 2d 308 (D. Del. 2013).
64. *Id.* at 315.
65. *Id.*
66. *Id.* at 316.
67. *Cascades Computer Innovation v. RPX Corp.*, No. 12-cv-01143, 2013 WL 316023 (N.D. Cal. Jan. 24, 2013).
68. *Proctor & Gamble Co. v. CAO Grp.*, No. 1:13-cv-337, 2013 WL 6061103 (S.D. Ohio Nov. 18, 2013).
69. *Id.* at *2.

between the patent and antitrust claims, and [the] overlap weighs strongly in favor of consolidated discovery and trial."[70] Further, the district court also determined that "[b]ifurcation would require duplicative presentations to two separate juries and would substantially delay resolution of the case"[71] and could prejudice the defendant.[72]

In *Lincoln Electric v. National Standard*,[73] a district court denied the plaintiffs' motion to bifurcate the patent claims from the defendant's antitrust counterclaims during the trial phase of the case.[74] The discovery phase of the case was conducted without bifurcation. Further, the factual issues and witnesses relevant to the patent claims and the antitrust claims overlapped.[75] The court concluded that bifurcation is "not warranted and would not expedite, economize, or make the trial(s) more convenient and/or less prejudicial."[76]

In *Otsuka Pharmaceutical v. Torrent Pharmaceuticals*,[77] the district court granted a motion to bifurcate and stay the antitrust counterclaim pending the outcome of a related patent infringement proceeding.[78] The court recognized that "[c]ritically, resolution of the patent infringement issues may render Torrent's antitrust Counterclaims moot, thereby serving the interests of judicial economy."[79]

§ 4.4 Legal Standards for Antitrust Claims

§ 4.4.1 Motions to Dismiss

A requirement for successfully bringing an antitrust action is to allege injury that the antitrust laws were enacted to prevent.[80] Failure to do so has been a frequent ground for dismissing antitrust claims and counterclaims in patent infringement litigation.

In *Cherdak v. Vock*,[81] the district court granted antitrust defendants' motion to dismiss the plaintiff's antitrust claims for failing to satisfy the antitrust injury requirement. Cherdak brought suit against defendants

70. *Id.* at *3.
71. *Id.*
72. *Id.* at *4.
73. *Lincoln Elec. Co. v. Nat'l Standard, LLC*, 2012 U.S. Dist. LEXIS 115847 (N.D. Ohio 2012).
74. *Id.* at *2–3.
75. *Id.* at *3.
76. *Id.* at *3.
77. *Otsuka Pharm. Co. v. Torrent Pharm., Inc.*, 2015 WL 3869677 (D.N.J. 2015).
78. *Id.* at *10.
79. *Id.*
80. *Associated Gen. Contractors of Cal., Inc. v. Cal. State Council of Carpenters*, 459 U.S. 519, 538 (1983).
81. *Cherdak v. Vock*, No. 1:11-cv-1311, 2012 WL 1427847 (E.D. Va. Apr. 23, 2012).

relating to U.S. Patent Nos. 5,636,146 and 5,960,380 relating to devices for use with Nike shoes that recorded exercise-related information. He alleged that the claims were unenforceable for inequitable conduct over his own U.S. Patent No. 5,343,445, alleging "but for" causation under *Therasense Inc. v. Becton, Dickinson and Co.*[82] The court disagreed, saying that the portions of the prosecution history Cherdak relied upon to support his inequitable conduct allegations were mere attorney argument. Citing *Innogenetics v. Abbott Labs*[83] and *Young v. Lumenis*,[84] the court stated that attorney argument, without more, does not amount to material information sufficient to satisfy the "but-for" materiality requirements under *Therasense* and granted summary judgment on the inequitable conduct claim.

The court also granted summary judgment against the plaintiff on the antitrust counts. The substantive allegations alleged to support the antitrust count of the complaint amounted to nothing more than the activity the court held was not inequitable conduct, and thus there was no support for the plaintiff's allegation that Nike and Apple acted in concert to achieve a monopoly. The plaintiff also did not adequately plead antitrust injury, according to the district court, because "the alleged conduct of which Plaintiff complains is not the sort that Congress intended to prevent when establishing the Sherman and Clayton Acts."[85] The court explained:

> "As the legislative history shows, the Sherman Act was enacted to assure customers the benefits of price competition, and [the Supreme Court's] prior cases have emphasized the central interest in protecting the economic freedom of participants in the relevant market." The ability to enforce a patent is a recognized exception to the antitrust laws. Here, Plaintiff seeks only to substitute the monopoly power inherent in his patent in place of the Defendants' monopoly power. The essence of Plaintiff's argument is that he, rather than the Defendants, is entitled to the royalties available from licensing his patents. The antitrust laws are directed at protecting market competition, not at protecting the inherent monopoly power and benefits provided under intellectual property laws. In sum, the antitrust laws are not a proper avenue for the Plaintiff to seek redress.[86]

82. *Id.* at *1; *see also Therasense, Inc. v. Becton, Dickinson & Co.*, 649 F.3d 1276, 1289 (Fed. Cir. 2011).

83. *Innogenetics, N.V. v. Abbott Labs.*, 512 F.3d 1363, 1379 (Fed. Cir. 2008).

84. *Young v. Lumenis, Inc.*, 492 F.3d 1336, 1349 (Fed. Cir. 2007).

85. *Cherdak*, 2012 WL 1427847, at *5 (citing *Associated Gen. Contractors of Cal., Inc. v. Cal. State Council of Carpenters*, 459 U.S. 519, 538 (1983)).

86. *Cherdak*, 2012 WL 14278, at *5 (quoting *Associated Gen. Contractors of Cal. v. Cal. State Council of Carpenters*, 459 U.S. 519, 538 (1983)).

In *Demodulation v. Applied DNA Sciences*,[87] the district court granted defendants' motion to dismiss plaintiff's antitrust claims for failure to satisfy the pleading requirements under *Twombly*.[88] Demodulation owned certain patents and other intellectual property related to an amorphous glass-coated metal microwire and entered into an agreement with the university defendant to commercialize the invention. Parts of this agreement were nondisclosure agreements between Demodulation and Applied DNA, the university, Corning, and ATRI (a startup company incubator). Demodulation alleged it had disclosed "extensive trade secrets" to defendants under these agreements.[89] In its complaint, Demodulation alleged conflicts of interest (and failure to disclose them) based on activities of defendants relating to development of the technology including activities with funding agencies and other business opportunities exploited by Applied DNA at Demodulation's expense.

The district court dismissed Demodulation's antitrust allegations for failure to allege facts relating to an agreement between the defendants in restraint of trade under section 1, or evidence of the relevant market with regard to either section 1 or section 2 allegations. In granting the motion to dismiss, the court stated that "[a] claim has 'facial plausibility when the plaintiff pleads factual content that allows the court to draw the reasonable inference that the defendant is liable for the misconduct alleged.'"[90] Under the facts plead in Demodulation's complaint, the court held that plaintiff had not satisfied this standard.

In *Eatoni Ergonomics v. Research In Motion* (RIM),[91] Eatoni Ergonomics alleged that RIM has monopoly power over QWERTY smartphones and acted anticompetitively to maintain that monopoly. In reviewing the district court's grant of the defendant's motion to dismiss, the Court of Appeals assumed that RIM has monopoly power but affirmed the district court because Eatoni did not sufficiently plead acts by RIM to maintain its monopoly. Eatoni alleged only that RIM refused to collaborate with Eatoni. But refusal to deal is not an antitrust violation absent other considerations, the court said, and distinguished *Aspen Skiing v. Aspen Highlands Skiing*[92] because Eatoni did not allege that RIM had discontinued a mutually beneficial preexisting course of conduct nor had forgone

87. *Demodulation, Inc. v. Applied DNA Scis., Inc.*, No. 2:11-cv-00296, 2012 WL 6204172 (D.N.J. Dec. 12, 2012).

88. *Bell Atl. Corp. v. Twombly*, 550 U.S. 544, 557 (2007).

89. *Demodulation, Inc.*, 2012 WL 6204172, at *2.

90. *Id.* at *3 (quoting *Ashcroft v. Iqbal*, 556 U.S. 662, 678 (2009)).

91. *Eatoni Ergonomics, Inc. v. Research In Motion Corp.*, No. 11-5328, 2012 WL 2348443 (2d Cir. June 21, 2012).

92. *Aspen Skiing Co v. Aspen Highlands Skiing Corp.*, 472 U.S. 585 (1985).

short-term profits to achieve anticompetitive ends. In this case, the only agreement between the parties was an agreement to collaborate in good faith prospectively. In addition, the court noted that in a prior arbitration, the arbitrator found that RIM's decision not to go forward in its collaboration with Eatoni was "a legitimate business judgment" that the proposed product was not commercially viable. Under these circumstances, mere refusal to go forward did not satisfy the "anti-competitive conduct" required to be a section 2 violation.[93]

Addressing another of Eatoni's allegations, the court held that refusing access to "essential facilities" as the basis for an antitrust violation requires more than mere inconvenience or "even some economic loss"; it requires that there is not a feasible alternative.[94] Because RIM was not the only possible partner, the court held that Eatoni could not prevail just because RIM was the most lucrative partner. And insofar as RIM provided a platform most compatible with Eatoni's patented technology, RIM's exercise of its right to exclude under its patents was lawful.

Finally, Eatoni alleged that the combination of several discrete acts by RIM constituted a course of anticompetitive conduct even though any one of those acts would not be independently anticompetitive. The appellate court agreed with the district court's conclusion that the combination of such acts in this case was not cumulatively anticompetitive, citing *City of Groton v. Conn. Light and Power*.[95]

In considering defendant's motion to dismiss, the plaintiffs' antitrust allegations and request for an injunction under the Clayton Act, the district court considered the standard: "plaintiffs 'must demonstrate a significant threat of injury from an impending violation . . . or from a contemporary violation likely to continue or recur.'"[96] Under this standard, "lingering monetary injury" is not sufficient.[97] Here, the '398 patent having been held unenforceable, there can be no "threat of future injury";[98] in addition, both Barr and Teva have generic equivalents of DDAVP on the market. The district court found that plaintiffs' prayer for relief in the form of an injunction was predicated on no facts demonstrating the risk of future injury and was "purely speculative" with regard not only to injury

93. *Eatoni Ergonomics*, 2012 WL 2348443, at 190.

94. *Id.* at 190 (citing *Twin Labs, Inc. v. Weider Health & Fitness*, 900 F.2d 566, 570 (2d Cir. 1990)).

95. *Id.* at 191 (citing *City of Groton v. Conn. Light & Power Co.*, 662 F.2d 921, 928–29 (2d. Cir. 1981)).

96. *Id.* at 209 (quoting *In re New Motor Vehicles Canadian Exp. Antitrust Litig.*, 522 F.3d 6, 13 (1st Cir. 2008)).

97. *Id.*; *compare Zenith Radio Corp. v. Hazeltine Research, Inc.*, 395 U.S. 100, 131–32 (1969), *with In re G-Fees Antitrust Litig.*, 584 F. Supp. 2d 26, 35 (D.D.C. 2008).

98. *In re DDAVP*, 903 F. Supp. 2d at 210.

but even as to the drug(s) involved. The court thus granted defendant's motion to dismiss.

The court did not dismiss the plaintiff's state antitrust law claims, however, saying that these were not preempted by federal law and that plaintiff's could use evidence of inequitable conduct and malfeasance with regard to the FDA Citizen Petition to support allegations under state law that Ferring had committed *Walker Process* fraud and brought sham litigation in filing its Abbreviated New Drug Application (ANDA) lawsuits against Barr and Teva.

In *Cascades v. RPX*,[99] Cascades alleged that the defendants, including several major telecommunications companies, conspired to refuse to deal with it and formed an illegal boycott to not license Cascades' patents. RPX is a defensive patent aggregator, or "antitroll," purportedly established to protect its 110 members from non-practicing entities like Cascades. Cascades claimed violations of the Sherman Act, sections 1 and 2 and California state antitrust violations. Defendants moved to dismiss for failure to state a claim.

Cascades exercised rights to thirty-eight patents related to technology for optimizing the Android operating system for use with mobile phones and tablet computers. The defendants, according to Cascades, "sell more than 95% of the devices sold in the United States that use the Android operating system[,]" which, Cascades alleged, gives them collectively market power sufficient to form a buyers' cartel.[100] RPX entered into negotiations with Cascades and none of the RPX member companies licensed any of Cascades patents. Cascades alleged that one of the company members of RPX refused to pay the proposed licensing fees causing the negotiations to break down. Cascades alleged that each of the named defendants was infringing some or all of Cascades' patents. Accordingly, the defendants' collective actions amounted to a conspiracy not to deal with RPX that constituted a group boycott in violation of the antitrust violations.

Cascades also alleged that coordinated actions taken by the defendants in defending patent infringement litigation were part of the alleged antitrust conspiracy. The anticompetitive actions included joint defense agreements having provisions that included: "do not settle with Cascades; do not discuss the possibility of a license; do not negotiate independently; and act consistently with each other."[101] Cascades even included RPX's law

---

99. *Cascades Computer Innovation v. RPX Corp.*, No. 12-cv-01143 YGR, 2013 WL 316023 (N.D. Cal. Jan. 24, 2013).

100. *Id.* at *2.

101. *Id.* at *3.

firm, Winston & Strawn, as part of the conspiracy, specifically as a conduit for sharing information.

As a consequence of the alleged illegal cartel and boycott, Cascades identified several harms to competition, including "(1) diminishing the value of licenses; (2) reducing NPEs' incentives to support innovation; (3) driving Cascades out of business; (4) raising prices and reducing output in products covered by Cascades' patents; and (5) raising barriers to entry in the market for licenses by implementing a plan to eliminate all NPEs" and markets including the markets for "(1) patents, (2) patented technology, (3) licenses for patents, (4) licenses for Cascades' patents, (5) licensing of Cascades' patented technology, (6) the 'Android market,' (7) mobile phones and tablets that use the Android operating system; and (8) products that use Cascades' patented technology."[102]

The district court granted defendants' motions to dismiss. As to the first prong of the analysis for section 1 and section 2 violations, the court considered the sufficiency of the pleadings regarding Cascades' allegation of "concerted action" by the defendants. The court noted that "an allegation of parallel conduct and a bare assertion of conspiracy will not suffice," citing Ninth Circuit law.[103] This requires allegations of facts "such as a 'specific time, place, or person involved in the alleged conspiracies'" in order to give the accused a basis for responding to antitrust allegations.[104] This does not amount to a "who, what, when, where pleading requirement," but cannot be "a mere conclusory allegation of agreement at some identified point" to show illegality.[105] Applying this standard, the court concluded that Cascades had not pled sufficient facts to properly allege an illegal conspiracy. Specifically, Cascades provided none of the "who, what, when, where" information required by Ninth Circuit precedent.[106] Instead, the court characterized Cascades' allegations as "threadbare recitals of conspiracy."[107] This was exactly the kind of generic pleading rejected in *Twombly*. As to defendant Dell, the court held that the generic allegations of conspiracy failed because Dell had in fact performed some or all of the actions, such as independent negotiations, that the conspirators allegedly agreed not to do.

102. *Id.* at *4.

103. *Id.* at *5 (quoting *Kendall v. Visa U.S.A., Inc.*, 518 F.3d 1042, 1047 (9th Cir. 2008) (both relying on *Twombly*, 550 U.S. at 556–57)).

104. *Id.* at *6 (quoting *Kendall*, 518 F.3d at 1047)).

105. *Id.* (citing *In re TFT-LCD (Flat Panel) Antitrust Litig.*, 599 F. Supp. 2d 1179, 1183 (N.D. Cal. 2009); *Twombly*, 550 U.S. at 556–57).

106. *See, e.g.*, *Rick-Mik Enters. v. Equilon Enters., LLC*, 532 F.3d 963, 976 (9th Cir. 2008).

107. *Cascades*, 2013 WL 316023, at *6.

As to the second element, directing the alleged conspiracy to an unreasonable restraint of trade, the court addressed Cascades' allegations of both per se restraints and restraints as assessed under the rule of reason. With regard to per se violations, because the harm to competition is presumed, the burden fell on defendants to rebut the presumption with evidence of pro-competitive effects of their behavior. The court found that the defendants did not address whether their conduct had any potential pro-competitive benefit or justification or that their conduct did not have "a predictable and pernicious anticompetitive effect."[108] Thus, the court denied this basis for dismissal.

Under the rule of reason, the district court found that Cascades, who has the burden under this standard of antitrust analysis, had failed to plead antitrust injury to the relevant market by defendants having market power under the standards established by the Supreme Court in *National Society of Professional Engineers v. United States*.[109] The first ground for the court's determination was that Cascades not only failed to define the relevant market but that it had "avoid[ed] its pleading obligation with subterfuge" and "further obfuscate[d] the analysis" by contending on the one hand that the market is "for patented technology" relating to "the Android industry" but, on the other hand, alleging that the market is "the entire mobile phone and tablet industry that uses the Android operating system."[110] Without a cogent market definition, the court asserts that it is "impossible to determine the actual effect the alleged challenged conduct has had on competition."[111] The court thus dismissed the complaint on the ground that Cascades had not defined the relevant market.

With regard to the alleged harm on competition and antitrust injury, the district court noted that Cascades had standing to allege antitrust violations as a private entity only if it established that it had suffered antitrust injury (defined as that injury the antitrust laws were enacted to prevent).[112] Cascades was required to satisfy four factors: "(1) unlawful conduct, (2) causing an injury to the plaintiff, (3) that flows from that which makes the conduct unlawful, and (4) that is of the type the antitrust laws were intended to prevent."[113] Although the court did not credit the defendants' attacks on Cascades' pleadings in this regard, neither did

108. *Id.* at *8.

109. *Nat'l Soc'y of Prof'l Eng'rs v. United States*, 435 U.S. 679, 690 (1978).

110. *Cascades*, 2013 WL 316023, at *9.

111. *Id.*

112. *Id.* at *10; *see also Brunswick Corp. v. Pueblo Bowl-O-Mat, Inc.*, 429 U.S. 477, 489 (1977).

113. *Cascades*, 2013 WL 316023, at *10 (quoting *Am. Ad Mgmt., Inc. v. Gen. Tel. Co. of Cal.*, 190 F.3d 1051, 1055 (9th Cir. 1999)).

it credit Cascades' allegations of group boycott, and accordingly could not find that Cascades had pled antitrust injury adequately. The injuries Cascades pled resulted from its inability to license its patents, and was not antitrust injury.

Finally, the district court noted that antitrust allegations must make economic sense and that an antitrust complaint must be dismissed if the allegations are not plausible economically. While this standard is not satisfied merely by showing that the accused monopolist's actions had "a plausible and justifiable reason . . . consistent with proper business behavior," the question in the context of a motion to dismiss is whether a defendant had "any rational motive" to join an alleged conspiracy consistent with its independent economic interests.[114] Here, the court found that the defendants offered "well-reasoned justifications" for refusing Cascades' proffered licenses, and that Cascades "has fastidiously avoided providing specific facts with respect to [the timing of the negotiations with regard to the filing of the patent infringement actions]."[115] In the absence of any "clarification and specificity, [t]he Court [refused to] presume economic rationality" for the alleged antitrust conduct, and dismissed Cascades' complaint on these grounds as well.[116]

Following the dismissal of Cascades' initial complaint, the court denied the defendants' motion to dismiss Cascades' amended complaint, finding that the amended complaint "alleges specific facts raising a reasonable inference that the [defendants] engaged in a so-called 'hub-and-spoke' conspiracy to force sub-competitive pricing for Cascades' patent licenses by monopsonizing the market."[117] Under this repleaded theory, RPX forms the hub of the conspiracy and each of the manufacturers operates as a spoke of the conspiracy. The rim connecting the spokes represents the horizontal conspiracy.

Cascades alleged four different Sherman Act claims: (1) a horizontal conspiracy to restrain trade in violation of section 1 of the Sherman Act; (2) a vertical conspiracy to restrain trade in violation of section 1; (3) a conspiracy to monopsonize in violation of section 2; and (4) against RPX only, a separate section 2 monopsonization claim. The court held that all four of these repleaded claims survived defendants' motion to dismiss for failure to state a claim.

The court rejected the defendants' arguments that Cascades failed to allege a plausible conspiracy. RPX argued that Cascades' overpricing of its

114. *Id.* at *11 (quoting *In re Citric Acid Litig.*, 191 F.3d 1090, 1094 (9th Cir. 1999)).

115. *Cascades*, 2013 WL 316023, at *11–12.

116. *Id.* at *12.

117. Order at 2, *Cascades Computer Innovation v. RPX Corp.*, No. 12-cv-01143, 2013 WL 316023 (N.D. Cal. Jan. 24, 2013) (No. 119).

licenses—and not any collusion—explained RPX's refusal to take a license from Cascades and such overpricing was a more plausible explanation for the refusal of RPX to license. But RPX had initially accepted a license from Cascades of close to $10 million for all manufacturers until one manufacturer vetoed that license. When Cascades approached the manufacturers independently about taking a license for as little as $2.5 million, none of them agreed. The court concluded from these facts that Cascades' inference of an agreement was plausible.[118]

The defendants also argued that Cascades' complaint alleged "no more than organizational membership and parallel conduct."[119] Although the court admitted that Cascades' initial complaint lacked sufficient factual allegations to rebut this argument, the court identified new facts that altered its conclusion: (1) "a named representative, Roesslein, of an alleged conspirator, Motorola, affirmatively expressed a desire to conduct business only through RPX"; and (2) "after Cascades and RPX reached an agreement as to price, RPX's representative, Barhydt, told Cascades that RPX members, in the plural, had raised the amounts necessary to fund the deal."[120] Taken together, these newly alleged facts could, if proved, constitute direct evidence of RPX's knowledge, and circumstantial evidence of RPX's members' knowledge, that the RPX members funding the deal had to agree upon a price for Cascades' licenses.[121]

Defendants also argued unsuccessfully that Cascades failed to plead an unreasonable restraint on trade within the meaning of Sherman Act section 1. The crux of this argument is that the manufacturers' subscription agreements with RPX permit members to negotiate licenses independent of RPX. The court rejected this argument summarily, recognizing that even if the RPX agreements permit the manufacturers to negotiate licenses separately, that does not mean that these manufacturers actually did negotiate separately. Indeed, Cascades' allegations to support the existence of an agreement suggests that manufacturers ignored their right to negotiate independently and agreed to act as a group in dealing with Cascades.[122]

The court also rejected RPX and the manufacturers' argument that RPX, or the manufacturers acting as a group, does not hold monopsony power. Cascades alleged that the manufacturing defendants "control more than 90% of the mobile phone business using the Android operating system and 75% of the combined mobile phone tablet business."[123] In response,

118. *Id.* at *11–15.
119. *Id.* at *16.
120. *Id.* at *17.
121. *Id.*
122. *Id.* at *20–21.
123. *Id.* at *26.

defendants argued that these allegations pertain only to the downstream product market for Android mobile devices but say "nothing about their buyer share in the upstream input market."[124] The court rejected that argument because "[n]othing in the FAC suggests that anyone would or could participate in the 'upstream' market for the '750 Patent except for the markets of the Android devices that the '750 Patent allegedly optimizes."[125]

Finally, the court did not address antitrust injury in the defendants' motion to dismiss the amended complaint because defendants did not expressly challenge Cascades' pleading of either the "willful acquisition" or "antitrust injury" prongs of the monopsonization claim.

A lawsuit between Intellectual Ventures and Capital One[126] presented an instance of a patent infringement defendant attempting to avoid patent infringement liability on the grounds that the plaintiff is a patent troll. In striking Capitol One's patent misuse defense and affirmative counterclaims of antitrust violations,[127] the district court found Capitol One's pleadings merely alleged that Intellectual Ventures was asserting "over 3,500 patents" against Capitol One and other financial services defendants. Absent well-pled facts showing that the assertions are objectively baseless, asserting presumptively valid patents is not an antitrust violation. The district court noted that a section 2 Sherman Act violation required market power and "willful acquisition or maintenance of that power as distinguished from growth or development as a consequence of a superior product, business acumen, or historic accident."[128] The court found that Capital One had not alleged facts showing monopoly power, because the "ex post market for technologies used to provide commercial banking services" did not identify a specific geographical market or marketed product.[129] In addition, the court found that Capital One "failed to allege facts that make plausible its claim that [Intellectual Ventures] wields unlawful monopoly power within that market."[130]

The court in *In re Nexium (Esomeprazole) Antitrust Litigation*[131] addressed the question of the types of evidence that could be used to support

---

124. *Id.* (emphasis in original).

125. *Id.*

126. *Intellectual Ventures I LLC, et al. v. Capital One Fin. Corp., et al.*, No. 13-cv-00740, 2013 WL 6682981 (E.D. Va. Dec. 18, 2013).

127. Including violation of section 2 of the Sherman Act and section 7 of the Clayton Act.

128. *Id.* at *4 (quoting *United States v. Grinnell Corp.*, 384 U.S. 563, 570–71 (1966)).

129. *Id.* at *5–6 ("Capital One's proposed market is not a 'relevant market' under any recognized antitrust jurisprudence.").

130. *Id.* at *6; *see also infra* pp. 142–145 providing fuller discussion of case in patent misuse context.

131. *In re Nexium (Esomeprazole) Antitrust Litig.*, 42 F. Supp. 3d 231 (D. Mass. 2014).

an allegation of antitrust violation under section 1 of the Sherman Act. At issue were three separate settlement agreements of ANDA litigation with three different generic challengers, and the antitrust plaintiffs argued that these agreements were evidence of "a single overarching conspiracy to illegally restrain trade."[132] The court held that, for purposes of defeating a motion to dismiss, circumstantial evidence could be sufficient to establish the existence of a single agreement, tacit or express, in restraint of trade by demonstrating, for example, "parallel behavior that would probably not result from chance, coincidence, independent responses to common stimuli, or mere interdependence unaided by an advance understanding among the parties."[133] Independent decisions by each of the generic challengers to enter into settlement with branded drugmaker AstraZeneca could be and were the equivalent of conspiracy, particularly where as here the individual agreements would not be in these generic companies' best interests unless the agreements each contained provisions to align their behavior.

In contrast, the district court in *King Drug Co. v. Cephalon, Inc.*[134] found that the antitrust plaintiffs had not pled the existence of a conspiracy in restraint of trade sufficient to avoid a motion to dismiss. In this case, the plaintiffs were a putative class of direct purchasers (King Drug), a putative class of end payors (Vista Healthplan), a generic drug company (Apotex, Inc.), and several individual direct purchasers that are not part of the putative class. The defendants included Cephalon, Inc., the brand-name pharmaceutical manufacturer, and four generic manufacturers: Teva Pharmaceuticals, Ranbaxy Laboratories, Mylan Pharmaceuticals, and Barr Laboratories, Inc. The court decided the plaintiffs had not satisfied the pleading requirements because there was "no evidence of significant motive for the Generics to collude amongst themselves. . . . Plaintiffs have difficulty positing exactly what the Generic Defendants stood to gain from an overall conspiracy that they could not achieve through the one-on-one settlements with Cephalon."[135]

§ 4.4.2 Failure to State a Claim

IGT v. Alliance Gaming[136] involved patents related to so-called wheel games (games where a wheel provides the opportunity for "bonus" payments). Bally and IGT are the only two competitors in the market for wheel games, IGT having used its patent position to drive other competitors out of the

132. *Id.* at 248.
133. *Id.* at 250–51 (quoting *Twombly*, 550 U.S. at 556 n.4).
134. *King Drug Co. v. Cephalon, Inc.*, No. 2:06-cv-1797, 2014 WL 2813312 (E.D. Pa. June 23, 2014) (*In re Modafinil Litig.*).
135. *Id.* at *13.
136. *IGT v. Alliance Gaming Corp.*, 702 F.3d 1338 (Fed. Cir. 2012).

market. IGT sued Bally for infringement of its wheel game patents, and Bally responded that the patents were invalid and not infringed and also counterclaimed, alleging that the infringement lawsuit was an attempt to monopolize the wheel game market by asserting patents that IGT knew to be invalid, unenforceable, and not infringed. Initially, the district court granted partial summary judgment against Bally because it presented no evidence about the gaming market as a whole; its evidence was limited to wheel games and thus the scope of its putative anticompetitive conduct was limited to that aspect of the game machine industry. As to this more limited market, the district court denied IGT's summary judgment motion on the grounds that there were disputed facts at issue that must be tried.

In the district court there was a "battle of the experts" as to the relevant market; Bally contended that the market is limited to wheel games, while IGT contended that the market includes all competing mechanical gambling gaming machines. In a first appeal of the district court's earlier denial of Bally's antitrust counterclaims, the Federal Circuit agreed that these differences raised a genuine issue of material fact. On remand, the district court ruled that wheel games are not the relevant market but that the relevant market included mechanical games in general, all of which compete with one another. Because Bally had conceded that there was competition between "wheel" and "non-wheel" games, the district court granted summary judgment against Bally because it did not show that IGT had market power in the relevant market.

The Federal Circuit affirmed, in an opinion by Judge Reyna joined by Judge Linn, based on the defendants' failure to allege facts sufficient to "establish the existence of a relevant antitrust market in wheel games."[137] Judge Bryson dissented. In the majority opinion, the court stated that Bally could prevail only if it established that the district court erred in its determination that the wheel game market was not the relevant market. Bally offered three arguments:

1. the court "improperly resolved" disputed fact issues;
2. the existence of some substitution between wheel and non-wheel games does not foreclose the existence of a "wheel game market"; and
3. the court focused on functional, rather than economic, substitution.[138]

The panel applied the law of the Ninth Circuit in reviewing the district court's decision, stating that defining the relevant market is a "threshold

137. *Id.* at 1341.
138. *Id.* at 1343.

issue" because "[t]he relevant market is the field in which meaningful competition is said to exist."[139] The panel majority rejected Bally's first argument because there was extensive evidence below that wheel games compete with all other games, and the district court did not err because there were no disputed facts.

The court rejected Bally's second argument, saying that the district court decided wheel games were not a relevant market because "a market limited to wheel games would not encompass all economic substitutions."[140] The standard, according to the court, in defining the relevant market is that "[t]he circle must be drawn narrowly to exclude any other product to which, within reasonable variations in price, only a limited number of buyers will turn; in technical terms, products whose cross-elasticities of demand are small."[141] Assessing the evidence Bally presented, the court stated that Bally failed to produce evidence that where the district court "drew the circle"—that is, encompassing all mechanical gaming machines and not just wheel games—was erroneous under this standard.

The Federal Circuit also rejected Bally's argument that the district court focused on functional, rather than economic, considerations in reaching its conclusion that the wheel game market was not the relevant market. The panel concluded that the district court "based its ultimate conclusion on competition, not on functionality, and that its recognition of meaningful competition [between wheel and non-wheel games] was not error."[142]

Finally, the court rejected Bally's argument that the wheel game market was a relevant "submarket," relying on the indicia for the existence of a submarket set forth in *Brown Shoe v. United States*,[143] which include "industry or public recognition of the submarket as a separate economic entity, the product's peculiar characteristics and uses, unique production facilities, distinct customers, distinct prices, sensitivity to price changes, and specialized vendors."[144] The court found no "peculiar characteristics and uses" for wheel games versus non-wheel games, nor are there any "distinct customers" for wheel games (all the customers are casinos, according to the court). The court specifically rejected Bally's reliance on the single factor of player preference for wheel games because that was not evidence that wheel games are a proper submarket for antitrust analysis. Rather, it

139. *Id.* at 1344 (quoting *Image Tech. Servs., Inc. v. Eastman Kodak Co.*, 125 F.3d 1195, 1202 (9th Cir. 1997)).

140. *Id.* at 1345.

141. *Id.* at 1345 (quoting *Times-Picayune Publ'g Co. v. United States*, 345 U.S. 594, 613 n.31 (1953), *rev'd on other grounds*, *Unitherm Food Sys. v. Swift-Eckrich, Inc.*, 546 U.S. 394 (2006)).

142. *IGT*, 702 F.3d at 1346.

143. *Brown Shoe Co. v. United States*, 370 U.S. 294 (1962).

144. *IGT*, 702 F.3d at 1346 (quoting *Brown Shoe*, 370 U.S. at 325).

was merely an indication that the market in gaming machines is a differentiated market and that wheel games compete with all other type of games.

In *In re DDAVP Indirect Purchaser*,[145] the district court dismissed the indirect drug purchasers' request for an injunction under the Clayton Act for failure to state a claim. The case involved the antidiuretic drug desmopressin acetate (sold as DDAVP) in a suit by indirect purchasers against drugmakers Ferring, Ferring Pharmaceuticals, Aventis Pharmaceuticals, and direct purchasers who had settled an earlier class action lawsuit against these defendants on the same facts.[146]

Also relevant to this action was previous ANDA litigation against Barr and Teva over Orange Book listed U.S. Patent No. 5,407,398 (formulation patent for absorbable tablet), where the issue was inequitable conduct. The allegation in the earlier case was that Ferring submitted declarations during patent prosecution to overcome prior art, but the declarants were purportedly unaffiliated experts. It was not disclosed during prosecution that some of these experts had been paid consultants for Ferring and were not independent. In ANDA litigation against Barr, the district court found that the withheld information was material and supported the generic companies' inequitable conduct claim. Barr prevailed both in the district court and at the Federal Circuit, and the '398 patent was held to be unenforceable.[147]

§ 4.4.3 Lack of Antitrust Standing

In *Ethypharm v. Abbott*,[148] the Third Circuit held that a foreign drug supplier who did not have FDA approval to sell in the United States also lacked antitrust standing to sue under sections 1 and 2 of the Sherman Act, as well as sections 4 and 16 of the Clayton Act. Plaintiff Ethypharm made fenofibrate sold by Reliant in the United States. Reliant had obtained FDA approval under section 505(b)(2) of the Food, Drug, and Cosmetic Act, an alternative route to generic entry from an ANDA filing under the Hatch-Waxman Act. Under a complicated settlement agreement with NDA holder Abbott, Reliant transferred its fenofibrate business and Abbot license to another generic drugmaker, but the agreement automatically increased the royalty rate upon transfer. Over time, Ethypharm's share

145. *In re DDAVP Indirect Purchaser Antitrust Litig.*, 903 F. Supp. 2d 198 (S.D.N.Y. 2012).

146. In the original case, the district court granted defendant drugmakers' motion under Federal Rule of Civil Procedure 12(b)(6) and the Second Circuit vacated and remanded. The direct purchasers and drug companies settled, and the indirect purchasers brought this suit against both under the Clayton Act and for Sherman Act violations. *In re DDAVP*, 903 F. Supp. 2d at 206–07.

147. *In re DDAVP*, 903 F. Supp. 2d at 206.

148. *Ethypharm S.A. v. Abbott Labs.*, 707 F.3d 223 (3d Cir. 2013).

of the market decreased at least in part due to other generic-drug entry. Ethypharm sued under the antitrust laws, claiming that the provisions of the settlement agreements were anticompetitive. The district court denied Abbott's motion to dismiss, but later granted its summary judgment motion against Ethypharm.

The Third Circuit affirmed, deciding that Ethypharm did not have standing because it did not suffer antitrust injury. The court noted that, in addition to Article III standing, antitrust allegations are burdened with a showing of "prudential standing" limitations, insofar as an antitrust plaintiff must show that it is entitled to bring a private cause of action.[149] These considerations of antitrust standing are based on *Associated General Contractors of California v. California State Council of Carpenters*,[150] which in the Third Circuit are enumerated as follows:

> (1) the causal connection between the antitrust violation and the harm to the plaintiff and the intent by the defendant to cause that harm, with neither factor alone conferring standing; (2) whether the plaintiff's alleged injury is of the type for which the antitrust laws were intended to provide redress; (3) the directness of the injury, which addresses the concerns that liberal application of standing principles might produce speculative claims; (4) the existence of more direct victims of the alleged antitrust violations; and (5) the potential for duplicative recovery or complex apportionment of damages.[151]

While there is conflicting Third Circuit precedent,[152] the fact that Ethypharm was unable to sell fenofibrate in the United States (because it did not seek or obtain FDA approval) was dispositive: "Ethypharm's inability to participate in the United States fenofibrate market makes all the difference."[153] The court held that because Ethypharm did not (indeed, could not) compete with Abbott, it did not have standing to complain that Abbott's settlement agreement was anticompetitive:

---

149. *Id.* at 232 (citing *City of Pittsburgh v. W. Penn Power Co.*, 147 F.3d 256, 264 (3d Cir. 1998)).

150. *Associated Gen. Contractors of Cal., Inc. v. Cal. State Council of Carpenters*, 459 U.S. 519 (1983).

151. *Ethypharm*, 707 F.3d at 232–33 (citing *In re Lower Lake Erie Iron Ore Antitrust Litig.*, 998 F.2d 1144, 1165–66 (3d Cir. 1993)).

152. Specifically, between *Barton & Pittinos, Inc. v. SmithKline Beecham Corp.*, 118 F.3d 178, 182 (3d Cir.1997), and *Carpet Grp. Int'l v. Oriental Rug Importers Assoc., Inc.*, 227 F.3d 62 (3d Cir. 2000), *abrogated on other grounds by Animal Sci. Prods., Inc. v. China Minmetals Corp.*, 654 F.3d 462 (3d Cir. 2011).

153. *Ethypharm*, 707 F.3d at 236.

> Ethypharm wants to have it both ways: it wants to pass on to a licensee the expense and risk of qualifying to compete in the United States pharmaceutical market, but, when that arrangement fails to achieve success, Ethypharm seeks to avail itself of the United States laws protecting fair competition. The rules of antitrust standing do not permit that tactic. We stress that it is not the general arrangement of manufacturer and distributor that is problematic; it is the fact that Ethypharm cannot sell Antara [fenofibrate]in the United States because of legal barriers particular to the pharmaceutical market, barriers that Ethypharm chose not to surmount. Ethypharm is literally not a lawful competitor in the United States fenofibrate market, and so it cannot be considered a competitor for purposes of antitrust injury.[154]

The question of antitrust standing arose in *Fido's Fences, Inc. v. Radio Systems Corp.* (RSC).[155] In this case, which was originally filed as a qui tam action, the plaintiff alleged antitrust injury with regard to the market for electrified fences used to restrict domestic animals to private lands. The court limited the market (and hence the potential damages) to the replacement battery market because this was the only antitrust injury established. According to the court, to establish antitrust standing, a plaintiff must not only allege injury-in-fact to its "business or property" caused by the antitrust violation, but must also plausibly allege "(a) that it suffered a special kind of 'antitrust injury,' and (b) that it is a suitable plaintiff to pursue the alleged antitrust violations and thus is an 'efficient enforcer' of the antitrust laws."[156] An antitrust plaintiff must also establish an "antitrust injury"; in the Second Circuit, the plaintiff must first allege that it has been injured by an illegal anticompetitive practice and "identify the practice complained of and the reasons such a practice is or might be anticompetitive"; the court then must "identify the actual injury the plaintiff alleges"; and finally, the court must consider how the "anticompetitive effect of the specific practice at issue" relates to "the actual injury the plaintiff alleges."[157] Finally with regard to standing, to determine whether an antitrust plaintiff is an "efficient enforcer" of the antitrust laws, the Second Circuit looks to the following factors: "(1) the directness or indirectness of the asserted violation; (2) whether other potential plaintiffs are more motivated to vindicate the public interest in antitrust enforcement; (3) whether

154. *Id.* (emphasis added).
155. *Fido's Fences, Inc. v. Radio Sys. Corp.*, 999 F. Supp. 2d 442 (E.D.N.Y. 2014).
156. *Id.* at 451.
157. *Id.*

the alleged injury is speculative; and (4) the difficulty of apportioning damages among direct and indirect victims so as to avoid duplicative recovery."[158] Considering the extent of RSC's market presence and power, as well as Fido's direct interest in selling replacement batteries for RSC's systems, the court held that Fido's had antitrust standing, but only to the extent of replacement battery sales and not complete system sales. In *Motorola Mobility v. AU Optronics*,[159] the Seventh Circuit held that defendants' sale of price-fixed LCD panels to Motorola Mobility's foreign subsidiaries did not give rise to an antitrust claim under the Sherman Act.[160] The alleged price-fixing defendants sold the LCD panels to Motorola Mobility's foreign subsidiaries, which then incorporated them into a finished product and passed the finished product to Motorola Mobility for U.S. domestic sale to Motorola Mobility's cellphone customers.[161] The court noted that to state an antitrust claim under the Sherman Act that meets the exception under the FTAIA for importing requires (1) "direct, substantial, and reasonably foreseeable effect on U.S. domestic commerce" and that (2) "the effect must give rise to a federal antitrust claim."[162] The court recognized that "[h]ad the defendants conspired to sell LCD panels to Motorola in the United States at inflated prices, they would be subject to the Sherman Act because of the exception in the [FTAIA] for importing."[163] Motorola Mobility argued that it and its foreign subsidiaries should be considered a "single integrated enterprise."[164] In response, the court determined that Motorola Mobility as an indirect purchaser has no right to seek relief in the United States on behalf of its foreign subsidiaries. Instead, the court stated that Motorola Mobility's foreign subsidiaries are direct purchasers with the right to "seek relief for restraints of trade under the laws either of the countries in which they are incorporated or do business or the countries in which their victimizers are incorporated or do business.[165] Further, as an indirect purchaser, the court recognized Motorola Mobility as a derivative victim, who lacks "antitrust standing."[166] Also, the court relied on "the indirect-purchaser doctrine" of *Illinois Brick v. Illinois*,[167] "which forbids a customer of the purchaser who paid a cartel price to sue the cartelist, even if his seller—the

158. *Id.* at 452.
159. *Motorola Mobility LLC v. AU Optronics Corp.*, 775 F.3d 816 (7th Cir. 2014).
160. *Id.* at 819.
161. *Id.*
162. *Id.* at 818.
163. *Id.*
164. *Id.* at 820.
165. *Id.*
166. *Id.* at 820–21.
167. *Ill. Brick Co. v. Illinois*, 431 U.S. 720 (1977).

direct purchaser from the cartelist—passed on to him some or even all of the cartel's elevated price."[168]

§ 4.4.4 Antitrust in ANDA Litigation (without Reverse Payment Provisions)

The Second Circuit also discussed the contours of the Supreme Court's decision in *Aspen Skiing Co. v. Aspen Highlands Skiing Corp.*[169] in the context of settlements of ANDA litigation in *In re Adderall XR Antitrust Litigation*.[170] In this case there was an agreement settling ANDA litigation over Adderall XR, wherein Teva and Impax agreed to refrain from marketing a generic version of the drug for three years, during which time Shire would be the exclusive manufacturer and distributor of the drug. If the FDA had not approved the generic companies' ANDAs by the end of the three-year term, then Shire agreed to sell unbranded Adderall to Teva and Impax to be distributed by them. In this case, this happened and two wholesale distributors filed suit against Shire alleging that shortfalls on delivery resulting from this arrangement substantially affected the end price paid by wholesalers; plaintiffs further alleged that by not delivering Teva and Impax's full orders, Shire had relegated only 50–60 percent of the market to its competitors, instead of the 90 percent they should have expected, should they have fulfilled the orders. The district court rejected the plaintiff's theory that the agreement created a "duty to deal," the failure of which would be a violation of section 2 of the Sherman Act. In affirming, the Second Circuit clarified the extent of Shire's "duty to deal" through *Aspen* as "[a] unilateral termination of a voluntary (*and thus presumably profitable*) course of dealing suggest[ing] a willingness to forsake short-term profits to achieve an anticompetitive end."[171] In this case, Shire did not "terminate any prior course of dealing—let alone a 'presumably profitable' one that had . . . 'originated in a competitive market and had persisted for several years.' . . . Indeed, the agreements [] were explicitly unprofitable—they introduced price competition into a market where none would otherwise have existed [creating] competition in the market for AXR *ex nihilo*."[172] According to the Second Circuit, "[t]he logical inference from plaintiff's allegations was that, unlike the defendant in *Aspen Skiing*, Shire accepted a below-retail price for its product. In short, the plaintiffs'

168. *Motorola Mobility*, 775 F.3d at 821.
169. *Aspen Skiing Co. v. Aspen Highlands Skiing Corp.*, 472 U.S. 585, 600 (1985).
170. *In re Adderall XR Antitrust Litig.*, 754 F.3d 128 (2d Cir. 2014).
171. *Id.* at 135.
172. *Id.* (quoting *Aspen Skiing*, 472 U.S. at 603).

allegations amount to the self-defeating claim that Shire monopolized the market by ceding its monopoly."[173]

One drug company (Abbott) unilaterally increasing the price of a drug subject to a contractual arrangement wherein the drug was co-administered with another company's (Glaxo Smith Kline, GSK) drug was found to be an antitrust violation under section 2 of the Sherman Act in *SmithKline Beecham Corp. v. Abbott Labs.*[174] GSK entered into a license with Abbott to recommend, label, market, use, sell, have sold, and offer to sell GSK protease inhibitors in co-prescription/administration with one of Abbott's Norvir drugs (ritonavir). After GSK entered the market with its combination drug, Lexira, Abbott increased the price of Norvir by 400 percent. As part of its breach of contract action, GSK asserted an antitrust claim and prevailed on this claim at trial. In the instant decision, the district court denied Abbott's motion under Rule 50, rejecting Abbott's contentions that GSK failed to prove (1) the possession of monopoly power in the relevant market and (2) the willful acquisition or maintenance of that power as distinguished from growth or other development as a consequence of a superior product, business acumen, or historic accident, as well as having a legitimate business justification.

§ 4.4.5 Antitrust and Professional Rights Organizations

The licensing activities of a performing rights organization (PRO), SESAC, Inc.,[175] raised antitrust allegations in *Radio Music License Comm., Inc. v. SESAC, Inc.*[176] and *Meredith Corp. v. SESAC LLC.*[177] In *Radio Music Licensing*, plaintiff Radio Music License Committee (RMLC), a nonprofit organization that negotiates performance licenses for radio stations, brought allegations of antitrust violations against SESAC for anticompetitive licensing practices, including offering only blanket licenses; making it difficult to identify individual works in its catalog; and compiling a critical mass of must-have, copyrighted works that radio stations cannot avoid broadcasting as a practical matter, thus requiring users to purchase the blanket license.[178] In its complaint, RMLC alleged three antitrust violations: horizontal price fixing (Count I), group boycott/refusal to deal

173. *Id.* (citations omitted).

174. *SmithKline Beecham Corp. v. Abbott Labs.*, No. 07-5702, 2014 WL 6664226 (N.D. Cal. Nov. 24, 2014).

175. As set forth in the opinion, "SESAC is one of three performing rights organizations ("PROs") that operate in the United States, the two others being the American Society of Composers, Authors and Publishers ("ASCAP") and Broadcast Music, Inc., ("BMI")." *Radio Music License Comm., Inc. v. SESAC, Inc.*, 29 F. Supp. 3d 487, 490 (E.D. Pa. 2014).

176. 29 F. Supp. 3d 487 (E.D. Pa. 2014).

177. *Meredith Corp. v. SESAC LLC*, 1 F. Supp. 3d 180 (S.D.N.Y. 2014).

178. *Radio Music License Comm.*, 29 F. Supp. 3d at 492–93.

(Count II), and monopolization (Count III). The court dismissed the first two counts with leave to amend, for failure to allege the agreement in furtherance of the illegal agreement (the "crucial question is whether the challenged anticompetitive conduct stems from independent decision or from an agreement"). The court permitted the suit to proceed on the third count as pled. A significant factor is that SESAC, unlike the other two PROs operating in the United States, was not party to a consent decree from the Department of Justice pursuant to an earlier antitrust action brought by the government.

The *Meredith* case involved a class action by local television affiliates alleging that SESAC engaged in anticompetitive licensing practices, including offering only blanket licenses encompassing "essential" works. Meredith's complaint alleged violations of section 1 of the Sherman Act by combining (with its 20,000 affiliated composers) to unlawfully restrain trade and section 2 of the Sherman Act by monopolizing and conspiring to monopolize the market for the performance rights to the musical works within SESAC's repertory. The court denied SESAC's motion for summary judgment but narrowed Meredith's claims by rejecting, as a matter of law, the plaintiff's per se theory of section 1 liability; and the claim of an agreement to restrain trade among all 20,000-plus SESAC affiliates, as opposed to among only those affiliates who were party to a supplemental affiliation agreement with SESAC.[179]

In a rather counterintuitive decision, the district court in *Retractable Technologies, Inc. v. Becton, Dickinson & Co.*[180] denied infringement defendant's motion for summary judgment that, as a matter of law, patent infringement cannot constitute anticompetitive conduct sufficient to incur antitrust liability. While citing no precedent supporting its opinion, the court relied on the Supreme Court for the principle that the Sherman Act covers "every conceivable act which could possibly come within the spirit or purpose of the prohibitions of the law."[181] At trial patent infringement was found to be anticompetitive conduct that was the basis for a finding of monopolization under section 2 of the Sherman Act.

§ 4.4.6 Antitrust and Professional Sports Leagues

Professional sports leagues have also seen their share of antitrust allegations. In *Dang v. San Francisco Forty Niners*,[182] a fan (on behalf of a class of fans) sued the National Football League, the San Francisco

179. *See also supra* pp. 35–37 discussing case.

180. *Retractable Techs., Inc. v. Becton, Dickinson & Co.*, No. 2:08-cv-16, 2013 WL 4806905 (E.D. Tex. Sept. 9, 2013).

181. *Id.* at *1 (citing *United States v. Am. Tobacco Co.*, 221 U.S. 106, 181 (1911)).

182. *Dang v. S.F. Forty Niners*, 964 F. Supp. 2d 1097 (N.D. Cal. 2013).

Forty-Niners, and the Players Association over the cost of league-approved athletic shoes. In denying the defendants' motion to dismiss, the court found that the plaintiff properly alleged antitrust standing pursuant to the factors set forth in *Associated General Contractors v. Carpenters*[183] to withstand the motion to dismiss. "These factors include: '(1) the nature of the plaintiff's alleged injury; that is, whether it was the type the antitrust laws were intended to forestall; (2) the directness of the injury; (3) the speculative measure of the harm; (4) the risk of duplicative recovery; and (5) the complexity in apportioning damages.'"[184] Antitrust injury was properly pled when the plaintiff consumer alleged he paid more for an article (the shoes) due to the antitrust violation,[185] and the relevant markets are not single-brand markets but "a market of several independent and competitive brands"[186] that compete with each other for market share and are not interchangeable (due to fan loyalty).

Judgment against the American Quarter Horse Association was reversed in a case involving registration of cloned horses, in *Abraham and Veneklasen Joint Venture v. American Quarter Horse Association*.[187] Plaintiffs sued the American Quarter Horse Association (AQHA) for violation of sections 1 and 2 of the Sherman Act and the Texas Free Enterprise and Antitrust Act, alleging that members of the Stud Book and Registration Committee conspired with the AQHA to block the registration of cloned horses from the market of "elite Quarter Horses." The issue on appeal was "whether [the plaintiffs] proved an actual conspiracy to restrain trade in violation of Section 1 of the Sherman Act, or illegal monopolization by AQHA of breed registration for the 'elite Quarter Horse' market in violation of Section 2."[188]

Under section 1 of the Sherman Act, the court found that "[r]easonable jurors . . . could not draw any inference of conspiracy from the evidence presented, because it neither tends to exclude the possibility of independent action nor does it suggest the existence of any conspiracy at all. In the absence of substantial evidence on the issue of an illegal conspiracy to restrain trade, AQHA's JMOL motion should have been granted."[189] Under section 2 of the Sherman Act, the court found that "the Section 2 claim

183. *Associated Gen. Contractors v. Carpenters*, 459 U.S. 519 (1983).

184. *Dang*, 964 F. Supp. at 1110 (quoting *Am. Ad Mgmt., Inc. v. Gen. Tel. Co. of Cal.*, 190 F.3d 1051, 1054–55 (9th Cir. 1999)).

185. *Id.* at 1111.

186. *Id.* at 1106.

187. *Abraham & Veneklasen Joint Venture v. Am. Quarter Horse Ass'n*, 776 F.3d 321 (5th Cir. 2015).

188. *Id.* at 326–27.

189. *Id.* at 334.

failed as a matter of law because AQHA is not a competitor in the allegedly relevant market for elite Quarter Horses."[190]

The district court enjoined the NCAA from prohibiting its member schools from offering "a limited share of the revenues generated by the use of [the] names, images and likenesses" to their "FBS football or Division I basketball recruits" in addition to full grants-in-aid in *O'Bannon v. National Collegiate Athletic Association*.[191] The case arose when a group of current and former college football and men's basketball players brought an antitrust class action against the National Collegiate Athletic Association (NCAA) alleging Sherman Act violations in restraint of trade with regard to use of the players' names, images, and likenesses.

The court parsed out the relevant markets to include the college education market; a group licensing market for live games; group licensing markets for videogames; and group licensing markets for rebroadcasts, highlight clips, and other archival footage, but found evidence of anticompetitive behavior or consequences only for the first group. The court recognized some balance of pro-competitive factors, including competitive balance, and to a lesser degree, amateurism (because the rigid rules regarding absolute restraints on compensation imposed by the NCAA were not justified), although the court found insufficient evidence that these rules promoted amateurism. Another purported pro-competitive factor, integration of academics and athletics was a "narrow" pro-competitive benefit that does not justify "sweeping prohibitions on [] student-athlete compensation," according to the opinion. There was no evidence that the school's athletic programs required free student athlete services to avoid financial ruin, so increased output was not an issue; and "a narrowly tailored trust payment system" would be a less restrictive alternative.[192] The court recognized two such less restrictive alternatives proposed by the plaintiffs. The court stated:

> First, the NCAA could permit FBS football and Division I basketball schools to award stipends to student-athletes up to the full cost of attendance, as that term is defined in the NCAA's bylaws, to make up for any shortfall in its grants-in-aid. Second, the NCAA could permit its schools to hold in trust limited and equal shares of its licensing revenue to be distributed to its student-athletes after they leave college or their eligibility expires. The NCAA could also prohibit schools from funding the stipends or payments held in trust with anything other than revenue generated from the use of

190. *Id.*
191. *O'Bannon v. Nat'l Collegiate Athletic Ass'n*, 7 F. Supp. 3d 955 (N.D. Cal. 2014).
192. *Id.* at 1006.

the student-athletes' own names, images, and likenesses. Permitting schools to award these stipends and deferred payments would increase price competition among FBS football and Division I basketball schools in the college education market (or, alternatively, in the market for recruits' athletic services and licensing rights) without undermining the NCAA's stated procompetitive objectives.[193]

§ 4.5 Counterclaims

Antitrust violations are often pled as counterclaims in patent infringement litigation. If an antitrust claim is not pled as a counterclaim, but is raised in another proceeding, courts must decide if it should be dismissed in the second proceeding because it was compulsory in the first. In *Cascades Computer Innovation v. RPX*,[194] a district court considered the relationship between a current antitrust proceeding and earlier patent infringement proceedings. One of the defendants argued that the plaintiff's antitrust claims against it must be dismissed because they were compulsory counterclaims under Rule 13(a) and should have been asserted in the related patent infringement proceedings.[195] The district court determined that "[t]he nature of the antitrust claims, the legal basis for recovery, the law involved, and the facts giving rise to the antitrust claims all differ from the patent infringement claim asserted" and, therefore, were not compulsory in the earlier proceeding.[196]

By contrast, in *MGA Entertainment v. Mattel*,[197] a district court dismissed MGA's sham litigation antitrust claim under the doctrine of res judicata. The court rejected MGA's argument that its antitrust claim was merely permissive in the prior lawsuit. Although Ninth Circuit law[198] provides an exception to the compulsory counterclaim rule in patent infringement cases, the prior lawsuit in this case included non-patent claims and the court declined to extend the compulsory counterclaim exception developed for patent infringement cases.[199]

193. *Id.* at 1005–06.

194. *Cascades Computer Innovation v. RPX Corp.*, No. 12-cv-01143 YGR, 2013 WL 316023 (N.D. Cal. Jan. 24, 2013).

195. *Id.* at *13.

196. *Id.*

197. *MGA Entm't v. Mattel, Inc.*, No. SACV 11-01063 DOC, 2012 WL 569389, at *1 (C.D. Cal. Feb. 21, 2012).

198. *See Destiny Tool v. SGS Tools Co.*, 344 F. App'x 320, 323 (9th Cir. 2009) ("although the antitrust and patent infringement claims are grounded in different statutes, they raise many of the same legal, factual, and evidentiary issues [such that] [j]udicial economy and efficiency counsel analysis of these issues in a single proceeding").

199. *MGA Entm't*, 2012 WL 569389, at *17.

In the context of granting leave to amend the defendant's answer and counterclaims the court assessed the sufficiency of the pleadings regarding a counterclaim of attempted monopolization, in *Nalco Co. v. Turner Designs, Inc.*[200] The court applied the Ninth Circuit standard, wherein in order to state a claim for attempted monopolization, the antitrust plaintiff must "allege facts that, if true, will prove: (1) that the defendant has engaged in predatory or anticompetitive conduct with (2) a specific intent to monopolize and (3) a dangerous probability of achieving monopoly power; moreover, an attempted monopolization claim also requires a showing of anticompetitive injury."[201] The court found that Turner adequately pled Nalco's unlawful conduct by alleging that (1) Nalco asserted a patent that no reasonable person would believe was infringed and that was fraudulently procured, (2) Nalco threatened Turner's customers with lawsuits if they did not discontinue purchasing Turner's product, and (3) Nalco subjected Turner to baseless litigation, the cost of which may have forced them out of the market. The court therefore granted the motion to leave and allowed Turner's proposed amendments because he "adequately pled that the injury—being forced to engage in costly litigation that may force Turner to discontinue its product and cede its ten percent market share to Nalco—is the type of anticompetitive injury that the antitrust laws were intended to prevent."[202]

A cease-and-desist letter can be enough to support an antitrust violation under the right circumstances, according to *Regional Multiple Listing Services of Minnesota v. American Home Realty Network*.[203] In this case, defendant American Home Realty Network (AHRN) counterclaimed against a charge of copyright infringement by Regional Multiple Listing Services (RMLS) involving pictures and descriptions of homes for sale. AHRN alleged group boycott and conspiracy in restraint of trade in refusing to deal, which was amply supported by the cease-and-desist letter. The court denied the antitrust defendant's motion to dismiss, stating that AHRN's counterclaim adequately stated a claim under section 1 of the Sherman Act. That defendants sent a cease-and-desist letter instead of filing a lawsuit was "immaterial here, as cease and desist letters typically initiate or give notice that copyright litigation may follow if the sender's

200. *Nalco Co. v. Turner Designs, Inc.*, No. 13-cv-02727 NC, 2014 WL 645365 (N.D. Cal. Feb. 19, 2014).

201. *Id.* at *9 (quoting *Coal. for ICANN Transparency, Inc. v. VeriSign, Inc.*, 611 F.3d 495, 506 (9th Cir. 2010)).

202. *Id.*

203. *Reg'l Multiple Listing Serv. of Minn., Inc. v. Am. Home Realty Network, Inc.*, 9 F. Supp. 3d 1032 (D. Minn. 2014).

demands are not met."[204] However, in its decision, the court noted that it is not a violation of the Sherman Act for a competitor to refuse to gratuitously share with a competitor.

§ 4.6 Pleading

The Supreme Court set forth the pleading requirements for an antitrust claim in *Bell Atlantic Corp. v. Twombly*.[205] To meet the threshold requirement under Federal Rule of Civil Procedure 8(a)(2), a party must plead a "plain statement of the claim showing that the pleader is entitled to relief."[206] To meet the standards under section 1 of the Sherman Act, "a claim requires a complaint with enough factual matter" to plausibly suggest that an illegal agreement was made.[207] However, "an allegation of parallel conduct and a bare assertion of conspiracy" are not sufficient unless adequate facts are also pled that place the parallel conduct "in a context that raises a suggestion of a preceding agreement."[208] A recent example of the application of these rubrics is *Evergreen Partnering Group, Inc. v. Pactiv Corp.*, where the court found that Evergreen's complaint satisfied the pleading requirements for an antitrust claim under *Twombly*.[209]

In *Samsung Electronics Co. v. Panasonic Corp.*,[210] the Ninth Circuit reversed a grant of a motion to dismiss based on the existence of "new and accumulating injury" tolling the statute of limitations. The technology at issue was flash memory (or "SD") cards produced and sold by Panasonic under a licensing agreement developed by "the SD Group" that contained a clause imposing a 6 percent royalty for cards using a proprietary format and entered into in 2003.[211] Thereafter, Panasonic developed two alternative formats (termed microSD and SDHC) that were later brought under the scope of this license by amendments adopted in 2006.[212] Samsung refused to sign the amended license, although it paid the 6 percent royalties and thereafter brought suit against Panasonic in 2010 (more than four years after Panasonic's demand for royalties under the amended agreement), alleging violation of sections 1 and 2 of the Sherman Act.[213] The district court dismissed on the grounds that the claims were time-barred,[214] and the Ninth Circuit reversed.

204. *Id.* at 1040.
205. *Bell Atl. Corp. v. Twombly*, 550 U.S. 544 (2007).
206. FED. R. CIV. P. 8(a)(2); *Towmbly*, 550 U.S. 544, 554–55 (2007).
207. *Twombly*, 550 U.S. at 556.
208. *Id.* at 556–57.
209. *Evergreen Partnering Grp., Inc. v. Pactiv Corp.*, 720 F.3d 33, 47 (1st Cir. 2013).
210. *Samsung Elecs. Co. v. Panasonic Corp.*, 747 F.3d 1199 (9th Cir. 2014).
211. *Id.* at 1201.
212. *Id.* at 1201–02.
213. *Id.* at 1202.
214. *Id.*

The court held that while the statute provides a four-year statute of limitations for bringing private actions under the Sherman Act,[215] "an exception to this time limit exists for continuing violations."[216] The asserted standard applied by the court was:

> To state a continuing violation of the antitrust laws in the Ninth Circuit, a plaintiff must allege that a defendant completed an overt act during the limitations period that meets two criteria: "(1) It must be a new and independent act that is not merely a reaffirmation of a previous act; and (2) it must inflict new and accumulating injury on the plaintiff."[217]

Under this standard, the court opined that an antitrust suit can be maintained "where a continuing violation is ongoing."[218] The court agreed with Samsung that Panasonic committed two "overt acts" during the limitations period: "the adoption of the 2006 license, which extended the license to cover the second-generation SD cards, and the attempt to enforce either license by collecting royalty payments from Samsung."[219] Adoption of the 6 percent royalty in the amended agreement was not dispositive, the court characterizing the amended agreement as merely an example of "conspirators [] fine-tun[ing] their cartel agreement" (here, to incorporate the after-developed technology).[220] Application of the requirement for royalty payments under the 2006 amended agreement was an "overt act" that restarted the limitations period because "those acts caused independent harm and accumulating injury."[221] Finally, the court also held that the antitrust injury alleged by Samsung was sufficiently speculative in 2003 (under the original agreement) to provide another exception to the statute of limitations.[222]

A similar conclusion was reached by the Ninth Circuit in a suit by a class of consumers against Panasonic and alleged coconspirators under the antitrust laws; in *Oliver v. SD-3C*,[223] the basis for the court's decision differed: because plaintiffs sought injunctive relief under Section 26 of the Clayton Act[224] (in contrast to Samsung's allegations under the Sherman Act

215. 15 U.S.C. § 15b.

216. *Samsung Elecs. Co.*, 747 F.3d at 1202 (citing *Zenith Radio Corp. v. Hazeltine Research, Inc.*, 401 U.S. 321, 398 (1971)).

217. *Id.* (citing *Pace Indus. Inc. v. Three Phx. Co.*, 813 F.2d 234, 238 (9th Cir. 1987).

218. *Id.*

219. *Id.* at 1203.

220. *Id.* at 1204 (quoting *Midwestern Mach. Co. v. Nw. Airlines, Inc.*, 392 F.3d 265, 269 (8th Cir. 2004)).

221. *Id.*

222. *Id.* (citing *Zenith Radio Corp. v. Hazeltine Research, Inc.*, 401 U.S. at 340).

223. *Oliver v. SD-3C LLC*, 751 F.3d 1081 (9th Cir. 2014).

224. 15 U.S.C. § 26.

in *Samsung Electronics Co. v. Panasonic Corp.*), the statute of limitations did not apply. Instead, the court held that the equitable doctrines of laches applied to the plaintiffs' claims.[225] Expressly "drawing liberally" from its *Samsung* opinion, the court focused on the portion of the agreement between defendants to charge a "fair market price" for SD cards, which plaintiffs alleged was price-fixing contrary to federal and state antitrust laws.[226] Although laches is applied with regard to the same time period specified under the limitations statute, laches is also subject to the same exceptions.[227] In the context of a consumer suit, "each time a defendant sells its price-fixed product, the sale constitutes a new overt act causing injury to the purchaser and the statute of limitations runs from the date of the act"[228] and thus the plaintiffs' claim was not time-barred under laches or the statute of limitations. The court also applied the "speculative damages" exception, because "it would have been pure speculation whether Plaintiffs would have been harmed by Defendants' alleged unlawful acts" and "[p]laintiffs should not be penalized for failing to foresee earlier that they would enter the market for SD cards and would therefore be harmed by Defendants' conduct."[229]

§ 4.7 Discovery

Twombly is also relevant to the question of antitrust discovery, which the Supreme Court characterized as a "sprawling, costly, and hugely time-consuming undertaking" often unsuccessful in "reveal[ing] relevant evidence to support a Section 1 claim."[230] These considerations were relevant to *In re Aspartame Antitrust Litigation*, in which the court awarded almost $500,000 in e-discovery costs to prevailing defendants under 28 U.S.C. § 1920(4).[231]

§ 4.8 Remedies

§ 4.8.1 Private Actions

The Clayton Act includes a private right of action for individuals or entities harmed by anticompetitive acts.[232] To encourage private enforcement, section 15 of the Clayton Act provides for mandatory award of treble damages,

225. *Id.* at 1084.
226. *Id.* at 1084–85.
227. *Id.* at 1086.
228. *Id.* (citing *Klehr v. A.O. Smith Corp.*, 521 U.S. 179, 189 (1997)).
229. *Id.* at 1087.
230. *Twombly*, 550 U.S. at 559, 560 n.6 (2007).
231. *In re Aspartame Antitrust Litig.*, 817 F. Supp. 2d 608 (E.D. Pa. 2011).
232. 15 U.S.C. § 15 (2013).

as well as the cost of the lawsuit, including reasonable attorney's fees.[233] The court may also, in its discretion, award interest on the actual damages sustained from the date of service of the complaint.[234] Furthermore, in cases where a civil action follows a successful civil or criminal action, the factual findings in the first action are given prima facie effect in the subsequent civil action and, if applicable, issue preclusive effect.[235] Injunctive relief may also be available to private parties upon a proper showing.[236]

While individual harm can form the basis for a private cause of action, the antitrust laws are intended to prevent harm to the market rather than a single individual. Thus, in *Ace Arts, LLC v. Sony/ATV Music Publishing, LLC*,[237] the court granted (in part) defendants' motion to dismiss. The action arose when Ace Arts filed multiple causes of action against Sony and Apple (the Beatles' Apple) alleging antitrust injury due to interference with Ace's distribution of *The Lost Concert* by asserting copyright claims against Ace for eight songs used within the film. The court determined Ace's complaint to be insufficiently specific to substantiate a Sherman Act section 1 claim:

> [A] plaintiff . . . must show that the challenged action "had an actual adverse effect on competition as a whole in the relevant market." Allegations that the plaintiff alone "has been harmed as an individual competitor will not suffice" to satisfy this requirement of adverse effect, or "antitrust injury." . . . The only injury alleged in the Amended Complaint is Defendants' interference with and prevention of the United States distribution of Plaintiff's film. . . . [the Plaintiff] alleges that the challenged restraints on trade "reduced output in the relevant market by completely precluding the distribution and exhibition of [The Lost Concert]." These allegations, even if accepted as true, are insufficient to plausibly establish any harm to the market for Beatles-related historical audio visual material as a whole, assuming for purposes of this analysis that such a market exists.[238]

A class of plaintiffs challenging the NCAA regulations prohibiting its member schools from offering "a limited share of the revenues generated by the use of [the] names, images and likenesses" to their "FBS football or

233. *Id.* § 15(a).
234. *Id.*
235. *Id.* § 16(a).
236. *Id.* § 26.
237. *Ace Arts, LLC v. Sony/ATV Music Publ'g, LLC*, 56 F. Supp. 3d 436 (S.D.N.Y. 2014).
238. *Id.* at 448–49.

Division I basketball recruits" in addition to full grants-in-aid obtained an injunction against the NCAA in *O'Bannon v. National Collegiate Athletic Association*.[239] The case arose when a group of current and former college football and men's basketball players brought an antitrust class action against the NCAA for alleging Sherman Act violations in restraint of trade with regard to use of the players' names, images, and likenesses. Although the court was able to parse several relevant markets, it was only in the college education market that the court found anticompetitive behavior, and there were insufficient pro-competitive factors for this behavior to, on balance, avoid antitrust liability. The court proposed alternatives that could be sufficiently pro-competitive to pass antitrust muster.[240]

§ 4.8.2 Government Actions

Government antitrust actions generally take the form of actions before the Federal Trade Commission under the Clayton Act[241] and the Federal Trade Commission Act.[242] The FTC also takes action for private acts such as so-called reverse payment settlement agreements in ANDA litigation.[243] Two recent decisions from the FTC illustrate the principles involved.

In *In re Corelogic, Inc.*,[244] the FTC brought an action for violation of section 5 of the Federal Trade Commission Act[245] and section 7 of the Clayton Act[246] regarding Corelogic's acquisition of TPG VI Ontario 1 AIV L.P. The grounds for FTC action were that the acquisition would "substantially lessen competition and tend to create a monopoly in the relevant market in violation of Section 7 of the Clayton Act" for a variety of expressly enumerated reasons and consequences.[247] As is the usual resolution of such an action, Corelogic entered into a consent agreement under which Corelogic agreed to make certain divestiture of assets, licenses, and agreements with competitors and its customers to ensure that the acquisition did not have an anticompetitive effect.

In *In re Nielsen Holdings N.V. and Arbitron, Inc.*,[248] the FTC brought an action for violation of section 5 of the Federal Trade Commission Act[249] and

239. 7 F. Supp. 3d 955 (N.D. Cal. 2014).
240. *Id.* at 1005–06; *see supra* note 193 and accompanying text.
241. 15 U.S.C. §§ 12–27; 29 U.S.C. §§ 52–53.
242. 15 U.S.C. §§ 41–58.
243. *See* Chapter 5.
244. *In re Corelogic, Inc.*, FTC Docket No. C-4458 (May 20, 2014).
245. 15 U.S.C. § 45.
246. 15 U.S.C. § 18.
247. *In re Corelogic, Inc.*, FTC Docket No. C-4458, at 3.
248. *In re Nielsen Holdings N.V. & Arbitron, Inc.*, FTC Docket No. C-4439 (Feb. 24, 2014).
249. 15 U.S.C. § 45.

section 7 of the Clayton Act[250] regarding Nielsen's acquisition of Arbitron. The grounds for FTC action were that the acquisition would "substantially lessen competition and tend to create a monopoly in the relevant market in violation of Section 7 of the Clayton Act" for a variety of expressly enumerated reasons and consequences.[251] As is the usual resolution of such an action, Nielsen entered into a consent agreement under which Nielsen agreed to make certain licenses and agreements with competitors to ensure that the acquisition did not have an anticompetitive effect.

§ 4.8.3 Equitable Relief

Courts have broad discretion to "create remedies 'effective to redress [antitrust] violations and to restore competition.'"[252] These remedies commonly include divestiture of an unlawful merger, which is an equitable remedy available in both government and private actions.[253]

§ 4.8.4 Disgorgement

The district court denied the defendant's motion to preclude the Federal Trade Commission from ordering disgorgement of five years' worth of profits for the drug Provigil in *FTC v. Cephalon, Inc.*[254] The patents at issue had been held invalid and to have been obtained through inequitable conduct, and the court in the antitrust action held that the FTC had statutory authority to seek disgorgement in cases brought under section 13(b) of the FTC Act.

IV. Enforcement

The Federal Circuit has made clear that when a patent holder, in good faith, seeks to protect its patent rights by bringing an infringement lawsuit or otherwise communicating its patent rights to potential infringers, this cannot constitute an antitrust violation under state or federal law.

In *Zenith Electronics Corp. v. Exzec, Inc.*,[255] a good-faith enforcement issue arose in the context of whether federal antitrust law preempts federal and state unfair competition claims. Exzec alleged that Zenith's

250. 15 U.S.C. § 18.

251. *In re Nielsen Holdings N.V. & Arbitron, Inc.*, FTC Docket No. C-4439, at 3.

252. *FTC v. Whole Foods Mkt., Inc.*, 548 F.3d 1028, 1033 (D.C. Cir. 2008) (quoting *Ford Motor Co. v. United States*, 405 U.S. 562, 573 (1972)).

253. *Ginsburg v. InBev NV-SA*, 623 F.3d 1229, 1234–35 (8th Cir. 2010); *Whole Foods Mkt., Inc.*, 548 F.3d at 1033–34.

254. *FTC v. Cephalon, Inc.*, No. 08-cv-2141, 2015 WL 1724597 (E.D. Pa. Apr. 15, 2015).

255. *Zenith Elecs. Corp. v. Exzec, Inc.*, 182 F.3d 1340, 1352–55 (Fed. Cir. 1999).

licensee, Elo Touchsystems, Inc., had falsely informed certain of its customers that Exzec's product infringed Zenith's licensed patents. The Federal Circuit affirmed the district court's denial of Zenith's motion to dismiss because, while federal patent and antitrust law governed its activities and their legality *vel non*, the protections of these laws could be lost if the patent holder acted in bad faith. On the other hand, the court noted that "communications to possible infringers concerning patent rights is not improper if the patentholder has a good faith belief in the accuracy of the communication."[256] It is the good-faith belief that a patent holder's patents are being infringed that distinguishes good-faith from bad-faith assertion of patent rights.[257]

§ *4.9* Noerr-Pennington

The *Noerr-Pennington* doctrine of antitrust immunity is based on two Supreme Court cases: *Eastern Railroad Presidents Conference v. Noerr Motor Freight*[258] and *United Mine Workers of America v. Pennington.*[259] These cases stand for the proposition that a party has the right to petition its government for redress of grievances or to influence public officials that is protected activity that cannot raise antitrust liability. These activities include, inter alia, filing suit including patent infringement lawsuits (other than baseless sham litigation) and submitting Citizen Petitions to the FDA regarding standards for approving generic drugs.

In *In re Skelaxin (Metaxalone) Antitrust Litigation*,[260] antitrust defendants King Pharmaceuticals and Mutual Pharmaceuticals moved to dismiss antitrust claims in a consolidated class action lawsuit by multiple plaintiffs regarding the drug metaxalone (Skelaxin), a prescription muscle relaxant. The grounds for plaintiffs' antitrust allegations included a settlement agreement between King and Mutual involving payment of $200 million from King to Mutual not to market a generic copy of the drug, as well as obtaining an Orange Book listing of additional patents, instituting additional ANDA litigation against several other generic-drug makers, and filing several Citizen Petitions with the FDA, all of which plaintiffs alleged to be sham or baseless. Defendants moved to dismiss the antitrust claims because their activities were immunized from antitrust liability under the

256. *Id.* at 1353 (quoting *Mikohn Gaming Corp. v. Acres Gaming, Inc.*, 165 F.3d 891, 897 (Fed. Cir. 1998)).

257. *Id.* (citing *Virtue v. Creamery Package Mfg. Co.*, 227 U.S. 8, 37–38 (1913); *Mallinckrodt, Inc. v. Medipart, Inc.*, 976 F.2d 700, 709 (Fed. Cir. 1992); *Va. Panel Corp. v. MAC Panel Co.*, 133 F.3d 860, 869 (Fed. Cir. 1997)).

258. *E. R.R. Presidents Conference v. Noerr Motor Freight, Inc.*, 365 U.S. 127, 136 (1961).

259. *United Mine Workers v. Pennington*, 381 U.S. 657 (1965).

260. *In re Skelaxin (Metaxalone) Antitrust Litig.*, No. 1:12-MD-2343, 2013 WL 2181185 (E.D. Tenn. May 20, 2013).

Noerr-Pennington doctrine. The district court denied defendants' motion finding that plaintiffs had plead antitrust injury with sufficient particularity under *Twombly*[261] when their allegations regarding defendants' several specific acts alleged to be anticompetitive are considered together so as to form a pattern of anticompetitive conduct. Moreover, recognizing that activity falling within *Noerr-Pennington* immunity cannot be included in any allegations of anticompetitive conduct,[262] the court found that while "[p]laintiffs will not have an easy task trying to prove both prongs of the *PRE Test*[263] as the case progresses," plaintiffs alleged sufficient facts to support both that the defendants' lawsuits were both objectively baseless and were an attempt to "interfere directly with the business relationships" of their competitors.[264] And while the district court could find no "binding Supreme Court or Sixth circuit precedent" that the principles applied in the litigation context under *Professional Real Estate Investors* should apply to petitions to administrative agencies like the FDA, the court was persuaded by authority from other district and circuit courts that sound reasoning supported the application of these principles to the Citizen Petitions at issue here. Under that standard, the district court found that plaintiffs had satisfied the *Twombly* standard and that the defendants' motion to dismiss should be denied.

Similarly, in the *Actavis* case, upon remand from the Supreme Court, the drugmaker defendants raised a *Noerr-Pennington* defense. Defendants argue that binding precedents demonstrate that *Noerr* applies to the court's consent judgment, which enjoined the generic companies, Parr and Paddock, from entering the market for generic AndroGel. In support, defendants cite *Noerr* and well as its progeny cases that expanded the doctrine to include protections for the rights of parties to petition courts, as well as the legislature. If defendants cannot be liable for their concerted petitioning of the court, it would make little sense for defendants to be liable for the resulting action by the court. Defendants argue that once the court acts, any harm caused by the court's injunction delaying entry of the generic drugs—is not attributable to the petitioners.[265]

261. *Bell Atl. Corp. v. Twombly*, 550 U.S. 544, 557 (2007).

262. *In re Skelaxin (Metaxalone) Antitrust Litig.*, 2013 WL 2181185, at *17 (citing *In re Neurontin Antitrust Litig.*, MDL 1479, 2009 WL 2751029, at *17 (D.N.J. Aug. 28, 2009)).

263. *Prof'l Real Estate Investors, Inc. (PRE) v. Columbia Pictures Indus., Inc.*, 508 U.S. 49 (1993) (which may be referred to as the *PRE Test*).

264. *In re Skelaxin*, 2013 WL 2181185, at *19–20.

265. Memorandum of Law in Support of Defendants Parr Pharmaceutical Companies, Inc. and Paddock Holdings, Inc.'s Motion to Dismiss the Second Amended Complaint, *FTC v. Actavis, Inc.*, No. 1:09-cv-00955, 2014 WL 1600331 (N.D. Ga. Apr. 21, 2014) (No. 239-1); *see Generic Companies in Actavis Case Urge Court To Adopt Noerr-Pennington Defense*, ABA Antitrust Section Intellectual Property E-bulletin, (Apr. 2014) (prior published version of *Actavis Noerr* defense arguments).

The FTC argued in opposition that the drugmakers' motion was flawed in at least three respects. First, the FTC objected to the application of *Noerr* to the private settlement between the parties because the defendants also petitioned the court to enter a consent judgment regarding their agreement. The FTC cited Supreme Court precedent that a contrary rule would lead to the absurdity that competitors would be immune from liability for a horizontal price-fixing agreement so long as they sought government approval for the agreed-upon prices. Second, the FTC rebuts the notion that the court's consent judgment constitutes "government action," thereby immunizing defendants. The FTC argues that consent judgments are not equivalent to statutes, regulations, or adjudicated court decisions because such judgments are voluntary and courts base their jurisdiction to enter such judgments solely upon the parties' agreement and not upon an independent review. Finally, the FTC argues, in the alternative, that the specific consent judgment entered for these drugmakers would not be immune because the agreement explicitly permits the parties to alter the agreement without court approval and the parties failed to disclose to the court how the delay payments would be computed.[266] The *Actavis* court has not yet resolved this motion.

The district court reached a similar decision in *In re Androgel Antitrust Litigation.*[267] In the context of settlement of ANDA litigation, the generic challengers argued that their agreement should be considered immune from antitrust scrutiny because the settlement agreement had been reviewed and approved by the district court and the subject of a final consent judgment. The district court denied any such immunity applied to the consent judgment because "[t]he judgment did not contain the full scope of the agreement between [the generic challengers] and [branded-drug maker] Solvay. Further, the full agreement . . . is precisely the sort of [reverse payment settlement] agreement the Supreme Court directed district courts to review with the rule of reason. Allowing the Defendants to shield themselves from antitrust scrutiny simply by obtaining a consent judgment would largely eliminate the application of the Supreme Court's decision in *Actavis*."[268]

In *Breville v. Storebound,*[269] the district court dismissed defendant Storebound's antitrust counterclaim under section 2 of the Sherman Act

266. FTC's Memorandum in Opposition to Defendants Par Pharmaceutical Companies, Inc., and Paddock Holdings, Inc.'s Motion to Dismiss Second Amended Complaint, *In re Androgel Antitrust Litig. (No. II)*, No. 1:09-cv-955 (N.D. Ga. Apr. 21, 2014) (No. 258).

267. *In re Androgel Antitrust Litig. (No. II)*, No. 1:09-cv-955, 2014 WL 1600331 (N.D. Ga. Apr. 21, 2014).

268. *Id.* at *9.

269. *Breville Pty Ltd. v. Storebound LLC*, No. 12-cv-01783-JST, 2013 WL 1758742 (N.D. Cal. Apr. 24, 2013).

for failing to satisfy the standards of objective and subjective baselessness mandated by the *Professional Real Estate Investors*.[270] The court found that the defendant had not pled sufficient facts to support its inequitable conduct counterclaim, and that the only basis pled for supporting the objectively baseless prong of the standard was the same facts that were insufficient with respect to the inequitable conduct affirmative defense. Thus, the counterclaim also must fail, and the court granted plaintiff's motion to dismiss under Federal Rule of Civil Procedure 12(b)(6).

In *Adobe v. Coffee Cup Partners*,[271] the district court granted plaintiff patent holder's motion to dismiss and rejected defendant's allegations that the *Noerr-Pennington* doctrine did not immunize the plaintiff from antitrust liability because the lawsuit was a sham. The court noted that in the Ninth Circuit the pleadings requirement for sham litigation were heightened because making such a determination necessarily interferes with a party's First Amendment rights.[272] Taking defendant's allegations as true, the court found that Coffee Cup had established the objective prong of the standard but failed to plead sufficient facts to establish the subjective prong; that is, the litigation was pursued in an attempt to "interfere directly with the business relationships" of their competitors "through the use of the governmental process—as opposed to the outcome of that process—as an anticompetitive weapon."[273] Moreover, the court further found that defendant had not alleged the elements of a Sherman Act section 2 violation—that is, that Adobe had market power and engaged in "predatory or anticompetitive" conduct with a specific intent to monopolize the relevant market and a "dangerous probability" of attaining that monopoly.[274]

Because this was a private cause of action, Coffee Cup was also required to allege antitrust injury, defined as an injury against which the antitrust laws were enacted to prevent. The district court stated that the defendant had failed to allege antitrust injury and thus its antitrust counterclaim must fail. While it pled injury to its own interests, Coffee Cup did not allege sufficient facts to support an inference of an injury to the market as a whole. The court characterized its pleadings in this regard as being no "more than the sweeping legal conclusion" that Adobe's purported

270. *Prof'l Real Estate Investors, Inc. v. Columbia Pictures Indus., Inc.*, 508 U.S. 49 (1993) (which may be referred to as the *PRE Test*).

271. *Adobe Sys. Inc. v. Coffee Cup Partners, Inc.*, No. C11-2243, 2012 WL 3877783 (N.D. Cal. Sept. 6, 2012).

272. *Kearney v. Foley & Lardner, LLP*, 590 F.3d 638, 643–44 (9th Cir. 2009).

273. *Adobe Sys.*, 2012 WL 3877783, at *9 (quoting *Prof'l Real Estate Investors, Inc.*, 508 U.S. at 60).

274. *Id.* at *10 (quoting *Spectrum Sports, Inc. v. McQuillan*, 506 U.S. 447, 456 (1993)).

anticompetitive actions have "caused injury to competition in the relevant market," which was not enough to survive a motion to dismiss.[275]

The issue of *Noerr-Pennington* immunity has also arisen in the so-called smartphone wars. *Apple v. Motorola Mobility*[276] is a case that originated in the International Trade Commission (ITC), where Motorola filed an infringement action aimed at obtaining an exclusion order for Apple products imported from abroad. Part of Apple's counterclaims recited antitrust violations by Motorola in bringing the ITC action and pursuing this lawsuit in district court. Motorola responded by asserting immunity under the *Noerr-Pennington* doctrine. The patents at issue were related to standards adopted by the European Telecommunications Standards Institute and were "essential" patents that were subject to being licensed under "fair, reasonable and nondiscriminatory [FRAND] terms to anyone who requests a license."[277] Apple contended that the *Noerr-Pennington* doctrine should not apply to immunize Motorola from its Sherman Act section 2 counterclaims because the basis for antitrust liability was not filing the ITC or district court actions but rather arose from Motorola's "abuse of the standard-setting process" and "Motorola's deceptive conduct and failure to offer a [fair, reasonable and nondiscriminatory] license."[278] In support of its position, Apple cited *ERBE v. Canady*,[279] where the Federal Circuit held that while "assertion of non-sham claims for 'patent infringement, trademark, and trade dress'" were immunized under the doctrine,[280] "other conduct," which Apple alleged included Motorola's conduct here, was not so immunized. The district court found that the weakness in Apple's position was that Motorola's behavior underlying Apple's antitrust counterclaim was, at root, based on its assertion of its "essential" patents and thus should fall within the immunity. Moreover, the court found that Apple failed to sufficiently allege that the litigation was a sham. The court further found that Apple did not allege sufficient antitrust injury to overcome the immunity. While the court was willing to find Motorola had *Noerr-Pennington* immunity to Apple's antitrust claims, it also found that the immunity did not extend to Apple's breach of contract and tort claims because, inter alia, Motorola provided no precedent for so applying the doctrine. Apple has appealed the court's decision on *Noerr-Pennington* to the Federal Circuit.

275. *Id.* at *10.

276. *Apple, Inc. v. Motorola Mobility, Inc.*, 886 F. Supp. 2d 1061 (W.D. Wis. 2012).

277. *Id.* at 1068.

278. *Id.* at 1076.

279. *ERBE Elektromedizin GmbH v. Canady Tech. LLC*, 629 F.3d 1278, 1292 (Fed. Cir. 2010).

280. *Motorola Mobility*, 886 F. Supp. 2d at 1076.

In *Clean Conversion v. CleanTech Biofuels*,[281] the district court denied defendant patent holder's motion to dismiss plaintiff's complaint based on *Noerr-Pennington* immunity. The plaintiff alleged violations of sections 1 and 2 of the Sherman Act, section 18 of the Clayton Act, and state antitrust law claims. The court based its decision on allegations in the complaint regarding CleanTech's efforts to aggregate all technology and patents related to methods for producing cellulosic biomass from municipal solid waste and to exclude all competition, including the plaintiff, from this market. Also pled were allegations that CleanTech's behavior involved canceling licenses to competitors upon acquisition of patent rights from third parties as evidence of predatory and anticompetitive conduct aimed at achieving a monopoly in the relevant market, including structuring its patent acquisitions to enlist the aid of the former patent owner in its efforts to monopolize the market. The court found plaintiff Clean Conversion had pled sufficient facts to support antitrust injury, including that Clean Conversion participates as a competitor in the relevant market and "alleges harms that are precisely the type that antitrust laws were designed to prevent."[282] These harms included that "CleanTech's conspiracy suppressed, eliminated, and interfered with competition and continues to do so through a scheme of strategic litigation, market manipulation, and back-room agreements to manipulate market participants out of the market—including CCT—and disrupt the natural competition in the relevant market for PSC conversion technology and services."[283] Finally, the court found that CleanTech had market power in the relevant market as the result of its predatory and anticompetitive activities. Accordingly, the defendant's anticompetitive activities extended beyond merely pursuing its rights and remedies through litigation and, therefore, *Noerr-Pennington* immunity did not shield it from antitrust liability:

> More importantly, CleanTech puts the cart before the horse. Litigation is only implicated in order to support an alleged scheme to violate antitrust law. CleanTech does not, however, provide any substantive analysis as to whether the Noerr-Pennington doctrine even applies. It neither specifically identifies any petitions sent directly to the court in the course of nor any conduct incidental to the prosecution of either litigation.[284] Rather, CleanTech merely starts its analysis from the presumption that the doctrine applies,

281. *Clean Conversion Techs., Inc. v. CleanTech Biofuels, Inc.*, No. 12-cv-239, 2012 WL 3585171 (S.D. Cal. Aug. 20, 2012).

282. *Id.* at *4.

283. *Id.*

284. *See Sosa v. DIRECTV, Inc.*, 437 F.3d 923, 934–35 (9th Cir. 2006).

> and then goes on to argue that the unalleged litigation between Vande Vegte and CCT does not fall within the "sham" exception.[285] CleanTech has not shown that it is entitled to the benefit of such a presumption. Simply put, CleanTech fails specifically identify any petitioning activity, and also fails to show that either litigation is entitled to Noerr-Pennington protection. Therefore, without more, the Court cannot conclude that either litigation is protected by the Noerr-Pennington doctrine.[286]

In re Wellbutrin XL Antitrust Litigation[287] involved antitrust allegations relating to conduct by Biovail and Glaxo Smith Kline in ANDA litigation over generic competition for the antidepressant bupriopion hydrochloride (Wellbutrin XL). Biovail owned the Orange Book–listed patents (U.S. Patent Nos. 6,096,341 and 6,143,327, which expire on October 30, 2018) and GSK was the NDA holder that listed these patents and sold the Welbutrin XL product. Prior to this litigation, Biovail separately sued four different generic ANDA filers, and reached settlement agreements with all four. Biovail also submitted Citizen Petitions to the FDA regarding proposed standards for generic extended release bupriopion hydrochloride. Plaintiffs in this lawsuit, direct and indirect purchasers of generic extended release bupriopion hydrochloride, alleged antitrust violations resulting from the ANDA litigation, the FDA Citizen Petitions, and the settlement agreements. Biovail and GSK countered asserting *Noerr-Pennington* immunity. The district court granted summary judgment to Biovail and GSK on the allegations relating to the ANDA litigations and the Citizen Petitions and deferred judgment on the settlement agreements.

With regard to the ANDA litigation, the court considered Biovail's conduct with regard to each of the ANDA litigations. In each, the generic challengers' Paragraph IV letters were based on non-infringement, inter alia because the generic formulation contained a stabilizer and the claims recited that the patented formulation was "free of stabilizer."[288] The court found that in two of the cases a hydrochloric acid stabilizer was present during formulation, but that it evaporated during formulation and was not a component of the finished drug product. On those facts, the court found that the ANDA litigation was not objectively baseless because Biovail

285. *See* Memorandum of Points and Authorities in Support of Motion to Dismiss Pursuant to Rule 12(b)(6), at 7:15–:19, 7:20–8:25, *Clean Conversion Techs., Inc. v. CleanTech Biofuels, Inc.*, No. 12-cv-239 (S.D. Cal. March 26, 2012), ECF No. 14-1.

286. *Clean Conversion*, 2012 WL 3585171, at *7.

287. *In re Wellbutrin XL Antitrust Litig.*, Nos. 08-2431, 08-2433, 2012 WL 1657734 (E.D. Pa. May 11, 2012).

288. U.S. Patent No. 6,096,341 col. 9 l. 51 (Claim 1) and col. 12 ll. 3–4 (Claim 30); U.S. Patent No. 6,143,327 col. 12 l. 15 (Claim 1) and col. 13 l. 11 (Claim 15).

proposed a reasonable claim construction that would have defeated the non-infringement allegations. In addition, the court found that insofar as there was any delay in generic drugs coming to market, such delay was based on the thirty-month stay, which was not antitrust injury because it was mandated by statute. In view of the court finding that Biovail's ANDA litigation was not objectively baseless, the delay did not trigger antitrust liability. The court reached the same conclusion regarding the 180-day exclusivity period for the first ANDA filer because it determined that the litigation was not objectively baseless as to this ANDA filer and thus the delay was not an antitrust violation.

As to the Citizen Petition, which was related to proposed FDA standards for evaluating ANDA applications directed towards generic bupriopion hydrochloride, the district court also found that this was not objectively baseless. The court found no binding case law that would strip a patent holder of *Noerr-Pennington* immunity if the FDA denied the Citizen Petition (and here the petition was granted in part and denied in part). With regard to any delay in generic-drug approval arising from the Citizen Petition amounting to antitrust injury, the court opined that the plaintiffs failed to show causation:

> An antitrust plaintiff must prove a causal connection between the antitrust violation and actual damages suffered.[289] In this case, the plaintiffs' theory of antitrust injury is that the Citizen Petition delayed ANDA approval, thus postponing generic entry and permitting the brand manufacturers to maintain monopoly prices of Wellbutrin XL. Having found that two of the Citizen Petition requests were successful non-sham requests entitled to Noerr-Pennington immunity, however, this Court must examine whether the plaintiffs have put forth evidence of injury attributable to the unsuccessful (and arguably sham) requests. . . .
>
> The plaintiffs have not pointed to any other evidence in the record from which a jury could reasonably conclude that the FDA would have approved the ANDAs earlier if the Citizen Petition had been limited to the successful, non-sham requests. In other words, even if the unsuccessful requests were sham petitions not entitled to Noerr-Pennington immunity, the plaintiffs have not met their burden to show causation of anticompetitive injury.[290]

289. *See In re Hydrogen Peroxide Antitrust Litig.*, 552 F.3d 305, 311 (3d Cir. 2008); *Rossi v. Standard Roofing, Inc.*, 156 F.3d 452, 483–84 (3d Cir. 1998).

290. *In re Wellbutrin*, 2012 WL 1657734, at *33–34.

The court also found insufficient evidence that Biovail and GSK conspired to achieve a monopoly either with regard to ANDA litigation or the FDA Citizen Petition.

In an interesting side note, the district court considered whether the standard for objective baselessness with regard to establishing sham litigation should be clear and convincing evidence or the preponderance standard. Acknowledging that the question is one of Federal Circuit law, and in absence of Federal Circuit authority, the court noted that analogy to cases "in other contexts" suggests the standard should be "clear and convincing evidence."[291] However, because in this case the ANDA litigation is not objectively baseless under either standard, the court concluded that it need not decide the question.

In *Cascades v. RPX*,[292] the plaintiff alleged that the defendants, including several major telecommunications companies, conspired to refuse to deal with it and forming an illegal boycott not to license the plaintiff's patents. The defendants' actions allegedly amounted to violations of the Sherman Act sections 1 and 2 and California state antitrust laws. Defendants moved to dismiss because the activities asserted in support of the antitrust allegations were protected by the *Noerr-Pennington* doctrine as a concerted effort to defend against Cascades' infringement allegations in a related action. The district court refused to grant defendants' motion to dismiss on these grounds. Instead, the court dismissed for the lack of specificity in the complaint regarding antitrust injury—including the timing of the infringement action and the instigation of the alleged conspiracy not to deal.

Following the filing of an amended complaint by Cascades, however, the court concluded that there were numerous factual issues that precluded resolving the applicability of *Noerr-Pennington* immunity. The defendants asserted that their decision whether to "accept or reject a licensing offer from Cascades" was a "decision whether or not to settle Cascades' patent claims" and therefore incidental to legitimate petition activity.[293] The court concluded that numerous factual issues must be resolved in order to determine the veracity of the defendants' *Noerr-Pennington* defense. "Determining whether the Manufacturing Defendants' alleged cooperative conduct falls within the ambit of Noerr-Pennington necessarily requires a close look at the timing of any decision to refuse Cascades'

---

291. *Id.* at *5 (citing *800 Adept, Inc. v. Murex Secs. Ltd.*, 539 F.3d 1354, 1370 (Fed. Cir. 2008)).

292. *Cascades v. RPX*, No. 12-cv-01143 YGR, 2013 WL 316023, at *1 (N.D. Cal. Jan. 24, 2013).

293. Order at 27, *Cascades*, No. 12-cv-01143 (No. 119).

individual licensing overtures, the timing of any perceived threats or demands pre-lawsuit, the scope of any perceived threat, and potentially other, unforeseen matters."[294]

The issue of sham litigation also arose in *AstraZeneca AB v. Glenmark Generics Ltd.*,[295] in which the district court dismissed the defendant's counterclaim for failure to allege sufficient facts to state an antitrust injury. The court explained that "alleging 'sham' litigation alone is not sufficient to state a claim for an antitrust violation under the Sherman Act, 15 U.S.C. §§ 1 & 2. Claimants must also allege an independent antitrust injury. . . . Not all injuries qualify—an antitrust injury must be of the type that the antitrust laws are specifically designed to prevent. . . . [T]o satisfy standing and state a justiciable claim, claimants' alleged injuries 'must be both "real and immediate," not "conjectural" or "hypothetical."'"[296]

The existence of a court-sanctioned consent judgment was raised in support of a motion to dismiss by antitrust defendants accused of antitrust violations with regard to a reverse payment settlement of ANDA litigation in *In re Nexium (Esomeprazole) Antitrust Litigation*.[297] The district court did not find the consent judgments in this case were sufficient because the district court did not play "an independent role in drafting the terms in the consent judgments . . . so it [was] unclear how much of the content found within the consent judgments is properly attributable to the New Jersey District Court judge's deliberation."[298]

In *TransWeb, LLC v. 3M Innovative Properties Co.*[299] the trial court denied defendant 3M's motion for judgment as a matter of law after a jury trial. The jury found the claims to 3M's patent for an environmental filter to be obvious and obtained by inequitable conduct. Although the jury also found 3M had engaged in *Walker Process* fraud in asserting its patent and had committed antitrust violations on those grounds, it did not find that 3M had mounted sham litigation and thus did not find 3M guilty of an antitrust violation on that basis.

In *Pearson Education v. Allen Air Conditioning*,[300] the district court granted plaintiffs' motion to dismiss the defendants' antitrust counterclaims. The case arose in the context of copyright litigation by several U.S.

294. *Id.*

295. *AstraZeneca AB v. Glenmark Generics Ltd.*, No. CV 14-665-GMS, 2014 WL 5366050 (D. Del. Oct. 9, 2014).

296. *Id.* at *1 n.1 (internal citations omitted).

297. *In re Nexium (Esomeprazole) Antitrust Litig.*, 968 F. Supp. 2d 367 (D. Mass. 2013).

298. *Id.* at 398.

299. *TransWeb, LLC v. 3M Innovative Props. Co.*, 16 F. Supp. 3d 385 (D.N.J. 2014).

300. *Person Educ., Inc. v. Allen Air Conditioning Co.*, No. 08-cv-6152, 2014 WL 2154099, at *1 (S.D.N.Y. May 22, 2014).

publishers against an individual who purchased textbooks abroad (sold by publishers at prices lower than U.S. prices) and then sold the reimported textbooks in the U.S. market at a discount over the publishers' U.S. prices. (The facts of this case are similar to those in *Kirtsaeng v. John Wiley & Sons, Inc.*[301]) After the Supreme Court handed down its *Kirtsaeng* decision, the court dismissed the plaintiffs' copyright infringement claims.[302] The court then granted plaintiffs' motion to dismiss the defendants' antitrust counterclaims because the allegations "fail[ed] to state a cognizable antitrust claim. There is nothing unlawful regarding the Publishers' coordinated commencement of litigation to protect their copyrights from a similar course of conduct."[303] The court recognized that defendants had antitrust standing, stating that:

> At a basic and high level, if it were the case that Pearson and Wiley agreed to undertake specific actions to prevent Liu from acquiring and selling foreign edition textbooks, such conduct could result in cognizable antitrust injury.[304]

However, defendants otherwise failed to assert sufficient facts to support the remainder of its antitrust allegations under section 1 of the Sherman Act. "Without more, parallel conduct does not suggest conspiracy, and a conclusory allegation of agreement at some unidentified point does not supply facts adequate to show illegality" according to the opinion.[305] In addition the court stated:

> [Counterclaim plaintiff] Liu does not allege any detail with regard to who has an agreement with whom, nor does she explain the relevant terms of such agreement. Thus, it is impossible to know whether the offending agreement is a horizontal agreement, a vertical agreement, a rimless conspiracy, a rimmed conspiracy, or none of the above.[306]

With regard to the section 2 claim, the court said it was dismissing this counterclaim because "Liu has failed to allege a cognizable relevant market; the relevant market she appears earlier in her counterclaims to be pursuing (relating to college textbook titles) has given way in the second Counterclaim to a generalized statement of conduct in no clear market."[307]

301. 133 S. Ct. 1351 (2013).
302. *Pearson Educ. v. Allen Air Conditioning*, 2014 WL 2154099, at *3.
303. *Id.* at *1.
304. *Id.* at *8.
305. *Id.* at *5 (quoting *Twombly*, 550 U.S. at 556–57).
306. *Id.* at *10.
307. *Id.* at *11.

§ 4.10 *Illegally Obtained Patents:* Walker Process

The classic basis for finding antitrust liability arising from the exercise of patent exclusivity is where the patent holder has procured patents as the result of fraud.[308] Under a *Walker Process* analysis, claims asserted from a knowingly fraudulently obtained patent, or *via* litigation known to be baseless and without legal or factual support can raise antitrust liability.

In *RB Rubber Products, Inc. v. Ecore International, Inc.*,[309] the district court dismissed with prejudice claims arising under section 2 of the Sherman Act, predicated on alleged inequitable conduct in the procurement of patents for rubber acoustical underlayments. The district court dismissed these claims because the U.S. Patent and Trademark Office had reissued the patent in suit (U.S. Patent No. 6,920,723) as RE41945 notwithstanding that prior art and information antitrust plaintiffs contended had been withheld with the intent to deceive the USPTO in obtaining the original patent. According to the district court:

> [T]he re-issuance of RE41945 is probative. Because the PTO reexamines re-issuance applications as if being presented for the first time, the fact that the PTO did re-issue [ECORE's] patent even with the prior art precludes [U.S. Rubber] from plausibly pleading Claim One. The fact that the court also stated that it had been unable to locate relevant precedent stating that reissue of a patent would always cure an alleged Walker Process violation does not undermine its conclusion that, under the facts of the case before it, the reissue of the [original] patent precluded the plaintiff from plausibly pleading but-for causation.[310]

This conclusion was further supported by the Federal Circuit's decision in *Therasense v. Becton.*[311] According to the district court, under that precedent, reissue of the patent in view of purportedly withheld material information would preclude "but for" causation and thus would fail to satisfy a necessary prong of the Federal Circuit's requirements for establishing inequitable conduct.

In *WesternGeco v. ION*,[312] the district court granted summary judgment against defendant ION Geophysical Corp.'s inequitable conduct defenses and antitrust counterclaims. The case involved five patents (U.S. Patent

308. *Walker Process Equip., Inc. v. Food Mach. & Chem. Corp.*, 382 U.S. 172 (1965).

309. *RB Rubber Prods., Inc. v. Ecore Int'l, Inc.*, No. 3:11-cv-319-AC, 2012 WL 860416 (D. Or. Mar. 13, 2012).

310. *Id.* at *8.

311. *Therasense, Inc. v. Becton, Dickinson & Co.*, 649 F.3d 1276, 1289 (Fed. Cir. 2011).

312. *WesternGeco LLC v. ION Geophysical Corp.*, No. 4:09-cv-1827, 2012 WL 567430 (S.D. Tex. Feb. 21, 2012).

Nos. 6,932,017; 7,080,607; 7,162,967; 7,293,520; and 6,691,038) relating to technology used for conducting offshore seismic surveys. The inequitable conduct and antitrust counterclaims were limited to the '038 patent. ION alleged that certain statements made to the PTO during prosecution of the '038 patent were material misrepresentations regarding the scope and content of a reference WesternGeco had submitted in an Information Disclosure Statement. The district court held that the purported misrepresentations were merely attorney argument and were not material and, thus, that ION would not be able to prove inequitable conduct under the standards enunciated by the Federal Circuit in *Therasense v. Becton*. The court distinguished cases where such (mis)representations have been held to be material, such as *Ring Plus v. Cingular Wireless*,[313] because in this case the art was before the examiner "who was then free to either accept or reject [the prosecuting attorney's] characterization of the prior art," citing *Young v. Lumenis*[314] and *Innogenetics v. Abbott Labs.*[315]

With regard to the antitrust counterclaims, the district court held that, as these allegations were based on the same purportedly "material facts" as ION's inequitable conduct defenses, WesternGeco was similarly entitled to summary judgment that its lawsuit was not subject to *Walker Process* antitrust liability.

The Federal Trade Commission raised the issue of *Walker Process* fraud in *FTC v. Cephalon, Inc.*,[316] in which the court had in prior ANDA litigation determined that the claims of certain Orange Book–listed patents had been obtained through inequitable conduct. The district court in the antitrust action declined to grant the FTC's motion to prohibit Cephalon from introducing evidence of validity and enforceability based upon the language in *Actavis*, relying instead on the doctrine of collateral estoppel. Cephalon contended that it should be able to argue validity and enforceability because the reverse payment negotiation was separate from the patent infringement case. According to Cephalon, there was "uncertainty and risk on both sides of the patent litigation when it negotiated the settlements with the Generic Defendants," and therefore they should not be barred for inclusion in the antitrust case.[317] The court precluded Cephalon from defending the antitrust claim on the grounds of litigation uncertainty, reasoning that "one who acted fraudulently in obtaining a patent

---

313. *Ring Plus, Inc. v. Cingular Wireless Corp.*, 614 F.3d 1354, 1361 (Fed. Cir. 2010).

314. *WesternGeco*, 2012 WL 567430, at *19 (citing *Young v. Lumenis, Inc.*, 492 F.3d 1336, 1348–49 (Fed. Cir. 2007)).

315. *Id.* at *19 (citing *Innogenetics, N.V. v. Abbott Labs.*, 512 F.3d 1363, 1379 (Fed. Cir. 2008)).

316. *FTC v. Cephalon, Inc.*, 36 F. Supp. 3d 527 (E.D. Pa. 2014).

317. *Id.* at 533.

necessarily knows its patent is unenforceable." The court further reasoned that Cephalon would not be allowed to "justify a reverse payment on the grounds that it resolved 'uncertainty and risk' that existed because of its own affirmative misconduct . . . [because] [w]ithout its misrepresentations and omissions—made with specific intent to deceive the PTO—Cephalon would never have been in the position to institute infringement litigation in the first place."[318]

The court denied defendants' motion to dismiss a complaint for antitrust violations under section 2 of the Sherman Act in *Moldex Metric, Inc. v. 3M Co.*[319] The basis of the complaint was a prior infringement action by 3M against Moldex involving ear protectors supplied to the U.S. military, which litigation Moldex contended was objectively baseless. The court found that, although a patent owner is usually protected by the *Noerr-Pennington* doctrine from antitrust liability for bringing an infringement suit against an alleged infringer, even if the patentee does not prevail in the action, there are two exceptions. The anticompetitive effects of an infringement suit can raise antitrust liability if the patent was obtained "through knowing and willful fraud" or the infringement suit was "a mere sham to cover what is actually nothing more than an attempt to interfere directly with the business relationships of a competitor."[320] In this case the court determined that Moldex had pled sufficiently that the prior infringement action against it was objectively baseless to withstand 3M's motion to dismiss.

While refusing to grant defendant's motion to dismiss antitrust allegations (based on defendants' assertion of *Noerr-Pennington* immunity), the district court discussed application of the doctrine in instances of aggressive patent litigation in *Kimberly-Clark Worldwide Inc. v. First Quality Baby Products LLC*.[321] This case was one in a long-running series of cases between the parties relating to the disposable diaper market, and antitrust plaintiff's allegations under section 2 of the Sherman Act were grounded in Kimberly-Clarke's litigation behavior. This included filing additional patent applications to encompass First Quality's products and basing these applications on patents found in other patent litigation between the parties to be obvious. The court noted that there was no allegation of *Walker Process* fraud or inequitable conduct and that the patent at issue was the

318. *Id.* at 535.

319. *Moldex Metric, Inc. v. 3M Co.*, No. CIV. 14-1821 JNE/FLN, 2015 WL 520722 (D. Minn. Feb. 9, 2015).

320. *Id.* at *6–7 (quoting *Q-Pharma, Inc. v. Andrew Jurgens Co.*, 360 F.3d 1295, 1304–05 (Fed. Cir. 2004)).

321. *Kimberly-Clark Worldwide Inc. v. First Quality Baby Prods. LLC*, No. 14-cv-1466, 2015 WL 1582368 (E.D. Wis. Apr. 9, 2015).

subject of infringement litigation in which invalidity had been pled. The court permitted the antitrust case to proceed while the validity *vel non* of the patent was litigated.[322]

The Federal Circuit affirmed grant of summary judgment against an antitrust plaintiff in *Tyco Healthcare Group LP v. Mutual Pharmaceutical Co.*[323] The case involved ANDA litigation over temazepam, a sleep-inducing drug that infringement defendant Mutual alleged was sham litigation and thus not protected from antitrust liability under the *Noerr-Pennington* doctrine. Although Tyco did not prevail in the underlying ANDA litigation (Mutual's product was found not to infringe and Tyco's patent was found invalid), the action was not a sham, according to the court: "It is not unreasonable for a patent owner to allege infringement under section 271(e)(2)(A) if the patent owner has evidence that the as-marketed commercial ANDA product will infringe, even though the hypothetical product specified in the ANDA could not infringe."[324] The court enunciated the standard:

> Given the presumption of patent validity and the burden on the patent challenger to prove invalidity by clear and convincing evidence, it will be a rare case in which a patentee's assertion of its patent in the face of a claim of invalidity will be so unreasonable as to support a claim that the patentee has engaged in sham litigation. We therefore affirm the district court's grant of summary judgment for Tyco with respect to the invalidity portion of Mutual's sham-litigation counterclaim.[325]

The court took a different view with regard to a Citizen Petition filed by Tyco and alleged to be fraudulent by Mutual; that issue required fact-finding on the question of whether the Citizen Petition delayed approval of Mutual's ANDA. Finally, the court affirmed the district court's judgment against Mutual's *Walker Process* counterclaim for failing to establish inequitable conduct.

§ 4.10.1 Handgards Presumption of Good Faith

Courts have struggled to find an appropriate balance between the rights afforded a patent holder through the patent laws and enforcement of the

322. *See also supra* pp. 26–27.
323. *Tyco Healthcare Grp. LP v. Mut. Pharm. Co.*, 762 F.3d 1338 (Fed. Cir. 2014).
324. *Id.* at 1345.
325. *Id.* at 1345–47.

antitrust laws. In *Handgards, Inc. v. Ethicon, Inc.*,[326] the court recognized the need to "prevent frustration of patent laws by the long reach of antitrust laws" through providing "the means whereby the bad faith infringement action can be identified *post hoc* with a sufficiently high degree of certainty to make it highly improbable that the action in fact was brought in good faith."[327] The *Handgards* court applied a presumption that a patent holder's infringement lawsuit was brought in good faith, and this presumption may only be overcome by clear and convincing evidence to the contrary.[328] This presumption is "necessary to provide reasonable protection for the honest patent holder who brings an infringement action to protect his legal monopoly."[329] The Federal Circuit has affirmed this presumption, for example, in *Zenith Electronics Corp. v. Exzec, Inc.*,[330] and *Nobelpharma AB v. Implant Innovations, Inc.*[331]

§ 4.11 *Other Examples of Inequitable Conduct: Pick-Barth Doctrine*

The *Pick-Barth* doctrine states that it is unnecessary to prove a public injury under a section 1 analysis in circumstances where there is a conspiracy to eliminate a competitor using unfair or anticompetitive means.[332] However, such activity is not per se anticompetitive conduct.[333] With regard to patents, the *Pick-Barth* doctrine is applied where a patent owner alleges that a defendant's infringing activity itself constitutes anticompetitive conduct. This application was rejected in *Eatoni Ergonomics, Inc. v. Research In Motion Corp.*,[334] in which the court declined to find patent infringement to be anticompetitive conduct.

---

326. *Handgards, Inc. v. Ethicon, Inc.*, 601 F.2d 986 (9th Cir. 1979).

327. *Id.* at 993.

328. *Id.* at 996.

329. *Id.*

330. 182 F.3d 1340, 1352 (Fed. Cir. 1999) (citing *Loctite Corp. v. Ultraseal Ltd.*, 781 F.2d 861, 876–77 (Fed. Cir. 1985)).

331. 141 F.3d 1059, 1068 (Fed. Cir. 1998) (holding that antitrust liability may apply to a patent holder who brings an infringement suit where the antitrust plaintiff "proves [among other things] (1) that the asserted patent was obtained through knowing and willful fraud . . . , or (2) that the infringement suit was 'a mere sham'").

332. *Albert Pick-Barth Co. v. Mitchell Woodbury Corp.*, 57 F.2d 96 (1st Cir. 1932), *cert. denied*, 286 U.S. 552 (1932).

333. *See Associated Radio Serv. Co. v. Page Airways, Inc.*, 624 F.2d 1342, 1354 (5th Cir. 1980); *Stifel, Nicolaus & Co. v. Dain, Kalman & Quail, Inc.*, 578 F.2d 1256, 1261 (8th Cir. 1978); *Nw. Power Prods., Inc. v. Omark Indus.*, 576 F.2d 83, 90 (5th Cir. 1978); *Craig v. Sun Oil Co. of Pa.*, 515 F.2d 221, 224 (10th Cir. 1975).

334. *Eatoni Ergonomics, Inc. v. Research In Motion Corp.*, 826 F. Supp. 2d 705 (S.D.N.Y. 2011).

V. Defenses

§ 4.12 Patent Misuse

The basic rule of patent misuse established by the Supreme Court is that, while the patent holder may exploit its patent, the patent holder may not "use it to acquire a monopoly not embraced in the patent."[335] This doctrine has a narrow scope, applying only to misuse of the patent in suit itself.[336] While wrongful conduct with an anticompetitive effect may prove an antitrust violation, it does not establish patent misuse "unless the conduct in question restricts the use of that patent and does so in one of the specific ways that have been held to be outside the otherwise broad scope of the patent grant."[337] Thus, a patent holder commits patent misuse only if the patent holder (1) increases the physical or temporal scope of his patent rights beyond the lawful scope and (2) this conduct has an anticompetitive effect.[338]

Congress and the courts have developed a three-tiered system to address allegations of patent misuse. First, Congress has defined five types of conduct that cannot provide the basis for a claim of patent misuse.[339] Second, courts have identified a group of practices that are per se illegal, including "tying" arrangements, where a license under the patent is conditioned upon the purchase of a separate, staple good, resale price-fixing of a patented good, and effective extension of a patent term by requiring royalties on an expired patent.[340] Finally, as to all other practices, courts must determine whether the conduct reasonably relates to the subject matter within the scope of the patent claims, or whether the conduct effectively extends the scope of the patent right and has an anticompetitive effect.[341] If a court determines the latter, this conduct is analyzed under the "rule of reason" by the fact-finder, which takes into account several factors to determine "whether the questioned practice imposes an unreasonable restraint on competition."[342]

In *Intellectual Ventures v. Capital One*,[343] defendants in patent infringement litigation involving online banking services filed an amended answer

335. *Transparent-Wrap Mach. Corp. v. Stokes & Smith Co.*, 329 U.S. 637, 643 (1947).

336. *See Princo Corp. v. ITC*, 616 F.3d 1318, 1329 (Fed. Cir. 2010) (en banc).

337. *Id.*

338. *Id.*

339. *See* 35 U.S.C. § 271(d).

340. *Va. Panel Corp. v. MAC Panel Corp.*, 133 F.3d 860, 869 (Fed. Cir. 1997); *see also Mallinckrodt v. Medipart, Inc.*, 976 F.2d 700, 704 (Fed. Cir. 1992).

341. *Va. Panel*, 133 F.3d at 869.

342. *Id.* (quoting *State Oil Co. v. Kahn*, 522 U.S. 3, 10 (1997)).

343. *Intellectual Ventures I LLC et al. v. Capital One Fin. Corp. et al.*, No. 14-111, 2015 WL 898146 (D. Md. Mar. 2, 2015).

to add antitrust counterclaims including monopolization and attempted monopolization under section 2 of the Sherman Act and unlawful asset acquisition under section 7 of the Clayton Act.[344] Intellectual Ventures, also referred to as "IV," is commonly considered a non-practicing entity (NPE) whose "businesses include purchasing important inventions from individual inventors and institutions and then licensing the inventions to those who need them" or bringing patent infringement actions against alleged infringers.[345]

With regard to the monopolization and attempted monopolization counterclaims, Intellectual Ventures argued that both counterclaims fail because "(1) they do not allege a plausible relevant market . . . ; (2) they do not allege sufficiently that [Intellectual Ventures has] monopoly power in such a market, . . . ; and (3) none of the purportedly unlawful acts of monopolization that [defendants] allege are indeed unlawful."[346]

Defendants submitted that Intellectual Ventures' "3,500-patent financial-services portfolio" is the relevant market in this case by alleging:[347]

> IV's financial-services portfolio in the United States constitutes a relevant licensing market because IV demands that banks license this portfolio to continue their commercial-banking services . . . , *threatening and suing those banks that resist*. Because IV sought and obtained such a large portfolio, banks do not have the option to license alternative portfolios, because such an alternative license would not eliminate *IV's threat of ceaseless litigation*. . . . In short, IV has eliminated banks' access to substitutes for IV's license, both in the form of other patent licenses and banking-product designs, through a *carefully orchestrated campaign of patent aggregation, concealment, and sham litigation*.[348]

The court recognized that the defendants' circumstances are similar to those under *Meredith v. SESAC*, "in which local stations could go only to the PROs, not the composers and musicians, and had to go to each PRO, as each amassed a distinct collection of music."[349] Further, the court noted that, "like the local stations, [defendants] already own products that (unknowingly) incorporate the allegedly patented products, and the patented products cannot be extracted from the online banking systems, just

344. *Id.* at *1.
345. *Id.*
346. *Id.* at *7.
347. *Id.* at *8.
348. *Id.* at *11 (emphasis added).
349. *Id.* at *10.

as the music cannot be removed from the television programs."[350] The court determined that the defendants adequately alleged a plausible relevant market, including by noting that the defendants had sufficiently alleged that their business necessity is "not only to avoid litigation but also to continue to provide the online services they already offer without paying the cost-prohibitive licensing fees to [Intellectual Ventures]."[351] As to monopoly power, the court recognized that monopoly power may be established "either through 'direct evidence of supracompetitive prices and restricted output' or by inference 'from the structure and composition of the relevant market.'"[352] Further, the court noted that "control of seventy percent or more of the relevant market is circumstantial evidence of monopoly power."[353] Also, the court noted that the use of market share to show monopoly power also "must show that new competitors face high market barriers to entry and that current competitors lack the ability to expand their output to challenge a monopolist's high prices,"[354] for which the court recognized patents as being "[c]ommon entry barriers."[355] The defendants not only offered direct evidence but also circumstantial evidence that "IV has a 100 percent share of the relevant market because it alone sells a license to what it contends to be an indispensable body of patents, and licenses to patents held by other entities cannot halt IV's activities with respect to its financial-services portfolio."[356] The court determined that the defendants sufficiently alleged a significant market share as the "entire market" and "high barriers to market entry" based on Intellectual Ventures' "3,500-patent financial-services portfolio."[357]

As to unlawful acts of monopolization, the defendants alleged that Intellectual Ventures' wrongful conduct included the "intentional acquisition of a 'massive patent portfolio,' encompassing 3,500 patents, 'that

350. *Id.*

351. *Id.* at *11; *see also Intellectual Ventures I LLC v. Capital One Fin. Corp.*, 2013 WL 6682981, at *5 (E.D. Va. Dec. 18, 2013) (The Eastern District of Virginia court noted that in the cases that the defendants cited, "the relevant market was defined in terms of what was a business necessity for the complaining businesses' lawful operation" instead of the "business necessity" alleged by the defendants of avoiding future litigation.).

352. *Intellectual Ventures I LLC*, 2015 WL 898146, at *11 (quoting *Intellectual Ventures I LLC*, 2013 WL 6682981, at *4).

353. *Id.* (*E.I. du Point de Nemours & Co. v. Kolon Indus., Inc.*, 637 F.3d 435, 450–51 (4th Cir. 2011)).

354. *Id.*

355. *Id.*

356. *Id.* at *12; *see also Intellectual Ventures I*, 2013 WL 6682981, at *6 (The Eastern District of Virginia court determined that the defendants had failed to state a plausible claim that Intellectual Ventures had unlawful monopoly power within the relevant market by failing to state the "share of the market" that Intellectual Ventures controls.).

357. *Intellectual Ventures I LLC*, 2015 WL 898146, at *12.

[IV] alleges reads, vaguely, on existing products in [the financial-services] industry, regardless of how those products are designed, so that it could hold up banks that have substantially invested in those existing product designs."[358] The court emphasized that Intellectual Ventures had no role in the market when it began acquiring patents and the associated products were already in place and used by the banking industry in contrast to the circumstances under *SCM Corp. v. Xerox Corp.*[359] where the allegedly wrongful patent acquisition preceded "the appearance of the relevant product market and submarket defined by SCM by at least eight years, such that it only 'eventually afforded it monopoly power.'"[360]

In *Masimo v. Philips*,[361] the district court denied Masimo's motion to strike Philips' affirmative defenses of patent misuse including allegations that Masimo "engaged in unlawful licensing activities by tying its patented articles to sales of commodity cables and sensors."[362] The court bifurcated and stayed Philips' antitrust counterclaims against Masimo for alleged violations of the Sherman Act and the Clayton Act.[363]

Philips argued that the sensors and cables are unpatented commodity products "with respect to which Masimo would otherwise face competition from a variety of others" and are like the commodity products of salt tablets used with patented machines in *Morton Salt*[364] and dry ice used with patented devices in *Carbice*.[365] Based on this reasoning, the court determined that Philips adequately stated a claim for per se patent misuse with respect to the tying arrangement relying on the Federal Circuit's en banc decision in *Princo*,[366] which restated the holding in *Carbice* as "a patentee may exploit his patent but may not 'use it to acquire a monopoly not embraced in the patent.'"[367] Masimo countered that its actions do not constitute patent misuse under § 271(d)'s[368] exemptions to patent misuse since it does not have "market power in the relevant market for the patent or patented product on which the license or sale is conditioned."[369] However,

358. *Id.* at *13.

359. 645 F.2d 1195 (2d Cir. 1981).

360. *Id.*

361. *Masimo Corp. v. Philips Elecs. N.A. Corp. et al.*, No. 09-80-LPS, 2015 WL 2406155 (D. Del. May 18, 2015).

362. *Id.* at *1–2.

363. *Id.* at *1.

364. *Morton Salt Co. v. G.S. Suppiger Co.*, 314 U.S. 488 (1942).

365. 2015 WL 2406155, at *6–7; *see Carbice Corp. of Am. v. Am. Patents Dev. Corp.*, 283 U.S. 27 (1931).

366. *Princo Corp. v. ITC*, 616 F.3d 1318 (Fed. Cir. 2010).

367. 2015 WL 2406155, at *6 (quoting *Transparent-Wrap Mach. Corp. v. Stokes & Smith Co.*, 329 U.S. 637, 643 (1947)).

368. 35 U.S.C. § 271(d).

369. 2015 WL 2406155, at *8.

the court determined that Philips had adequately alleged that Masimo had the requisite market power.[370]

Furthermore, Masimo contended that Philips' theory of patent misuse contradicted settled law"[371] by emphasizing Philips' request to certify the following question by the Federal Circuit for interlocutory review: "Whether a patent holder, wielding economic monopoly power over a patented article, may rely on a 'system claim' to exclude aftermarket competition from commodity components of the claimed system."[372] However, the court determined that any lack of clarity in the law as evidenced by Philips' request provides further reason not to affirmatively bar as a matter of law Philips' theory of patent misuse.[373]

In addition, Masimo contended that Philips' claims must fail because Philips had not alleged that commodity cables and sensors are "entirely separate products" and not a "necessary concomitant of the invention," basing its arguments on *Senza-Gel*.[374] However, the court rejected Masimo's interpretation of *Senza-Gel* by noting that the Federal Circuit in *Senza-Gel, having a similar fact pattern to the present case,* affirmed summary judgment that the patentee engaged in patent misuse by never licensing its process patent without leasing its machine, which was a staple good usable in performing a step of the process.[375] Further, the court was swayed by Philips' argument that "if Masimo's contention were correct, it would follow that patentees could exercise control over a market well beyond the scope of their invention—and immunize themselves against misuse claims—merely by drafting system claims that include every non-patented article that might possibly interact with the patented article."[376]

The court also noted that the language quoted from *Senza-Gel* by Masimo addressed "the distinction between what a court must look to in the 'separate products' analysis for tying in the context of antitrust compared to patent misuse." As explained by the Federal Circuit in *Senza Gel*:[377]

> The law of patent misuse in licensing need not look to consumer demand (which may be non-existent) but need look only to the nature of the claimed invention as the basis for determining whether a product is a necessary concomitant of the invention or an entirely separate product. The law of antitrust violation, tailored

370. *Id.*
371. *Id.*
372. *Id.* at *9.
373. *Id.*
374. *Id.* at *9 (quoting *Senza-Gel*, 803 F.2d at 670).
375. *Id.*
376. *Id.*
377. *Id.* at *10.

for situations that may or may not involve a patent, looks to a consumer demand test for determining product separability.[378]

§ 4.13 Copyright Misuse

Copyright misuse is a judicially created affirmative defense to copyright infringement aimed at preventing copyright holders "from leveraging their limited monopoly to allow them control of areas outside the monopoly."[379] While earlier copyright misuse cases required a finding of a violation of the antitrust laws, recent cases rely on copyright policy, rather than antitrust policy, and have found that "a defendant in a copyright infringement suit need not prove an antitrust violation to prevail on a copyright misuse defense."[380]

In *IDI Design v. A.O.D. Jewelry*,[381] the district court granted plaintiff IDI Design's motion to dismiss for failure to state a cause of action. The case involved IDI Design's assertion of its copyrighted jewelry designs that included specific designs having federal copyright protections and other designs without specifically identified registrations. Defendant's alleged that IDI Design had "been engaged in a pattern of threats and intimidation against small jewelry dealers to extract money on no valid legal basis."[382] The basis for these allegations was that IDI Design violated the antitrust laws by misusing its copyright, because it had "engaged in interfering with commerce by expanding the scope of its Copyright Registration beyond a reasonable scope to intimidate and inhibit commerce in the jewelry business."[383] The court dismissed this counterclaim because "Defendant A.O.D. Jewelry has pleaded no facts to support an allegation of a violation of the antitrust laws" and had not even pled facts from which the court could draw a reasonable interest against IDI Design with regard to violating the antitrust laws.[384] In particular the court criticized the defendant for not identifying the relevant market with particularity ("[t]he 'jewelry business,' in which Plaintiff is purportedly trying to 'intimidate and inhibit commerce,' is not a bounded market").[385]

In *Malibu Media v. Doe*,[386] the district court refused to grant plaintiff's motion to dismiss. The case involved the plaintiff's allegation that

378. *Id* (quoting *Senza-Gel*, 803 F.2d at 670).
379. *Apple Inc. v. Psystar Corp.*, 658 F.3d 1150, 1157 (9th Cir. 2011).
380. *Id.* at 1158.
381. *IDI Design Inc. v. A.O.D. Jewelry Co.*, No. 1:13-cv-08266, 2014 WL 661355 (S.D.N.Y. Feb. 19, 2014).
382. *Id.* at *1.
383. *Id.*
384. *Id.* at *2.
385. *Id.*
386. *Malibu Media v. Doe*, No. 13-11432, 2014 WL 2616902 (E.D. Mich. June 12, 2014).

defendants (originally unnamed) were infringing its copyright in pornographic videos by using BitTorrent to stream the videos online.[387] The court found that *Twombly* and *Iqbal* did not require heightened pleading to state an affirmative defense such as copyright misuse here and that such defenses "need only be pleaded such that they give fair notice of the nature of the defense."[388] Enunciating the standard, that a motion to dismiss must be granted only when the defense could not succeed under any circumstances, the court held that while defendants' asserted basis for the defense was insufficient, the plaintiff had not shown that there were no circumstances under which the defense could succeed and thus refused to grant the motion to dismiss.[389]

Oracle America, Inc. v. Terix Computer Co.[390] involved allegations of antitrust violations and copyright misuse involving the Solaris operating system, originally developed by Sun Microsystems and later acquired by Oracle. The case arose over operating system updates, which Sun had provided without significant cost but Oracle made subject to exclusive availability from Oracle ("once Plaintiffs Oracle America, Inc. and Oracle International Corporation were in charge, customers had to make a choice—either buy their Solaris support services from Oracle, or find themselves cut off from any updates or firmware they might need to keep their servers up and running").[391] The defendants' allegations were grounded in four distinct tying allegations having to do with patches and bug fixes, updates to support services, firmware and hardware support services, and critical and non-critical server support services.[392] The court set out the principles applied by the Ninth Circuit regarding tying claims:

> First, the law permits an antitrust claimant to restrict the relevant market to a single brand of the product at issue (as in Eastman Kodak [v. Image Technical Services, Inc.]). Second, the law prohibits an antitrust claimant from resting on market power that arises solely from contractual rights that consumers knowingly and voluntarily gave to the defendant (as in Queen City Pizza and Forsyth). Third, in determining whether the defendant's market power falls in the Queen City Pizza category of contractually-created market power or in the Eastman Kodak category of economic market power,

387. *Id.* at *1.

388. *Id.* at *2 (citing *Paducah River Painting, Inc. v. Mcnational, Inc.*, No. 5:11-cv-00135, U.S. Dist. LEXIS 131291, at *4 (N.D. Ky. Nov. 12, 2011)).

389. *Id.* at *3.

390. *Oracle Am., Inc. v. Terix Computer Co.*, No. 5:13-cv-03385, 2014 WL 5847532 (N.D. Cal. Nov. 7, 2014).

391. *Id.* at *1–3.

392. *Id.* at *3.

the law permits an inquiry into whether a consumer's selection of a particular brand in the competitive market is the functional equivalent of a contractual commitment, giving that brand an agreed-upon right to monopolize its consumers in an aftermarket.[393]

The district court refused to dismiss defendants' antitrust counterclaims regarding the first three of these tying allegations, finding that defendants' had pled a relevant market (actually, an aftermarket) where Oracle's actions indicated market power. "Defendants' counterclaims clearly meet the Ninth Circuit standard," opined the court, because "Oracle's operative complaint is targeted at ensuring that hardware owners only can obtain access to Solaris updates if they also purchase support services from Oracle. Defendants' counterclaims allege that this same policy constitutes copyright misuse and a violation of the antitrust laws. The parties' allegations thus are logically connected" and thus satisfy the standard for surviving the motion to dismiss.[394]

Conversely, the court granted Oracle's motion to dismiss the defendants' copyright misuse counterclaim, reasoning that under Ninth Circuit precedent such counterclaims are applied "sparingly."[395] "Because Defendants do not allege any such restriction on use of a competitive product as a condition of licensing Oracle's copyrighted software, Defendants do not plead a plausible copyright misuse defense here" according to the opinion.[396]

In a later decision in this same litigation, *Oracle America, Inc. v. Terix Computer Co.*,[397] the court revisited the sufficiency of the pleadings. In this opinion, the district court applied the heightened pleading standards from the Supreme Court (in *Bell Atlantic Corp. v. Twombly* and *Ashcroft v. Iqbal*) to the amended counterclaims asserted by the defendant.[398] The Ninth Circuit motions to strike were evaluated under a two-step standard: "First, a court should 'identif[y] pleadings that, because they are no more than conclusions, are not entitled to the assumption of truth.'"[399] "Then, a court should 'assume the[ ] veracity' of 'well pleaded factual allegations' and 'determine whether they plausibly give rise to an entitlement to relief.'"[400] The court denied Oracle's motion to dismiss the defendant's

393. *Id.* at *5.

394. *Id.* at *7.

395. *Id.* at *8 (citing *Oracle Am. Inc. v. Google, Inc.*, 750 F.3d 1339, 1355–56 (Fed. Cir. 2014)).

396. *Id.*

397. *Oracle Am., Inc. v. Terix Computer Co.*, No. 5:13-cv-03385-PSG, 2015 WL 1886968 (N.D. Cal. Apr. 24, 2015).

398. *Id.* at *2.

399. *Id.* at *3 (citing *Eclectic Props. E., LLC v. Marcus & Millichap Co.*, No. 12-cv-16526, 2014 WL 1797676, at *2 (9th Cir. May 7, 2014)).

400. *Id.*

amended copyright misuse counterclaim, stating that "contrary to Oracle's assertions, Defendants' copyright misuse defense is more robust than its previous iteration and is sufficient to pass muster."[401] While not refuting Oracle's argument that Ninth Circuit precedent (*Triad Systems Corp. v. Southeastern Exp. Co.*[402]) was dispositive (because, unlike in *Triad*, "Oracle did not curtail Defendants' ability develop their own services platform"), the court held that "[a]t the pleadings stage, Defendants have sufficiently alleged copyright misuse by demonstrating that Solaris license terms specifically curtailed the ability of third parties to access software or patches to repair or provide technical services to Solaris users"[403] and refused to strike the defense.

§ 4.14 Trademark Misuse

In *RJ Machine v. Canada Pipeline*,[404] the district court granted antitrust defendant's motion to dismiss allegations that it had violated section 2 of the Sherman Act.[405] The case involved patented flow regulators used in the petroleum industry and known throughout the industry as "50E" regulators. Although the patent on the device had expired, antitrust defendant Canada Pipeline had obtained trademark registrations for the "50E" designation and asserted trade dress protection for regulators configured as disclosed in the expired patents.[406] RJ Machine brought suit after Canada Pipeline threatened to enforce its trademarks and trade dress should RJ Machine enter the market using either.[407] The court dismissed RJ Machine's antitrust counts because RJ Machine did not establish antitrust injury (and thus did not have standing) and that the injury alleged was not the sort of action the antitrust laws were enacted to prevent.[408] The court recognized the quandary Canada Pipeline had created but found this was not enough for RJ Machine to bring an action under section 2 of the Sherman Act:

> [T]he Court acknowledges the potential anticompetitive effect of Canada Pipeline's alleged activity. Canada Pipeline suggests RJ Machine is free to compete with its 50E flow conditioners; RJ Machine just cannot use the trademarks "50E" or "CPA-50E" nor can it market a product which mimics the trade dress of the CPA-

401. *Id.* at *5.
402. 64 F.3d 1330 (9th Cir. 1995).
403. *Oracle Am.*, 2015 WL 1886968, at *5.
404. *RJ Mach. v. Can. Pipeline*, No. 13-579, 2013 WL 8115445 (W.D. Tex, Nov. 22, 2013).
405. *Id.* at *4.
406. *Id.* at *1.
407. *Id.* at *2
408. *Id.* at *3.

> 50E flow conditioner. This suggestion rings hollow considering the nature of the market and the claimed trademarks. RJ Machine forcefully points out it cannot meaningfully compete in the market if it cannot use the term "50E" to describe its product or the design of the 50E flow conditioner, i.e. what Canada Pipeline claims as trade dress. More specifically, RJ Machine contends the term "50E," based on the history and development of the market for this product, is the only term consumers associate with this flow conditioner. In addition, according to RJ Machine's allegations, Canada Pipeline has been able to "lock in" consumers of 50E conditioners because they can only be replaced by flow conditioners with the same 50E design. The anticompetitive argument is even more persuasive when it comes to trade dress. If the 50E design is as functional as RJ Machine alleges, it would be difficult, if not impossible, for RJ Machine to compete in the flow conditioner market without using the same functional design Canada Pipeline is claiming to be its trade dress. Nevertheless, these potential anti-competitive effects do not transform this trademark dispute into an antitrust case, no matter how clever the argument may be.[409]

The court also noted that there were no cases cited by RJ Machine where trademark litigation "formed the basis for an antitrust claim."[410]

---

409. *Id.* at *4.
410. *Id.*

chapter 5

Antitrust Issues in ANDA Litigation

I. Introduction

A specialized area of particular focus at the intersection of patent and antitrust law is Abbreviated New Drug Application (ANDA) litigation under the Hatch-Waxman Act. ANDA is an application for approval of a U.S. generic drug typically for an existing brand-name drug. The ANDA is submitted to the U.S. Food and Drug Administration's (FDA) Center for Drug Evaluation and Research, Office of Generic Drugs, which provides for the review and approval of a generic drug. Once approved, an applicant may manufacture and market the generic drug in the United States to provide an alternative for the corresponding brand-name drug. All approved drugs, including generic drugs, are listed in the FDA's Approved Drug Products with Therapeutic Equivalence Evaluations, which is also referred to as the Orange Book.

In 2013, the Supreme Court resolved an unsettled question regarding the legality of "reverse payment" settlement agreements, which involve a payment from a patent holder to an accused infringer in exchange for an agreement by the accused infringer not to compete with the patent holder.[1] While not finding such agreements presumptively illegal, the Court held that they were susceptible to antitrust scrutiny and should be evaluated under a "rule of reason" analysis. In so holding, the Court overruled the majority of courts of appeal that had deemed the practice free of antitrust implications, for reasons directly related to the nature of the activities giving rise to such litigation.

1. *FTC v. Actavis, Inc.*, 133 S. Ct. 2223 (2013).

II. ANDA Litigation Basics

§ 5.1 "Reverse Payment" Settlement Agreements

The Hatch-Waxman Act[2] makes it an act of infringement to file an ANDA with the FDA in the face of a patent holder/innovator having regulatory approval to market a drug and a patent or patents on said drug, a formulation of the drug or methods of making or using the drug. Generally, a generic-drug maker filing an ANDA triggers this infringement provision by asserting that the patent or patents listed with the FDA in the Orange Book for an approved drug is not infringed, invalid, or unenforceable. The patent holder then has forty-five days to file suit, and if filed, invokes a thirty-month stay in any approval of the generic-drug maker's ANDA by the FDA.

The nature of this litigation is unlike any other patent infringement case. The accused infringer's product is not on the market in the United States and accordingly is not at risk for a damages assessment, and may not have investment at risk of an injunction. As noted by the Eleventh Circuit in *Schering-Plough v. FTC*:[3]

> It is uncontested that parties settle cases based on their perceived risk of prevailing in and losing the litigation. Pre–Hatch-Waxman, [the generic challengers] normally would have had to enter the market with their products, incurring the costs of clinical trials, manufacturing and marketing. This market entry would have driven down [the patent holder]'s profits, as it took sales away. As a result, [the patent holder] would have sued [the generics challengers], seeking damages for lost profits and willful infringement. Assuming the patent is reasonably strong, and the parties then settled under this scenario, the money most probably would flow from the infringers to [the patent holder] because the generics would have put their companies at risk by making infringing sales.

In ANDA litigation, it is the patent holder who has all the risk, specifically that the patent holder's patent will be found invalid or unenforceable. As a consequence, there has developed over the past decade a greater tendency for the patent holder/drug innovator to settle ANDA litigation on terms where the generics challenger enters the marketplace later than it would have if it had prevailed in the litigation but generally earlier than if the challenger had lost, with the exchange of cash or other payment of

2. Drug Price Competition and Patent Term Restoration Act, 35 U.S.C. § 271(e)(2)(A).
3. *Schering-Plough Corp. v. Fed. Trade Comm'n*, 402 F.3d 1056, 1073–74 (11th Cir. 2005).

value from the patent holder to the accused infringer. This situation has raised antitrust concerns not only from consumers but also especially by the FTC, who has not only participated as a plaintiff or amicus in antitrust suits but has also originated antitrust suits.

§ 5.1.1 The FTC's Objections to "Reverse Payment" Settlement Agreements

The FTC's original position was that "reverse payment" settlement agreements are per se violations of section 1 of the Sherman Act as naked agreements in restraint of trade. It should be noted that proponents of "reverse payment" agreements commonly refer to these agreements as such while detractors like the FTC commonly refer to these agreements as "pay for delay" agreements. Accordingly, the FTC called for an outright ban on these agreements.[4] Having universally lost in the courts on this theory, as set forth in more detail below, the FTC has moderated its position, more recently advocating that these agreements are presumptively illegal and should be reviewed for antitrust liability under the "rule of reason."

The FTC's reasoning and the basis for its crusade against such practices are as follows. First, generic drug competition decreases the costs of drugs to consumers and, more importantly, to the federal government, the largest drug purchaser in the United States if not the world. Second, generic drug companies are motivated under the Hatch-Waxman Act to challenge patents, because the "first to file" an ANDA with a certification that the generic drug does not infringe or, more commonly, that the innovator's patents are invalid or unenforceable, will garner a 180-day exclusivity period as the only generic drug on the market. Third, reverse payment settlements upset the statutory arrangement, permitting "bad" patents to remain in effect and delaying generic drug entry. On the contrary, courts have found generally that reverse payment arrangements *reduce* the delay in generic drug entry (see later in chapter). Fourth, generic drug companies prevailed in ANDA litigation against brand-name drug companies 75 percent of the time between 1992 and 2002.[5] Finally, the FTC contends that branded drug companies enter into reverse payment arrangements because they know that their patents are invalid or unenforceable and the agreement permits them to undeservedly collect "monopoly" profits. This contention has been almost universally rejected by the courts of appeal

4. *See* FTC, PAY-FOR-DELAY: HOW DRUG COMPANY PAY-OFFS COST CONSUMERS BILLIONS 2 (2010).

5. *See* FTC, GENERIC DRUG ENTRY PRIOR TO PATENT EXPIRATION: AN FTC STUDY, at viii (2002) (providing incentives for brand-name companies to pursue these types of agreements).

until very recently.[6] As a result (in part) of FTC advocacy against these agreements, Congress enacted provisions requiring all such agreements to be filed with the FTC as part of the Medicare Prescription Drug, Improvement, and Modernization Act of 2003.[7]

The factual underpinnings of the FTC's contentions that reverse payment settlement agreements of ANDA litigation require antitrust scrutiny are set forth in detail in a series of reports on the subject—those issued in 2010–2013 are illustrative. In 2010, the *FTC Pay-for-Delay Report* characterized these agreements as harming consumers while enriching both innovator and generic-drug makers, due in large part to a delay in the up to 90 percent reduction in the cost of a branded drug upon generic drug competitor entry.[8] The FTC's *Pay-for-Delay* report notes that the FTC had "deterred" the use of such agreements between April 1999 and 2004, buttressed by a single decision by a regional court of appeals[9] that these agreements were per se illegal.[10] However, later decisions, including by the Federal Circuit[11] and other courts of appeal,[12] upheld these agreements, "missappl[ying] the antitrust law[s]," according to the commission.[13] As a consequence, the report contends that generic-drug entry has been delayed for on average seventeen months and pay-for-delay agreements "protect at least $20 billion in sales of brand-name pharmaceuticals from generic competition."[14] The report estimated that the "cost [to] American consumers [is] $3.5 billion per year."[15]

The 2010 report noted that there have been 66 agreements that "involved some form of compensation" for delayed entry between FY 2004–2009, and that in the same time period, ANDA litigation was settled in 152 instances without pay-for-delay agreements.[16] Of the 66 agreements involving delayed generic entry, 51 of them (77 percent) were between the

---

6. *See Ark. Carpenters Health & Welfare Fund v. Bayer AG*, 604 F.3d 98, 105 (2d Cir. 2010); *In re Ciprofloxacin Hydrochloride Antitrust Litig.*, 544 F.3d 1323, 1337 (Fed. Cir. 2008); *In re Tamoxifen Citrate Antitrust Litig.*, 466 F.3d 187, 206 (2d Cir. 2006); *Schering-Plough*, 402 F.3d at 1075–76; *Valley Drug Co. v. Geneva Pharms., Inc.*, 344 F.3d 1294, 1311 (11th Cir. 2003).

7. *See* 42 U.S.C. § 1395w-101 note (2009) (§ 110 of the Act); 21 U.S.C. § 355 note (2009) (§§ 1111–1118 of the Act); 21 U.S.C. § 355(j)(5) (2009) (§ 1102 of the Act).

8. FTC, PAY-FOR-DELAY, *supra* note 4, at 1.

9. *In re Cardizem CD Antitrust Litig.*, 332 F.3d 896 (6th Cir. 2003).

10. *Id.*

11. *See In re Ciprofloxacin Hydrochloride Antitrust Litig.*, 544 F.3d 1323, 1341 (Fed. Cir. 2008).

12. *See Schering-Plough Corp. v. Fed. Trade Comm'n*, 402 F.3d 1056, 1076 (11th Cir. 2005); *see also In re Tamoxifen Citrate Antitrust Litig.*, 466 F.3d 187, 216 (2d Cir. 2006).

13. FTC, PAY-FOR-DELAY, *supra* note 4, at 1.

14. *Id.* at 2.

15. *Id.*

16. *Id.* at 4.

brand-name pharmaceutical company and the first ANDA filer.[17] This data is significant, because as the report notes, "[s]ettlements with first-filer generics can prevent *all* generic entry," since the generic company to first file an ANDA has a 180-day exclusivity period under the Hatch-Waxman Act.[18] Thus, any subsequent ANDA filer is delayed from entering the market until the first filer has utilized the 180-day exclusivity period.

However, these agreements do not all involve direct cash payments to the generic drug companies. Other arrangements described in the report include an agreement from the brand-name pharmaceutical company not to introduce an "authorized generic"—that is, a generic version of the drug made by the brand-name company, which is not excluded by the 180-day exclusivity period awarded to the first to file an ANDA.[19] These types of agreements were included in about 25 percent of the "pay for delay" agreements discussed in the report.[20]

The situation was no better a year later. In its 2011 report, the FTC provided a tabulation of reverse payment settlement agreements per year up to 2011.[21]

Table 5.1

	FY 2004	FY 2005	FY 2006	FY 2007	FY 2008	FY 2009	FY 2010	FY 2011
Final Settlement	14	11	28	33	66	68	113	156
Potential Pay-for-Delay	0	3	14	14	16	19	31	28
Potential Pay-for-Delay Involving First Filers	0	2	9	11	13	15	26	18

Finally, by the time of its 2013 report, the FTC's data indicated that the "vast majority of patent settlements (greater than 70%) continued to be resolved without compensation to the generic manufacturer."[22] This trend reflects an adaptation to the FTC's campaign against these agreements, wherein the majority of agreements contain, instead of a cash payment, an agreement from the innovator not to bring an "authorized generic" version of the drug to market in competition with the generic-drug maker.

17. *Id.* at 5.

18. *Id.* (emphasis in original).

19. *Id.*

20. *Id.*

21. *See* Federal Trade Comm'n, Overview of Agreements Filed in FY 2011, A Report by the Bureau of Competition 2 (2011).

22. Fed. Trade Comm'n, Overview of Agreements filed in FY 2012, A Report by the Bureau of Competition 2 (2013), *available at* http://www.ftc.gov/os/2013/01/130117mmareport.pdf.

Such provisions are particularly important to the "first filer" generics challenger, insofar as authorized generics made under the regulatory auspices of the innovator do not fall within the 180-day exclusivity and thus provide a direct competitor to the first-filing generic-drug maker.

Not surprisingly, the FTC has taken the position that agreements involving a promise by the innovator not to market an authorized generic drug should also be presumptively illegal, applying the following reasoning.[23] First, authorized generics (AG) destroy a significant amount of the value that a generic company otherwise would obtain from the 180-day exclusivity period.[24] Second, a branded company's agreement not to market an AG enables the generic company to maximize its revenues during the first-filer exclusivity period.[25] Finally, these "economic realities" compel the conclusion that a no-AG commitment is without a doubt a method of paying a generic drug company for delayed entry.[26]

The factual grounds for all the FTC's arguments have been challenged if not rebutted by a report by the Generic Pharmaceutical Association (GPhA) on the value of generic drugs to the U.S. consumer and economy.[27] The statistics and policy arguments discussed in the report on the benefits of generic drugs included a defense of reverse payment agreements between brand-drug makers and generic-drug entrants to the marketplace. The principal argument made in the report is that one-third of the annual savings that result from pharmaceutical products that entered the marketplace after 2001 implicate such agreements, because "most new generics get to market as the result of a settlement."[28] The report also asserted that, over the past ten years, settlements of patent litigation over generic drugs "has resulted in billions of dollars in savings" due to the generic drugs at issue entering the market before they would otherwise—that is, "prior to patents expiring on the counterpart brand drugs." The report characterized such settlements as being "pro-consumer" due to the decrease in the time consumers must wait for a generic version of branded drugs involved in patent settlement agreements. The report asserts in support of this conclusion that "[o]ver the past 10 years, patent settlements have enabled dozens of first-time generics to come to market many months and even many years before patents on the counterpart brand drugs

23. *See In re K-Dur Antitrust Litig.*, 686 F.3d 197, 207 (3d Cir. 2012).

24. Fed. Trade Comm'n Motion for Leave to File *Amicus Curiae* Brief, *In re Effexor XR Antitrust Litig.*, No. 11-cv-5479, 2014 WL 4988410 (D.N.J. Oct. 6, 2014).

25. *Id.* at 7.

26. *Id.* at 9.

27. *See* Generic Pharm. Ass'n, Savings $1 Trillion Over 10 Years: Generic Drug Savings in the U.S. (4th ed. 2012), *available at* http://www.gphaonline.org/media//cms/IMSStudyAug2012WEB.pdf.

28. *Id.* at 7.

expires," citing the seventeen of twenty-two new generic drugs expected to launch in 2011 that were the result of such settlements.[29] The report also cites a study by RBC Capital Markets, which "found that generic companies are successful, [and] thus able to market the generic product before patent expiration, in just 48 percent of cases," and that "when factoring in settlements, generics are successful in bringing the generic product to market before patent expiration in 76 percent of cases."[30] While recognizing (but not acknowledging) the identities of "some who contend such generic-brand agreements are anticompetitive," the report declares that "[t]he record is clear: settlements allow generic drugs to come to market long before patents on the counterpart brands expire," and that this results in "billions of dollars in annual savings."[31]

These conclusions parallel decisions by the courts that have until recently rejected the FTC's position unless there have been additional factors that change the nature of the agreement to be on balance anticompetitive, as set forth in more detail below.

§ 5.1.2 Decisions by Courts of Appeal on "Reverse Payment" Settlement Agreements

The first appellate decision regarding reverse payment settlement agreements, in the Sixth Circuit, supported the FTC's position, but had several aspects not found in later cases where these agreements have been upheld.[32]

This case was brought by a variety of patient groups as plaintiffs against Hoechst Marion Roussel (HMR) and Andrx over a "reverse payment" settlement agreement in ANDA litigation over U.S. Patent No. 5,470,584 for HMR's Cardizem CD product.[33] The active ingredient in Cardizem is diltiazem hydrochloride, used for treating angina and hypertension and as a preventative for heart attack and stroke. Andrx filed an ANDA for Cardizem CD and HMR sued triggering the thirty-month stay of FDA approval of the generic drug. Andrx filed antitrust counterclaims and stated its intention to launch upon approval, and after expiration of the thirty-month stay, the FDA approved Andrx's generic Cardizem CD. According to the court:

> On June 9, 1999, the FDA approved Andrx's reformulated product. That same day, HMR and Andrx entered into a stipulation settling

29. *Id.*
30. *Id.*
31. *Id.*
32. *See In re Cardizem CD Antitrust Litig.*, 332 F.3d 896 (6th Cir. 2003).
33. *Id.* at 902, 904.

the patent infringement case and terminating the Agreement. On June 23, 1999, Andrx began to market its product under the trademark Cartia XT, and its 180-day period of marketing exclusivity began to run.[34]

The terms of the agreement were as follows:

- Andrx agreed not to market a generic version of Cardizem CD until Andrx received a final determination in its favor in the patent infringement lawsuit, HMR or Andrx entered into a licensing agreement, or HMR entered into a licensing agreement with a third party, with the trigger date being the earliest of these events.
- Andrx agreed to dismiss its counterclaims for unfair competition and antitrust violations.
- Andrx further agreed to pursue its ANDA and not to relinquish or transfer its 180-day exclusivity period or any other right.
- HMR agreed to pay Andrx $40 million per year (paid $10 million every calendar quarter) beginning on the date when the FDA approved Andrx's ANDA, and $100 million per year (less the interim $40 million payments) once either there was a final judgment that the '584 patent was not infringed, or HMR dismissed the patent infringement lawsuit, or there was another resolution of the lawsuit between the parties that did not finally resolve issues of invalidity, unenforceability, or infringement, and HMR did not refile or pursue the lawsuit.
- HMR also agreed not to seek preliminary injunctive relief during the ANDA suit.[35]

The FDA approved Andrx's generic Cardizem CD formulation on June 9, 1998, one day after the end of the thirty-month stay, and HMR began paying Andrx the $40 million per year payment in $10 million quarterly payments.[36] Andrx then filed a supplement to its ANDA specifying that it had reformulated the product and certified that its reformulated product did not infringe the claims of the '584 patent. The FDA approved this reformulated product on June 9, 1999, and the parties settled the infringement suit and terminated the agreement that day. HMR also paid Andrx a final sum of $50.7 million, for a total of payments equaling $89.83 million. Two weeks later, Andrx began to market its generic product, starting the

34. *Id.* at 903.
35. *Id.* at 902–03.
36. *Id.* at 903.

180-day exclusivity period.[37] This date of market entry was almost twelve years before the expiration date of the '584 patent, February 15, 2011.

The agreement contained a number of provisions not found in other legal agreements. First, Andrx was the first ANDA filer, and the agreement did not require the generic company to change its Paragraph IV certification. Since the parties settled the ANDA litigation, the 180-day exclusivity period could not begin to run until Andrx entered the marketplace—a date delayed by the agreement. Moreover, the agreement contained a provision where Andrx agreed neither to relinquish nor transfer its right to the exclusivity period. In addition, plaintiffs alleged that the agreement covered generic Cardizem products that did not satisfy the dissolution limitations in the patent claims and thus did not infringe the '584 patent.[38]

The lawsuit against HMR and Andrx was consolidated from a number of complaints from individuals, states, and other groups. These complaints were brought under section 1 of the Sherman Act and section 4 of the Clayton Act (including its treble damages provisions), based on the "but for" argument that a generic Cardizem would have been on the market but for the agreement, and that the exercise of its 180-day exclusivity barred other generics from coming to market.[39] Plaintiffs fell into three groups:[40]

1. the "State Law Class Plaintiffs," indirect purchasers, and class representatives, from various states (California, Michigan, Minnesota, New York, North Carolina, Tennessee, and Wisconsin) and the District of Columbia whose complaints, initially filed in state court and then removed to federal district court by defendants, alleged violations of state antitrust and consumer protection statutes
2. the "Sherman Act Class Plaintiffs," direct purchasers, and class representatives, whose complaint, filed in federal district court, alleged a violation of federal antitrust law
3. the "Individual Sherman Act Plaintiffs," two groups of purchasers, not representatives of any class, whose complaints, filed in federal district court, alleged violations of federal antitrust law (one filed by the Kroger Co., Albertson's, Inc., the Stop and Shop Supermarket Co., and Eckerd Corp. and the other filed by CVS Meridian, Inc. and Rite Aid Corp.); the plaintiffs from seven states (California, Michigan, Minnesota, New York, North

37. *Id.*
38. *Id.* at 915.
39. *Id.* at 904.
40. *Id.*

> Carolina, Tennessee, and Wisconsin) and the District of Columbia claiming violations of state antitrust law

The district court held that the agreement was per se illegal, because the reverse payment provisions and actual payments from HMR to Andrx delayed generic entry and constituted a naked, horizontal restraint of trade.[41] The court certified the following question for interlocutory appeal to the Sixth Circuit:

> In determining whether Plaintiffs' motions for partial judgment were properly granted, whether the Defendants' September 24, 1997 Agreement constitutes a restraint of trade that is illegal per se under Section 1 of the Sherman Antitrust Act, 15 U.S.C. § 1, and under the corresponding state antitrust laws at issue in this litigation.[42]

In its opinion, the appellate court noted that while the literal meaning of section 1 of the Sherman Act would render per se illegal every agreement in restraint of trade, the Supreme Court has "long recognized" that the statute is meant only to prohibit unreasonable restraints, and that courts assess whether a restraint is unreasonable using a rule of reason.[43] According to the court:

> Under this approach, the "finder of fact must decide whether the questioned practice imposes an unreasonable restraint on competition, taking into account a variety of factors, including specific information about the relevant business, its condition before and after the restraint was imposed, and the restraint's history, nature, and effect."[44]

However, there are some agreements, the court noted, that "have such predictable and pernicious anti-competitive effect[s], and such limited potential for procompetitive benefit," that they are "deemed unlawful *per se*."[45] Courts have recognized that certain kinds of agreements cannot satisfy the rule of reason under any circumstances, and such agreements have a "conclusive presumption" of illegality.[46] For such agreements, "no consideration is given to the intent behind the restraint, to any claimed procompetitive justifications, or to the restraint's actual effect on competition,"

---

41. *See In re Cardizem CD Antitrust Litig.*, 105 F. Supp. 2d 682, 705-06 (E.D. Mich. 2000).
42. *In re Cardizem*, 332 F.3d at 900.
43. *Id.* at 906 (citing *State Oil Co. v. Khan*, 522 U.S. 3, 10 (1997)).
44. *Id.* (quoting *State Oil*, 522 U.S. at 10 (citing *Arizona v. Maricopa Cty. Med. Soc'y*, 457 U.S. 332, 343 & n.13 (1982))).
45. *Id.* (quoting *N. Pac. Ry. Co. v. United States*, 356 U.S. 1, 5 (1958)).
46. *Id.* (citing *Arizona v. Maricopa Cty. Med. Soc'y*, 457 U.S. at 344).

the court opined.[47] The Supreme Court is cited as being almost dismissive of such instances: "a *per se* rule reflects the judgment that such cases are not sufficiently common or important to justify the time and expense necessary to identify them."[48]

Citing *National Collegiate Athletic Association v. Board of Regents of the University of Oklahoma*, the Sixth Circuit identified naked, horizontal price restraints as being per se illegal according to this line of Supreme Court precedent.[49] This type of agreement is defined as "an agreement between competitors at the same level of the market structured to allocate territories in order to minimize competition," stating that "[t]his Court has reiterated time and time again that horizontal territorial limitations . . . are naked restraints of trade with no purpose except stifling of competition. Such limitations are *per se* violations of the Sherman Act."[50]

With this analytical framework in mind, the Sixth Circuit listed facts it termed "undisputed and dispositive."[51] First, under the agreement, HMR was assured that Andrx, at the time the only potential competitor in the marketplace for Cardizem, would remain off the market at a cost of $10 million per quarter even after Andrx had obtained FDA approval for its generic version of the drug.[52] Second, as a consequence of this agreement, not only Andrx but all other generic competitors were kept off the market in view of Andrx's 180-day exclusivity period and the provisions of the agreement that Andrx would not relinquish or transfer the right, which commenced only when Andrx first entered the marketplace.[53] Thus, there was a direct nexus between the agreement's provisions keeping Andrx off the market and the delay in generic Cardizem coming to the marketplace from any source.[54]

This was enough for the court to characterize this as a naked horizontal restraint that is per se illegal.[55] In a footnote, the court addressed the consequences of a per se determination, instead of applying a rule of reason analysis.

> The risk that the application of a *per se* rule will lead to the condemnation of an agreement that a rule of reason analysis would

47. *Id.* (citing *Nat'l Coll. Athletic Ass'n v. Bd. of Regents of the Univ. of Okla.*, 468 U.S. 85, 100 (1984)).
48. *Id.* at 907 (quoting *Cont'l T.V., Inc. v. GTE Sylvania Inc.*, 433 U.S. 36, 50 n.6 (1977)).
49. *Id.*
50. *Id.* (citing *United States v. Topco Assocs.*, 405 U.S. 596, 608 (1972)).
51. *Id.*
52. *Id.*
53. *Id.* at 907–08.
54. *Id.*
55. *Id.* at 908.

> permit has been recognized and tolerated as a necessary cost of this approach.[56]

The Sixth Circuit was not persuaded by the arguments to the contrary. Specifically, the court rejected defendants' argument that the agreement was a proper exercise of the patent right. According to the court, "the Agreement cannot be fairly characterized as merely an attempt to enforce patent rights or an interim settlement of the patent litigation,"[57] and "[a] s the plaintiffs point out, it is one thing to take advantage of a monopoly that naturally arises from a patent, but another thing altogether to bolster the patent's effectiveness in inhibiting competitors by paying the only potential competitor $40 million per year to stay out of the market."[58] In addition, arguments that there were pro-competitive effects that offset the anticompetitive effects were unavailing because of the court's determination that the agreement was per se illegal.

The court also determined that the plaintiffs had pleaded sufficiently to satisfy the requirement of asserting an antitrust injury.[59] Part of the court's decision was based on the standard of review, where all allegations in the complaint are taken as true and all inferences are drawn in plaintiffs' favor. These included:

> (1) Andrx had developed and was ready to market a generic version of Cardizem CD; (2) Andrx had certified to the FDA that its generic product did not infringe any of the patents associated with Cardizem CD; (3) the patent infringement litigation was a "sham"; (4) prior to entering into the Agreement, Andrx had represented to the federal district court presiding over the patent infringement litigation that it intended to market and sell its generic version of Cardizem CD as soon as it received final FDA approval; (5) the Agreement entered into by Andrx and HMR provided, among other things, that once the FDA approved Andrx's ANDA, HMR would commence making quarterly payments of $10 million in exchange for Andrx not bringing its generic product to market; (6) Andrx did

---

56. *Id.* at 906 n.11; *see, e.g.*, *Arizona v. Maricopa Cty. Med. Soc'y*, 457 U.S. at 344 ("As in every rule of general application, the match between the presumed and the actual is imperfect. For the sake of business certainty and litigation efficiency, we have tolerated the invalidation of some agreements that a full-blown inquiry might have proved to be reasonable."); *Topco*, 405 U.S. at 609 ("Whether or not we would decide this case the same way under the rule of reason used by the District Court is irrelevant to the issue before us.").

57. *Id.* at 908.

58. *Id.*

59. *Id.* at 909; *see Brunswick Corp. v. Pueblo Bowl-O-Mat, Inc.*, 429 U.S. 477, 489 (1977) ((1) "injury of the type the antitrust laws were intended to prevent" and (2) injury "that flows from that which makes defendants' acts unlawful").

> not enter the market upon receiving FDA approval on July 9, 1998; (7) pursuant to the Agreement, HMR ultimately paid Andrx $89.83 million; (8) "but for" the Agreement and the payment, Andrx would have begun to market its generic version of Cardizem CD on or shortly after July 9, 1998; (9) the Agreement effectively eliminated generic competition in the market for Cardizem CD from July 1998 through July 1999, when the Agreement was terminated; and (10) due to the lack of a competitive market, the plaintiffs were deprived of the option of purchasing a generic lower-priced drug and paid more than they otherwise would have for Cardizem CD.[60]

The Sixth Circuit affirmed the district court's determination that these allegations satisfy the *Brunswick* requirements and that plaintiffs had alleged sufficient antitrust injury that the district court properly denied defendants' motion to dismiss. The antitrust injury was to consumers who "were deprived of a less expensive generic product, forcing them to purchase the higher-priced brand name product, because of a *per se* illegal horizontal market restraint." Preventing such an outcome was "undoubtedly a *raison d'etre*" for passage of the Sherman Act.[61] In addition, the injury "flows from that which makes defendants' act unlawful"—that is, causing consumers to pay more for branded Cardizem CD than they would have paid for Andrx's generic version.[62] Moreover, the court found "incredible" the argument that Andrx would not have entered the market for fear of patent infringement liability in the absence of the $89 million paid by HMR under the agreement.[63]

There are several distinctions that can be used to explain the different outcomes in this case and the other cases that did not find a reverse payment agreement to be per se illegal. For example, in the three cases that did not find an antitrust violation in a reverse payment agreement (discussed later) the courts were careful to state that there were circumstances in which the agreement *could* be illegal. These included an extension of the exclusionary right of the patent in excess of the proper scope of the claims, initiation, or continuance of "sham" litigation in which the patent holder knew that the patent was invalid or unenforceable—that is, *Walker Process*-type violations—or that the accused product did not infringe the asserted claims.

Here, the court found that Andrx's reformulated product did *not* infringe the claims of the '584 patent. From that conclusion, payment

60. *Id.* at 910.
61. *Id.*
62. *Id.* at 911.
63. *Id.*

from HMR to Andrx was not a legitimate exercise of the patent's exclusionary right. Moreover, in other instances, the first ANDA filer changed its certification from Paragraph IV to Paragraph III, and thus gave up its 180-day exclusivity period; that was not the case here. Not only did Andrx not change its certification, but the reverse payment agreement contained an affirmative requirement that Andrx would neither relinquish nor transfer the right. The effect of this provision was to keep other potential generic entrants from the marketplace. Finally, in other cases the change in certification permitted other generic-drug companies to file their own ANDAs and to thus be able to obtain FDA approval, and in some of those cases that is precisely what occurred, although the patent holder sometimes prevailed and other generics companies did not enter the market. Here the reverse payment agreement had a preclusive effect on other potential generic entrants.

It is likely, although not expressly stated in the opinion, that the fact that Andrx's reformulated product did not infringe the '584 patent and that the agreement was at least in part responsible for delaying entry of the reformulated product were important factors precluding the Sixth Circuit from crediting other considerations that were important in the decisions of the other appellate courts that the reverse payments in those cases were not illegal. As in those cases of legal reverse payment agreements, Andrx's generic Cardizem CD product entered the marketplace significantly earlier than the expiration date of the '584 patent. Moreover, the court noted that Andrx's generic reformulated product, sold as Cartia XT, had "captured a substantial portion of the market" and "sold for a much lower price than Cardizem CD."[64] From a "big picture" approach, as has been applied by other circuit courts of appeal for other reverse payment agreements, the period of delay from the time the parties entered into the agreement (September 24, 1997) until Andrx first entered the marketplace with its Cartia XT product (July 9, 1999)—that is, less than twenty-two months, is significantly shorter than the difference between the time Cartia XT was first marketed and the expiration date of the '584 patent (February 15, 2011)—that is, eleven years, seven months. This "advantage" to the public evaporates under circumstances where the patent holder had no right to exclude the generic entrant from the marketplace since the generic drug product does not infringe the patent claims. That appears to have been the case here, and no doubt influenced the court's decision.

The Eleventh Circuit came to a different conclusion. In *Schering-Plough v. FTC*,[65] the FTC issued a "cease and desist" order prohibiting

64. *Id.* at 903.
65. *Schering-Plough Corp. v. Fed. Trade Comm'n*, 402 F.3d 1056 (11th Cir. 2005).

Schering-Plough from settling any patent infringement lawsuit with a generic drug company where Schering-Plough gave the generic drug company "anything of value" and "agree[d] to suspend research, development, manufacture, marketing, or sales of [the generic drug] product."[66] The basis of the order was the FTC's determination that the "reverse payment" settlement agreement between Schering-Plough and Upsher Pharmaceuticals was an unreasonable restraint of trade in violation of section 1 of the Sherman Antitrust Act[67] and section 5 of the FTC Act.[68]

The drug product at issue was an extended-release formulation of a potassium supplement claimed in U.S. Patent No. 4,863,743. Schering-Plough filed suit in response to Upsher's ANDA filing on a generic version of Schering-Plough's formulation product, and the parties settled before trial. The agreement contained a $60 million initial licensing fee, $10 million in milestone royalty payments, and 10–15 percent running royalties on five drugs owned by the generic company, including an anticholesterol drug having an estimated net present value of $250 million. In addition, Upsher agreed to a compromise date for market entry of it generic potassium product.

The administrative law judge (ALJ) hearing the case in the first instance found both these agreements legal and dismissed the FTC complaint.[69] The ALJ's reasoning was that, unless the patent was invalid or the generic products did not infringe, the agreements were not violations of the antitrust laws. Significantly, the FTC adduced no evidence before the ALJ that these agreements were anything other than arm's-length transactions between the parties. The ALJ found that the FTC did not prove that, without the payment, either a better settlement agreement or litigation would have resulted in earlier generic market entry.[70]

The case was then heard by the full commission, who reversed the ALJ. The FTC backed off its initial position that reverse payment agreements are per se illegal, but held that the quid pro quo of payment was for delayed generic market entry, which "would injure competition and consumers."[71] The commission based its decision on generic market entry that "might have been" agreed upon between the parties in the absence of payments.[72] Even though the commission could not tie the delayed entry dates to the monetary compensation, it developed the rule that reverse

66. *Id.* at 1058.
67. 15 U.S.C. § 1.
68. 15 U.S.C. § 45(a).
69. *Schering-Plough Corp.*, 402 F.3d at 1061.
70. *Id.* at 1061–62.
71. *Id.* at 1062.
72. *Id.*

payments were illegal, with an exception for litigation costs to be capped at $2 million and a requirement that the FTC must be notified of the existence and terms of the agreement, a requirement adopted in the 2003 Medicare Prescription Drug, Improvement, and Modernization Act.[73]

The Eleventh Circuit reversed, in an opinion that gave less deference to the commission's decision that it might have otherwise, absent the different results before the ALJ and the commission as a whole. The court made its determination in view of an earlier Eleventh Circuit case. In *Valley Drug v. Geneva Pharmaceuticals*,[74] the court reversed a district court determination regarding an interim settlement agreement between a branded pharmaceutical company and a generic containing a monthly payment ($4.5 million) from the branded company to the generic that kept the generic drug off the market until the underlying patent infringement suit was concluded. The district court found this per se anticompetitive, but the court of appeals reversed, based on the exclusionary powers of a patent.[75] Patents, according to the court, intrinsically distort the competitive landscape, and thus defeat a determination that the agreement was per se illegal. Per the court's opinion:

> In the context of patent litigation . . . the anticompetitive effect may be no more broad than the patent's own exclusionary power. To expose those agreements to antitrust liability would "obviously chill such settlements."[76]

The commission did not use a per se standard against Schering-Plough, however, but instead applied a "rule of reason" analysis. This rule "tests 'whether the restraint imposed is such as merely regulates and perhaps thereby promotes competition or whether it is such as may suppress or even destroy competition.'"[77] Here, the commission differed from the ALJ merely by showing "a detrimental market effect," which the court characterized as "a low threshold" for making a finding of antitrust liability.

> Thus, under the Commission's standard, once the FTC met the low threshold of demonstrating the anticompetitive nature of the agreements, it found that Schering and Upsher did not sufficiently establish that the challenged activities were justified by procompetitive benefits. Despite the appearance that it openly considered Schering and Upsher's procompetitive affirmative defense, the

73. *Id.*
74. *Valley Drug Co. v. Geneva Pharm., Inc.*, 344 F.3d 1294, 1303–04 (11th Cir. 2003).
75. *Id.* at 1312–13.
76. *Schering-Plough*, 402 F.3d at 1064 (quoting *Valley Drug*, 344 F.3d at 1309).
77. *Id.* (quoting *FTC v. Ind. Fed'n of Dentists*, 476 U.S. 447, 457 (1986) (quoting *Bd. of Trade of City of Chi. v. United States*, 246 U.S. 231, 238 (1918)).

> Commission immediately condemned the settlements because of their absolute anti-competitive nature, and discounted the merits of the patent litigation. It would seem as though the Commission clearly made its decision before it considered any contrary conclusion.[78]

The court stated that when patents are involved *neither* per se illegality nor rule-of-reason analysis is appropriate in assessing antitrust liability "because they seek to determine whether the challenged conduct had an anticompetitive effect on the market."[79]

> By their nature, patents create an environment of exclusion, and consequently, cripple competition. The anticompetitive effect is already present. "What is required here is an analysis of the extent to which antitrust liability might undermine the encouragement of innovation and disclosure, or the extent to which the patent laws prevent antitrust liability for such exclusionary effects." Valley Drug Co. v. Geneva Pharm., Inc. Therefore, in line with Valley Drug, we think the proper analysis of antitrust liability requires an examination of: (1) the scope of the exclusionary potential of the patent; (2) the extent to which the agreements exceed that scope; and (3) the resulting anticompetitive effects.[80]

It is the legitimate exclusionary power of the patent that the court said must be considered in making an antitrust determination. "Although the exclusionary power of a patent may seem incongruous with the goals of antitrust law," the court stated:

> [A] delicate balance must be drawn between the two regulatory schemes. Indeed, application of antitrust law to markets affected by the exclusionary statutes set forth in patent law cannot discount the rights of the patent holder.[81]

Turning to the patent at issue and the agreement between the parties, the court noted that the FTC's characterization of the agreements as linking the payments to the delayed market entry was not supported by substantial evidence.[82] Indeed, in the proceedings before the ALJ, FTC counsel "acknowledged that it could not prove that Upsher [and ESI,

---

78. *Schering-Plough*, 402 F.3d at 1065.

79. *Id.*

80. *Id.* at 1066.

81. *Id.* at 1067; *see Simpson v. Union Oil Co.*, 377 U.S. 13, 24 (1964). (patent laws "are in *pari materia* with the antitrust laws and modify them pro tanto" (as far as the patent laws go)).

82. *Schering-Plough*, 402 F.3d at 1071.

another generic entrant] could have entered the market on their own prior to the '743 patent's expiration on September 5, 2006," which "reinforces the validity and strength of the patent."[83] Indeed, the court found that the evidence before the ALJ was directly contrary to the FTC's position—that Schering-Plough's personnel evaluating the value of the license of Upsher's products were "unaware of" the litigation, and the reverse payment was "a bona fide fair-value payment" for rights to market these drugs (particularly the anticholesterol drug).[84] The commission credited a staff economist (purportedly an "expert" in pharma industry licensing) who testified that the reverse payment amounts were "grossly excessive."[85] The court was unimpressed.

> We are troubled by [expert] Levy's testimony. Interestingly, Levy arrived at his conclusions without performing a quantitative analysis of Niacor [the anticholesterol product] or any of the other Upsher products licensed by Schering. Additionally, Levy lacked expertise in the area of cholesterol-lowering drugs and niacin supplements. Finally, Levy's unpersuasive appraisal of the post-settlement behavior blatantly ignored the parties' ongoing communications and the fact that the niacin market essentially bottomed out.[86]

The court found even less evidence for the commission's decision with regard to the other agreement with Lederle—the FTC presented no factual witnesses and "little" expert testimony and "spen[t] little time" in its opinion and order justifying its conclusions.[87]

The court stated that "[t]he FTC did not rebut [Schering-Plough's] testimony, but rather ignored it," and that "all of the evidence" supports the ALJ's conclusion that the settlement did not contain a "naked payment" merely intended to delay generic entry.[88] The Eleventh Circuit also noted that the Supreme Court has endorsed the practice for litigants in a patent lawsuit to "exchange consideration to settle their litigation" without any antitrust liability,[89] and the Eleventh Circuit panel noted a general policy position that encourages settling litigation. Affirming the commission's decision, the court commented that to decide otherwise "would leave settlements, including those endorsed and facilitated by a federal court, with little confidence."[90]

83. *Id.* at 1068.
84. *Id.* at 1069.
85. *Id.*
86. *Id.*
87. *Id.* at 1071.
88. *Id.* at 1072.
89. *Id.* (citing *Standard Oil Co. v. United States*, 283 U.S. 163, 170–71 n.5 (1931)).
90. *Id.*

Turning to the allegations that the agreement violated the FTC Act, whether the agreements represented an "unfair method of competition," the court commented that this requires that there be an actual anticompetitive effect, not one that is "hypothetical or presumed."[91] The court based its decision in part on the limited effect of the agreement, to the specific controlled-release potassium chloride formulation and limited in scope to the extent of the exclusionary right stemming from the patent. Interestingly, the court opined that the certainty resulting from the settlement would lead to "more intense competition."[92] Citing *Valley Drug*,[93] the court fashioned the idea that litigation can be a more costly means to achieve the same exclusion reached by settlement, contrary to the "logic" employed by the commission that payment was merely a quid pro quo for delayed generic market entry.[94]

The court's opinion also contained an interesting analysis regarding the effects of the Hatch-Waxman Act:

> It is uncontested that parties settle cases based on their perceived risk of prevailing in and losing the litigation. Pre-Hatch-Waxman, Upsher and ESI normally would have had to enter the market with their products, incurring the costs of clinical trials, manufacturing and marketing. This market entry would have driven down Schering's profits, as it took sales away. As a result, Schering would have sued ESI and Upsher, seeking damages for lost profits and willful infringement. Assuming the patent is reasonably strong, and the parties then settled under this scenario, the money most probably would flow from the infringers to Schering because the generics would have put their companies at risk by making infringing sales.[95]
>
> "By contrast, the Hatch-Waxman Amendments grant generic manufacturers standing to mount a validity challenge without incurring the cost of entry or risking enormous damages flowing from" any possible infringement.[96]

The Hatch-Waxman Act substantially redistributes the relative risk assessments and explains the flow of settlement funds and their magnitude.[97] Because of the Hatch-Waxman scheme, ESI and Upsher gained

91. *Id.*
92. *Id.* at 1073.
93. *Valley Drug Co. v. Geneva Pharm., Inc.*, 344 F.3d 1294 (11th Cir. 2003).
94. *Schering-Plough*, 402 F.3d at 1073.
95. *Id.* at 1073–74.
96. *Id.* at 1074; *see In re Ciprofloxacin Hydrochloride Antitrust Litig.*, 261 F. Supp. 2d 188, 251 (E.D.N.Y. 2003).
97. *Id.*

considerable leverage in patent litigation—the exposure to liability amounted to litigation costs, but paled in comparison to the immense volume of generic sales and profits. This statutory scheme could then cost Schering its patent.

> By entering into the settlement agreements, Schering realized the full potential of its infringement suit—a determination that the '743 patent was valid and that ESI and Upsher would not infringe the patent in the future. Furthermore, although ESI and Upsher obtained less than what they would have received from successfully defending the lawsuits (the ability to immediately market their generics), they gained more than if they had lost. A conceivable compromise, then, directs the consideration from the patent owner to the challengers. . . . Ultimately, the consideration paid to Upsher and ESI was arguably less than if Schering's patent had been invalidated, which would have resulted in the generic entry of potassium chloride supplements.[98]

Following this line of reasoning, the court posed a "pre-Hatch-Waxman" hypothetical regarding settlement of a similar lawsuit, wherein if the patent holder settled for less than the damages it was entitled to, the "windfall" garnered by the generic would be like the reverse payment here, since presumably the settlement would effect a delay in generic market entry.[99] Moreover, looking long-term, the court acknowledged that a ban on reverse payments would remove the incentive for settlement, and in some percentage of the cases the patent holder would prevail; thus, delaying generic market entry even longer. Accordingly, the court noted that the anticompetitive cost to consumers of litigation needed to be considered.[100]

Finally, the caustic environment of patent litigation may actually decrease product innovation by amplifying the period of uncertainty around the drug manufacturer's ability to research, develop, and market the patented product or allegedly infringing product. According to the court, the intensified guesswork involved with lengthy litigation cuts against the benefits proposed by a rule that forecloses a patent holder's ability to settle its infringement claim.[101] Similarly, Hatch-Waxman settlements, like the ones at issue in this case, which resulted in the patent holder's purchase of

98. *Schering-Plough*, 402 F.3d at 1074.

99. *Id.*

100. *Id.* at 1075.

101. *See In re Tamoxifen Citrate Antitrust Litig.*, 277 F. Supp. 2d 121, 133 (E.D.N.Y. 2003) (noting that the settlement resolved the parties' complex patent litigation, and in so doing, "cleared the field" for other ANDA filers).

a license for some of the alleged infringer's other products may benefit the public by introducing a new rival into the market, facilitating competitive production, and encouraging further innovation.

The Eleventh Circuit's decision found the commission to have ignored or discounted evidence contrary to its inclination to find that settlement agreements containing reverse payments constitute an antitrust violation, and rejected its legal determinations that the specific agreement at issue in this case was improperly anticompetitive—that is, outside the scope of the legitimate exclusionary scope of the patent grant.[102]

The Second Circuit, in a lawsuit involving the anticancer drug tamoxifen, agreed with the analysis by the Eleventh Circuit in the *Schering-Plough* case.[103] In this case, the FTC (representing multiple plaintiffs) sued a number of related companies collectively designated "Zeneca" and Barr Laboratories over a settlement agreement of ANDA litigation regarding tamoxifen, a breast cancer treatment. The reverse payment amounted to $21 million and an agreement between the companies wherein Barr became the source of an "authorized generic" version of the drug—that is, that Zeneca would act as a supplier of tamoxifen for Barr to be resold in the United States at a price higher than would typically occur when a generic version of a drug enters the marketplace. The district court in the underlying ANDA litigation found the patent invalid, and the parties' agreement was contingent on getting a vacatur of this judgment.[104] The basis for the district court's invalidity decision was non-disclosure of material prior art and inequitable conduct.[105] While this judgment was being appealed to the Federal Circuit, the parties settled.

An additional fact relevant to the court's decision was that Barr, the first ANDA filer, reasserted its 180-day data exclusivity period that prevented other generic drugs that were preparing to enter the market. Prior to Barr's action, several other generic drug companies filed ANDAs and Zeneca prevailed in all three of these lawsuits. The FDA permitted Barr to recoup its 180-day exclusivity period, which was subsequently challenged and overturned by the district court. The FTC's position was that the settlement agreement and the district court's vacatur of the underlying ANDA litigation amounted to "reviving" an invalid patent, continuing Zeneca's "monopoly" over tamoxifen, prevented other generics from entering

102. *Schering-Plough*, 402 F.3d at 1074–76.

103. *See In re Tamoxifen Citrate Antitrust Litig.*, 466 F.3d 187 (2d Cir. 2006), *abrogated by F.T.C. v. Actavis, Inc.*, 133 S. Ct. 2223 (2013).

104. *Id.* at 190.

105. *Imperial Chem. Indus., PLC v. Barr Labs.*, 795 F. Supp. 619, 626 (S.D.N.Y. 1992) vacated pursuant to settlement sub nom. *Imperial Chem. Indus., PLC v. Heumann Pharma GmbH & Co.*, 991 F.2d 811 (Fed. Cir. 1993).

the marketplace, maintained a high price on tamoxifen, and amounted to the companies "sharing of unlawful monopoly profits."[106]

In the district court case brought by plaintiffs and the FTC and the judgment before the Second Circuit, the court dismissed the complaint based on the existence of a patent, U.S. Patent No. 4,536,516. The district court held that only by misusing a patent could the patent holder be liable for an antitrust violation.[107] The district court suggested that a reverse payment merely to keep a generic drug off the market might have a different character than an agreement, as here, that settles active litigation.[108] In addition, Barr's petition to extend its 180-day exclusivity period was also not illegal, being exempt from antitrust liability under the *Noerr-Pennington* doctrine, and no antitrust violation by petitioning the government (see earlier). Specifically, the court held that regulatory agency action, taken or petitioned in good faith, does not raise antitrust injury if it is "the result of the legal monopoly that a patent holder possesses."[109] Moreover, "forcing" the other ANDA filers to "prove" that the patent was invalid was not an antitrust injury, particularly since Zeneca prevailed in these actions, implying that the patents were not invalid.[110]

The Second Circuit's opinion began with an express recognition that there is a tension between antitrust law and patent law.[111] The court further recognized that there were competing legal principles between consumer protection under the antitrust law and the exclusivity conferred to patent holders under patent law.[112] However, unlike the FTC, the court did not believe that a ban on reverse payments was the answer.[113] Rather, the court substantively considered the several allegations made by plaintiffs and the FTC.[114]

Plaintiffs' first allegation discussed in the Second Circuit's opinion was that the district court should have considered the patent presumptively invalid based on the earlier determination of invalidity.[115] The Second Circuit rejected this view, saying that the established principle is that courts should encourage settlement in the public interest. The court says it is unwilling to presume what decision would have been made at the Federal

106. *In re Tamoxifen Citrate*, 466 F.3d at 196–97.

107. *See In re Tamoxifen Citrate Antitrust Litig.*, 277 F. Supp. 2d 121, 136 (E.D.N.Y. 2003), *aff'd*, 466 F.3d 187 (2d Cir. 2006).

108. *Id.* at 133.

109. *Id.* at 138.

110. *Id.*

111. *In re Tamoxifen Citrate*, 466 F.3d at 201.

112. *Id.* at 202.

113. *Id.* at 202–05.

114. *Id.*

115. *Id.* at 202.

Circuit if the district court's original invalidity opinion had been reviewed in an appeal of the underlying ANDA litigation.[116] The panel was not willing to presume that the Federal Circuit would have affirmed the invalidity determination.

Secondly, the court found that the timing of the settlement agreement, after an invalidity decision in the ANDA litigation, was irrelevant, noting that both parties had reason to settle before having the decision reviewed by the Federal Circuit.[117]

Third, plaintiffs and the FTC contended that the amount of the reverse payment greatly exceeded the value of the settlement even under a "best case scenario."[118] This argument differs from the FTC's position that the very existence of a reverse payment is per se unlawful, an opinion supported by academic commentary. The Second Circuit expressly refused to hold that a reverse payment is a per se antitrust violation.[119] Indeed, the court said that the Hatch-Waxman regime encourages settlements having reverse payments, because the statute reverses the usual positions of the parties.[120] Typically, according to the court, the risk is with the accused infringer (the generic-drug maker), who must develop the competing generic drug, obtain approval, and then enter the marketplace "at risk" of patent infringement litigation.[121] The provisions of Hatch-Waxman changed this calculus, the court opined, because the generic-drug maker does not need to expend very much of its resources in developing its ANDA. As a consequence, in the court's view, the generic-drug maker has relatively "little to lose" in ANDA litigation.[122] The situation of the generic-drug maker is in contrast to the patent holder, who has lost the possibility of damages from the generic-drug maker and can, at best, effectively obtain an injunction either from the court or by the refusal of the FDA to provide regulatory approval until its Orange Book–listed patent(s) expire(s). The patent holder's incentive is to prevent infringement, and a patent holder may be willing to reach this result even if it needs to incur certain costs in the short term—that is, reverse payments. In the court's view, reverse payments are expected consequences of the incentives created under the Hatch-Waxman system.[123]

116. *Id.* at 203.

117. *See id.* at 204 (noting that "it takes no citation to authority to conclude that appellants prevail with some frequency in federal courts of appeals even when a high degree of deference is accorded the district courts from which the appeals are taken").

118. *Id.* at 205.

119. *Id.* at 206.

120. *Id.*

121. *Id.*

122. *Id.* at 207.

123. *Id.*

The Second Circuit also said that "excessive" reverse payments can be a violation if it is merely "a device for circumventing antitrust law."[124] The court recognized that "at first blush" a reverse payment may look per se anticompetitive, but stated that "upon reflection" suspicion abates "so long as the patent litigation is neither a sham nor otherwise baseless."[125] Under the circumstances here and generally absent sham litigation or assertion of patent(s) known to be invalid or unenforceable, settlements are a way to protect what the patent holder is lawfully entitled to—the patent monopoly: "[t]he anticipated profits of the patent holder in the absence of generic competition are greater than the sum of its profits and the profits of the generic entrant when the two compete."[126] The court stated:

> It might therefore make economic sense for the patent holder to pay some portion of that difference to the generic manufacturer to maintain the patent-monopoly market for itself. And, if that amount exceeds what the generic manufacturer sees as its likely profit from victory, it seems to make obvious economic sense for the generic manufacturer to accept such a payment if it is offered.[127]

To the extent that an "excessive" reverse payment indicates a lack of confidence in the patent's strength or validity, the court opined:

> [W]e doubt the wisdom of deeming a patent effectively invalid on the basis of a patent holder's fear of losing it. . . . It is not "bad faith" to assert patent rights that one is not certain will be upheld in a suit for infringement pressed to judgment and to settle the suit to avoid risking the loss of the rights. No one can be certain that he will prevail in a patent suit.[128]

The court went on to say that a rule that would penalize a patent holder for settling a lawsuit neglects to consider that there is always a risk that a court will invalidate a patent, and that a patent holder might legitimately decide to insure against that risk by settling. Using this case as an illustration, the court noted that settlement occurred *after* the district court had invalidated the patent.[129] Zeneca could not have counted on the Federal Circuit to reverse the invalidity decision any more than Barr could count on the appellate court to affirm. Thus, both parties had an incentive

---

124. *Id.* at 208.

125. *Id.*

126. *Id.* at 209 (quoting *In re Schering-Plough Corp.*, slip op. at 27, 2003 WL 22989651 (Fed. Trade Comm'n Dec. 8, 2003)).

127. *Id.*

128. *Id.* at 210 (quoting *Asahi Glass Co. v. Pentech Pharm. Inc.*, 289 F. Supp. 2d 986, 992–93 (N.D. Ill. 2003) (Posner, J.) (emphasis in original)).

129. *Id.* at 211.

to settle. In addition, it was reassuring at the least that the subsequent litigation history found Zeneca suing successfully on the patent multiple times against other ANDA filers.

Speaking generally on the FTC's position, the court commented:

> We are unsure, too, what would be accomplished by a rule that would effectively outlaw payments by patent holders to generic manufacturers greater than what the latter would be able to earn in the market were they to defend successfully against an infringement claim. A patent holder might well prefer such a settlement limitation—it would make such a settlement cheaper—while a generic manufacturer might nonetheless agree to settle because it is less risky to accept in settlement all the profits it expects to make in a competitive market rather than first to defend and win a lawsuit, and then to enter the marketplace and earn the profits.[130]

However, the court stated:

> We are not unaware of a troubling dynamic that is at work in these cases. The less sound the patent or the less clear the infringement, and therefore the less justified the monopoly enjoyed by the patent holder, the more a rule permitting settlement is likely to benefit the patent holder by allowing it to retain the patent. But the law allows the settlement even of suits involving weak patents with the presumption that the patent is valid and that settlement is merely an extension of the valid patent monopoly. So long as the law encourages settlement, weak patent cases will likely be settled even though such settlements will inevitably protect patent monopolies that are, perhaps, undeserved.[131]

The court further noted:

> If courts do not discount the exclusionary power of the patent by the probability of the patent's being held invalid, then the patents most likely to be the subject of exclusion payments would be precisely those patents that have the most questionable validity. This concern, on its face, is quite powerful. But the answer to this concern lies in the fact that, while the strategy of paying off a generic company to drop its patent challenge would work to exclude that particular competitor from the market, it would have no effect on other challengers of the patent, whose incentive to mount a

130. *Id.*
131. *Id.*

> challenge would also grow commensurately with the chance that the patent would be held invalid.[132]
>
> There is, of course, the possibility that the patent holder will continue to buy out potential competition such that a settlement with one generic manufacturer protecting the patent holder's ill-gotten patent monopoly will be followed by other settlements with other generic manufacturers should a second, third, and fourth rise to challenge the patent. We doubt, however, that this scenario is realistic.[133]

Every settlement payment to a generic manufacturer reduces the profitability of the patent monopoly. The point will come when there are simply no monopoly profits with which to pay the new generic challengers.

> [I]t is unlikely that the holder of a weak patent could stave off all possible challengers with exclusion payments because the economics simply would not justify it.[134]

In this regard, the court noted that Zeneca settled its first tamoxifen lawsuit against the first generic manufacturer, Barr, but did not settle or attempt to settle, the litigation it brought against the subsequent challenging generics, Novopharm, Pharmachemie, and Mylan.[135]

The court considered the alternative, what the FTC advocated.

> But such a requirement would be contrary to well-established principles of law. As we have rehearsed at some length above, settlement of patent litigation is not only suffered, it is encouraged for a variety of reasons even if it leads in some cases to the survival of monopolies created by what would otherwise be fatally weak patents. It is too late in the journey for us to alter course.[136]

The court also considered the terms of the agreement, specifically whether the exclusionary terms of the agreement exceeded the scope of the patent protection—that is, to enlarge the patent right. The answer here is that it did not, in part because the patent at issue was to a composition rather than a formulation. Under these circumstances, the patent scope was broader and the exclusionary right accordingly more expansive. In addition, the court noted that, unlike other instances of reverse payments,

---

132. *Id.* (quoting *In re Ciprofloxacin Hydrochloride Antitrust Litig.*, 363 F. Supp. 2d 514, 534 (E.D.N.Y. 2005)).

133. *Id.* at 211–12.

134. *In re Ciprofloxacin Hydrochloride Antitrust Litig.*, 363 F. Supp. 2d at 535.

135. *In re Tamoxifen Citrate*, 466 F.3d at 211–12.

136. *Id.* at 212.

there was no generic bottleneck, since several other generic companies filed ANDAs on Zeneca's drug.[137] Moreover, Barr entered the market under license from Bayer, so there was competition in the marketplace, albeit as an "authorized generic" that sold for about 5 percent less than the branded.

Finally, while the court was "not so sure" that Barr's later attempts to recover its 180-day exclusivity period as the first ANDA filer was immune from antitrust considerations under the *Noerr-Pennington* doctrine, the scope of the anticompetitive aspects of the agreement was not illegally excessive, and the court could discern no antitrust injury.[138]

Once again, the circuit court in this case appeared to carefully consider the agreement as a whole, and to reject the FTC's call for substantially per se determination that reverse payments are illegal and should be banned in all circumstances.

The Federal Circuit followed this trend in *In re Ciprofloxacin Hydrochloride Antitrust Litigation*.[139] In this case, several union and other patient groups, as well as individual patients, sued defendants including Bayer, Hoechst Marion Roussel, Watson Pharmaceuticals, and Barr Labs. The patent-in-suit, U.S. Patent No. 4,670,444, encompassed ciprofloxacin hydrochloride ("Cipro"), Bayer's product, with Barr being the first ANDA filer. Litigation pursuant to 35 U.S.C. § 271(e)(2) ensued.

Under the terms of the settlement agreement, defendants agreed not to challenge the validity or enforceability of the '444 patent, and Barr would convert its Paragraph IV certification to a Paragraph III certification, agreeing not to enter the market until the '444 patent expired. The reverse payment from Bayer to Barr totaled $398.1 million. Bayer also agreed to make quarterly "reverse payments" or supply Barr with Cipro for resale until after the '444 patent expired.[140]

Plaintiffs alleged antitrust violations under sections 1 and 2 of the Sherman Act, illegal contracts in restraint of trade, as well as state antitrust and consumer protection laws. Later plaintiffs added a *Walker Process* claim despite the fact that the '444 patent had been through a re-exam with a claim specific to ciprofloxacin hydrochloride exiting unamended.[141]

The district court granted summary judgment against the plaintiffs, holding that any anticompetitive effects "were within the exclusionary zone of [the patent]."[142] This decision was based on a rule of reason analysis

137. *Id.* at 215.

138. *Id.* at 217.

139. *In re Ciprofloxacin Hydrochloride Antitrust Litig.*, 544 F.3d 1323 (Fed. Cir. 2008), *abrogated by F.T.C. v. Actavis, Inc.*, 133 S. Ct. 2223 (2013).

140. *Id.* at 1328–29 & n.5.

141. *Id.* at 1329.

142. *Id.* at 1330 (citing *In re Ciprofloxacin Hydrochloride*, 363 F. Supp. 2d at 523–40).

that did not get past the first step: any anticompetitive effects fell within the ambit of the patent exclusionary right and hence were not illegal.

The Federal Circuit affirmed, in an opinion by Judge Prost, joined by Judge Schall and Judge Ward.[143] The panel reviewed the judgment de novo on all issues, the grant of summary judgment as well as defendants' motion to dismiss and the decision that the state law claims were preempted by federal patent and antitrust laws.[144] The plaintiffs asserted five points of error:

> 1. That the agreement was per se illegal, or illegal under a proper application of the rule of reason; 2. That the agreement improperly extended the exclusionary zone of patent; 3. That the District Court should have considered the law of regional circuits and government agencies (FTC); 4. That the District Court should have considered the effects of these kinds of agreements on other generic entrants; and, 5. The effects on competition of Barr's 180-day exclusivity period.[145]

As to the first asserted point of error, Judge Prost's opinion reminded plaintiffs that the Supreme Court has not interpreted the Sherman Act as prohibiting all agreements in restraint of trade, just unreasonable restraints:

> Only agreements that have a "predictable and pernicious anticompetitive effect, and . . . limited potential for procompetitive benefit" are deemed to be per se unlawful under the Sherman Act.[146]

The Federal Circuit found no basis for finding the agreement to be per se illegal and instead applied a rule of reason analysis under the law of the Second Circuit.[147] This is a three-step process, according to the Federal Circuit, where plaintiffs have the initial burden of showing an actual (not speculative) adverse effect on competition. If the plaintiffs make such a showing, the burden shifts to the defendant to "establish the procompetitive redeeming virtues of the action."[148] Finally, the plaintiffs get the opportunity to "show that the same pro-competitive effect could be achieved through an alternative means that is less restrictive of competition."[149] The panel performed this analysis by first identifying the relevant

143. District Judge for the Eastern District of Texas, sitting by designation.
144. *In re Ciprofloxacin Hydrochloride Antitrust Litig.*, 544 F.3d at 1330–31.
145. *Id.* at 1331.
146. *Id.* at 1331–32 (quoting *State Oil Co. v. Khan*, 522 U.S. 3, 10 (1997)).
147. *Id.* at 1332.
148. *Id.* (quoting *Clorox Co. v. Sterling Winthrop, Inc.*, 117 F.3d 50, 56 (2d Cir. 1997)).
149. *Id.* (quoting *Clorox*, 117 F.3d at 56).

market and deciding whether defendants possess market power in that relevant market. Judge Prost opined that the district court performed the rule-of-reason analysis properly under this Second Circuit standard, including its conclusion that "there was no evidence that the Agreements created a bottleneck on challenges to the '444 patent or otherwise restrained competition outside the 'exclusionary zone' of the patent."[150]

Regarding the second allegation of error, that the settlement agreement improperly extended the exclusionary scope of the '444 patent, the Federal Circuit set forth plaintiffs' argument to the contrary.

> The appellants assert, however, that the district court erred in concluding that the Agreements were within the "exclusionary zone" of the '444 patent, in essence treating them as per se legal. According to the appellants, the patent holder's right to exclude competition is not defined by the facial scope of the patent, but rather is limited to the right to exclude others from profiting from the patented invention. Under the Agreements, the appellants argue, Bayer is seeking not simply to enforce its patent rights, but to insulate itself from competition and avoid the risk that the patent is held invalid.[151]

However, the Federal Circuit noted that the district court had cited many Supreme Court and circuit courts of appeal decisions that "any adverse anti-competitive effects within the scope of the '444 patent could not be redressed by antitrust law."[152] According to the district court, citing 35 U.S.C. § 154(a)(1), "[t]his is because a patent by its very nature is anticompetitive; it is a grant to the inventor of 'the right to exclude others from making, using, offering for sale, or selling the invention,'" and concluding "[t]hus, 'a patent is an exception to the general rule against monopolies and to the right of access to a free and open market.'"[153]

The Federal Circuit agreed.

> [T]he essence of the Agreements was to exclude the defendants from profiting from the patented invention. This is well within Bayer's rights as the patentee.[154]

The court noted that "[s]ettlement of patent claims by agreement between the parties—including exchange of consideration—rather than by

150. *Id.*
151. *Id.* at 1332–33.
152. *Id.* at 1333.
153. *Id.* (quoting *Precision Instrument Mfg. Co. v. Auto. Maint. Mach. Co.*, 324 U.S. 806, 816 (1945)).
154. *Id.*

litigation is not precluded by the Sherman Act even though it may have some adverse effects on competition."[155]

The Federal Circuit found no difference between the anticompetitive effects of this settlement and settlements in patent cases in general. Of special importance to this decision is the court's discounting the allegation that the settlements hinder challenges to the '444 patent, in view of the fact that four other generics manufacturers had challenged the '444 patent after the settlement at issue.

As to the "legal standards applied by the regional circuits and government agencies,"[156] particularly the Sixth Circuit decision in *In re Cardizem CD*,[157] and the FTC's position that reverse payments should be per se illegal, the court declined plaintiffs' invitation to apply the legal opinions of other regional circuits, administrative agencies, or legal commentators.

> In [the district court's rule-of-reason] analysis, it considered whether there was evidence of sham litigation or fraud before the PTO, and whether any anticompetitive effects of the Agreements were outside the exclusionary zone of the patent. The application of a rule of reason analysis to a settlement agreement involving an exclusion payment in the Hatch-Waxman context has been embraced by the Second Circuit, and advocated by the FTC and the Solicitor General. And, although the Sixth Circuit found a per se violation of the antitrust laws in In re Cardizem, the facts of that case are distinguishable from this case and from the other circuit court decisions. In particular, the settlement in that case included, in addition to a reverse payment, an agreement by the generic manufacturer to not relinquish its 180-day exclusivity period, thereby delaying the entry of other generic manufacturers.[158] Furthermore, th[at] agreement provided that the generic manufacturer would not market non-infringing versions of the generic drug.[159] Thus, th[at] agreement clearly had anti-competitive effects outside the exclusion zone of the patent.[160] To the extent that the Sixth Circuit may have found a per se antitrust violation based solely on the reverse payments, we respectfully disagree.[161]

155. *Id.* (quoting *Standard Oil Co. v. United States*, 283 U.S. 163, 171 & n.5 (1931)).

156. *Id.* at 1334.

157. *In re Cardizem CD Antitrust Litig.*, 332 F.3d 896 (6th Cir. 2003).

158. *In re Ciprofloxacin Hydrochloride Antitrust Litig.*, 544 F.3d at 1335 (citing *In re Cardizem*, 332 F.3d at 907).

159. *Id.* (citing *In re Cardizem*, 332 F.3d at 908 n.13).

160. *Id.* at 1335; *see* Brief for the United States at *16 n.7, *Joblove v. Barr Labs., Inc.*, 127 S. Ct. 3001 (No. 06-830); Brief for the United States as Amicus Curiae at *17, *FTC v. Schering-Plough Corp.*, 548 U.S. 919 (2006) (No. 05-273), 2006 WL 1358441.

161. *In re Ciprofloxacin Hydrochloride Antitrust Litig.*, 544 F.3d at 1335.

The court also distinguished the Sixth Circuit's decision that reverse payment agreements were per se illegal "because the court failed to consider the exclusionary power of the patent in its antitrust analysis."[162]

The Federal Circuit turned instead to decisions from the Eleventh Circuit (*Schering-Plough v. Andrx Pharmaceuticals*) and by the Second Circuit (*In re Tamoxifen*) that follow its approach that antitrust violations occur in reverse-settlement-containing ANDA settlement agreements when the patent is invalid or unenforceable due to inequitable conduct or litigation is a sham (or "objectively baseless").

> [The Second Circuit] concluded that the presence of a reverse payment, or the size of a reverse payment, alone is not enough to render an agreement violative of the antitrust laws unless the anticompetitive effects of the agreement exceed the scope of the patent's protection . . . .
>
> We conclude that in cases such as this, wherein all anticompetitive effects of the settlement agreement are within the exclusionary power of the patent, the outcome is the same whether the court begins its analysis under antitrust law by applying a rule of reason approach to evaluate the anti-competitive effects, or under patent law by analyzing the right to exclude afforded by the patent. The essence of the inquiry is whether the agreements restrict competition beyond the exclusionary zone of the patent. This analysis has been adopted by the Second and the Eleventh Circuits and by the district court below and we find it to be completely consistent with Supreme Court precedent.[163]

The Federal Circuit also opined that, absent fraud on the PTO or sham litigation, patent validity does not need to be considered in the application of a rule-of-reason analysis—ironically, citing an FTC position to this effect: "it would not be necessary, practical, or particularly useful for the Commission to embark on an inquiry into the merits of the underlying patent dispute when resolving antitrust issues in patent settlements."[164] It seems, however, that the FTC has changed its position on this point, because it argued that the "expected value" of the lawsuit at the time of settlement be considered in the rule of reason antitrust analysis.[165] The

162. *Id.*

163. *Id.* at 1336; *see Walker Process Equip., Inc. v. Food Mach. & Chem. Corp.*, 382 U.S. 172, 175–77 (1965) (holding that there may be a violation of the Sherman Act when a patent is procured by fraud, but recognizing that a patent is an exception to the general rule against monopolies).

164. *Id.* (quoting *In re Schering-Plough Corp.*, No. 9297, 2003 WL 22989651, slip op. at 19 (F.T.C. Dec. 8, 2003)).

165. *Id.* at 1337.

court disagreed, based on the presumption of validity: "the district court correctly concluded that there is no legal basis for restricting the right of a patent holder to choose its preferred means of enforcement and no support for the notion that the Hatch-Waxman Act was intended to thwart settlements."[166]

Even circuit court Judge Richard Posner, a leader in the "law and economics" movement, seems to agree.

> As Judge Posner remarked, if "there is nothing suspicious about the circumstances of a patent settlement, then to prevent a cloud from being cast over the settlement process a third party should not be permitted to haul the parties to the settlement over the hot coals of antitrust litigation."[167]

The Federal Circuit disregarded the plaintiffs' argument that the effects of these kinds of agreements on other generic entrants should be considered, particularly insofar as it was based on the expense of filing an ANDA with a Paragraph IV certification.[168] In addition, the final argument, regarding Barr's attempts to retain its 180-day exclusivity period, is mooted by the section of the agreement in which Barr changed its Paragraph IV certification to a Paragraph III certification.[169] The court also noted that this outcome has been changed by provisions of the 2003 Medicare Modernization Act that strips from a first filer any right to the 180-day exclusivity if a reverse payment agreement was found to be anticompetitive.

The Second Circuit also followed its own and the other circuit's precedent in a case involving the antibiotic Cipro.[170] In this decision, the court ruled that the reverse payment settlement agreement between defendants Bayer AG and several generic-drug makers, including the Rugby Group, Watson Pharmaceuticals Inc., and Barr Laboratories Inc., was not illegal under U.S. antitrust law and prevailing precedent.[171]

The opinion arose from the plaintiffs' appeal of summary judgment for defendants by the U.S. District Court for the Eastern District of New York that defendants were not guilty of violating section 1 of the Sherman

---

166. *Id.*

167. *Id.* (quoting *Asahi Glass Co. v. Pentech Pharm., Inc.*, 289 F. Supp. 2d 986, 992 (N.D. Ill. 2003)).

168. *Id.* at 1338.

169. *Id.* at 1338–39.

170. *See Ark. Carpenters Health & Welfare Fund v. Bayer AG*, 625 F.3d 779 (2d Cir. 2010).

171. *Ark. Carpenters Health & Welfare Fund v. Bayer AG*, 604 F.3d 98, 106 (2d Cir. 2010), *abrogated by F.T.C. v. Actavis, Inc.*, 133 S. Ct. 2223 (2013).

Act by agreeing to a "reverse exclusionary payment" settlement of patent infringement litigation. The panel's opinion cited the earlier determination that such "reverse payments" were not illegal.[172]

As the consolidated case name indicates, the drug at issue was ciprofloxacin (or "Cipro"), a patented antibiotic owned by Bayer, U.S. Patent No. 4,670,444.[173] The other defendants were generic-drug makers capable of making generic versions of Cipro who had filed ANDAs with the FDA to obtain regulatory approval for selling generic Cipro. Under the provisions of the Hatch-Waxman Act,[174] Bayer sued each of these generic-drug makers to block FDA approval until the conclusion of the patent litigation.[175] The court recognized that "the Hatch-Waxman Act redistributes the relative risks between the patent holder and the generic manufacturer, allowing generic manufacturers to challenge the validity of the patent without incurring the costs of market entry or the risks of damages from infringement."[176]

The terms of the pay-for-delay agreement between Bayer and Barr, the first ANDA filer, had Bayer paying Barr $49.1 million in a lump sum and then quarterly payments of $12.5 million to $17.125 million until six months prior to patent expiry, for a total payment of $398.1 million and a guarantee that the generic manufacturers could sell "brand name" Cipro for six months prior to the expiration date of the '444 patent.[177] Bayer received Barr's promise and the promise of the other generic manufacturers not to enter the marketplace with a generic version of Cipro and concessions regarding the validity and enforceability of the '444 patent, thereby ending the ANDA lawsuit.[178] Barr "reserved its right to reinstate its ANDA-IV [lawsuit] if Bayer's ['444] patent [was] later held to be invalid."[179] There were four later challenges to the '444 patent by Ranbaxy, Schein, Carlsbad, and Mylan, none of which were successful in invalidating it.[180]

Plaintiffs responded with "over thirty antitrust lawsuits," which were consolidated in the Eastern District of New York for trial, granting

172. *Id.* at 105; *see Joblove v. Barr Labs., Inc.*, 466 F.3d 187, 208–12 (2d Cir. 2005) (*In re Tamoxifen Citrate Antitrust Litigation*).

173. *Id.* at 100.

174. Drug Price Stabilization and Patent Term Restoration Act of 1984, Pub. L. No. 98-417, 98 Stat. 1585.

175. 35 U.S.C. § 271(e)(2)(A).

176. *Ark. Carpenters Health & Welfare Fund v. Bayer AG*, 604 F.3d at 101.

177. *Id.* at 102.

178. *Id.*

179. *Id.* at 102 n.9.

180. *Id.*

defendants' summary judgment motion.[181] The panel quoted from the District Court opinion:

> The ultimate question—and this is the crux of the matter—is not whether Bayer and Barr had the power to adversely affect competition for ciprofloxacin as a whole, but whether any adverse effects on competition stemming from the Agreements were outside the exclusionary zone of the '444 Patent. It goes without saying that patents have adverse effects on competition. However, any adverse effects within the scope of a patent cannot be redressed by antitrust law.[182]

Specifically, the court rejected what it called a "*post hoc* determination of the potential validity" *vel non* of the '444 patent, which would be contrary to the statutory presumption of validity and "would work a revolution in patent law."[183] Further, from the district court's reasoning:

> In the absence of any evidence that the Agreements created a bottleneck on challenges to the '444 Patent, or that they otherwise restrained competition beyond the scope of the claims of the '444 Patent, the Agreements have not had any anti-competitive effects on the market for ciprofloxacin beyond that which are permitted under the '444 Patent. The fact that Bayer paid what in absolute numbers is a handsome sum to Barr to settle its lawsuit does not necessarily reflect a lack of confidence in the '444 Patent, but rather the economic realities of what was at risk. There is simply no precedent for plaintiffs' argument that the parties to a settlement are required to preserve the public's interest in lower prices. Such a rule would only result in parties being less likely to reach settlements, aside from undermining well-settled principles of patent law. Finally, to even attempt to quantify the public's interest in a patent settlement between private parties would require devaluing patents across the board, a result that would contravene the presumption of validity afforded by Congress and impact the very way patent licenses are handled in countless daily transactions.[184]

In an interesting footnote, the Second Circuit explained that the "indirect purchaser plaintiffs" had included *Walker Process* antitrust claims,

---

181. *Id.* at 102.

182. *Id.* at 103 (quoting *In re Ciprofloxacin Hydrochloride Antitrust Litig.*, 363 F. Supp. 2d 514, 548 (E.D.N.Y. 2005)).

183. *Id.* (quoting *In re Ciprofloxacin Hydrochloride*, 363 F. Supp. 2d at 529) (emphasis in original).

184. *Id.* (quoting *In re Ciprofloxacin Hydrochloride*, 363 F. Supp. 2d at 540–41).

based on the willful assertion of an unenforceable patent, pursuant to *Walker Process Equipment v. Food Machinery & Chemical Corp.*[185] Transfer was necessary because *Walker Process* claims "arise under" U.S. patent law and are thus within the exclusive province of the Federal Circuit.[186] That court affirmed the district court's grant of summary judgment for defendants.[187]

In the instant case, the Second Circuit panel analyzed the defendants' behavior in the context of the prohibitions of the Sherman Act.[188] Its consideration of the question was informed by the opinions of other circuit courts of appeal as well as the arguments put forward by the FTC, whose position is that reverse payment arrangements are per se illegal restraints of trade.[189] Putting it mildly, the court noted that "[a]uthorities are divided on this question."[190] Notably, while academic commentators and FTC economists take the per se illegal view, most courts have applied the "rule of reason" and held that such agreements are not sufficiently anticompetitive, if at all, to raise antitrust liability.[191] The most relevant of these judicial determinations finding no antitrust liability was *Joblove v. Barr Labs*,[192] being binding precedent on this court. In that case, the Second Circuit panel determined as a matter of law that the reverse-payment agreement was not anticompetitive to a degree that raised antitrust liability.[193] Here, the panel noted the similarities between the *Tamoxifen* court's reasoning and the analysis supplied by the district court here. In *Tamoxifen*, the court stated:

> Unless and until the patent is shown to have been procured by fraud, or a suit for its enforcement is shown to be objectively baseless, there is no injury to the market cognizable under existing antitrust law, as long as competition is restrained only within the scope of the patent.[194]

---

185. *Id.* at 103 n.10.

186. *Id.*

187. *Id.* (citing *In re Ciprofloxacin Antitrust Litig.*, 544 F.3d 1323, 1333 (Fed. Cir. 2008)).

188. 15 U.S.C. §§ 1–3.

189. *See* Kevin E. Noonan, *FTC Disapproves of "Pay-for-Delay" Drug Deals*, PATENTDOCS (Feb. 15, 2010), *available at* http://www.patentdocs.org/2010/02/ftc-disapproves-of-payfordelay-drug-deals.html.

190. *Ark. Carpenters Health*, 604 F.3d at 105.

191. *See* Kevin E. Noonan, *Reverse Payments in Generic Drug Settlements*, PATENTDOCS (Feb. 22–23, 25, 2010), *available at* http://www.patentdocs.org/2010/02/reverse-payments-in-generic-drug-settlements.html.

192. *Joblove v. Barr Labs. Inc.*, 466 F.3d 187, 216 (2d Cir. 2006) (*In re Tamoxifen Citrate Antitrust Litig*ation).

193. *Id.*

194. *Ark. Carpenters Health*, 604 F.3d at 106 (quoting *In re Tamoxifen Citrate Antitrust Litig.*, 466 F.3d at 213).

Under the *Tamoxifen* precedent, there is a three-prong test for determining that a reverse payment agreement is legal: "where (1) there was no restriction on marketing noninfringing products; (2) a generic version of the branded drug would necessarily infringe the branded firm's patent; and (3) the agreement did not bar other generic manufacturers from challenging the patent."[195]

The opinion noted the binding nature of this precedent, and thus applied this test to the facts here. The court noted that there was no allegation that Bayer's assertion of the '444 patent was a sham or that Bayer procured the '444 patent by fraud. Thus, the court commented that "the only reasonable basis for distinguishing *Tamoxifen* would be if plaintiffs demonstrated that the settlement agreement here, unlike in *Tamoxifen*, exceeded the scope of the Cipro patent."[196] Which plaintiffs cannot do, of course, since a generic version of Cipro would "necessarily infringe" the '444 patent, so the exercise of the patent to exclude generic Cipro is precisely within the scope of the patent's exclusionary right.[197] In this regard, the court distinguished "formulation patents," which are limited to certain formulations of an active pharmaceutical ingredient, with "compound patents" such as the '444 patent, which encompass all formulations of a drug.[198] Moreover, while plaintiffs argued on appeal that the settlement agreement involved or at least permitted "manipulation" of the 180-day exclusivity period and precluded subsequent ANDA-IV challenges, there was no evidence to support these allegations. Indeed, here there were four "subsequent" ANDA-IV challenges to the '444 patent.[199] In addition, the court noted that Barr forfeited its 180-day exclusivity period under the law in effect at that time, which required the ANDA filer to prevail in litigation invalidating an Orange Book–listed patent.[200]

Perhaps as a hedge against the likelihood that legal arguments would prove unavailing, plaintiffs also argued on policy grounds that reverse payment settlements are contrary to the "purpose" of the Hatch-Waxman Act—that is, "to make available more low cost generic drugs."[201] Market entry of generic drugs "arising from successful Hatch-Waxman challenges can result in significant savings to consumers," the plaintiffs contended, citing data contained in an amicus brief filed by AARP.[202] However, the

195. *Id.*
196. *Id.*
197. *Id.*
198. *Id.*
199. *Id.*
200. *Id.* at 107.
201. *Id.* at 108 (quoting H.R. Rep. No. 98-857, pt. 1, at 14 (1984), *reprinted in* 1984 U.S.C.C.A.N. 2647, 2647).
202. *Id.* at 108.

panel held that such policy arguments could not be addressed by a panel, in view of the precedential *Tamoxifen* opinion.[203] Moreover, this situation prompted the panel to suggest "several reasons why this case might be appropriate for reexamination by our full court," including that the United States in an *amicus* brief "urged us to repudiate *Tamoxifen*."[204] The U.S. argued:

> This Court's Tamoxifen standard inappropriately permits patent holders to contract their way out of the statutorily imposed risk that patent litigation could lead to invalidation of the patent while claiming antitrust immunity for that private contract. . . . [T]his standard effectively bars considering whether the agreement might violate the antitrust laws, and so offers no protection to the public interest in eliminating undeserved patents.[205]

The government would have such settlements be presumptively illegal unless a patent holder could show that their cost does "not greatly exceed anticipated litigation costs."[206]

The court also noted that the "practice of entering into reverse exclusionary payment settlements has increased" since the *Tamoxifen* decision—fourteen settlements prior to the *Tamoxifen* decision, none of which contained reverse payment provisions, compared with twenty-seven settlements after the decision, in which twenty contained reverse payment provisions.[207] It should be noted that this data was gleaned from *amicus* briefs arguing against the legality of reverse-payment provisions in settlement agreements. Also significant for the panel were remarks from Senator Orrin Hatch to the effect that he found reverse payment provisions "appalling."[208] Finally, and perhaps most significantly, the court considered the *Tamoxifen* decision to have been based on "an erroneous characterization" of the law, specifically that the 180-day exclusivity period would be ceded by the first ANDA filer upon entering into a reverse-payment-containing settlement of ANDA litigation.[209]

The panel's sentiments, noted above, were patent in its conclusion.

> In sum, as long as Tamoxifen is controlling law, plaintiffs' claims cannot survive. Accordingly, we AFFIRM the judgment of the district court. However, we believe there are compelling reasons to

203. *Id.*
204. *Id.*
205. *Id.*
206. *Id.* at 109.
207. *Id.*
208. *Id.*
209. *Id.*

> revisit Tamoxifen with the benefit of the full Court's consideration of the difficult questions at issue and the important interests at stake. We therefore invite the plaintiffs-appellants to petition for rehearing in banc.[210]

The last of this series of negative judicial responses to the FTC's position came in the Eleventh Circuit's decision in *FTC v. Watson Pharmaceuticals, Inc. et al.*, with the "*et al.*" including the ANDA filer, Paddock Pharmaceuticals, and its licensee, Par Pharmaceuticals.[211] The case involved a reverse payment settlement between New Drug Application (NDA) holder Solvay Pharmaceuticals and ANDA filers Watson Pharmaceuticals and Paddock Pharmaceuticals over AndroGel, a prescription testosterone formulation prescribed for treating hypogonadism.[212] Unimed, acquired by Solvay and later acquired by Abbott, and Besins Healthcare S.A. held the NDA, as well as Orange Book–listed U.S. Patent No. 6,503,894 directed to the formulation, which will expire in August 2020.[213] Watson and Paddock filed separate ANDAs having Paragraph IV certifications that the '894 patent was invalid or unenforceable, and Unimed/Besins timely filed suit pursuant to 35 U.S.C. § 271(e)(2) in the U.S. District Court for the Northern District of Georgia.[214] The lawsuit was pending longer than the statutory thirty-month stay, and the FDA approved Watson's ANDA, but neither Watson nor Paddock launched "at risk"—that is, before the lawsuit had been decided. As part of the suit, both Watson and Paddock did not contest that their products would infringe the '894 patent, but rather that the patent was invalid or unenforceable. However, the parties settled before the court could rule on the defendants' summary judgment motions after a *Markman* hearing—the district court entered a stipulation of dismissal against Watson and a permanent injunction against Paddock.[215]

In addition to these actions by the district court, the parties agreed that the § 271(e)(2) defendants would "respect" the '894 patent, and that both were entitled to launch in August 2015, five years before the '894 patent was scheduled to expire.[216] Moreover, Watson and Paddock agreed that their sales forces would promote Unimed's (later Solvay's) AndroGel product until the agreed time for their own product launch, and that

---

210. *Id.* at 110.

211. *FTC v. Watson Pharm., Inc.*, 677 F.3d 1298 (11th Cir. 2012), *cert. granted*, *FTC v. Watson Pharm., Inc.*, 133 S. Ct. 787 (U.S. 2012), *abrogated by F.T.C. v. Actavis, Inc.*, 133 S. Ct. 2223 (2013).

212. *Id.* at 1304–05.

213. *Id.* at 1304.

214. *Id.*

215. *Id.* at 1305.

216. *Id.*

Unimed would make annual payments to the parties of ~$20–$30 million to Watson and ~$10 million to Par/Paddock.[217] In addition, Par/Paddock agreed to supply AndroGel to Unimed in a "backup capacity" for an additional $2 million annually.[218]

The case on appeal arose pursuant to an investigation by the FTC of these settlement agreements under 21 U.S.C. § 355 note (2003).[219] The FTC alleged violations of section 5a of the FTC Act.[220] The suit was transferred from the Central District of California to the Northern District of Georgia, where the district court granted defendants' motion to dismiss pursuant to Federal Rule of Civil Procedure 12(b)(6), failure to state a claim.[221] In doing so, the district court rejected the FTC's contentions in its complaint that (1) the settlement agreement between Solvay and Watson is an unfair method of competition; (2) the settlement agreement among Solvay, Paddock, and Par is an unfair method of competition; and (3) Solvay engaged in unfair methods of competition by eliminating the threat of generic competition to AndroGel and thereby monopolizing the market.[222] The basis for the district court's action was that, in this circuit, reverse payments did not constitute anticompetitive behavior "so long as the terms of the settlement remain within the scope of the exclusionary potential of the patent, *i.e.*, do not provide for exclusion going beyond the patent's term or operate to exclude clearly noninfringing products, regardless of whether consideration flowed to the alleged infringer."[223]

The Eleventh Circuit affirmed, in an opinion by Judge Carnes joined by Circuit Judge Kravitch and Ninth Circuit Court Judge Farris (sitting by designation) and applying the Eleventh Circuit standard of de novo review of granted motions to dismiss. The opinion from the outset showed little patience with the FTC's theories, saying that new drugs are produced in the United States under the maxims "no risk, no reward" and "more risk, more reward," and that "[n]o rational actor," the economists' archetype, "would take [the] risk" of investing more than "$1.3 billion" on a potential drug where "[o]nly one in every 5,000 medicines tested . . . is eventually approved for patient use" "without the prospect of a big reward."[224] Under this system, the court recognized that the successful drugmaker who patents its drug will "usually[] recoup its investment and gain a profit,

217. *Id.*

218. *Id.*

219. *Id.*

220. 15 U.S.C. § 45(a)(1).

221. *Watson Pharm., Inc.*, 677 F.3d at 1306.

222. *See* Complaint ¶¶ 106–13, *FTC v. Watson Pharm. Co.*, No. CV-09-00598 (C.D. Cal. Jan. 29, 2009).

223. *Id.*

224. *Watson Pharm., Inc.*, 677 F.3d at 1300.

sometimes a super-sized one."[225] The court also noted that "more money, more problems" is the result, with the profits "frequently attract[ing] competitors in the form of generic drug manufacturers that challenge or try to circumvent the pioneer's monopoly in the market."[226] The court recognized as the "key allegation in the FTC's complaint" that "the patent holder [is] 'not likely to prevail' in the [patent] infringement actions" that arise in the Hatch-Waxman context.[227] The court also recognized the FTC's position that reverse payments are per se anticompetitive as "unlawful restraints of trade" and hence violations of section 1 of the Sherman Act, and cited (albeit in a footnote) the economic rationale advanced by the FTC in this and other contexts.

> According to a study conducted by the FTC of the industry as a whole . . . , a branded manufacturer typically loses about 90 percent of its unit sales over the course of generic entry. While generic entrants gain that unit volume, they do not gain all the revenues lost by the branded manufacturer because, as generic competition sets in, the price falls, on average, to about 15 percent of what the branded manufacturer was charging. Thus, a branded manufacturer can expect that, if a drug is earning $1 billion a year before generic entry, the manufacturer will only earn about $100 million a year once generic competition has matured, and all the generic companies put together will only earn about $135 million a year (90% x 15% x $1 billion), thus leaving approximately $765 million a year for the public through the benefits of competition. The parties have a strong economic incentive to avoid that result.[228]

The court set forth both the statutory basis of the Hatch-Waxman regime and the specific facts of this case.[229] In its explication of the law, the court stated that "Federal law encourages generic drug manufacturers to file Paragraph IV certifications."[230]

The court got to the heart of the FTC's contentions. Since the FTC's complaint was dismissed under Federal Rule of Civil Procedure 12(b)(6), all factual allegations in the complaint were accepted as true. The court returned to its previously stated analysis of the FTC's position, commenting that "[t]he lynchpin of the FTC's complaint is its allegation that Solvay

225. *Id.*
226. *Id.*
227. *Id.* at 1301.
228. *Id.* at 1301 n.2.
229. *Id.* at 1303.
230. *Id.*

probably would have lost the underlying patent infringement action" and that "Solvay was *not likely to prevail*" in the patent litigation because "Watson and Par/Paddock developed persuasive arguments and amassed substantial evidence that their generic products did not infringe the ['894] patent and that the patent was invalid and/or unenforceable."[231] According to the court, "[t]he difficulty [] is in deciding how to resolve the tension between the pro-exclusivity tenets of patent law and the pro-competition tenets of antitrust law," a difficulty that "is made less difficult [] by the law's pro-precedent tenets" and "[o]ur earlier decisions[,]" which "carry us much of the way to a resolution [of the] case."[232] In reviewing Eleventh Circuit precedent, all of which reject the FTC's position, the court discussed the bases for these earlier decisions.

While noting that generally agreements between competitors that keep one competitor from the market to the benefit of the other and that increase costs to the public would be barred under the antitrust laws, the panel held that reverse payment cases were "atypical cases because 'one of the parties own[s] a patent.'"[233] This "[makes] all the difference" in the panel's view because the patent holder "[has] a 'lawful right to exclude others'" from the marketplace.[234] Said another way, "[t]he anticompetitive effect is already present" due to the existence of a patent.[235] Further citing *Valley Drug*, the court said that even subsequent invalidation of the patent would not render the agreement unlawful, since its lawfulness must be considered at the time of settlement, where the patent holder had "the right to exclude others."[236] What counts is the "*potential* exclusionary power" of the patent at the time of the reverse payment settlement, not its "*actual* exclusionary power" *unless* a court had rendered a negative judgment of invalidity or unenforceability prior to the settlement, which is an unlikely but not impossible scenario.[237] But the court noted that the mere existence of a patent did not give the parties to a reverse payment settlement *carte blanche*; the settlement cannot "exclude[] more competition than the patent has the potential to exclude."[238] Such agreements remain "vulnerable to antitrust attack," according to the opinion, and are subject to a "three-prong analysis" that requires an evaluation of "(1) the scope of

231. *Id.* at 1305–06 (emphasis in original).

232. *Id.* at 1306.

233. *Id.* at 1307 (quoting *Valley Drug Co. v. Geneva Pharm., Inc.*, 344 F.3d 1294, 1304 (11th Cir. 2003)).

234. *Id.* (quoting *Valley Drug*, 344 F.3d at 1304).

235. *Id.* (citing *Schering-Plough Corp. v. FTC*, 402 F.3d 1056, 1065–66 (11th Cir. 2005)).

236. *Id.* at 1308 (quoting *Valley Drug*, 344 F.3d at 1305).

237. *Id.* at 1308 (emphasis in original).

238. *Id.*

the exclusionary potential of the patent; (2) the extent to which the agreements exceed that scope; and (3) the resulting anticompetitive effects."[239]

In another footnote, the court also clarified the meaning of the term "strength of the patent" as used in the *Schering-Plough* case:

> The FTC's brief in this case places great weight on our statement in Schering-Plough that a proper antitrust analysis of reverse payment agreements needs to "evaluate the strength of the patent."[240]
>
> The FTC argues that evaluating the "strength of the patent" means evaluating "the strength of the patent holder's claims of validity and infringement, as objectively viewed at the time of settlement." We disagree. When read in the context of the facts and the reasoning of Schering-Plough, the phrase "strength of the patent" refers to the potential exclusionary scope of the patent—that is, the exclusionary rights appearing on the patent's face and not the underlying merits of the infringement claim. Nowhere in the Schering-Plough opinion did we actually evaluate the merits of the infringement claim when defining how much competition the patent could potentially exclude from the market.[241]

The court also provided useful contrast between these earlier cases denying antitrust liability and another case, *Andrx Pharmaceuticals v. Elan*,[242] in which the court reversed dismissal of an antitrust case brought by a private party.[243] In that case, the generic-drug maker "had agreed 'to refrain from *ever* marketing a generic' version of the patented drug," and the generic-drug maker was permitted to "retain its 180 day exclusivity period" despite having "no intention of marketing the drug" in this country.[244] This resulted in the generic-drug maker's 180-day exclusivity period to "act[] like a cork in a bottle" preventing another generic-drug maker from entering the market.[245] This tactic was eliminated by later amendments to the statute wherein the first ANDA filer can forfeit its exclusivity rights if it fails to market a generic version of a patented drug "within certain time periods."[246]

The court then synthesized the rule from these cases:

> [A]bsent sham litigation or fraud in obtaining the patent, a reverse payment settlement is immune from antitrust attack so long as

239. *Id.* at 1308, 1310 (citing *Schering-Plough*, 402 F.3d at 1066).
240. *Schering-Plough*, 402 F.3d at 1076 (emphasis added).
241. *Watson Pharm., Inc.*, 677 F.3d at 1311 n.8.
242. *Andrx Pharm., Inc. v. Elan Corp.*, 421 F.3d 1227 (11th Cir. 2005).
243. *Watson Pharm., Inc.*, 677 F.3d at 1312.
244. *Id.* at 1311–12 (quoting *Andrx Pharm.*, 421 F.3d at 1231, 1235).
245. *Id.* at 1311.
246. 21 U.S.C. § 355(j)(5)(D).

> its anticompetitive effects fall within the scope of the exclusionary potential of the patent.[247]

The court assessed the FTC's allegations under this standard, noting those allegations to be that (1) Solvay was "not likely to prevail" in the underlying patent infringement litigation; (2) accordingly the patent has "*no* exclusionary potential" (emphasis in original); and (3) if a patent has no exclusionary potential, the reverse payment arrangement "necessarily" exceeds its "potential exclusionary scope" and thus is tantamount to "'buying off' a serious threat to competition."[248] The FTC urged the court, according to the opinion, "to adopt 'a rule that an exclusion payment is unlawful if, viewing the situation objectively as of the time of the settlement, it is more likely than not that the patent would not have blocked generic entry earlier than the agreed-upon entry date.'"[249]

The court "decline[d] the FTC's invitation and reject[ed] its argument," saying that to adopt either would "equate[] a likely result (failure of an infringement claim) with an actual result."[250] In this context, according to the court, if Solvay was "likely" to fail to survive litigation that meant its chances were 51 percent to 49 percent; under these circumstances "as many as 49 out of 100 times that an infringement claim is 'likely' to fail it actually will succeed and keep the competitor out of the market."[251] Under these circumstances the court reasoned that "[r]ational parties settle to cap the cost of litigation and to avoid the chance of losing," noting that "[o]ne side or the other almost always has a better chance of prevailing, but a chance is only a chance, not a certainty."[252] The rationality, rather than possible perfidy, of this behavior is illustrated colorfully as follows:

> A party likely to win might not want to play the odds for the same reason that one likely to survive a game of Russian roulette might not want to take a turn. With four chambers of a seven-chamber revolver unloaded, a party pulling the trigger is likely (57% to 43%) to survive, but the undertaking is still one that can lead to undertaking.[253]

Patent litigation is analogous, according to the opinion, and "[w]hen both sides of a dispute have a substantial chance of winning and losing, especially when their chances may be 49% to 51%, it is reasonable for them

247. *Watson Pharm., Inc.*, 677 F.3d at 1312.
248. *Id.*
249. *Id.*
250. *Id.*
251. *Id.*
252. *Id.* at 1313.
253. *Id.*

to settle" without incurring antitrust liability for doing so.[254] The court continued its theme of the rationality of this behavior, citing the opinion in *In re Ciprofloxacin Hydrochloride*.

> No matter how valid a patent is—no matter how often it has been upheld in other litigation or successfully reexamined—it is still a gamble to place a technology case in the hands of a lay judge or jury. Even the confident patent owner knows that the chances of prevailing in patent litigation rarely exceed seventy percent. Thus, there are risks involved even in that rare case with great prospects.[255]

In addition, the court noted practical difficulties with the FTC's approach, including "an after-the-fact calculation of how 'likely' a patent holder was to succeed in a settled lawsuit if it had not been settled," calling it a "retrospective predict-the-likely-outcome-that-never-came approach" and noting that "[p]redicting the future is precarious at best; retroactively predicting from a past perspective a future that never occurred is even more perilous."[256] "And it is too perilous an enterprise to serve as a basis for antitrust liability and treble damages."[257] The court also emphasized the burden on the parties and the courts in this approach, noting that it would discourage settlements against the general consensus that settlements of litigation should be encouraged. The court further noted that the FTC itself had voiced concerns over the approach now espoused in appeal:

> An after-the-fact inquiry by the Commission into the merits of the underlying litigation is not only unlikely to be particularly helpful, but also likely to be unreliable. As a general matter, tribunals decide patent issues in the context of a true adversary proceeding, and their opinions are informed by the arguments of opposing counsel. Once a case settles, however, the interests of the formerly contending parties are aligned. A generic competitor that has agreed to delay its entry no longer has an incentive to attack vigorously the validity of the patent in issue or a claim of infringement.[258]

Finally, the court suggested that the FTC's concerns are likely to be overstated because of "the reality that there usually are many potential challengers to a patent, at least to drug patents" and other generic

254. *Id.*

255. *Id.* (citing *In re Ciprofloxacin Hydrochloride Antitrust Litig.*, 261 F. Supp. 2d 188, 208 (E.D.N.Y. 2003)).

256. *Id.* at 1313–14.

257. *Id.*

258. *Id.* at 1314 (quoting *In re Schering-Plough Corp.*, No. 9297, 2003 WL 22989651, at *22 (F.T.C. Dec. 8, 2003)).

competitors will arise to challenge the patent.[259] If the FTC is correct that reverse payment arrangements indicate a "weak" or vulnerable patent, the "[b]lood in the water" will likely provoke a "feeding frenzy" of other challenges in the court's view.[260] "Although a patent holder may be able to escape the jaws of competition by sharing monopoly profits with the first one or two generic challengers, those profits will be eaten away as more and more generic companies enter the waters by filing their own paragraph IV certifications attacking the patent."[261]

Together, these cases defined what became known as "the scope of the patent" test for reverse settlement payment agreements. Under this test, an agreement that did not exceed the legitimate scope of the patent, presumed valid by statute, did not raise antitrust concerns or liability.

This position was soundly rejected in *In re K-Dur*, from the Third Circuit, where a three-judge panel agreed with the FTC that such agreements should be presumptively illegal.[262] The facts of the case are these. The drug K-Dur 20 is a specific formulation of potassium chloride sold by Schering-Plough Co. (now owned by Merck) and protected by a formulation patent, U.S. Patent No. 4,863,743.

The action in this case named as plaintiffs drug wholesalers (Louisiana Wholesale Drug Co.) and retailers (CVS Pharmacy, Rite Aid, Walgreens, Eckerd, Safeway, Kroger, Albertson's, Hy-Vee and Maxi Drug) against Merck & Co. (the successor-in-interest to Schering-Plough) and Upsher-Smith Laboratories. Characterized as "separate from the FTC's challenge" but no doubt motivated by it, the plaintiffs here filed various lawsuits that were consolidated in the District of New Jersey by the Judicial Panel on Multidistrict Litigation, fortuitously for plaintiffs and the FTC, in an appellate circuit that had not ruled on the reverse payment practice.[263] A special master appointed by the court filed a report and recommendation that the lawsuits be dismissed, based on Schering's right under the patents to "exclude infringing products until the end of [the patent's] term," and that reverse payment agreements warrant antitrust scrutiny only if they either exceeded the scope of the underlying patents or if the patent infringement lawsuits brought under the authority of the

259. *Id.* at 1315.

260. *Id.*

261. *Id.*; also noting Herbert Hovenkamp, *Sensible Antitrust Rules for Pharmaceutical Competition*, 39 U. S.F. L. Rev. 11, 25 (2004) ("In a world in which there are numerous firms willing and able to enter the market, an exit payment to one particular infringement defendant need not have significant anticompetitive effects. If there is good reason for believing the patent [is] invalid others will try the same thing.").

262. *See In re K-Dur Antitrust Litig.*, 686 F.3d 197, 218 (3d Cir. 2012), *cert. granted*, 133 S. Ct. 2849, 186 L. Ed. 2d 904 (2013), *vacated and remanded sub nom. Upsher–Smith Labs., Inc. v. Louisiana Wholesale Drug Co.*, 133 S. Ct. 2849 (2013).

263. *Id.* at 207.

patents were objectively baseless, grounds that other appellate circuits had also considered in assessing the legality of reverse payment agreements.[264]

The Third Circuit rejected the precedent of its sister circuits, finding reverse payment agreements to be presumptively illegal.[265] The court set forth its opinion that the proper approach is to evaluate any agreement alleged to be one that restrains trade by the "rule of reason," following its appreciation of applicable Supreme Court precedent. In doing so, the opinion stated that "the finder of fact must decide whether the questioned practice imposes an unreasonable restraint on competition, taking into account a variety of factors, including specific information about the relevant business, its condition before and after the restraint was imposed, and the restraint's history, nature, and effect."[266] This inquiry has three parts, according to the Third Circuit: there must be a showing of an anticompetitive effect on the market, which if established, shifts the burden "to the defendant to show that the challenged conduct promotes a sufficiently pro-competitive effect."[267] The antitrust plaintiff can rebut this showing if it can establish that the restraint on trade is not "reasonably necessary to achieve the [purportedly] pro-competitive objective" asserted by the antitrust defendant.[268]

The opinion rejected what it termed "precedent from other circuits"—namely, cases that have almost unanimously found reverse payment agreements to be lawful.[269] The opinion noted that in each case, the appellate court found the reverse payments to be lawful based on the patent's presumption of validity and the patent holder's right to exclude, and that the agreements did not involve an improper extension of that exclusionary right, as well as the policy considerations involving favoring settlements. The panel opinion termed these considerations the "scope of the patent" test. In a footnote, the panel acknowledged these decisions, but finding that they are persuasive and not binding authority and that the panel does not find the arguments persuasive, they "decline to follow [them]."[270]

The panel then explained that it did not believe that the "scope of the patent" test was the appropriate test and should not entitle reverse

---

264. *Id.* at 208.

265. *Id.* at 209–14.

266. *Id.* at 209 (citing *State Oil Co. v. Khan*, 522 U.S. 3, 10 (1997)).

267. *Id.*

268. *Id.*

269. *Id.* at 211–12; *see Valley Drug Co. v. Geneva Pharm., Inc.*, 344 F.3d 1294 (11th Cir. 2003); *Schering-Plough Corp. v. FTC*, 402 F.3d 1056 (11th Cir. 2005); *In re Tamoxifen Citrate Antitrust Litig.*, 466 F.3d 187 (2d Cir. 2006), *Ark. Carpenters Health & Welfare Fund v. Bayer AG*, 604 F.3d 98, 105 (2d Cir. 2010); *In re Ciprofloxacin Hydrochloride Antitrust Litig.*, 544 F.3d 1323 (Fed. Cir. 2008).

270. *In re K-Dur Antitrust Litig.*, 686 F.3d.at 211 n.8.

payments to avoid antitrust scrutiny. The opinion formed this conclusion because "that test [in the panel's view] improperly restricts the application of antitrust law and is contrary to the policies underlying the Hatch-Waxman Act and a long line of Supreme Court precedent on patent litigation and competition."[271] The opinion provided three grounds for this conclusion. First, the opinion stated that it creates "an almost unrebuttable presumption of patent validity," due to the fact that the settlement "forces a presumption that the patent holder would have prevailed" in the underlying and settled ANDA litigation.[272] This presumption has or should have no substantive vitality, according to the panel, because it is merely "a procedural device and is not a substantive right of the patent holder."[273] The opinion also believed using the presumption of validity to uphold reverse payment agreements was "particularly misguided" when the basis for the underlying patent infringement defense is non-infringement as it was in this case, because the burden is properly on the patent holder, not the challenger, to prove infringement.[274] The panel opinion further "question[ed] the assumption" that subsequent ANDA filers will come forward to challenge "weak" patents.[275]

The Third Circuit panel considered perceived pernicious effects on reverse settlements as being directed to first ANDA filers, which it asserts are the "most motivated" due to the promise of 180 days of market exclusivity.[276] The panel also cited several Supreme Court cases for the proposition that patent rights are "a limited exception to a general rule of the free exploitation of ideas" that indicate that "the public interest supports judicial testing and elimination of weak patents." This is in contrast to the Eleventh Circuit's recognition that:

> No matter how valid a patent is—no matter how often it has been upheld in other litigation or successfully reexamined—it is still a gamble to place a technology case in the hands of a lay judge or jury. Even the confident patent owner knows that the chances of prevailing in patent litigation rarely exceed seventy percent. Thus, there are risks involved even in that rare case with great prospects.[277]

---

271. *Id.* at 214.
272. *Id.* at 214–15.
273. *Id.* at 214 (citing *Stratoflex, Inc. v. Aeroquip Corp.*, 713 F.2d 1530, 1534 (Fed. Cir. 1983)).
274. *Id.* at 214.
275. *Id.* at 215.
276. *Id.*
277. *See In re Ciprofloxacin Hydrochloride Antitrust Litig.*, 261 F. Supp. 2d 188, 208 (E.D.N.Y. 2003).

The panel explicitly limited the scope of its decision to "reverse payments between patent holders and would be [*sic*] generic competitors in the pharmaceutical industry."[278] It is clear that the panel was motivated at least in part by its perception, as argued by the FTC, that reverse payment settlement agreements were contrary to and in contravention of congressional goals of "increas[ing] the availability of low cost generic drugs" (despite findings in other circuits that in some circumstances reverse payment settlements do just that).[279] Nevertheless, the panel found that "[t]he line that Congress drew between these competing objectives [of stimulating innovation and furthering the public interest] strongly supports the application of rule of reason scrutiny of reverse payment settlements in the pharmaceutical industry."[280] Moreover, the panel limited the scope of its decision only to settlements that involve payments from the patent holder to the putative generic drug competitor:

> Nothing in the rule of reason test that we adopt here limits the ability of the parties to reach settlements based on a negotiated entry date for marketing of the generic drug: the only settlements subject to antitrust scrutiny are those involving a reverse payment from the name brand manufacturer to the generic challenger.[281]

According to the court, "the vast majority of pharmaceutical patent settlement [will be] unaffected" by its ruling.[282]

The proper procedure under Third Circuit law is thus to use a "quick look" rule of reason analysis "based on the economic realities of the reverse payment settlement rather than the labels applied by the settling parties" and that "any payment from a patent holder to a generic patent challenger who agrees to delay entry into the market as *prima facie* evidence of an unreasonable restraint of trade." In doing so, the court also "agree[d] with the FTC that there is no need to consider the merits of the underlying patent suit because '[a]bsent proof of other offsetting consideration, it is logical to conclude that the *quid pro quo* for the payment was an agreement by the generic to defer entry beyond the date that represents an otherwise reasonable litigation compromise,'" citing the commission's final order in this matter, which was overturned by the Eleventh Circuit.

The FTC as well as the parties, both the brand-name and generic-drug makers, petitioned for certiorari, but the commission asked the Supreme Court to grant certiorari in a different case, *FTC v. Watson*

278. *In re K-Dur Antitrust Litig.*, 686 F.3d at 216.
279. *Id.* at 217.
280. *Id.*
281. *Id.* at 217–18.
282. *Id.* at 218.

Pharmaceuticals, Inc., from the Eleventh Circuit. The question presented in the FTC's certiorari petition is prefaced by a long prelude, and eventually reads as follows:

> Federal competition law generally prohibits an incumbent firm from agreeing to pay a potential competitor to stay out of the market.[283] This case concerns agreements between (1) the manufacturer of a brand-name drug on which the manufacturer assertedly holds a patent, and (2) potential generic competitors who, in response to patent-infringement litigation brought against them by the manufacturer, defended on the grounds that their products would not infringe the patent and that the patent was invalid. The patent litigation culminated in a settlement through which the seller of the brand-name drug agreed to pay its would be generic competitors tens of millions of dollars annually, and those competitors agreed not to sell competing generic drugs for a number of years. Settlements containing that combination of terms are commonly known as "reverse payment" agreements.
>
> The question presented is as follows: Whether reverse-payment agreements are per se lawful unless the underlying patent litigation was a sham or the patent was obtained by fraud (as the court below held), or instead are presumptively anticompetitive and unlawful (as the Third Circuit has held).[284]

The commission's brief recited many of the same reasons supporting a certiorari grant that have been raised by the parties and amici in the certiorari petition in the *K-Dur* case: the circuit split, the importance of the issues to healthcare and the drug industry, and the substantive question of whether the Third Circuit's approach of presumptive illegality, or the Second, Eleventh, and Federal Circuits' approach of legality within the boundaries of the "scope of the patent," is the correct basis for assessing these agreements. However, the commission brought its own unique perspective to each question.

With regard to the circuit split, the commission argued, with no apparent irony, the likelihood of forum shopping should the court not step in to resolve the circuit split it tried very hard to create by forum shopping itself.[285] The petition also bemoaned that "[t]he near certainty of facing judicial review in a circuit that applies the scope-of-the-patent approach

283. *See Palmer v. BRG of Ga., Inc.*, 498 U.S. 46, 49–50 (1990).

284. Petition for Writ of Certiorari, *FTC v. Watson Pharm., Inc.*, 2012 WL 4750283 (11th Cir. 2012) *cert. granted*, 133 S. Ct. 787 (U.S. 2012).

285. *Id.* at *15.

has effectively disabled the FTC from proceeding administratively against any reverse-payment agreement," in the face of the commissioner affirmatively stating that the FTC will be filing all its reverse payment cases in district courts in the Third Circuit.[286] The "important question" argument is based entirely on the FTC's views of the economics of the branded and generic-drug marketplace, citing only academic studies and its own reports in support of its argument. In this regard it also cited some dated (vintage 1992–2000) statistics to the effect that generic-drug manufacturers prevail ~75 percent of the time in ANDA litigation.[287] In addition, its arguments regarding the "scope of the patent" test and its purported legal error were based predominantly on cases that relate to "naked" restraints of trade and that ignore the exclusionary rights of the patent holder and the regulatory framework imposed on Hatch-Waxman litigation.

The FTC's principal new argument was that the *Watson* case provides a "superior vehicle" for Supreme Court review, supported by four arguments. First, the brief argued, the *K-Dur* case is a private cause of action and the *Watson* case is an FTC enforcement action, brought by the government agency "charged by Congress with challenging unfair methods of competition, see 15 U.S.C. § 45, and responsible for reviewing agreements settling litigation under the Hatch-Waxman Amendments."[288] "The Court would benefit from the experienced presentation that the FTC, represented by the Solicitor General, would offer as a party" rather than an amicus, the brief argues.[289]

The FTC's second argument was that the *Watson* case has a "simpler" procedural history, arising from a motion to dismiss under Federal Rule of Civil Procedure 12(b)(6) rather than from a grant of a summary judgment motion.[290]

The third argument set forth by the FTC was that the *K-Dur* case is about post hoc damages (the agreements expired long ago), whereas the *Watson* case is about injunctive relief on agreements that will keep the generic parties off the market until 2015.[291] The FTC summarized its position by stating:

> That makes this case the more attractive vehicle because whatever uncertainties may arise in fixing the damages caused by a reverse-payment agreement—a question no court of appeals has confronted or passed upon—the FTC unquestionably will be enti-

286. *Id.*
287. *Id.* at *16.
288. *Id.* at *29–30.
289. *Id.* at *30.
290. *Id.*
291. *Id.* at *31–32.

tled to the remedy of an injunction if it proves that the reverse-payment agreements here are unfair methods of competition.[292]

The FTC's fourth and final argument was that the *K-Dur* case does not involve a Paragraph IV allegation of invalidity, which at first blush appears to provide an attractive reason for the Court to preferentially consider these issues by granting *certiorari* in the *Watson* case.[293] However, the *grounds* for deciding whether the agreement is anticompetitive and thus illegal should not depend on whether the product does not infringe or the patent is invalid. Those considerations are only relevant to the type of arguments the FTC petitioner wants to make, which at root are that the litigation is based on a "bad" patent and thus the patent should not be entitled to the presumption of validity.

§ 5.1.3 The Supreme Court Decision in *Actavis*

The Supreme Court granted certiorari in the *Watson* case, which is now styled *FTC v. Actavis*,[294] heard oral argument and ruled five to three in favor of the FTC. Writing for the majority that included Justices Kennedy, Ginsburg, Sotomayor and Kagan, Justice Breyer's opinion reversed the decision of the Eleventh Circuit Court of Appeals dismissing the FTC's complaint that a "reverse payment" settlement agreement between an innovator drugmaker and generics challengers in ANDA litigation was anticompetitive and violated the antitrust laws. The Court refused to accept the FTC's position that such agreements are presumptively unlawful, holding that lower courts should apply an antitrust "rule of reason" analysis when evaluating such agreements.

In the majority opinion, Justice Breyer wrote that reverse payment settlement agreements can "sometimes violate the antitrust laws,"[295] and thus that the district court should not have dismissed the case brought by the FTC. After discussing the Hatch-Waxman statutory scheme and the facts of the case below, the opinion focused on the risk to the consuming public posed by such settlements in cases where the patent is invalid or not infringed. According to the majority, although the Court was willing to accept that the agreement's "anticompetitive effects fall within the scope of the exclusionary potential of the patent," this fact was not sufficient to "immunize the agreement from antitrust attack."[296] The majority's concern was that while the holder of a valid patent may be exempt from antitrust

292. *Id.* (citing *Blue Cross & Blue Shield United v. Marshfield Clinic*, 152 F.3d 588, 591 (7th Cir. 1998)).

293. *Id.* at *32–33.

294. 133 S. Ct. 2223 (2013).

295. *Id.* at 2227.

296. *Id.* at 2230.

liability when enforcing the exclusionary right, ANDA litigation involves an allegation that either the patent is invalid, in which case the immunization is lost, or the generic product does not infringe, in which case the patent cannot be enforced against the non-infringing generic drug. Accordingly, such agreements "tend to have significant adverse effects on competition."[297] For this reason, the majority believed that "it would be incongruous to determine antitrust legality by measuring the settlement's anticompetitive effects solely against patent law policy, rather than by measuring them against procompetitive antitrust policies as well."[298] Support for this proposition, which was vigorously disputed by the dissenting justices (discussed later), can be found in Justice Breyer's reading of several of the Court's earlier cases.[299] Consequently:

> [R]ather than measure the length or amount of a restriction solely against the length of the patent's term or its earning potential, as the Court of Appeals apparently did here, this Court answered the antitrust question by considering traditional antitrust factors such as likely anticompetitive effects, redeeming virtues, market power, and potentially offsetting legal considerations present in the circumstances, such as here those related to patents.[300]

The opinion also cited several earlier cases in which settlement agreements not in the Hatch-Waxman context were held to violate the antitrust laws.[301] The question of whether any of these situations are at all relevant to reverse payment settlement agreements was not addressed in the opinion, which merely seemed content to find cases where the Court has in the past found that settlement agreements are not outside the scope of antitrust scrutiny and does not consider whether the circumstances surrounding this prior approbation is in any way related to the question before the Court. The majority seemed to be seeking some sort of "balance" with regard to accommodating patent and antitrust policies, reminiscent

---

297. *Id.* at 2231.

298. *Id.*

299. *See Walker Process Equip., Inc. v. Food Mach. & Chem. Corp.*, 382 U.S. 172 (1965) (incongruously, a case that established one of the grounds for finding reverse payment settlement agreements unlawful, i.e., asserting a patent obtained by "fraud on the Patent Office"), *United States v. Line Materials Co.*, 333 U.S. 287 (1948) (retail price-setting between patent holders); *United States v. U.S. Gypsum Co.*, 333 U.S. 364 (1948) (both cases where the only patents that were valid were those the Court had not yet ruled upon).

300. *FTC v. Actavis, Inc.*, 133 S. Ct. at 2231.

301. *See United States v. Singer Mfg. Co.*, 374 U.S. 174 (1963) (where the issue was collusion between three patent holders to enforce the strongest patent against their competitors); *United States v. New Wrinkle, Inc.*, 342 U.S. 371 (1952) (price fixing); *Standard Oil Co. (Ind.) v. United States*, 283 U.S. 163 (1931) (patent holders setting royalty rates).

of Justice Breyer's statements in *Mayo v. Prometheus*[302] that there needs to be a balance in patent law between sufficient patenting to creating incentives to innovation and avoiding excessive patenting that could inhibit innovation.[303] Finally, the Court found that the "procompetitive" purposes of the Hatch-Waxman Act are consistent with having courts apply antitrust principles to reverse payment settlement agreements in ANDA litigation.[304]

Turning to the "general legal policy favoring the settlement of disputes," Justice Breyer's opinion did not find sufficient force in this policy to override the majority's concerns regarding anticompetitive effects of reverse payment settlement agreements, even though the majority recognized the Eleventh Circuit's concern that "antitrust scrutiny of a reverse payment agreement would require the parties to litigate the validity of the patent in order to demonstrate what would have happened to competition in the absence of the settlement," an outcome that "will prove time consuming, complex, and expensive."[305] In response to this concern, the majority offered five "considerations" as its basis for its holding that the FTC should be permitted to establish an antitrust violation.

> First, the specific restraint at issue has the "potential for genuine adverse effects on competition." . . . The payment in effect amounts to a purchase by the patent holder of the exclusive right to sell its product, a right it already claims but would lose if the patent litigation were to continue and the patent were held invalid or not infringed by the generic product.[306]

The opinion also stated this concern as "[t]he patentee and the challenger gain; the consumer loses," citing academic sources and amicus briefs for the proposition that "there are indications that patentees sometimes pay a generic challenger a sum even larger than what the generic would gain in profits if it won the paragraph IV litigation and entered the market."[307] Under these circumstances, "a payment of this size . . . may [] provide strong evidence that the patentee seeks to induce the generic challenger to abandon its claim with a share of its monopoly profits that would otherwise be lost in the competitive market."[308] Moreover, the majority disparaged the idea that entering into such an agreement would merely

302. *Mayo Collaborative Servs. v. Prometheus Labs., Inc.*, 132 S. Ct. 1289 (2012).
303. *Actavis*, 133 S. Ct. at 2231–32.
304. *Id.* at 2234.
305. *Id.*
306. *Id.* (quoting *F.T.C. v. Indiana Fed'n of Dentists*, 476 U.S. 447, 460-61 (1986)).
307. *Actavis*, 133 S. Ct. at 2235.
308. *Id.*

entice other generic challengers to get in line to be bought off by the patent holder, based on the loss of the 180-day exclusivity for later ANDA filers and the thirty-month delay in FDA approval raised by ANDA litigation against such a subsequent filer. These considerations convinced the majority that, rather than producing an untenable situation in which the owner of a weak patent cannot possibly "buy off" all potential competitors, the Hatch-Waxman regime in fact produces a critical generic challenger, the first filer, who if successfully bought off by a reverse payment settlement agreement will effectively chill future challenges by other generic-drug makers.

> *Second*, these anticompetitive consequences will at least sometimes prove unjustified. [The majority's concern is that a court cannot tell without inquiry whether a particular reverse payment settlement agreement is or is not "justified" under antitrust principles.] . . . Where a reverse payment reflects traditional settlement considerations, such as avoided litigation costs or fair value for services, there is not the same concern that a patent holder is using its monopoly profits to avoid the risk of patent invalidation or a finding of noninfringement. In such cases, the parties may have provided for a reverse payment without having sought or brought about [] anticompetitive consequences.[309]

This uncertainty formed the basis for the majority to conclude that the district court erred in dismissing the FTC's complaint, because by doing so it denied the commission the chance to establish whether or not there were such justifications for the agreement.

> *Third*, where a reverse payment threatens to work unjustified anticompetitive harm, the patentee likely possesses the power to bring that harm about in practice.[310]

Once again the majority is concerned with the size of the payment, which a court can use to be "a strong indicator of [market] power."[311]

> *Fourth*, an antitrust action is likely to prove more feasible administratively than the Eleventh Circuit believed.[312]

Here, the majority finds the Eleventh Circuit "throws the baby out with the bathwater" by refusing to apply antitrust principles due to the difficulties of litigating patent infringement and validity, when of course

309. *Id.* at 2235–36.
310. *Id.*
311. *Id.* at 2236.
312. *Id.* at 2236–37.

the appellate court was merely recognizing that the impetus for these settlements would disappear should the parties be required to litigate in an antitrust context what they avoided litigating in an ANDA context.[313]

According to the majority, "it is normally not necessary to litigate patent validity to answer the antitrust question" (except for sham litigation), because "[a]n unexplained large reverse payment itself would normally suggest that the patent holder has serious doubts about the patent's survival."[314]

> *Fifth*, the fact that a large, unjustified reverse payment risks antitrust liability does not prevent litigating parties from settling their lawsuit.[315]

Here, the majority posits that the parties can settle an ANDA dispute in "other ways, [] by allowing the generic manufacturer to enter the patentee's market prior to the patent's expiration, without the patentee paying the challenger to stay out prior to that point."[316] Once again, the majority returns to the existence of a payment, saying that "the basic antitrust question" comes down to the reasons for the payment and, of course, a court's determination of whether those reasons are valid.

The majority summarized these considerations as follows:

> In sum, a reverse payment, where large and unjustified, can bring with it the risk of significant anticompetitive effects; one who makes such a payment may be unable to explain and to justify it; such a firm or individual may well possess market power derived from the patent; a court, by examining the size of the payment, may well be able to assess its likely anticompetitive effects along with its potential justifications without litigating the validity of the patent; and parties may well find ways to settle patent disputes without the use of reverse payments. In our view, these considerations, taken together, outweigh the single strong consideration—the desirability of settlements—that led the Eleventh Circuit to provide near-automatic antitrust immunity to reverse payment settlements.[317]

Simply put, these concerns amount to

1. the size of the payment;
2. whether there are "legitimate justifications" for the agreement;

313. *Id.* at 2236.
314. *Id.* at 2236.
315. *Id.* at 2237.
316. *Id.*
317. *Id.*

3. whether the patent holder has "market power";
4. the size of the reverse payment and whether it is "unexplained"; and
5. if there are other ways to settle, why the parties chose to a settlement agreement that includes a reverse payment.

The FTC did not entirely win the day with the majority. However, the majority rejected the commission's suggestion that these agreements should be presumptively unlawful and that the rule of reason be applied using a "quick look" or other shortcut, which the majority noted was permissible only in instances where "an observer with even a rudimentary understanding of economics could conclude that the arrangements in question would have an anticompetitive effect on customers and markets."[318] This treatment is not justified for reverse payment settlement agreements according to the majority, because "the likelihood of a reverse payment bringing about anticompetitive effects depends upon its size, its scale in relation to the payor's anticipated future litigation costs, its independence from other services for which it might represent payment, and the lack of any other convincing justification."[319] Instead, these justices held that the FTC must establish antitrust liability using a "rule of reason" analysis, and in doing so, district courts can structure the inquiry to avoid litigating patent validity, leaving it to these "lower" courts to determine exactly how that may be accomplished.

The Chief Justice wrote the dissent, joined by Justices Scalia and Thomas (Justice Alito recused himself from this case). Applying much of the same precedent, the dissent came to the opposite conclusion: the existence of a patent, properly cabined within its proper scope, should be enough to justify a reverse payment settlement of ANDA litigation. Instead of following "well-established" principles of patent law, the dissent asserted that the majority would "use antitrust law's amorphous rule of reason to inquire into the anticompetitive effects of such settlements."[320] Besides finding no support in the patent law or other statute, the dissent objected to the majority's ruling because it "will discourage the settlement of patent litigation."[321] According to the Chief Justice, patent law "provides an exception to antitrust law, and the scope of the patent—*i.e.*, the rights conferred by the patent—forms the zone within which the patent holder may operate without facing antitrust liability," and "[t]his should

318. *Id.* at 2237 (citing Justice Breyer's concurring-in-part and dissenting-in-part opinion in *Cal. Dental Ass'n v. FTC*, 526 U.S. 756, 770 (1999)).
319. *Id.* at 2237.
320. *Id.* at 2238.
321. *Id.*

go without saying, in part because we've said it so many times."[322] The dissent also noted that the only time a settlement was found to violate antitrust law in past Supreme Court precedent was when the settlement went beyond the boundaries of the patent grant unless the patents are obtained by fraud or the patent holder engaged in sham litigation.[323] The dissenting opinion dissected the authority cited by the majority and provided context or other statements from these cases that contradicted or threw a different light on these decisions contrary to the majority's views. In addition, the history of the application of antitrust law in the patent context is telling.

> The majority is therefore right to suggest that these "precedents make clear that patent-related settlement agreements can *sometimes* violate the antitrust laws." The key word is sometimes. And those some times are spelled out in our precedents. Those cases have made very clear that patent settlements—and for that matter, any agreements relating to patents—are subject to antitrust scrutiny if they confer benefits beyond the scope of the patent. This makes sense. A patent exempts its holder from the antitrust laws only insofar as the holder operates within the scope of the patent. When the holder steps outside the scope of the patent, he can no longer use the patent as his defense. The majority points to *no* case where a patent settlement was subject to antitrust scrutiny merely because the validity of the patent was uncertain. Not one. It is remarkable, and surely worth something, that in the 123 years since the Sherman Act was passed, we have never let antitrust law cross that Rubicon.[324]

According to the Chief Justice, "settling a patent claim *cannot possibly* impose unlawful anticompetitive harm if the patent holder is acting within the scope of a valid patent and therefore permitted to do precisely what the antitrust suit claims is unlawful."[325]

Thus, the dissenting justices contended that the majority's fancy that the antitrust question can be answered without considering the validity of the patent is unrealistic, and "depriving [the patent holder] of such a defense—if that's what the majority means to do—defeats the point of the

322. *Id.* (citing *Walker Process Equip., Inc. v. Food Mach. & Chem. Corp.*, 382 U.S. 172 (1965); *United States v. Line Mineral Co.*, 333 U.S. 287, 300 (1948); *United States v. Gen. Elec. Co.*, 272 U.S. 476, 485 (1926); *Simpson v. Union Oil Co. of Cal.*, 377 U.S. 13, 24 (1964)).

323. *Id.* at 2239 (citing *United States v. Singer Mfg. Co.*, 374 U.S. 174, 196–97 (1963); *Walker Process*, 382 U.S. at 177; *Prof'l Real Estate Investors, Inc. v. Columbia Pictures Indus., Inc.*, 508 U.S. 49, 60–61 (1993)).

324. *Id.* at 2242.

325. *Id.* at 2244 (emphasis in opinion).

patent, which is to confer a *lawful* monopoly on its holder."[326] Moreover, the dissent evinced little faith in the many presumptions underlying the majority opinion, regarding the mechanics and purpose of the Hatch-Waxman Act or how district courts will apply the Court's decision.

> Good luck to the district courts that must, when faced with a patent settlement, weigh the "likely anticompetitive effects, redeeming virtues, market power, and potentially offsetting legal considerations present in the circumstances."[327]

The policy implications are bleak regarding benefits to the consumer.

> The irony of all this is that the majority's decision may very well discourage generics from challenging pharmaceutical patents in the first place. Patent litigation is costly, time consuming, and uncertain. . . . Generics "enter this risky terrain only after careful analysis of the potential gains if they prevail and the potential exposure if they lose." . . . Taking the prospect of settlements off the table—or limiting settlements to an earlier entry date for the generic, which may still be many years in the future—puts a damper on the generic's expected value going into litigation, and decreases its incentive to sue in the first place. The majority assures us, with no support, that everything will be okay because the parties can settle by simply negotiating an earlier entry date for the generic drug manufacturer, rather than settling with money. . . . But it's a matter of common sense, confirmed by experience, that parties are more likely to settle when they have a broader set of valuable things to trade.[328]

The Court's decision will subject settlement of ANDA litigation to increased antitrust scrutiny and, as a consequence, likely harm generics competition. With settlement raising the risk of antitrust liability for both branded pharmaceutical companies and generic-drug makers, there will be increased incentives to litigate every case to conclusion, to avoid antitrust scrutiny involving the same or similar infringement and validity questions better settled in ANDA litigation. If inclined to settle, companies are likely to agree to non-monetary consideration (such as agreements over "branded generics") rather than the types of "reverse payments" at issue in the *Watson* case. The success of this strategy will be almost immediately tested, in view of the FTC's position that transfer of "anything of

326. *Id.* (emphasis in opinion).
327. *Id.* at 2245.
328. *Id.* at 2247 (citations omitted).

value" from the brand-name-drug maker to a generics competitor should also merit scrutiny for antitrust liability. The Court's decision has reduced incentives to settle, but it remains to be seen whether the lack of reverse payment settlement agreement options will be enough to counter the conventional economic incentives favoring settlements (after all, ANDA litigation is settled with or without reverse payments as a function of both high litigation costs, risk of patent invalidation, and timing in the lifecycle of a particular branded drug). Depending on how these different incentives influence the timing of generic drug entry will determine whether the consequences that the majority envisioned (cheaper generic drugs coming on the market faster) actually come to pass.

In the meantime, while awaiting the Supreme Court's decision, at least one district court applied the Third Circuit's standard in the *K-Dur* litigation and granted a motion to dismiss under Federal Rule of Civil Procedure 12(b)(6). Regarding ANDA litigation of the Orange Book–listed U.S. Patent 4,602,017 for the drug lamotrigine, Lactomal, prescribed for epilepsy and bipolar disorder, the district court in *In re Lamictal Direct Purchaser Antitrust Litigation*[329] considered the legality, for antitrust purposes, of a settlement agreement between Glaxo-Smith Kline (GSK) and Teva having the following provisions:

- Teva was permitted to sell generic lamotrigine chewables approximately thirty-seven months before the expiration of the '017 patent, and also before the FDA approved Teva's ANDA for lamotrigine tablets. GSK supplied the chewables to Teva and Teva began selling them on May 25, 2005.
- Teva was permitted to sell generic lamotrigine tablets on July 21, 2008, the expiration date of the '017 patent. At this time, the FDA had requested GSK to conduct pediatric studies and GSK intended to comply. If GSK did not receive pediatric exclusivity, Teva would be allowed to market and sell the tablets six months earlier, on March 1, 2008.
- GSK granted Teva an exclusive waiver of any pediatric exclusivity that might be granted to GSK.
- GSK further agreed not to launch its own authorized generic versions of Lamictal products until January 2009 by giving Teva an exclusive license.

The plaintiff, in a putative class action lawsuit, contended that the agreement constituted a "reverse payment" settlement that the court

329. *In re Lamictal Direct Purchaser Antitrust Litig.*, Civ. No. 12–995, 2012 WL 6725580 (D.N.J. Dec. 6, 2012).

should assess under the "quick look" rule of reason according to the Third Circuit's decision in the *K-Dur* opinion. Had the district court done so, any decision stemming from such an analysis would be subject to reversal under the Supreme Court's *Actavis* decision. The district court disagreed, finding that the *K-Dur* precedent was directly related to reverse payments, and that whereas here there were no payments then the "scope of the patent" test was the appropriate measure of the legality of the agreement. The district court expressly rejected plaintiffs' argument that the provisions in the agreement amounted to a payment as being synonymous with "significant consideration, incentives, and benefits," stating that:

> Without doubt Teva received consideration in the settlement. Otherwise, there would be no incentive to settle. A law student learns in the first semester that consideration is an essential element of any enforceable contract. In this sense, there is "payment" in every settlement.[330]

The district court held that the Third Circuit's *K-Dur* opinion did not require antitrust scrutiny for the agreement between GSK and Teva because it did not involve a cash payment, an interpretation the court supported by looking to the factual bases the Third Circuit used in rendering its decision. These included both the express language of the *K-Dur* decision,"[t]he scope of the patent test is criticized because it 'enable[s] the holder of a patent . . . to *buy* its way out of both competition with the challenging competitor and possible invalidation of the patent.'"[331] And included other factors such as the Third Circuit's reliance upon the 2010 FTC Study that showed 75 percent of ANDA settlement agreements did not include a cash payment from the branded-drug maker to the generic manufacturer, and thus that according to the circuit court's decision "'the vast majority of pharmaceutical patent settlements' will remain 'unaffected.'"[332]

However, in another case, it is likely that the district court may need to revisit its decision, provided that antitrust plaintiffs are not outside the procedural times for appealing the court's decision. In *Louisiana Wholesale Drug v. Shire*,[333] the district court applied the "scope of the patent" test under the Second Circuit's *Tamoxifen* decision in granting the ANDA parties' motion to dismiss an action brought by a class of wholesale drug suppliers and others. The case involved settlement of ANDA litigation between Shire and two generic companies, Teva and Impax, over Adderall XR, a drug used for treating attention deficit hyperactivity disorder

330. *In re Lamictal*, 2012 WL 6725580, at *6.
331. *Id.* (emphasis in opinion).
332. *Id.* at *7.
333. *La. Wholesale Drug Co. v. Shire LLC*, 929 F. Supp. 2d 256 (S.D.N.Y. 2013).

(ADHD). Under the terms of the agreement, the generic companies agreed not to launch their generic versions of Adderall for about three years after the settlement. Thereafter, Shire agreed to license both generic companies to sell generic Adderall XR, and moreover agreed to supply the totality of Teva's and Impax's needs for generic Adderall XR (these provisions of the licenses were supported by separate agreements). The plaintiffs distinguished the circumstances in this case from the *Tamoxifen* and other reverse payment settlement agreement cases because Shire reneged on its promise to supply Teva and Impax with all the generic Adderall XR they required, behavior that plaintiffs alleged was anticompetitive. The district court's reasoning in granting the motion to dismiss was that, under circumstances where the patent right permitted Shire not to settle or, alternatively, settle merely by making a cash payment, Shire's failure to live up to the entirety of its agreement could not raise antitrust liability. After the Supreme Court's *Actavis* decision, both the agreement and Shire's behavior should be subject to antitrust scrutiny under the rule of reason.

§ 5.1.4 Post-*Actavis* Decisions

In the years since the Supreme Court handed down its decision in *Actavis*, courts (predominantly district courts) have grappled with how to apply the principles enunciated in the decision. The biggest challenge has come from instances where there is no reverse payment in the traditional sense (i.e., with the innovator paying the generics company or companies to remain off the market), but rather where something else of value is transferred. As might be expected, the results of courts' decisions on whether such arrangements warrant antitrust scrutiny have been mixed.

Some courts have taken the position that the Supreme Court's *Actavis* decision is limited to cash payments. Thus, in *In re Lamictal Direct Purchaser Antitrust Litigation*,[334] the court granted the defendant's motion to dismiss based on the absence of a tradition reverse payment. The case involved Teva's generic versions of Glaxo-Smith Kline's Lamotrigine drug and the court considered the question in view of an earlier (January 2005) decision that claim 1 of the patent was invalid as anticipated by prior art. The settlement agreement contained three provisions wherein, in exchange for settling ANDA litigation asserting challenges to GSK's patents, Teva would be allowed to market generic Lamotrigine before the relevant patent expired and ensured that its generic tablets and chewables would not face competition from GSK's own "authorized generic." Plaintiffs then filed an

334. *In re Lamictal Direct Purchaser Antitrust Litig.*, 18 F. Supp. 3d 560 (D.N.J. 2014), *vacated and remanded sub nom. King Drug Co. of Florence v. Smithkline Beecham Corp.*, 791 F.3d 388 (3d Cir. 2015).

antitrust action alleging violations of federal antitrust law prior to the Supreme Court's *Actavis* decision, which the district court dismissed the claim, reasoning that because the settlement did not involve a transfer of *money*, it "[was] not subject to antitrust scrutiny" under the Third Circuit's *K-Dur* decision.[335] In considering the issue in view of *Actavis*, the district court attempted to interpret and apply the actual holding of *Actavis* as a three-part test:

> Step One, a district court must ask, is there a reverse payment? As the Court discusses below, the answer hinges on what the parties exchanged in the settlement and must include money. In Step Two, a district court must ask, is that reverse payment large and unjustified? As the Supreme Court explained, only *certain* reverse payments will actually warrant scrutiny. *See, e.g.*, Actavis, 133 S. Ct. at 2237 (explaining that "the likelihood of a reverse payment bringing about anticompetitive effects" is not presumed but "depends upon its size, its scale in relation to the payor's anticipated future litigation costs, its independence from other services for which it might represent payment, and the lack of any other convincing justification"). Step Three is the rule of reason.[336]

The court concluded that even though *Actavis* substantially changed the patent antitrust landscape, it "applie[d] to patent settlements that contain an *unjustified reverse payment of money*"[337] and the court dismissed the antitrust allegations as inappropriate because no money had been transferred.

In like manner the district court in *In re Effexor XR Antitrust Litigation*[338] held that money must change hands in order for an ANDA settlement agreement to warrant antitrust scrutiny under *Actavis*. In this case, Teva filed its ANDA to make a generic version of Wyeth's Effexor XR product, the parties settling after the *Markman* hearing. As part of the settlement, Teva allegedly agreed to delay market entry (among other contractual obligations). The antitrust plaintiff claimed that Wyeth fulfillment of its contractual obligations to Teva that it would not compete by marketing an authorized generic operated as a reverse payment, and as a result, the plaintiffs were injured because they were deprived of price-

---

335. *In re K-Dur Antitrust Litig.*, 686 F.3d at 218 (3d Cir. 2012).

336. *In re Lamictal Direct Purchaser Antitrust Litig.*, 18 F. Supp. 3d at 565 (emphasis in opinion).

337. *Id.* at 570 (emphasis added).

338. *In re Effexor XR Antitrust Litig.*, No. 11-cv-5479, 2014 WL 4988410 (D.N.J. Oct. 6, 2014).

reducing benefits of competition. The district court applied the *Twombly* and *Iqbal* standards against the factors of *Actavis* in analyzing the plaintiff's complaint. Specifically, the court considered the question of whether there was a "large and unjustified" reverse payment where, as here, the anticompetitive effects of a settlement agreement might fall within the scope of the exclusionary potential of a patent. In doing so, the court considered four factors: what constituted a payment; was it a "reverse payment" (i.e., did the generic company benefit to a greater extent than the branded company?); how large was the payment; and was it otherwise unexplained (i.e., did the parties fail to provide evidence of precompetitive effects?). For the first factor, the court added "any consideration" from the branded-drug maker to the generic minus "avoided litigation costs" and also less the value of goods and services provided by the generic to the patentee.[339] The court found the antitrust plaintiffs had "fail[ed] to provide appropriate evidence for the Court to determine the value of the payment," so that "the allegations in the Complaint [did] not reach the plausibility standard established in *Iqbal* and *Twombly*."[340]

And in *In re Loestrin 24 Fe Antitrust Litigation*,[341] the court granted antitrust defendants motion to dismiss because there was no reverse payment between the parties as part of the ANDA settlement agreement.

The New Jersey District Court applied a slightly more nuanced analysis to the question in dismissing antitrust allegations against two different classes of antitrust plaintiffs in *In re Lipitor Antitrust Litigation*.[342] The settlement agreement in this case was exceedingly complex, involving three different drugs (Lipitor, Caduet, and Accupril) and effectuating settlement of twenty-six different litigations worldwide. The agreement did not contain a reverse payment provision, but rather absolved one of the ANDA defendants (Ranbaxy) for damages arising from an "at-risk" launch as well as avoiding litigation costs. The court held that the Supreme Court's *Actavis* decision was not limited solely to the transfer of money from the branded-drug maker to a generic company but should be reviewed for the value to the parties of the agreement. Thus, *if* the plaintiffs (albeit

339. "[T]he total payment here is seen as the value of the no authorized generic promise for Effexor XR for eleven months (as Plaintiffs also allege that Wyeth kept all other generic companies off the market until June 2011), added to the value of the allowing Teva to release a generic of Effexor IR before the expiration of the Husbands patent, subtracted by the value of the avoided litigation costs and the royalties Teva would pay to Wyeth during those eleven months." *Id.* at *22.

340. *Id.* at *23.

341. *In re Loestrin 24 Fe Antitrust Litig.*, 45 F. Supp. 3d 180 (D.R.I. 2014), *vacated*, No. 14-2071, 2016 WL 698077 (1st Cir. Feb. 22, 2016).

342. *In re Lipitor Antitrust Litig.*, 46 F. Supp. 3d 523 (D.N.J. 2014).

not *these* plaintiffs) could properly plead the economic value of what was transferred then a court could assess, under the *Actavis* rubrics, whether the agreement constituted an antitrust violation using the rule of reason. However, the burden was on plaintiffs to plead sufficient facts to support their antitrust contentions, citing the Supreme Court in *Bell Atlantic Corp. v. Twombly*[343] and *Ashcroft v. Iqbal*.[344] Plaintiffs not satisfying the court with any reliable assessment of the value of the settlement sufficient to satisfy the *Actavis* standard, the court dismissed the complaint with prejudice.

Courts uniformly found that the *Actavis* standards for antitrust scrutiny had been met when a large reverse payment had been made by a branded-drug maker to one or more generics challengers to settle ANDA litigation. In *United Food and Commercial Workers Local 1776 and Participating Employers Health and Welfare Fund v. Teikoku Pharma USA, Inc.*,[345] the branded drug companies, Endo and Teikoku, provided consideration of more that $250 million[346] in exchange for generic-drug maker Watson's agreement to delay introduction of its generic version of Lidoderm. The court stated that, post-*Actavis*: "(i) the term must be a 'payment'; (ii) the payment must be 'reverse'; (iii) the reverse payment must be 'large'; and (iv) the large reverse payment must be 'unexplained,'" in addition to the five considerations expressly set forth in *Actavis*.[347] Viewing the evidence, the court could not find "any scenario" in which the size of the payment approximated the avoided litigation costs or where Endo/Teikoku would not have perceived generic competition to be a "viable" threat, and concluded that "the solution [] was to take strong anticompetitive action through such aggressive settlement terms." In addition, Endo/Teikoku did not provide "much, if any" proof of countervailing precompetitive effect of the agreement, and the court denied their summary judgment motion on those grounds.[348]

343. *Bell Atl. Corp. v. Twombly*, 550 U.S. 544 (2007).

344. *Ashcroft v. Iqbal*, 556 U.S. 662 (2009).

345. *United Food & Commercial Workers Local 1776 & Participating Employers Health & Welfare Fund v. Teikoku Pharma USA, Inc.*, 2014 WL 6465235 (N.D. Cal. 2014).

346. These payments constituted approximately $96 million in free drug product from patentees, as well as deferred competition (worth $170 million) with Watson's generic product.

347. *United Food & Commercial Workers*, 2014 WL 6465235, at *7.

348. Somewhat ironically, the court granted summary judgment that there was no properly pled Sherman Act violation in the complaint, because both companies were named together instead of individually. The court stated that "[p]laintiffs d[id] not cite any case where a court held a manufacturer and its distributor jointly liable for violating Section 2," and that a "monopoly, by definition, consists of a single firm, and both monopolization and attempted monopolization are single-firm violations . . . [t]he very phrase 'shared monopoly' is paradoxical." *Id.* at *17.

Similarly, in *King Drug Co. of Florence v. Cephalon, Inc.*,[349] cash payments by Cephalon to four generics challengers amounting to approximately $300 million was enough for the court to apply the rule of reason to the antitrust allegations.

But other courts have found that large cash payments are not required. In *In re Aggrenox Antitrust Litigation*,[350] Boehringer and three generics companies (Teva Israel, Barr, and Duramed) agreed that generic drug entry would be delayed by eighteen months and the parties entered into a co-promotion agreement. Antitrust plaintiffs defeated a motion to dismiss when the court determined that "the total payment [under the agreement was] far greater than the fair value of the services falling under the Co-Promotion Agreement, and therefore, constitutes a large and unjustifiable reverse payment."[351]

Such non-cash contractual arrangements also provided the basis for the court to apply antitrust scrutiny to an ANDA settlement in *In re Niaspan Antitrust Litigation*.[352] In this case, the agreement contained three separate contractual provisions: a "Settlement and Licensing" provision, wherein the ANDA parties (Kos and Barr) agreed to drop all claims and counterclaims pending against each other in the patent lawsuits and Kos gave Barr a license for all of the patents related to its Niaspan drug product on the condition that Barr would not bring a generic equivalent of Niaspan to market until September 20, 2013; a "co-promotion agreement," wherein Kos agreed to pay Barr a royalty on all of Kos's sales of Niaspan as long as Barr kept its generic equivalent of Niaspan off the market, in return for which Barr agreed to promote Niaspan to obstetricians, gynecologists, and other doctors specializing in women's health; and a "license and manufacturing agreement," wherein Kos made a non-refundable lump-sum payment to Barr, ostensibly as compensation for Barr's investment in developing FDA-approved manufacturing processes for Niaspan and in which Kos agreed to make quarterly payments to Barr for every quarter that Barr remained ready to manufacture Niaspan, as Barr had agreed to serve as a ready back-up supplier to Kos for those products. The court found the economic consequences of these agreements to the parties constituted a reverse payment and that the absence of a "large" and "unjustified" cash payment was not enough to avoid antitrust scrutiny, stating that defendants' arguments that they could avoid answering the plaintiff's

349. *King Drug Co. of Florence v. Cephalon, Inc.*, 88 F. Supp. 3d 402 (E.D. Pa. Jan. 28, 2015).

350. *In re Aggrenox Antitrust Litig.*, No. 3:14-MD-2516 SRU, 2015 WL 1311352 (D. Conn. Mar. 23, 2015).

351. *Id.* at *13.

352. *In re Niaspan Antitrust Litig.*, 42 F. Supp. 3d 735 (E.D. Pa. 2014).

antitrust allegations because such a payment was absent was inconsistent ("particularly anomalous") with the tradition focus of antitrust law on "economic realities."[353]

The court came to a similar conclusion in denying antitrust defendants' motion to dismiss in *In re Nexium (Esomeprazole) Antitrust Litigation*.[354] In this case, the ANDA settlement agreement contained no cash payments but the generic companies were compensated for agreeing not to enter the market by allegedly "outsized" payments for other services as well as forgiveness for "potential" liabilities to branded-drug maker AstraZeneca. The court found that antitrust plaintiffs had adequately pled antitrust violations under the Sherman Act in the face of not "a shred of affirmative evidence tending to show that the agreements into which they allegedly entered produced any countervailing procompetitive benefits whatsoever."[355]

Other considerations can also be sufficient to satisfy the *Actavis* standards, particular agreements where the branded-drug maker agrees not to market a competing branded generic. In *In re Wellbutrin XL Antitrust Litigation*,[356] the court considered the question and suggested that such an agreement could meet the *Actavis* standard, based on the value to the generic of the agreement wherein the challenger would receive the full benefit of its 180-day exclusivity period under the Hatch-Waxman Act with no other generic competition, but has not yet decided the issue.

§ 5.2 Other ANDA-Related Antitrust Violations

§ 5.2.1 Life Cycle Management

Settlement agreements have not been the only aspect of ANDA litigation subject to antitrust challenges. Another behavior that has raised antitrust liability is so-called "life cycle management," by which branded-drug makers develop "next generation" (and patent-protected) versions of their products to compete with the generic versions of their earlier product when patent protection for said earlier product expires. While not constituting a per se violation, *how* life cycle management is effected can raise antitrust liability, particularly if the branded-drug maker's behavior can be characterized as "product hopping"—that is, changing the product in a way that discourages or prevents generic competition from the older version of the drug.

353. *Id.* at 751.

354. *In re Nexium (Esomeprazole) Antitrust Litig.*, 968 F. Supp. 2d 367 (D. Mass. 2013).

355. *Id.* at 392–93.

356. *In re Wellbutrin XL Antitrust Litig.*, No. 08-2431, 2014 WL 10435333 (E.D. Pa. Jan. 17, 2014) (No. 534).

In *In re Suboxone (Buprenorphine Hydrochloride and Naloxone) Antitrust Litigation*,[357] the branded-drug maker Reckitt Benckiser, Inc. switched its branded formulation from one sublingual form (tablets, protected by Orphan Drug exclusivity but not patented) to another sublingual formulation (a film, that was protected by Orange Book–listed patents). While ruling that merely changing formulations from one to another was not by itself enough to classify as exclusionary conduct when viewed in the relatively new light of "product hopping," as well as the pharmaceutical industry as a whole, here Reckitt also falsely disparaged the tablet through fabricated safety concerns and ultimately removed Suboxone tablets from the market just as generic Suboxone tablets were able to begin competing. Moreover, "[t]he threatened removal of the tablets from the market in conjunction with the alleged fabricated safety concerns could plausibly coerce patients and doctors to switch from tablet to film[, because] patient[s] that preferred the tablets despite the safety concerns might be further persuaded to switch to the film, believing that their favored product would soon be removed from the market."[358] Alongside other "coercive" measures, its behavior was enough to constitute exclusionary conduct that could incur antitrust liability.

Behavior seemingly more egregious was the subject of *New York v. Actavis PLC*.[359] Defendants Actavis and Forest Laboratories, LLC were accused of switching the Alzheimer's drug Namenda from an immediate release (IR) formulation (patents protecting these formulations expired in July 2015) to an extended release (XR) formulation (protected by patents expiring later); associated with this switch the defendants purportedly intended to discontinue the IR form. This was characterized in the pleadings as a "forced" switch for current patients, because physicians would not be able to substitute generic IR forms of the drugs on prescriptions written on the branded XR form. The court granted antitrust plaintiffs a preliminary injunction, ordering the defendants to continue to make Namenda IR available. Defendants appealed the injunction, but it was upheld by the Second Circuit on May 28, 2015, ruling that "[i]n sum, we conclude that the combination of withdrawing a successful drug [IR] from the market and introducing a reformulated version of that drug [XR], which has the dual effect of forcing patients to switch to the new version and impeding generic competition, without a legitimate business justification, violates

357. *In re Suboxone (Buprenorphine Hydrochloride & Naloxone) Antitrust Litig.*, 64 F. Supp. 3d 665 (E.D. Pa. Dec. 3, 2014).

358. *Id.* at 682.

359. *New York v. Actavis PLC*, No. 1:14-cv-7473, 2014 WL 5353774 (S.D.N.Y.) Ct. App. No. 14-4624 (S.D.N.Y.).

§ 2 of the Sherman Act."[360] In upholding the injunction, the court mandated that the defendants continue to make available the IR version of the drug indefinitely.

Other changes in drug product have not been found to constitute product hopping. In *Mylan Pharmaceuticals v. Warner Chilcott PLC*,[361] the court granted summary judgment to defendants on a factual record containing extensive modification of the drugs formulation. The drug involved, Doryx capsules, was first approved in 1985 and marketed by Mayne Pharmaceuticals (which also produced an authorized generic version of the drug), albeit without any Orange Book–listed patents. Facing weak sales, Mayne entered into an exclusive license agreement with Warner Chilcott, in which Mayne agreed to withdraw the generic version from the market and act as an exclusive manufacturer and supplier to Warner Chilcott of branded Doryx in the United States. The agreement remains in force. Over the years, defendants have reformulated and modified Doryx in several ways, resulting in conduct Mylan alleges constitutes product hopping. This behavior included the following: in 2005, Mayne introduced 75 mg and 100 mg delayed release tablet versions (instead of capsules) of the drug, which had increased shelf life. Three years later, defendants introduced a 150 mg strength tablet with a single score, allowing the tablet to be broken into two 75 mg doses. Then, in 2009, defendants added a single score to their already developed 75 mg and 100 mg tablets. Finally, in 2011, defendants changed the 150 mg tablet from having a single score to having two scores, allowing it to be broken into 50 mg, 100 mg, and 150 mg doses. Mylan developed generic versions of the 75 mg, 100 mg, and 150 mg tablets, and was granted FDA approval shortly thereafter. Despite Mylan's allegations of product hopping, however, the court granted summary judgment that Mayne's frequent changes to its formulation did not amount to anticompetitive behavior falling within the purview of the antitrust laws.

§ 5.2.2 REMS Abuses

Another area where courts are examining the behavior of branded-drug makers for antitrust violations is related to Risk Evaluation and Mitigation Strategies (REMS) decisions. REMS is an FDA program imposed upon drugmakers who obtain marketing approval for drugs "that pose a significant safety risk"; thalidomide is an obvious example.[362] Because

---

360. *New York v. Actavis PLC*, No. 1:14-cv-7473 (S.D.N.Y.) Ct. App. No. 14-4624, slip op. at 50–51 (2d Cir. May 22, 2015).

361. *Mylan Pharm. v. Warner Chilcott PLC*, 2015 WL 1736957 (E.D. Pa. Apr. 16, 2015).

362. *See* FOOD & DRUG ADMIN., MEDICATION GUIDES—DISTRIBUTION REQUIREMENTS AND INCLUSION IN RISK EVALUATION AND MITIGATION STRATEGIES (REMS) at 2 (2011).

these programs impose restrictions on drug availability, branded-drug makers have been accused of limiting access to potential generic challengers, making it difficult if not impossible for such generic companies to have the necessary comparator for performing FDA-mandated studies for ANDA approval. While not all such restrictions raise antitrust concerns or liability, the scope of legal behavior has been tested in the courts.

In *Mylan Pharmaceuticals, Inc. v. Celgene Corp.*,[363] the court granted in part and denied in part Celgene's motion to dismiss Mylan's violations of sections 1 and 2 of the Sherman Act. Mylan alleged violation of section 2 of the Sherman Act by Celgene's refusal to permit the generic company to obtain drug samples needed for bioequivalence studies and also violation of section 1 of the Sherman Act for unreasonable restraint of trade as a result of Celgene's exclusive distribution agreements with wholesalers. The court found that Mylan had pled facts "plausibly giv[ing] rise to a duty to deal" in the face of the general rule that there is no such duty and that Celgene was permitted to dominate the market provided that the evidence was consistent with growth or development as a consequence of a superior product, business acumen, or historic accident rather than monopolization resulting from willful acquisition or maintenance of monopoly power. Consequently, the court denied Celgene's motion to dismiss as to section 2 of the Sherman Act. The court granted Celgene's motion to dismiss the section 1 count of Mylan's complaint, the court noting that the plaintiff must assert a concerted action by defendants that produced anticompetitive effects within the relevant product and geographic markets, that the concerted actions were illegal, and that plaintiff was injured as a proximate result of the concerted action. The court held that Mylan failed to plead that there was agreement to a common scheme or design between Celgene and its distributors, and thus granted the motion to dismiss the section 1 claims.

Additional cases involving these facts were recently consolidated in *Thalomid and Revlimid Antitrust Litigation*[364] but are far from being decided.

In another still pending case, *Natco Pharma Ltd. v. Gilead Science, Inc. and Express Scripts Holding Co.*,[365] generic-drug maker Natco sued

363. *Mylan Pharm., Inc. v. Celgene Corp.*, No. 2:14-cv-2094-ES-MAH (D.N.J.).

364. *Thalomid & Revlimid Antitrust Litig.*, No. 2:14-cv-06997-KSH-CLW (D.N.J.). These include *International Union of Bricklayers and Allied Craft Workers Local 1 Health Fund v. Celgene Corp.*, No. 2:14-cv-06997 (D.N.J.), and *City of Providence v. Celgene Corp.*, No. 14-cv-1605 (D.N.J.).

365. *Natco Pharma Ltd. v. Gilead Sci., Inc. & Express Scripts Holding Co.*, No. 14-cv-3247 (D. Minn. Aug. 22, 2014).

Gilead and Express Scripts for refusing to deal regarding a potential generic version of ambrisentan (sold under the brand name Letairis). Gilead implemented an REMS program for the drug, which restricts drug availability to females due to the risk of birth defects if taken while pregnant. However, the REMS program had no restrictions on the use of Letairis for clinical studies in males. Natco in its complaint asserted six counts sounding in antitrust, including a Sherman Act section 1 violation for conspiring, combining, and/or agreeing to restrain trade in the market for FDA-approved ambrisentan drug products, a Sherman section 2 violation for improperly maintaining and extending monopoly power in the ambrisentan market, a Sherman section 2 violation because Gilead controls an "essential facility" (ambrisentan) required for bioequivalence testing corresponding to monopolization of the relevant market, and Minnesota state law claims, as well as a plea for declaratory relief obliging Gilead to sell to Natco sufficient quantities of Letairis.

On the other hand, the court in *In re Suboxone (Buprenorphine Hydrochloride and Naloxone) Antitrust Litigation*[366] dismissed an antitrust claim involving REMs on the basis that "antitrust laws do not impose a duty on [branded-drug maker] Reckitt to aid the Generics in obtaining expeditious approval of an ANDA."[367]

366. *In re Suboxone (Buprenorphine Hydrochloride & Naloxone) Antitrust Litig.*, 64 F. Supp. 3d 665 (E.D. Pa. 2014).

367. *Id.* at 688.

chapter 6

Antitrust Issues for Standard Essential Patents

I. Introduction

Recent litigation has brought to light the complex legal issues confronted when patented technology is standardized. Well-known standard setting organizations (SSOs) such as the European Telecommunications Standards Institute (ETSI), International Telecommunications Union (ITU) and the Institute of Electrical and Electronics Engineers (IEEE) have been proposing and setting rules to help alleviate conflicts that arise with respect to the open access dichotomy that exists between a patent monopoly and open standards that incorporate patented technology.[1] A patent normally grants a monopoly for twenty years to its owner to exclude others from practicing the claimed technology. However, incorporating such patented technology into a standard is meant to provide open, but not free, access to the technology for all users and implementers. The courts have been construing SSO rules designed to bridge this dichotomy with more frequency. This chapter will address important legal precedent at the intersection of standards, patent law, and antitrust law

II. Private Actions Related to Standard Essential Patents

§ 6.1 *FRAND Commitments*

In one of a series of lawsuits between Microsoft and Motorola, a district court held that a licensee does not have to make a first contact for a fair,

1. J. Contreras & D. Newman, *Developing a Framework for Arbitrating Standard Essential Patent (SEP) Disputes*, 2014 J. Disp. Resol. 2–3.

reasonable, and non-discriminatory (FRAND) commitment to apply.[2] It should be noted that FRAND commitments may also be referred to as reasonable and non-discriminatory (RAND) commitments or as F/RAND commitments, and the terms may be interchangeably used. The district court held that an initial offer by a patent holder need not be FRAND, but must comport with principles of good faith and fair dealing in order to comply with a FRAND commitment.[3] On appeal, the Ninth Circuit held that the district court's conclusion that a FRAND agreement created a contract enforceable by Microsoft was not "legally erroneous."[4] On remand, Judge Robart extensively reviewed Motorola's patent portfolios regarding Wi-Fi and video coding technology and their importance to their respective standards.[5] Relying upon the fifteen-factor *Georgia-Pacific* test,[6] Judge Robart computed the RAND royalty rates for both patent portfolios.[7] Judge Robart's ruling was subsequently incorporated into a jury trial regarding Microsoft's breach of contract claim against Motorola for allegedly failing to comply with FRAND.[8] The jury entered a verdict for Microsoft and, pursuant to Federal Rule of Civil Procedure 54(b), the case is now on appeal to the Federal Circuit.

In *In re Innovatio IP Ventures*,[9] the parties agreed to have the court determine the RAND royalty amount in the event that infringement was established, so that the parties would have a clearer framework for potential settlement. The court relied heavily upon Judge Robart's *Microsoft* opinion, in applying the *Georgia-Pacific* factors to the Innovatio standard-essential patents (SEPs) at issue. The court also adopted the three-step approach utilized by Judge Robart:

1. Consider the importance of the patent portfolio to the standard, considering both the proportion of all patents essential to the standard that are in the portfolio, and also the technical contribution of the patent portfolio as a whole to the standard.
2. Consider the importance of the patent portfolio as a whole to the alleged infringer's accused products.
3. Examine other licenses for comparable patents to determine a RAND rate. Based on this framework, the court set the RAND

2. *Microsoft Corp. v. Motorola, Inc.*, 864 F. Supp. 2d 1023 (W.D. Wash. 2012).
3. *Id.*
4. *Microsoft Corp. v. Motorola, Inc.*, 696 F.3d 872 (9th Cir. 2012).
5. *Microsoft Corp. v. Motorola, Inc.*, 2013 U.S. Dist. LEXIS 60233 (W.D. Wash. Apr. 25, 2013).
6. *Ga.-Pac. Corp. v. U.S. Plywood Corp.*, 318 F. Supp. 1116, 1120 (S.D.N.Y. 1970).
7. *Microsoft*, 2013 U.S. Dist. LEXIS 60233.
8. *Id.*
9. *In re Innovatio IP Ventures, LLC Patent Litig.*, No. 11 C 9308, 2013 WL 5593609 (N.D. Ill. Oct. 3, 2013).

royalty rate that would be due to Innovatio if infringement were found.

The *Innovatio* court noted, however, a few differences between its context and the task in Judge Robart's *Microsoft* case. The court here had to set a single RAND rate instead of a RAND range because the procedural posture of the case was a damages calculation, not whether the party had breached an obligation to negotiate for a RAND license. The *Innovatio* court was also able to avoid determining a discount to the RAND royalty based upon how essential the patent was to the standard because the court had already determined that Innovatio's patents were essential to the standard. In using Judge Robart's RAND rate for Microsoft to benchmark its RAND rate for Innovatio, the court found that its proposed rate of 9.56 cents per unit, about three times the 3.471 cents per unit proposed as the high end of the range in *Microsoft*, reflected a proper multiplier given the relative higher importance of Innovatio's patent portfolio to its standard.[10]

In *Ericsson v. D-Link*,[11] the court instructed the jury on the *Georgia-Pacific* factors for determining a proper RAND royalty and the jury determined that defendants were obligated to pay Ericsson $0.15 per unit for use of Ericsson's patents. Defendants sought to have the court independently determine the RAND rate post-trial, but the court concluded that defendants should have raised any RAND-based royalty arguments with the jury and declined to disturb the jury's determined RAND rate. The court noted, in support, that it had instructed the jury that it must ensure that any damages award is consistent with and does not exceed the amounts permitted under Ericsson's RAND obligations. In the *Innovatio* case, discussed earlier, the court relied upon the Ericsson jury's RAND verdict as a proper benchmark for setting similar RAND rates.

The defendants also argued that the courts should find Ericsson in violation of its RAND obligation because Ericsson had proposed a RAND rate of $0.50 per unit at the outset, which defendants claimed was outside the range of RAND rates. The court reviewed Ericsson's internal processes for setting RAND rates, including how Ericsson factored its RAND obligation into the rate and had considered the feedback from other licensees. Combined with the fact that there was no evidence of royalty stacking or bad faith by Ericsson, the court concluded that merely making a RAND rate offer that licensees consider too high is not a violation of a RAND commitment.

10. *See* M. Scott Donahey & D. Newman, *Alternative Dispute Resolution Process That Can Resolve FRAND Disputes Better Than District Court Litigations*, 3 I.P. & TECH. L.J., June 2014.

11. *Ericsson Inc. v. D-Link Sys.*, 2013 U.S. Dist. LEXIS 110585 (E.D. Tex. Aug. 6, 2013).

In the *Certain Gaming and Entertainment Consoles* International Trade Commission (ITC) case,[12] in its initial determination regarding Microsoft's alleged infringement of various Motorola patents related to the Xbox videogame console, an ITC administrative law judge (ALJ) found that Microsoft had infringed certain Motorola patents and, further, refused Microsoft's request to bar Motorola from seeking an exclusion order with respect to those infringed patents that were also FRAND-encumbered SEPs. Microsoft argued that Motorola should be precluded from seeking an exclusion order for any FRAND-encumbered SEPs. Microsoft advanced numerous legal theories to support this conclusion, including a "RAND obligation defense" based on the "subordination of equity" implied license, implied waiver of the right to seek equitable or exclusionary relief, and equitable estoppel. The judge rejected all of Microsoft's theories principally because Motorola had not agreed to a fixed license under FRAND, but only to negotiate in good faith toward a FRAND license.

Microsoft did convince the judge that Motorola's offer to license its patents for a 2.25 percent royalty on the end price of Microsoft's customer products was a "sham" because the evidence showed that such a royalty rate "could not possibly have been accepted by Microsoft." However, this fact did not support a finding of equitable estoppel because the judge identified no evidence that Microsoft detrimentally relied upon Motorola's FRAND licensing commitments when it developed its Xbox product and failed to find any other basis on which to deprive Motorola of its entitlement to standard exclusionary relief.

Notably, the ITC's decision regarding Motorola's right to exclusionary relief did not ultimately result in an exclusion order against Microsoft's products because Microsoft obtained a remand order from the ITC on the infringement issues in the case and Motorola later withdrew its SEPs from the litigation, possibly in response to pressure from U.S. competition authorities, as indicated by Motorola's consent order with the FTC, entered in 2013 (discussed later).

In a series of lawsuits between Apple and Motorola Mobility, in response to various patent infringement claims brought by Motorola in the ITC regarding essential patents for wireless communications devices, Apple filed counterclaims against Motorola based upon breach of contract and the Sherman Act for Motorola's failure to properly disclose their patents to the SSO and refusal to negotiate royalty rates under RAND terms.[13]

---

12. *Certain Gaming & Entm't Consoles, Related Software & Components Thereof*, USITC Inv. No. 337-TA-752 (Apr. 23, 2012) (*Microsoft v. Motorola*, Notice of Initial Determination).

13. *Apple, Inc. v. Motorola Mobility, Inc.*, No. 11-CV-178-BBC, 2011 WL 7324582 (W.D. Wis. June 7, 2011).

Apple removed its counterclaims to the Western District of Wisconsin.[14] The court dismissed Apple's antitrust claims under the *Noerr-Pennington* doctrine, and Apple stipulated that it would only seek nominal damages for its contract claims.[15] The judge refused to hold a trial to determine the RAND value of Motorola's patents when Apple made it clear that they would not agree to be bound by the court's RAND determination, but would simply use it as the ceiling for a RAND negotiation with Motorola.[16] The court subsequently dismissed Apple's claims with prejudice.[17]

In *Ericsson, Inc. v. D-Link Systems, Inc.*[18] the Federal Circuit determined that when defining appropriate RAND terms it is not required that each of the *Georgia-Pacific* factors (or modified *Georgia-Pacific* factors) be considered. More importantly, the court held that a jury should be instructed as to the actual RAND commitment of the patentee. Further, the court held that a jury must be instructed that a royalty must be apportioned from the value of the standard as a whole and the royalty must be based on the invention, not any value added by the standardization of the invention.

§ 6.2 Duty to Disclose Obligations

In *Apple v. Samsung*,[19] a jury verdict of over $1 billion in Apple's favor made headlines. Judge Koh also ruled Apple could not enjoin Samsung's infringing products because Apple failed to prove a nexus between the claimed features of the infringed patent claims and its irreparable harm. In May 2015, the Federal Circuit affirmed the jury's verdict on the design patent infringements, the validity of two utility patent claims, and the damages awarded for the design and utility patent infringements appealed by Samsung. The Federal Circuit reversed the jury's findings that the asserted trade dresses are protectable and vacated the jury's damages awards against the Samsung products that were found liable for trade dress dilution and remanded to the district court.[20]

In *Barnes & Noble v. LSI*,[21] the district court held that a standard adopter can seek to avoid the need for a license, by raising an inequitable conduct defense with respect to a previous owner's intentional deception regarding a patent that can be imputed to the successor in interest to render the patent unenforceable. The district court held that "[i]mposing

14. *Id.*
15. *Apple, Inc. v. Motorola Mobility, Inc.*, 886 F. Supp. 2d 1061 (W.D. Wis. 2012).
16. *Id.*
17. *Id.*
18. 773 F.3d 1201 (Fed. Cir. 2014).
19. *Apple Inc. v. Samsung Elec.*, 909 F. Supp. 2d 1147 (N.D. Cal. 2012).
20. *Apple Inc. v. Samsung Elec.*, 786 F.3d 983, 989 (Fed. Cir. 2015).
21. *Barnes & Noble, Inc. v. LSI Corp.*, 849 F. Supp. 2d 925 (N.D. Cal. 2012).

liability for tort-like conduct of a predecessor is an entirely different proposition than assessing the validity and enforceability of a property right obtained from a predecessor."[22]

III. Remedies for Standard Essential Patents

§ 6.3 Royalties

In *Realtek v. LSI*,[23] Realtek filed an action against LSI and its subsidiary alleging that they "breached their RAND licensing obligations by initiating an ITC Section 337 action naming Realtek as a respondent before approaching Realtek with a RAND licensing offer."[24] The district court held an eleven-day jury trial to determine Realtek's breach of contract damages and RAND rates for two of LSI's SEPs under the IEEE 802.11 standard, commonly referred to as the Wi-Fi standard.[25] The jury awarded $3.825 million to Realtek for LSI's breach of contract and determined RAND royalty rates of 0.12 percent and 0.07 percent for the two SEPs.[26] After trial, Realtek moved in the present case for a permanent injunction enjoining LSI from demanding further royalties from Realtek and from enforcing LSI's two SEPs in the ITC.[27] Further, Realtek moved for a declaratory judgment that if LSI fails to offer Realtek an ongoing license to LSI's SEPs on RAND terms and conditions, then such SEPs are unenforceable against Realtek and its products.[28] As to the permanent injunction, the court determined that the ITC's holding in a related case that LSI did not prove patent infringement of its SEPs by Realtek rendered the irreparable-harm prong of a permanent injunction sufficiently speculative to deny Realtek's request for a permanent injunction.[29] However, the court entered the declaratory judgment that upon Realtek's request for a license, to be in compliance with its RAND commitment, LSI must offer Realtek a license to LSI's SEPs on RAND terms, including the royalty rate determined by the jury on Realtek's accused products.[30]

---

22. *Id.* at 931.
23. *Realtek Semiconductor Corp. v. LSI Corp.*, 2014 WL 2738226 (N.D. Cal. 2014).
24. *Id.* at *1.
25. *Id.* at *1–2.
26. *Id.* at *2.
27. *Id.*
28. *Id.*
29. *Id.**3–4.
30. *Id.* at *6.

In *Ericsson v. D-Link*,[31] as discussed earlier, the jury determined that defendants were obligated to pay Ericsson $0.15 per unit for use of Ericsson's patents. To arrive at the RAND royalty rate the court relied on the *Georgia-Pacific* factors. The court determined that a proper RAND royalty could be determined by following the fifteen *Georgia-Pacific* factors.

In *CSIRO v. Cisco*,[32] Judge Davis of the Eastern District of Texas extrapolated from the damage expert report of the plaintiff (proposing an approximately $30 million reasonable royalty calculation) and defendant Cisco (proposing an approximately $1 million reasonable royalty calculation) to arrive at damages of $16.2 million. Finding error with the patent owner's use of a chip as the smallest saleable unit covered by the patent. Instead, the court used access points and network interface card products as the base for the royalty calculation. The court relied on licenses negotiated between the parties to provide comparable rates for the reasonable royalty calculation, even though those license negotiations occurred after the date that traditionally would have been the date for the hypothetical negotiation.

Judge Davis had been aware of other courts modifying the traditional *Georgia-Pacific* factors when determining a reasonable royalty rate for a SEP. However, the court did not use modified *Georgia-Pacific* factors because the SEP infringement under the 802.11a Wi-Fi standard made up "an incredibly small percentage of the total products at issue."[33] Therefore, the patent owner's RAND commitment under IEEE's patent policy played a small role in the damages calculation despite the court's ruling that the patent owner's letters sent to several wireless industry companies and its RAND commitment to IEEE that resulted in the patent owner waiving any written license request requirement. As a result, the patent was bound to offer the defendant a license on RAND terms for the 802.11a products.[34]

§ 6.4 Injunctions and Exclusion Orders

As evidenced in the conflicting decisions that follow, whether a patent holder holding a SEP subject to a RAND obligation may pursue injunctive relief to enforce its patent is a difficult question. As the *Innovatio* court put it, "whether a RAND obligation precludes an injunction is 'muddled' and 'the subject of substantial, often contradictory, academic commentary.'"[35]

31. *Ericsson, Inc. v. D-Link Sys.*, 773 F.3d 1201 (Fed. Cir. 2014).

32. *Commonwealth Sci. & Indus. Research Org. v. Cisco Sys., Inc.*, 2014 WL 3805817 (E.D. Tex. 2014).

33. *Id.* at *12.

34. *Id.*

35. *In re Innovatio IP Ventures, LLC Patent Litig.*, 2013 WL 5593609 (N.D. Ill. 2013).

Notably, there is an important feedback loop between the availability of injunctive relief for RAND-bound SEPs and the computation of a RAND rate because the availability of injunctive relief suggests that the patent holder during the hypothetical negotiation for the RAND royalty rate would have had more leverage over the licensee due to the credible threat of a court-ordered injunction, thereby justifying an increase in the court-determined RAND rate.

In response to the growing number of cases in which patent holders holding SEPs sought exclusion orders, the DOJ and USPTO issued a statement in 2013.[36] After acknowledging the sizeable benefits of voluntary consensus standards set by SSOs as well as the risk of hold-up behavior posed by the inclusion of patents in such standards, the agencies sought to identify the circumstances under which injunctive relief would be appropriate. For example, the agencies noted that injunctive relief might be improper where "the holder of a F/RAND-encumbered, standards-essential patent had attempted to use an exclusion order to pressure an implementer of a standard to accept more onerous licensing terms than the patent holder would be entitled to receive with the F/RAND commitment." However, an exclusion order may be proper where "a putative licensee refuses to pay what has been determined to be a F/RAND royalty, or refuses to engage in a negotiation to determine F/RAND terms."

The agencies also strongly recommended that the ITC carefully consider the factors identified in their joint statement, as a part of the ITC's usual public interest factors, before issuing an exclusion order or, alternatively, delay the issuance of exclusion orders for a period of time during which parties have the opportunity to pursue RAND licenses.

In connection with the *Certain Gaming and Entertainment Consoles* ITC case (described earlier),[37] the FTC issued a statement on the public interest with respect to the availability of exclusionary relief for RAND-encumbered SEPs.[38] In short, the FTC urged the ITC to consider the harm to consumers caused by an exclusion order based on a SEP. The FTC noted that such exclusion orders have "the potential to cause substantial harm to U.S. competition, consumers and innovation." The concern, it noted, is that "a royalty negotiation that occurs under the threat of an exclusion order

36. U.S. Dep't of Justice & U.S. Patent & Trademark Office, Policy Statement on Remedies for Standard-Essential Patents Subject to Voluntary F/RAND Commitments (Jan. 8, 2013).

37. *Certain Gaming & Entm't Consoles, Related Software & Components Thereof*, USITC Inv. No. 337-TA-752 (Apr. 23, 2012).

38. Third Party FTC Statement on Public Interest to ITC, June 6, 2012 (D. Clark); *Certain Gaming & Entm't Consoles, Related Software & Components Thereof*, USITC Inv. No. 337-TA-752.

may be weighted heavily in favor of the patent holder in a way that is in tension with the RAND commitment" and, ultimately, "could raise prices to consumers while undermining the standard setting process."

The FTC admonished the ITC to consider its statutory obligation to weigh "competitive conditions in the United States economy . . . and United States consumers" when granting an exclusion order for a FRAND-encumbered SEP. For example, the ITC could condition a grant of an exclusion order to a patent holder on whether "the holder of the RAND-encumbered SEP has made a reasonable royalty offer." The FTC recommended that for the *Microsoft v. Motorola* case, the ITC could delay the effective date of any remedy "until the parties mediate in good faith for damages for past infringement and/or an ongoing royalty for future licensed use," with the infringer facing the risk that the exclusion order will go into effect if a reasonable royalty offer is made and the infringer turns it down and the patent holder facing the risk that if no reasonable offer is made, then the exclusion order will be unavailable.

The FTC acknowledged, in closing, "an appropriately granted exclusion order preserves the exclusivity that forms the foundation of the patent system's incentives to innovate, and the threat of an exclusion order can provide a significant deterrent to infringement." However, the FTC also implored the ITC to recognize that "RAND-encumbered SEPs present considerably different issues" because, in sum, "[a] RAND commitment provides evidence that the SEP owner planned to monetize its IP through broad licensing on reasonable terms rather than through exclusive use." Thus, it is appropriate for the ITC to consider the impact on consumers.

In a separate matter, Joseph F. Wayland, acting assistant attorney general of the Department of Justice Antitrust Division, echoed the FTC's comments about the use of exclusionary orders for FRAND-encumbered SEPs.[39]

> The law of injunctions in patent cases must be flexible and sensitive to the concern that opportunistic rights holders can exploit the threat of an injunction to extract royalties well in excess of the value of their intellectual property. To my mind, a patent holder who makes a licensing commitment to a standards body is implicitly saying that she will license the patent claims that must be used to implement the standard to any licensee that is willing and able to comply with the licensing terms embodied in the commitment.[40]

39. Dep't of Justice Comments from J. Wayland (Fordham Competition Law Inst. Sept. 21, 2012).

40. *Id.*

He further identified the Supreme Court's *eBay*[41] injunction factors as the appropriate test for evaluating an injunction for SEP FRAND cases.

Wayland also described the DOJ's recent actions with respect to two recent purchases of patent pools containing a large number of FRAND-encumbered SEPs: the acquisition by Rockstar Bidco—a partnership that included Apple, Microsoft, Research In Motion, Sony, and Ericsson—of 6,000 patents and patent applications from Nortel at a bankruptcy auction; and Google's acquisition of Motorola Mobility, the holder of 17,000 issued patents and 6,800 patent applications. In each case, the DOJ focused on whether the acquiring firm would have the "incentive and ability to exploit ambiguities in commitments the sellers made to license their patents on RAND terms to hold up implementers of the standard by raising rivals' costs or foreclosing competition, to the detriment of consumers." This might include raising "rivals' costs by demanding higher licensing rates, compelling cross licenses to differentiating patents valued in excess of the RAND rate, charging licensees the entire portfolio rate when licensing only a subset of the patents in its portfolio, or seeking to prevent or exclude products that infringed these patents from the market altogether." The DOJ concluded that neither acquisition materially posed these risks.

One key factor that allayed the DOJ's concerns in these two acquisitions was that Microsoft and Apple both publicly committed that they would not seek injunctions or exclusion orders based on FRAND-encumbered SEPs. Google offered a more watered-down commitment, agreeing not to seek injunctive relief only if the potential licensee (1) forgoes certain defenses such as challenging the validity of the patent, (2) pays the full disputed licensing amount into escrow, and (3) agrees to a reciprocal process regarding injunctions.

Wayland offered up two final thoughts on standard setting around patented technologies. First, he disclosed that DOJ has been working with standard-setting organizations to change their patent policies in ways that will better ensure consumer protection. This includes, for example, "[m]aking it clear that licensing commitments bind both the current patent holder and subsequent purchasers of the patents" and "[p]lacing some limitations on the right to exclude a willing and able licensees by, for example, requiring a commitment that a RAND-encumbered patent declared essential to a standard may be used to exclude only after litigation/arbitration of disputed issues has concluded." Second, he made clear the DOJ's view on ITC exclusion orders regarding FRAND-encumbered SEPs.

41. *eBay Inc. v. MercExchange, LLC*, 547 U.S. 388 (2006).

> The department believes that the ITC may tailor its relief in a manner that protects patent holders' rights in individual cases while taking into consideration the impact on consumers and on the competitive conditions in the United States economy.[42]

In *Apple v. Motorola*,[43] a recent opinion by Judge Posner, sitting as a trial court judge, reflects the barrier that FRAND-encumbered SEPs pose to a patent holder seeking injunctive relief. Motorola sought injunctive relief against Apple for infringing certain of its standard essential patents, which were all subject to FRAND licensing obligations. According to Judge Posner:

> I don't see how, given FRAND, I would be justified in enjoining Apple from infringing the '898 unless Apple refuses to pay a royalty that meets the FRAND requirement. By committing to license its patents on FRAND terms, Motorola committed to license the '898 to anyone willing to pay a FRAND royalty and thus implicitly acknowledged that a royalty is adequate compensation for a license to use that patent.[44]

Thus, under the *eBay* factors for injunctive relief, a FRAND-encumbered patent necessarily cannot qualify for an injunction. To buttress his conclusion, Judge Posner cited to the FTC's Statement on the Public Interest filed in connection with the ITC's resolution of the *Microsoft v. Motorola* case,[45] which "implies that injunctive relief is indeed unavailable for infringement of a patent governed by FRAND."

Judge Posner rejected two of Motorola's counterarguments. First, Motorola argued that Apple lost the "safe harbor" of the FRAND license by failing to negotiate Motorola's 2.25 percent royalty offer. Judge Posner rejected this view because Motorola's FRAND obligation "does not claim to have conditioned agreement on prospective licensees' making counter-offers in license negotiations." Thus, Motorola continues to be bound by its FRAND obligation to Microsoft. Second, Motorola argued that without injunctive relief available, it will not be able to extract a reasonable royalty form Microsoft. Here, Judge Posner calls Motorola out for essentially complaining about the litigation discount that both sides must weigh if they are unable to broker a license fee. The "deeper objection" is a complaint about the "American rule," which generally forces the winning side

42. *Id.*
43. *Apple Inc. v. Motorola, Inc.*, 869 F. Supp. 2d 901 (N.D. Ill. June 22, 2012 (Posner, J.).
44. *Id.*
45. *Apple, Inc. v. Motorola Mobility, Inc.*, 886 F. Supp. 2d 1061 (W.D. Wis. 2012).

in a litigation to pay its own costs. Nevertheless, the fact of litigation costs should not compel a court to provide relief that is otherwise unavailable, or courts would have to grant injunctions in contract suits to prevent unfair litigation costs there, too.

In the end, Judge Posner concluded that neither Motorola nor Apple could sustain a claim for equitable relief under the *eBay* factors because monetary relief would be adequate. With respect to Motorola's SEPs, this conclusion was at least somewhat simpler because "[a] FRAND royalty would provide all the relief to which Motorola would be entitled if it proved infringement [of its FRAND patent], and thus it is not entitled to an injunction."

On appeal, the Federal Circuit reversed Judge Posner with respect to Apple's request for injunctive relief and affirmed with respect to Motorola's request. The court determined that the refusal to grant injunctive relief to Apple had to be reversed because the decision rested upon an improperly narrow scope of infringement and, in light of the Federal Circuit's conclusion that Apple's infringement claim was more expansive, the trial court would need to reevaluate the need for injunctive relief.

The Federal Circuit affirmed the trial court's decision to deny injunctive relief to Motorola. As an initial matter, the court noted:

> To the extent that the district court applied a per se rule that injunctions are unavailable for SEPs, it erred. While Motorola's FRAND commitments are certainly criteria relevant to its entitlement to an injunction, we see no reason to create . . . a separate rule or analytical framework [different from the eBay factors].

Nevertheless, the court agreed that the factors relevant to Motorola's request militated against injunctive relief. Motorola had already licensed a large number of parties under the same patent, reflecting both that money compensation would be adequate and that adding a single additional license would not cause irreparable harm, and the evidence did not show that Apple was unilaterally refusing to deal with Motorola.

In 2014, the DOJ closed its investigation of Samsung's attempts to use its SEPs to obtain exclusion orders from the ITC.[46]

---

46. Press Release, U.S. Dep't of Justice, Office of Pub. Affairs, Statement of the Department of Justice Antitrust Division on Its Decision to Close Its Investigation of Samsung's Use of Its Standards-Essential Patents (Feb. 7, 2014), *available at* http://www.justice.gov/opa/pr/statement-department-justice-antitrust-division-its-decision-close-its-investigation-samsung.

IV. Government Actions Related to Standard Essential Patents

§ 6.5 U.S. Government Actions

Recent U.S. patent enforcement investigations and litigations regarding SEPs demonstrate that whether obligations to offer licenses on FRAND terms will prevent the patent owner from broadly pursing an injunction is dependent upon the U.S. jurisdiction undertaking the investigation. U.S. courts and the DOJ have raised the injunction issue as a key to evaluating antitrust violations by SEP owners. The FTC has filed a statement with the ITC regarding its investigation concerning its assertion of SEPs against Microsoft and Apple, where the FTC requested that the ITC refrain from issuing an exclusion order with respect to the importation of Microsoft and Apple products due to Motorola Mobility's FRAND commitments.

Many SSOs such as the IEEE require the submission of disclosures regarding patents that are likely to be essential to a standard being considered by the SSO—for example, a SEP. Most SSOs also require, as part of the disclosure, that the SEP owner commit to providing licenses under RAND terms. The ramifications of these RAND obligations are hotly investigated and litigated in many U.S. jurisdictions.

§ 6.5.1 U.S. Department of Justice Actions

Microsoft and Apple have apparently taken notice of the potential for intensified antitrust scrutiny and have taken positions that they will not seek injunctive relief in the enforcement of a SEP.

> This means that Microsoft will not seek an injunction or exclusion order against any firm on the basis of those essential patents.[47]
>
> Likewise, Apple stated:
>
> A party who made a FRAND commitment to license its cellular standards essential patents or otherwise acquired assets/rights from a party who made the FRAND commitment must not seek injunctive relief on such patents. Seeking an injunction would be a violation of the parties' commitment to FRAND licensing.[48]

47. Microsoft Statement, Feb. 8, 2012, *reported in* News Release, Dep't of Justice, Statement of Department of Justice's Anti-Trust Division on Its Decision to Close Its Investigation of Google Inc.'s Acquisition of Motorola Mobility Holdings, Inc. and the Acquisitions of Certain Patents by Apple Inc., Microsoft Corp. and Research in Motion Limited (Feb. 13, 2012).

48. Apple Letter to the European Telecommunications Standards Institute (ETSI) (Nov. 11, 2011) *cited in* DOJ Statement (Feb. 13, 2012).

In view of such commitments, the DOJ did not intervene in the Apple acquisition of patents formerly owned by Novell nor the deal by Microsoft, Apple, RIM, and others, *i.e.,* the Rock-Star Consortium, who acquired the patents out of the Nortel bankruptcy. The DOJ stated:

> In its analysis of its transactions, the division took into account the fact that during the pendency of these investigations, Apple, Google and Microsoft each made public statements explaining their respective SEP licensing practices. Both Apple and Microsoft made clear that they will not seek to prevent or exclude rivals' products from the market in exercising their SEP rights.[49]

§ 6.5.2 U.S. Federal Trade Commission Actions

Google provided a public statement on February 8, 2012, directed to the IEEE and other standards bodies.[50] The statement primarily addressed Google's position with respect to its acquisition of Motorola Mobility including Motorola Mobility patents and its commitment to uphold Motorola Mobility's FRAND obligations. The statement did not directly address Google's policy with respect to seeking injunctions. The DOJ stated:

> [B]ut how Google may exercise its patents in the future remains a significant concern.[51]

Possibly as a precursor to independent action, the FTC, on June 6, 2012, provided a statement to the ITC regarding its investigation no. 337-TA-745, in *In re Certain Wireless Communication Devices, Portable Music and Data Processing Devices, Computers and Components Thereof*, involving Motorola's assertion of its patents against Microsoft and Apple.[52] In the statement, the FTC stated:

> A RAND commitment provides evidence that the SEP owner planned to monetize its IP through broad licensing on reasonable terms rather than through exclusive use.

The FTC was highlighting the distinction between SEP and non-SEP-type patents—for which the ITC normally issues exclusion orders. The FTC stated:

---

49. DOJ Statement, *supra* note 47.

50. Google Letter from Allen Lo, Deputy Gen. Counsel, to Mr. Gordon Day, President IEEE (Feb. 8, 2012).

51. DOJ Statement, *supra* note 47.

52. FTC, Third Party US Federal Trade Commission's Statement of the Public Interest (2012), *available at* http://www.ftc.gov/os/2012/06/1206ftcgamingconsole.pdf.

> [I]nteroperability standards can create enormous value for consumers by increasing competition, innovation, product quality and choice.

In view of those parameters, the FTC asked the ITC to consider refraining from issuing an exclusion order in these cases involving SEPs. The FTC asked the ITC to consider its range of remedies to give effect to its statutory obligations to consider "competitive conditions in the United States economy . . . and the United States consumers." The weighing in on this issue by the FTC should raise a red flag for SEP owners who are pursuing injunctive relief in a broad-ranging manner such as an ITC action. For example, a new investigation regarding Samsung's activities in asserting SEPs may have been initiated.[53]

An important draft settlement between the DOJ and Google was announced January 3, 2013, that requires Google to complete a specific arbitration process before it can pursue injunctions under its standard essential patents acquired from Motorola Mobility, LLC.[54] The FTC arbitration process importantly may provide a roadmap for other standard essential patent owners to follow prior to seeking an injunction under its SEPs.

In *In re Motorola Mobility and Google*,[55] notwithstanding Motorola and Google's extensive litigation of its SEPs, Motorola Mobility entered into a consent decree with the FTC in mid-2013 under which it has recommitted to license its SEPs relating to smartphones, laptops, tablet computers, and gaming consoles on RAND terms. Motorola Mobility agreed that it would not pursue or threaten to pursue injunctions and exclusion orders against companies that use these patents and are willing to license the patents on RAND terms. The FTC's order also sets out an optional framework for Motorola Mobility and its prospective licensees to use for negotiating RAND licenses with the assistance of arbitration.

The FTC's decision comes only a few months after its decision in *In re Robert Bosch*,[56] in which the FTC similarly determined that a company being acquired by Bosch called SPX must cease and desist from "initiating,

53. *In re Certain Electronic Devices, Including Wireless Commc'n Devices, Portable Music & Data Processing Devices, & Tablet Computers*, ITC Inv. No. 337-TA-794; Respondent Apple Inc.'s Submission Pursuant to the Commission's Request for Statements on the Public Interest at 2 (Oct. 22, 2012).

54. The FTC Google settlement was finalized on July 24, 2013, without significant change.

55. Decision and Order, *In re Motorola Mobility LLC and Google, Inc.*, No. C-4410 (F.T.C. July 24, 2013).

56. *In re Robert Bosch GmbH*, No. C-4377 (F.T.C. Apr. 24, 2013).

or threatening to initiate, any Action demanding injunctive relief against any Third Party," with respect to any of SPX's SEPs.[57]

In addition to the actions highlighted, there are other suits pending between parties involved in the wireless, smartphone, and tablet computer industries involving SEPs. This level of litigation and controversy should indicate to the SSOs that their efforts to provide a streamlined process for promulgating standards are deficient—forcing individual parties to wage complex and costly patent battles. In fact, the DOJ has been encouraging SSOs to implement alternative dispute resolution policies to better deal with these conflicts.[58]

§ 6.6 *Foreign Actions*

Recent international patent enforcement investigations and litigations regarding SEPs demonstrate whether obligations to offer licenses on FRAND terms will prevent the patent owner from broadly pursing an injunction are dependent upon the international jurisdiction undertaking the investigation. A German court has allowed an injunction to be pursued for the assertion of a SEP. Separately, the European Commission has indicated that it may prevent pursuit of an injunction where there is a failure to negotiate in good faith. A recent ruling by the United Kingdom's High Court has indicated that an injunction should not be available when a FRAND obligation has been made with respect to a SEP. Many SSOs such as ETSI require the submission of disclosures regarding patents that are likely to be SEPs. Most SSOs also require, as part of the disclosure, that the SEP owner commits to providing licenses under FRAND terms. The ramifications of these FRAND obligations are hotly investigated and litigated in many international jurisdictions.

§ 6.6.1 European Commission Actions

Earlier in 2012, the European Commission provided a clearance decision on Google's proposed acquisition of Motorola Mobility. In providing its decision not to block or delay Google's acquisition of Motorola Mobility, the European Commission discussed the effect of the antitrust abuse paragraph of EU law.

> [T]he Commission considers that Google's incentives to use the threat of injunctions to forcibly extract cross-licenses from good

---

57. *See also supra* pp. 9–28; discussing other aspects of proposed merger.

58. R. Hesse, U.S. Dept. of Justice, Six Small Proposals (Oct. 10, 2012, ITU-T Patent Roundtable); *see* Kai-Uwe Kühn, Fiona Scott Morton & Howard Shelanski, *Standard Setting Organizations Can Help Solve the Standard Essential Patents Licensing Problem*, CPI Antitrust Chron., Mar. 2013.

> faith licensees are most likely to be constrained by the prospect of an investigation based on Article 102 TFEU.[59]

With the threat of investigation antitrust issues, the European Commission felt that any improper behavior of a SEP owner could be impeded.

> Furthermore, the seeking of enforcement of injunctions on the basis of SEP is also not, of itself, anti-competitive. In particular, and depending on the circumstances, it may be legitimate for the holder of SEP to seek an injunction against a potential licensee which is not willing to negotiate in good faith on FRAND terms.[60]

It is likely that the European Commission would require good-faith negotiations to occur on behalf of both parties.

> In the event licensing discussions fail, the SEP holder may ultimately take its counterparty to court and seek an injunction.[61]

Thus, under the ruling of the European Commission, it is likely that where good faith negotiations have occurred but have failed, the patent owner may seek an injunction.

§ 6.6.2 United Kingdom Actions

The European Commission's approach has not been followed in the United Kingdom. In *IPCom v. Nokia*,[62] the U.K. High Court reviewed an IPCom patent covering an ITU 3G standard and analyzed a declaration by IPCom made in 2009 to provide FRAND terms. Justice Roth stated:

> I have to say in those circumstances I am very uncertain, to put it mildly, to see why a permanent injunction should be granted in this case at all or indeed any injunction.[63]
>
> In reaction to this decision, Nokia stated:
>
> Nokia is pleased that the UK high court has finally dismissed IPCom's attempts to obtain an injunction. Mr. Justice Roth has confirmed that IPCom must abide by the commitments that it made to the European Commission and cannot seek injunctions under standard essential patents against companies such as Nokia

59. Commission Regulation (EC) No. 139/2004 of 13 February 2012, ¶ 132, *available at* http://ec.europa.eu/competition/mergers/cases/decisions/m6381_20120213_20310_2277480_EN.pdf.

60. *Id.* ¶ 126.

61. *Id.* ¶ 106.

62. *Nokia Corp. v. IP Com Gmbh & Co., KG* 2011 EWHC 1470 [10 May 2012].

63. *UK High Court Denies Patent Injunction Against Nokia in Light of a FRAND Commitment*, Foss Patents (May 30, 2012), http://www.fosspatents.com/2012/05/uk-high-court-denies-patent-injunction.html.

> who are prepared to take a license on fair, reasonable and non-discriminatory terms.[64]

§ 6.6.3 German Actions

The ruling by the U.K. High Court is in stark contrast to a recent court ruling in Germany. In a suit in the Mannheim Regional Court in Germany, Motorola was asserting patents against Microsoft involving the H.264 Video CODEC standard that apply to Windows 7 and the Xbox 360. In reaching its decision to allow Motorola to pursue an injunction, Judge Dr. Kircher started his analysis with respect to Motorola's FRAND pledge. He stated:

> [FRAND] cannot be understood as a binding license offer to any number of third parties unknown to the [p]laintiff, requiring only acceptance by a third party, but as a request to license seekers to submit their own FRAND offers.[65]

Therefore, the court viewed Motorola's FRAND pledge not as a license or contract between it and potential licensees but merely as an invitation to potential licensees to begin a negotiation and provide their FRAND offer.

Following its decision that a FRAND pledge is not a contractual obligation, the Mannheim Court stated that a FRAND pledge does not constitute a "waiver by the patent holder of injunctive relief as a means of enforcing its patent claims against an unknown number of potential patent infringers . . . a patent holder who submits a [p]atent [s]tatement and [l]icensing [d]eclaration [f]orm merely offers to waive its exclusivity rights under the patent by establishing a license agreement—and not unconditionally."[66]

The Mannheim Court also determined that "[i]n the judicial division's view, this review can be limited to the question of whether the rejection of the offer constituted an obvious violation of anti-trust law."[67] Therefore, in the view of the Mannheim Court, the SEP holder who has made a FRAND commitment and has made some attempts to negotiate a license but such negotiations have failed—whether or not the SEP holder made a good-faith attempt to license—it can seek injunctive relief unless its actions are blatantly or obviously a violation of antitrust laws. To sue under the contract,

---

64. *Id.*

65. *The German Approach to FRAND: Let's Err on the Side of Injunctions*, Foss Patents (May 23, 2012), http://www.fosspatents.com/2012/05/german-approach-to-frand-lets-err-on.html.

66. *Id.*

67. *Id.*

there must be an intended beneficiary of the FRAND commitment by examining the language of the SSO Intellecutal Property Rights policy. We note that in *ESS v. PC-Tel*,[68] the court held that the commitment applied to nonstandard members and also noted that specific performance may be an option for enforcing FRAND agreement.

In late 2013, the Mannheim Court announced that it was staying Motorola's case against Apple due to the European Commission's ongoing antitrust investigation of Motorola's use of SEPs against Apple. The court also invited the European Commission to participate in its German FRAND suit.

68. *ESS Tech., Inc. v. PC-Tel, Inc.*, No. C-99-20292 RMW, 1999 WL 33520483 (N.D. Cal. Nov. 4, 1999).

appendix A

Antitrust Guidelines for the Licensing of Intellectual Property

Antitrust Guidelines for the Licensing of Intellectual Property

Issued by the
U.S. Department of Justice*
and the
Federal Trade Commission

April 6, 1995

* These Guidelines supersede section 3.6 in Part I, "Intellectual Property Licensing Arrangements," and cases 6, 10, 11, and 12 in Part II of the U.S. Department of Justice 1988 Antitrust Enforcement Guidelines for International Operations.

Table of Contents

1. Intellectual property protection and the antitrust laws

1.0 These Guidelines state the antitrust enforcement policy of the U.S. Department of Justice and the Federal Trade Commission (individually, "the Agency," and collectively, "the Agencies") with respect to the licensing of intellectual property protected by patent, copyright, and trade secret law, and of know-how.[1] By stating their general policy, the Agencies hope to assist those who need to predict whether the Agencies will challenge a practice as anticompetitive. However, these Guidelines cannot remove judgment and discretion in antitrust law enforcement. Moreover, the standards set forth in these Guidelines must be applied in unforeseeable circumstances. Each case will be evaluated in light of its own facts, and these Guidelines will be applied reasonably and flexibly.[2]

In the United States, patents confer rights to exclude others from making, using, or selling in the United States the invention claimed by the patent for a period of seventeen years from the date of issue.[3] To gain patent protection, an invention (which may be a product, process, machine, or composition of matter) must be novel, nonobvious, and useful. Copyright protection applies to original works of authorship embodied in a tangible medium of expression.[4] A copyright protects only the expression, not the underlying

[1] These Guidelines do not cover the antitrust treatment of trademarks. Although the same general antitrust principles that apply to other forms of intellectual property apply to trademarks as well, these Guidelines deal with technology transfer and innovation-related issues that typically arise with respect to patents, copyrights, trade secrets, and know-how agreements, rather than with product-differentiation issues that typically arise with respect to trademarks.

[2] As is the case with all guidelines, users should rely on qualified counsel to assist them in evaluating the antitrust risk associated with any contemplated transaction or activity. No set of guidelines can possibly indicate how the Agencies will assess the particular facts of every case. Parties who wish to know the Agencies' specific enforcement intentions with respect to any particular transaction should consider seeking a Department of Justice business review letter pursuant to 28 C.F.R. § 50.6 or a Federal Trade Commission Advisory Opinion pursuant to 16 C.F.R. §§ 1.1–1.4.

[3] *See* 35 U.S.C. § 154 (1988). Section 532(a) of the Uruguay Round Agreements Act, Pub. L. No. 103-465, 108 Stat. 4809, 4983 (1994) would change the length of patent protection to a term beginning on the date at which the patent issues and ending twenty years from the date on which the application for the patent was filed.

[4] *See* 17 U.S.C. § 102 (1988 & Supp. V 1993). Copyright protection lasts for the author's life plus 50 years, or 75 years from first publication (or 100 years from creation, whichever expires first) for works made for hire. *See* 17 U.S.C. § 302 (1988). The principles stated in these Guidelines also apply to protection of mask works fixed in a semiconductor chip product (*see* 17 U.S.C. § 901 *et seq.* (1988)), which is analogous to copyright protection for works of authorship.

ideas.[5]Unlike a patent, which protects an invention not only from copying but also from independent creation, a copyright does not preclude others from independently creating similar expression. Trade secret protection applies to information whose economic value depends on its not being generally known.[6] Trade secret protection is conditioned upon efforts to maintain secrecy and has no fixed term. As with copyright protection, trade secret protection does not preclude independent creation by others.

The intellectual property laws and the antitrust laws share the common purpose of promoting innovation and enhancing consumer welfare.[7] The intellectual property laws provide incentives for innovation and its dissemination and commercialization by establishing enforceable property rights for the creators of new and useful products, more efficient processes, and original works of expression. In the absence of intellectual property rights, imitators could more rapidly exploit the efforts of innovators and investors without compensation. Rapid imitation would reduce the commercial value of innovation and erode incentives to invest, ultimately to the detriment of consumers. The antitrust laws promote innovation and consumer welfare by prohibiting certain actions that may harm competition with respect to either existing or new ways of serving consumers.

2. General principles

2.0 These Guidelines embody three general principles: (a) for the purpose of antitrust analysis, the Agencies regard intellectual property as being essentially comparable to any other form of property; (b) the Agencies do not presume that intellectual property creates market power in the antitrust context; and (c) the Agencies recognize that intellectual property licensing allows firms to combine complementary factors of production and is generally procompetitive.

---

[5] *See* 17 U.S.C. § 102(b) (1988).

[6] Trade secret protection derives from state law. *See generally Kewanee Oil Co. v. Bicron Corp.*, 416 U.S. 470 (1974).

[7] "[T]he aims and objectives of patent and antitrust laws may seem, at first glance, wholly at odds. However, the two bodies of law are actually complementary, as both are aimed at encouraging innovation, industry and competition." *Atari Games Corp. v. Nintendo of America, Inc.*, 897 F.2d 1572, 1576 (Fed. Cir. 1990).

2.1 Standard antitrust analysis applies to intellectual property

The Agencies apply the same general antitrust principles to conduct involving intellectual property that they apply to conduct involving any other form of tangible or intangible property. That is not to say that intellectual property is in all respects the same as any other form of property. Intellectual property has important characteristics, such as ease of misappropriation, that distinguish it from many other forms of property. These characteristics can be taken into account by standard antitrust analysis, however, and do not require the application of fundamentally different principles.[8]

Although there are clear and important differences in the purpose, extent, and duration of protection provided under the intellectual property regimes of patent, copyright, and trade secret, the governing antitrust principles are the same. Antitrust analysis takes differences among these forms of intellectual property into account in evaluating the specific market circumstances in which transactions occur, just as it does with other particular market circumstances.

Intellectual property law bestows on the owners of intellectual property certain rights to exclude others. These rights help the owners to profit from the use of their property. An intellectual property owner's rights to exclude are similar to the rights enjoyed by owners of other forms of private property. As with other forms of private property, certain types of conduct with respect to intellectual property may have anticompetitive effects against which the antitrust laws can and do protect. Intellectual property is thus neither particularly free from scrutiny under the antitrust laws, nor particularly suspect under them.

The Agencies recognize that the licensing of intellectual property is often international. The principles of antitrust analysis described in these Guidelines apply equally to domestic and international licensing arrangements. However, as described in the 1995 Department of Justice and Federal Trade Commission Antitrust Enforcement Guidelines for International Operations, considerations particular to international operations, such as jurisdiction and comity, may affect enforcement decisions when the arrangement is in an international context.

[8] As with other forms of property, the power to exclude others from the use of intellectual property may vary substantially, depending on the nature of the property and its status under federal or state law. The greater or lesser legal power of an owner to exclude others is also taken into account by standard antitrust analysis.

2.2 Intellectual property and market power

Market power is the ability profitably to maintain prices above, or output below, competitive levels for a significant period of time.[9] The Agencies will not presume that a patent, copyright, or trade secret necessarily confers market power upon its owner. Although the intellectual property right confers the power to exclude with respect to the *specific* product, process, or work in question, there will often be sufficient actual or potential close substitutes for such product, process, or work to prevent the exercise of market power.[10] If a patent or other form of intellectual property does confer market power, that market power does not by itself offend the antitrust laws. As with any other tangible or intangible asset that enables its owner to obtain significant supracompetitive profits, market power (or even a monopoly) that is solely "a consequence of a superior product, business acumen, or historic accident" does not violate the antitrust laws.[11] Nor does such market power impose on the intellectual property owner an obligation to license the use of that property to others. As in other antitrust contexts, however, market power could be illegally acquired or maintained, or, even if lawfully acquired and maintained, would be relevant to the ability of an intellectual property owner to harm competition through unreasonable conduct in connection with such property.

2.3 Procompetitive benefits of licensing

[9] Market power can be exercised in other economic dimensions, such as quality, service, and the development of new or improved goods and processes. It is assumed in this definition that all competitive dimensions are held constant except the ones in which market power is being exercised; that a seller is able to charge higher prices for a higher-quality product does not alone indicate market power. The definition in the text is stated in terms of a seller with market power. A buyer could also exercise market power (e.g., by maintaining the price below the competitive level, thereby depressing output).

[10] The Agencies note that the law is unclear on this issue. *Compare Jefferson Parish Hospital District No. 2 v. Hyde*, 466 U.S. 2, 16 (1984) (expressing the view in dictum that if a product is protected by a patent, "it is fair to presume that the inability to buy the product elsewhere gives the seller market power") *with id.* at 37 n.7 (O'Connor, J., concurring) ("[A] patent holder has no market power in any relevant sense if there are close substitutes for the patented product."). *Compare also Abbott Laboratories v. Brennan*, 952 F.2d 1346, 1354–55 (Fed. Cir. 1991) (no presumption of market power from intellectual property right), *cert. denied*, 112 S. Ct. 2993 (1992) *with Digidyne Corp. v. Data General Corp.*, 734 F.2d 1336, 1341–42 (9th Cir. 1984) (requisite economic power is presumed from copyright), *cert. denied*, 473 U.S. 908 (1985).

[11] *United States v. Grinnell Corp.*, 384 U.S. 563, 571 (1966); *see also United States v. Aluminum Co. of America*, 148 F.2d 416, 430 (2d Cir. 1945) (Sherman Act is not violated by the attainment of market power solely through "superior skill, foresight and industry").

Intellectual property typically is one component among many in a production process and derives value from its combination with complementary factors. Complementary factors of production include manufacturing and distribution facilities, workforces, and other items of intellectual property. The owner of intellectual property has to arrange for its combination with other necessary factors to realize its commercial value. Often, the owner finds it most efficient to contract with others for these factors, to sell rights to the intellectual property, or to enter into a joint venture arrangement for its development, rather than supplying these complementary factors itself.

Licensing, cross-licensing, or otherwise transferring intellectual property (hereinafter "licensing") can facilitate integration of the licensed property with complementary factors of production. This integration can lead to more efficient exploitation of the intellectual property, benefiting consumers through the reduction of costs and the introduction of new products. Such arrangements increase the value of intellectual property to consumers and to the developers of the technology. By potentially increasing the expected returns from intellectual property, licensing also can increase the incentive for its creation and thus promote greater investment in research and development.

Sometimes the use of one item of intellectual property requires access to another. An item of intellectual property "blocks" another when the second cannot be practiced without using the first. For example, an improvement on a patented machine can be blocked by the patent on the machine. Licensing may promote the coordinated development of technologies that are in a blocking relationship.

Field-of-use, territorial, and other limitations on intellectual property licenses may serve procompetitive ends by allowing the licensor to exploit its property as efficiently and effectively as possible. These various forms of exclusivity can be used to give a licensee an incentive to invest in the commercialization and distribution of products embodying the licensed intellectual property and to develop additional applications for the licensed property. The restrictions may do so, for example, by protecting the licensee against free-riding on the licensee's investments by other licensees or by the licensor. They may also increase the licensor's incentive to license, for example, by protecting the licensor from competition in the licensor's own technology in a market niche that it prefers to keep to itself. These benefits of licensing restrictions apply to patent, copyright, and trade secret licenses, and to know-how agreements.

Example 1[12]

Situation: ComputerCo develops a new, copyrighted software program for inventory management. The program has wide application in the health field. ComputerCo licenses the program in an arrangement that imposes both field of use and territorial limitations. Some of ComputerCo's licenses permit use only in hospitals; others permit use only in group medical practices. ComputerCo charges different royalties for the different uses. All of ComputerCo's licenses permit use only in specified portions of the United States and in specified foreign countries.[13] The licenses contain no provisions that would prevent or discourage licensees from developing, using, or selling any other program, or from competing in any other good or service other than in the use of the licensed program. None of the licensees are actual or likely potential competitors of ComputerCo in the sale of inventory management programs.

Discussion: The key competitive issue raised by the licensing arrangement is whether it harms competition among entities that would have been actual or likely potential competitors in the absence of the arrangement. Such harm could occur if, for example, the licenses anticompetitively foreclose access to competing technologies (in this case, most likely competing computer programs), prevent licensees from developing their own competing technologies (again, in this case, most likely computer programs), or facilitate market allocation or price-fixing for any product or service supplied by the licensees. (*See* section 3.1.) If the license agreements contained such provisions, the Agency evaluating the arrangement would analyze its likely competitive effects as described in parts 3–5 of these Guidelines. In this hypothetical, there are no such provisions and thus the arrangement is merely a subdivision of the licensor's intellectual property among different fields of use and territories. The licensing arrangement does not appear likely to harm competition among entities that would have been actual or likely potential competitors if ComputerCo had chosen not to license the software program. The Agency therefore would be unlikely to object to this arrangement. Based on these facts, the result of the antitrust analysis would be the same whether the technology was protected by patent, copyright, or trade secret. The Agency's conclusion as to likely competitive effects could differ if, for example, the license barred licensees from using any other inventory management program.

[12] The examples in these Guidelines are hypothetical and do not represent judgments about, or analysis of, any actual market circumstances of the named industries.

[13] These Guidelines do not address the possible application of the antitrust laws of other countries to restraints such as territorial restrictions in international licensing arrangements.

3. Antitrust concerns and modes of analysis

3.1 Nature of the concerns

While intellectual property licensing arrangements are typically welfare-enhancing and procompetitive, antitrust concerns may nonetheless arise. For example, a licensing arrangement could include restraints that adversely affect competition in goods markets by dividing the markets among firms that would have competed using different technologies. *See, e.g.*, Example 7. An arrangement that effectively merges the research and development activities of two of only a few entities that could plausibly engage in research and development in the relevant field might harm competition for development of new goods and services. *See* section 3.2.3. An acquisition of intellectual property may lessen competition in a relevant antitrust market. *See* section 5.7. The Agencies will focus on the actual effects of an arrangement, not on its formal terms.

The Agencies will not require the owner of intellectual property to create competition in its own technology. However, antitrust concerns may arise when a licensing arrangement harms competition among entities that would have been actual or likely potential competitors[14] in a relevant market in the absence of the license (entities in a "horizontal relationship"). A restraint in a licensing arrangement may harm such competition, for example, if it facilitates market division or price-fixing. In addition, license restrictions with respect to one market may harm such competition in another market by anticompetitively foreclosing access to, or significantly raising the price of, an important input,[15] or by facilitating coordination to increase price or reduce output. When it appears that such competition may be adversely affected, the Agencies will follow the analysis set forth below. *See generally* sections 3.4 and 4.2.

3.2 Markets affected by licensing arrangements

Licensing arrangements raise concerns under the antitrust laws if they are likely to affect adversely the prices, quantities, qualities, or varieties of goods and services[16] either currently or potentially available. The competitive effects of licensing arrangements often can be

[14] A firm will be treated as a likely potential competitor if there is evidence that entry by that firm is reasonably probable in the absence of the licensing arrangement.

[15] As used herein, "input" includes outlets for distribution and sales, as well as factors of production. *See, e.g.*, sections 4.1.1 and 5.3–5.5 for further discussion of conditions under which foreclosing access to, or raising the price of, an input may harm competition in a relevant market.

[16] Hereinafter, the term "goods" also includes services.

adequately assessed within the relevant markets for the goods affected by the arrangements. In such instances, the Agencies will delineate and analyze only goods markets. In other cases, however, the analysis may require the delineation of markets for technology or markets for research and development (innovation markets).

3.2.1 Goods markets

A number of different goods markets may be relevant to evaluating the effects of a licensing arrangement. A restraint in a licensing arrangement may have competitive effects in markets for final or intermediate goods made using the intellectual property, or it may have effects upstream, in markets for goods that are used as inputs, along with the intellectual property, to the production of other goods. In general, for goods markets affected by a licensing arrangement, the Agencies will approach the delineation of relevant market and the measurement of market share in the intellectual property area as in section 1 of the U.S. Department of Justice and Federal Trade Commission Horizontal Merger Guidelines.[17]

3.2.2 Technology markets

Technology markets consist of the intellectual property that is licensed (the "licensed technology") and its close substitutes—that is, the technologies or goods that are close enough substitutes significantly to constrain the exercise of market power with respect to the intellectual property that is licensed.[18] When rights to intellectual property are marketed separately from the products in which they are used,[19] the Agencies may rely on technology markets to analyze the competitive effects of a licensing arrangement.

Example 2

Situation: Firms Alpha and Beta independently develop different patented process technologies

---

[17] U.S. Department of Justice and Federal Trade Commission, Horizontal Merger Guidelines (April 2, 1992) (hereinafter "1992 Horizontal Merger Guidelines"). As stated in section 1.41 of the 1992 Horizontal Merger Guidelines, market shares for goods markets "can be expressed either in dollar terms through measurement of sales, shipments, or production, or in physical terms through measurement of sales, shipments, production, capacity or reserves."

[18] For example, the owner of a process for producing a particular good may be constrained in its conduct with respect to that process not only by other processes for making that good, but also by other goods that compete with the downstream good and by the processes used to produce those other goods.

[19] Intellectual property is often licensed, sold, or transferred as an integral part of a marketed good. An example is a patented product marketed with an implied license permitting its use. In such circumstances, there is no need for a separate analysis of technology markets to capture relevant competitive effects.

to manufacture the same off-patent drug for the treatment of a particular disease. Before the firms use their technologies internally or license them to third parties, they announce plans jointly to manufacture the drug, and to assign their manufacturing processes to the new manufacturing venture. Many firms are capable of using and have the incentive to use the licensed technologies to manufacture and distribute the drug; thus, the market for drug manufacturing and distribution is competitive. One of the Agencies is evaluating the likely competitive effects of the planned venture.

Discussion: The Agency would analyze the competitive effects of the proposed joint venture by first defining the relevant markets in which competition may be affected and then evaluating the likely competitive effects of the joint venture in the identified markets. (*See* Example 4 for a discussion of the Agencies' approach to joint venture analysis.) In this example, the structural effect of the joint venture in the relevant goods market for the manufacture and distribution of the drug is unlikely to be significant, because many firms in addition to the joint venture compete in that market. The joint venture might, however, increase the prices of the drug produced using Alpha's or Beta's technology by reducing competition in the relevant market for technology to manufacture the drug.

The Agency would delineate a technology market in which to evaluate likely competitive effects of the proposed joint venture. The Agency would identify other technologies that can be used to make the drug with levels of effectiveness and cost per dose comparable to that of the technologies owned by Alpha and Beta. In addition, the Agency would consider the extent to which competition from other drugs that are substitutes for the drug produced using Alpha's or Beta's technology would limit the ability of a hypothetical monopolist that owned both Alpha's and Beta's technology to raise its price.

To identify a technology's close substitutes and thus to delineate the relevant technology market, the Agencies will, if the data permit, identify the smallest group of technologies and goods over which a hypothetical monopolist of those technologies and goods likely would exercise market power—for example, by imposing a small but significant and nontransitory price increase.[20] The Agencies recognize that technology often is licensed in ways that are not readily quantifiable in monetary terms.[21] In such

[20] This is conceptually analogous to the analytical approach to goods markets under the 1992 Horizontal Merger Guidelines. *Cf.* § 1.11. Of course, market power also can be exercised in other dimensions, such as quality, and these dimensions also may be relevant to the definition and analysis of technology markets.

[21] For example, technology may be licensed royalty-free in exchange for the right to use other technology, or it may be licensed as part of a package license.

circumstances, the Agencies will delineate the relevant market by identifying other technologies and goods which buyers would substitute at a cost comparable to that of using the licensed technology.

In assessing the competitive significance of current and likely potential participants in a technology market, the Agencies will take into account all relevant evidence. When market share data are available and accurately reflect the competitive significance of market participants, the Agencies will include market share data in this assessment. The Agencies also will seek evidence of buyers' and market participants' assessments of the competitive significance of technology market participants. Such evidence is particularly important when market share data are unavailable, or do not accurately represent the competitive significance of market participants. When market share data or other indicia of market power are not available, and it appears that competing technologies are comparably efficient,[22] the Agencies will assign each technology the same market share. For new technologies, the Agencies generally will use the best available information to estimate market acceptance over a two-year period, beginning with commercial introduction.

3.2.3 Research and development: innovation markets

If a licensing arrangement may adversely affect competition to develop new or improved goods or processes, the Agencies will analyze such an impact either as a separate competitive effect in relevant goods or technology markets, or as a competitive effect in a separate innovation market. A licensing arrangement may have competitive effects on innovation that cannot be adequately addressed through the analysis of goods or technology markets. For example, the arrangement may affect the development of goods that do not yet exist.[23] Alternatively, the arrangement may affect the development of new or improved

---

[22] The Agencies will regard two technologies as "comparably efficient" if they can be used to produce close substitutes at comparable costs.

[23] *E.g.*, *Sensormatic*, FTC Inv. No. 941-0126, 60 Fed. Reg. 5428 (accepted for comment Dec. 28, 1994); *Wright Medical Technology, Inc.*, FTC Inv. No. 951-0015, 60 Fed. Reg. 460 (accepted for comment Dec. 8, 1994); *American Home Products*, FTC Inv. No. 941-0116, 59 Fed. Reg. 60,807 (accepted for comment Nov. 28, 1994); *Roche Holdings Ltd.*, 113 F.T.C. 1086 (1990); *United States v. Automobile Mfrs. Ass'n*, 307 F. Supp. 617 (C.D. Cal. 1969), *appeal dismissed sub nom. City of New York v. United States*, 397 U.S. 248 (1970), *modified sub nom. United States v. Motor Vehicles Mfrs. Ass'n*, 1982–83 Trade Cas. (CCH) ¶ 65,088 (C.D. Cal. 1982).

goods or processes in geographic markets where there is no actual or likely potential competition in the relevant goods.[24]

An innovation market consists of the research and development directed to particular new or improved goods or processes, and the close substitutes for that research and development. The close substitutes are research and development efforts, technologies, and goods[25] that significantly constrain the exercise of market power with respect to the relevant research and development, for example by limiting the ability and incentive of a hypothetical monopolist to retard the pace of research and development. The Agencies will delineate an innovation market only when the capabilities to engage in the relevant research and development can be associated with specialized assets or characteristics of specific firms.

In assessing the competitive significance of current and likely potential participants in an innovation market, the Agencies will take into account all relevant evidence. When market share data are available and accurately reflect the competitive significance of market participants, the Agencies will include market share data in this assessment. The Agencies also will seek evidence of buyers' and market participants' assessments of the competitive significance of innovation market participants. Such evidence is particularly important when market share data are unavailable or do not accurately represent the competitive significance of market participants. The Agencies may base the market shares of participants in an innovation market on their shares of identifiable assets or characteristics upon which innovation depends, on shares of research and development expenditures, or on shares of a related product. When entities have comparable capabilities and incentives to pursue research and development that is a close substitute for the research and development activities of the parties to a licensing arrangement, the Agencies may assign equal market shares to such entities.

---

[24] *See* Complaint, *United States v. General Motors Corp.*, Civ. No. 93-530 (D. Del., filed Nov. 16, 1993).

[25] For example, the licensor of research and development may be constrained in its conduct not only by competing research and development efforts but also by other existing goods that would compete with the goods under development.

Example 3

Situation: Two companies that specialize in advanced metallurgy agree to cross-license future patents relating to the development of a new component for aircraft jet turbines. Innovation in the development of the component requires the capability to work with very high tensile strength materials for jet turbines. Aspects of the licensing arrangement raise the possibility that competition in research and development of this and related components will be lessened. One of the Agencies is considering whether to define an innovation market in which to evaluate the competitive effects of the arrangement.

Discussion: If the firms that have the capability and incentive to work with very high tensile strength materials for jet turbines can be reasonably identified, the Agency will consider defining a relevant innovation market for development of the new component. If the number of firms with the required capability and incentive to engage in research and development of very high tensile strength materials for aircraft jet turbines is small, the Agency may employ the concept of an innovation market to analyze the likely competitive effects of the arrangement in that market, or as an aid in analyzing competitive effects in technology or goods markets. The Agency would perform its analysis as described in parts 3–5.

If the number of firms with the required capability and incentive is large (either because there are a large number of such firms in the jet turbine industry, or because there are many firms in other industries with the required capability and incentive), then the Agency will conclude that the innovation market is competitive. Under these circumstances, it is unlikely that any single firm or plausible aggregation of firms could acquire a large enough share of the assets necessary for innovation to have an adverse impact on competition.

If the Agency cannot reasonably identify the firms with the required capability and incentive, it will not attempt to define an innovation market.

Example 4

Situation: Three of the largest producers of a plastic used in disposable bottles plan to engage in joint research and development to produce a new type of plastic that is rapidly biodegradable. The joint venture will grant to its partners (but to no one else) licenses to all patent rights and use of know-how. One of the Agencies is evaluating the likely competitive effects of the proposed joint venture.

Discussion: The Agency would analyze the proposed research and development joint venture using an analysis similar to that applied to other joint ventures.[26] The Agency would begin by defining the relevant markets in which to analyze the joint venture's likely competitive effects.

[26] *See, e.g.*, U.S. Department of Justice and Federal Trade Commission, Statements of Enforcement Policy and Analytical Principles Relating to Health Care and Antitrust 20–23, 37–40, 72–74 (September 27, 1994). This type of transaction may qualify for treatment under the National Cooperative Research and Production Act of 1993, 15 U.S.C.A §§ 4301–05.

In this case, a relevant market is an innovation market—research and development for biodegradable (and other environmentally friendly) containers. The Agency would seek to identify any other entities that would be actual or likely potential competitors with the joint venture in that relevant market. This would include those firms that have the capability and incentive to undertake research and development closely substitutable for the research and development proposed to be undertaken by the joint venture, taking into account such firms' existing technologies and technologies under development, R&D facilities, and other relevant assets and business circumstances. Firms possessing such capabilities and incentives would be included in the research and development market even if they are not competitors in relevant markets for related goods, such as the plastics currently produced by the joint venturers, although competitors in existing goods markets may often also compete in related innovation markets.

Having defined a relevant innovation market, the Agency would assess whether the joint venture is likely to have anticompetitive effects in that market. A starting point in this analysis is the degree of concentration in the relevant market and the market shares of the parties to the joint venture. If, in addition to the parties to the joint venture (taken collectively), there are at least four other independently controlled entities that possess comparable capabilities and incentives to undertake research and development of biodegradable plastics, or other products that would be close substitutes for such new plastics, the joint venture ordinarily would be unlikely to adversely affect competition in the relevant innovation market (*cf.* section 4.3). If there are fewer than four other independently controlled entities with similar capabilities and incentives, the Agency would consider whether the joint venture would give the parties to the joint venture an incentive and ability collectively to reduce investment in, or otherwise to retard the pace or scope of, research and development efforts. If the joint venture creates a significant risk of anticompetitive effects in the innovation market, the Agency would proceed to consider efficiency justifications for the venture, such as the potential for combining complementary R&D assets in such a way as to make successful innovation more likely, or to bring it about sooner, or to achieve cost reductions in research and development.

The Agency would also assess the likelihood that the joint venture would adversely affect competition in other relevant markets, including markets for products produced by the parties to the joint venture. The risk of such adverse competitive effects would be increased to the extent that, for example, the joint venture facilitates the exchange among the parties of competitively sensitive information relating to goods markets in which the parties currently compete or facilitates the coordination of competitive activities in such markets. The Agency would examine whether the joint venture imposes collateral restraints that might significantly restrict competition among the joint venturers in goods markets, and would examine whether such collateral restraints were reasonably necessary to achieve any efficiencies that are likely to be attained by the venture.

3.3 Horizontal and vertical relationships

As with other property transfers, antitrust analysis of intellectual property licensing arrangements examines whether the relationship among the parties to the arrangement is primarily horizontal or vertical in nature, or whether it has substantial aspects of both. A licensing arrangement has a vertical component when it affects activities that are in a complementary relationship, as is typically the case in a licensing arrangement. For example, the licensor's primary line of business may be in research and development, and the licensees, as manufacturers, may be buying the rights to use technology developed by the licensor. Alternatively, the licensor may be a component manufacturer owning intellectual property rights in a product that the licensee manufactures by combining the component with other inputs, or the licensor may manufacture the product, and the licensees may operate primarily in distribution and marketing.

In addition to this vertical component, the licensor and its licensees may also have a horizontal relationship. For analytical purposes, the Agencies ordinarily will treat a relationship between a licensor and its licensees, or between licensees, as horizontal when they would have been actual or likely potential competitors in a relevant market in the absence of the license.

The existence of a horizontal relationship between a licensor and its licensees does not, in itself, indicate that the arrangement is anticompetitive. Identification of such relationships is merely an aid in determining whether there may be anticompetitive effects arising from a licensing arrangement. Such a relationship need not give rise to an anticompetitive effect, nor does a purely vertical relationship assure that there are no anticompetitive effects.

The following examples illustrate different competitive relationships among a licensor and its licensees.

Example 5

Situation: AgCo, a manufacturer of farm equipment, develops a new, patented emission control technology for its tractor engines and licenses it to FarmCo, another farm equipment manufacturer. AgCo's emission control technology is far superior to the technology currently owned and used by FarmCo, so much so that FarmCo's technology does not significantly constrain the prices that AgCo could charge for its technology. AgCo's emission control patent has a broad scope. It is likely that any improved emissions control technology that FarmCo could develop in the foreseeable future would infringe AgCo's patent.

Discussion: Because FarmCo's emission control technology does not significantly constrain AgCo's competitive conduct with respect to its emission control technology, AgCo's and FarmCo's emission control technologies are not close substitutes for each other. FarmCo is a consumer of AgCo's technology and is not an actual competitor of AgCo in the relevant market for superior emission control technology of the kind licensed by AgCo. Furthermore, FarmCo is not a likely potential competitor of AgCo in the relevant market because, even if FarmCo could develop an improved emission control technology, it is likely that it would infringe AgCo's patent. This means that the relationship between AgCo and FarmCo with regard to the supply and use of emissions control technology is vertical. Assuming that AgCo and FarmCo are actual or likely potential competitors in sales of farm equipment products, their relationship is horizontal in the relevant markets for farm equipment.

Example 6

Situation: FarmCo develops a new valve technology for its engines and enters into a cross-licensing arrangement with AgCo, whereby AgCo licenses its emission control technology to FarmCo and FarmCo licenses its valve technology to AgCo. AgCo already owns an alternative valve technology that can be used to achieve engine performance similar to that using FarmCo's valve technology and at a comparable cost to consumers. Before adopting FarmCo's technology, AgCo was using its own valve technology in its production of engines and was licensing (and continues to license) that technology for use by others. As in Example 5, FarmCo does not own or control an emission control technology that is a close substitute for the technology licensed from AgCo. Furthermore, as in Example 5, FarmCo is not likely to develop an improved emission control technology that would be a close substitute for AgCo's technology, because of AgCo's blocking patent.

Discussion: FarmCo is a consumer and not a competitor of AgCo's emission control technology. As in Example 5, their relationship is vertical with regard to this technology. The relationship between AgCo and FarmCo in the relevant market that includes engine valve technology is vertical in part and horizontal in part. It is vertical in part because AgCo and FarmCo stand in a complementary relationship, in which AgCo is a consumer of a technology supplied by FarmCo. However, the relationship between AgCo and FarmCo in the relevant market that includes engine valve technology is also horizontal in part, because FarmCo and AgCo are actual competitors in the licensing of valve technology that can be used to achieve similar engine performance at a comparable cost. Whether the firms license their valve technologies to others is not important for the conclusion that the firms have a horizontal relationship in this relevant market. Even if AgCo's use of its valve technology were solely captive to its own production, the fact that the two valve technologies are substitutable at comparable cost means that the two firms have a horizontal relationship.

As in Example 5, the relationship between AgCo and FarmCo is horizontal in the relevant markets for farm equipment.

3.4 Framework for evaluating licensing restraints

In the vast majority of cases, restraints in intellectual property licensing arrangements are evaluated under the rule of reason. The Agencies' general approach in analyzing a licensing restraint under the rule of reason is to inquire whether the restraint is likely to have anticompetitive effects and, if so, whether the restraint is reasonably necessary to achieve procompetitive benefits that outweigh those anticompetitive effects. *See Federal Trade Commission v. Indiana Federation of Dentists*, 476 U.S. 447 (1986); *NCAA v. Board of Regents of the University of Oklahoma,* 468 U.S. 85 (1984); *Broadcast Music, Inc. v. Columbia Broadcasting System, Inc.*, 441 U.S. 1 (1979); 7 Phillip E. Areeda, *Antitrust Law* § 1502 (1986). *See also* part 4.

In some cases, however, the courts conclude that a restraint's "nature and necessary effect are so plainly anticompetitive" that it should be treated as unlawful per se, without an elaborate inquiry into the restraint's likely competitive effect. *Federal Trade Commission v. Superior Court Trial Lawyers Association*, 493 U.S. 411, 433 (1990); *National Society of Professional Engineers v. United States*, 435 U.S. 679, 692 (1978). Among the restraints that have been held per se unlawful are naked price-fixing, output restraints, and market division among horizontal competitors, as well as certain group boycotts and resale price maintenance.

To determine whether a particular restraint in a licensing arrangement is given per se or rule of reason treatment, the Agencies will assess whether the restraint in question can be expected to contribute to an efficiency-enhancing integration of economic activity. *See Broadcast Music*, 441 U.S. at 16–24. In general, licensing arrangements promote such integration because they facilitate the combination of the licensor's intellectual property with complementary factors of production owned by the licensee. A restraint in a licensing arrangement may further such integration by, for example, aligning the incentives of the licensor and the licensees to promote the development and marketing of the licensed technology, or by substantially reducing transactions costs. If there is no efficiency-enhancing integration of economic activity and if the type of restraint is one that has been accorded per se treatment, the Agencies will challenge the restraint under the per se rule. Otherwise, the Agencies will apply a rule of reason analysis.

Application of the rule of reason generally requires a comprehensive inquiry into market conditions. (*See* sections 4.1–4.3.) However, that inquiry may be truncated in certain circumstances. If the Agencies conclude that a restraint has no likely anticompetitive effects, they will treat it as reasonable, without an elaborate analysis of market power or the justifications for the restraint. Similarly, if a restraint facially appears to be of a kind that would always or almost always tend to reduce output or increase prices,[27] and the restraint is not reasonably related to efficiencies, the Agencies will likely challenge the restraint without an elaborate analysis of particular industry circumstances.[28] *See Indiana Federation of Dentists*, 476 U.S. at 459–60; *NCAA*, 468 U.S. at 109.

Example 7

Situation: Gamma, which manufactures Product X using its patented process, offers a license for its process technology to every other manufacturer of Product X, each of which competes world-wide with Gamma in the manufacture and sale of X. The process technology does not represent an economic improvement over the available existing technologies. Indeed, although most manufacturers accept licenses from Gamma, none of the licensees actually uses the licensed technology. The licenses provide that each manufacturer has an exclusive right to sell Product X manufactured using the licensed technology in a designated geographic area and that no manufacturer may sell Product X, however manufactured, outside the designated territory.

Discussion: The manufacturers of Product X are in a horizontal relationship in the goods market for Product X. Any manufacturers of Product X that control technologies that are substitutable at comparable cost for Gamma's process are also horizontal competitors of Gamma in the relevant technology market. The licensees of Gamma's process technology are technically in a vertical relationship, although that is not significant in this example because they do not actually use Gamma's technology.

The licensing arrangement restricts competition in the relevant goods market among manufacturers of Product X by requiring each manufacturer to limit its sales to an exclusive territory. Thus, competition among entities that would be actual competitors in the absence of the licensing arrangement is restricted. Based on the facts set forth above, the licensing arrangement does not involve a useful transfer of technology, and thus it is unlikely that the restraint on sales outside the designated territories contributes to an efficiency-enhancing integration of economic activity. Consequently, the evaluating Agency would be likely to challenge the arrangement under the per se rule as a horizontal territorial market allocation scheme and to view the intellectual property aspects of the arrangement as a sham intended to cloak its true nature.

---

[27] Details about the Federal Trade Commission's approach are set forth in *Massachusetts Board of Registration in Optometry*, 110 F.T.C. 549, 604 (1988). In applying its truncated rule of reason inquiry, the FTC uses the analytical category of "inherently suspect" restraints to denote facially anticompetitive restraints that would always or almost always tend to decrease output or increase prices, but that may be relatively unfamiliar or may not fit neatly into traditional per se categories.

[28] Under the FTC's *Mass. Board* approach, asserted efficiency justifications for inherently suspect restraints are examined to determine whether they are plausible and, if so, whether they are valid in the context of the market at issue. *Mass. Board*, 110 F.T.C. at 604.

If the licensing arrangement could be expected to contribute to an efficiency-enhancing integration of economic activity, as might be the case if the licensed technology were an advance over existing processes and used by the licensees, the Agency would analyze the arrangement under the rule of reason applying the analytical framework described in this section.

In this example, the competitive implications do not generally depend on whether the licensed technology is protected by patent, is a trade secret or other know-how, or is a computer program protected by copyright; nor do the competitive implications generally depend on whether the allocation of markets is territorial, as in this example, or functional, based on fields of use.

4. General principles concerning the Agencies' evaluation of licensing arrangements under the rule of reason

4.1 Analysis of anticompetitive effects

The existence of anticompetitive effects resulting from a restraint in a licensing arrangement will be evaluated on the basis of the analysis described in this section.

4.1.1 Market structure, coordination, and foreclosure

When a licensing arrangement affects parties in a horizontal relationship, a restraint in that arrangement may increase the risk of coordinated pricing, output restrictions, or the acquisition or maintenance of market power. Harm to competition also may occur if the arrangement poses a significant risk of retarding or restricting the development of new or improved goods or processes. The potential for competitive harm depends in part on the degree of concentration in, the difficulty of entry into, and the responsiveness of supply and demand to changes in price in the relevant markets. *Cf.* 1992 Horizontal Merger Guidelines §§ 1.5, 3.

When the licensor and licensees are in a vertical relationship, the Agencies will analyze whether the licensing arrangement may harm competition among entities in a horizontal relationship at either the level of the licensor or the licensees, or possibly in another relevant market. Harm to competition from a restraint may occur if it anticompetitively forecloses access to, or increases competitors' costs of obtaining, important inputs, or facilitates coordination to raise price or restrict output. The risk of anticompetitively foreclosing access or increasing competitors' costs is related to the proportion of the markets affected by the licensing restraint; other characteristics of the relevant markets, such as concentration, difficulty of entry, and the responsiveness of supply and demand to changes in price in the relevant markets; and the duration of the restraint. A licensing arrangement does not foreclose competition merely because some or all of the potential licensees in an industry choose to use the licensed technology to the exclusion of other technologies. Exclusive use may be an efficient consequence of the licensed technology having the lowest cost or highest value.

Harm to competition from a restraint in a vertical licensing arrangement also may occur if a licensing restraint facilitates coordination among entities in a horizontal relationship to raise prices or reduce output in a relevant market. For example, if owners of competing technologies impose similar restraints on their licensees, the licensors may find it easier to coordinate their pricing. Similarly, licensees that are competitors may find it easier to coordinate their pricing if they are subject to common restraints in licenses with a common licensor or competing licensors. The risk of anticompetitive coordination is increased when the relevant markets are concentrated and difficult to enter. The use of similar restraints may be common and procompetitive in an industry, however, because they contribute to efficient exploitation of the licensed property.

4.1.2 Licensing arrangements involving exclusivity

A licensing arrangement may involve exclusivity in two distinct respects. First, the licensor may grant one or more *exclusive licenses*, which restrict the right of the licensor to license others and possibly also to use the technology itself. Generally, an exclusive license may raise antitrust concerns only if the licensees themselves, or the licensor and its licensees, are in a horizontal relationship. Examples of arrangements involving exclusive licensing that may give rise to antitrust concerns include cross-licensing by parties collectively possessing market power (*see* section 5.5), grantbacks (*see* section 5.6), and acquisitions of intellectual property rights (*see* section 5.7).

A non-exclusive license of intellectual property that does not contain any restraints on the competitive conduct of the licensor or the licensee generally does not present antitrust concerns even if the parties to the license are in a horizontal relationship, because the non-exclusive license normally does not diminish competition that would occur in its absence.

A second form of exclusivity, *exclusive dealing*, arises when a license prevents or restrains the licensee from licensing, selling, distributing, or using competing technologies. *See* section 5.4. Exclusivity may be achieved by an explicit exclusive dealing term in the license or by other provisions such as compensation terms or other economic incentives. Such restraints may anticompetitively foreclose access to, or increase competitors' costs of obtaining, important inputs, or facilitate coordination to raise price or reduce output, but they also may have procompetitive effects. For example, a licensing arrangement that prevents the licensee from dealing in other technologies may encourage the licensee to develop and market the licensed technology or specialized applications of that technology. *See, e.g.*, Example 8. The Agencies will take into account such procompetitive effects in evaluating the reasonableness of the arrangement. *See* section 4.2.

The antitrust principles that apply to a licensor's grant of various forms of exclusivity to and among its licensees are similar to those that apply to comparable vertical restraints outside the licensing context, such as exclusive territories and exclusive dealing. However, the fact that intellectual property may in some cases be misappropriated more easily than other forms of property may justify the use of some restrictions that might be anticompetitive in other contexts.

As noted earlier, the Agencies will focus on the actual practice and its effects, not on the formal terms of the arrangement. A license denominated as non-exclusive (either in the sense of exclusive licensing or in the sense of exclusive dealing) may nonetheless give rise to the same concerns posed by formal exclusivity. A non-exclusive license may have the effect of exclusive licensing if it is structured so that the licensor is unlikely to license others or to practice the technology itself. A license that does not explicitly require exclusive dealing may have the effect of exclusive dealing if it is structured to increase significantly a licensee's cost when it uses competing technologies. However, a licensing arrangement will not automatically raise these concerns merely because a party chooses to deal with a single licensee or licensor, or confines his activity to a single field of use or location, or because only a single licensee has chosen to take a license.

Example 8

Situation: NewCo, the inventor and manufacturer of a new flat panel display technology, lacking the capability to bring a flat panel display product to market, grants BigCo an exclusive license to sell a product embodying NewCo's technology. BigCo does not currently sell, and is not developing (or likely to develop), a product that would compete with the product embodying the new technology and does not control rights to another display technology. Several firms offer competing displays, BigCo accounts for only a small proportion of the outlets for distribution of display products, and entry into the manufacture and distribution of display products is relatively easy. Demand for the new technology is uncertain and successful market penetration will require considerable promotional effort. The license contains an exclusive dealing restriction preventing BigCo from selling products that compete with the product embodying the licensed technology.

Discussion: This example illustrates both types of exclusivity in a licensing arrangement. The license is exclusive in that it restricts the right of the licensor to grant other licenses. In addition, the license has an exclusive dealing component in that it restricts the licensee from selling competing products.

The inventor of the display technology and its licensee are in a vertical relationship and are not actual or likely potential competitors in the manufacture or sale of display products or in the sale or development of technology. Hence, the grant of an exclusive license does not affect competition between the licensor and the licensee. The exclusive license may promote competition in the manufacturing and sale of display products by encouraging BigCo to develop and promote the new product in the face of uncertain demand by rewarding BigCo for its efforts if they lead to large sales. Although the license bars the licensee from selling competing products, this exclusive dealing aspect is unlikely in this example to harm competition by anticompetitively foreclosing access, raising competitors' costs of inputs, or facilitating anticompetitive pricing because the relevant product market is unconcentrated, the exclusive dealing restraint affects only a small proportion of the outlets for distribution of display products, and entry is easy. On these facts, the evaluating Agency would be unlikely to challenge the arrangement.

4.2 Efficiencies and justifications

If the Agencies conclude, upon an evaluation of the market factors described in section 4.1, that a restraint in a licensing arrangement is unlikely to have an anticompetitive effect, they will not challenge the restraint. If the Agencies conclude that the restraint has, or is likely to have, an anticompetitive effect, they will consider whether the restraint is reasonably necessary to achieve procompetitive efficiencies. If the restraint is reasonably necessary, the Agencies will balance the procompetitive efficiencies and the anticompetitive effects to determine the probable net effect on competition in each relevant market.

The Agencies' comparison of anticompetitive harms and procompetitive efficiencies is necessarily a qualitative one. The risk of anticompetitive effects in a particular case may be insignificant compared to the expected efficiencies, or vice versa. As the expected anticompetitive effects in a particular licensing arrangement increase, the Agencies will require evidence establishing a greater level of expected efficiencies.

The existence of practical and significantly less restrictive alternatives is relevant to a determination of whether a restraint is reasonably necessary. If it is clear that the parties could have achieved similar efficiencies by means that are significantly less restrictive, then the Agencies will not give weight to the parties' efficiency claim. In making this assessment, however, the Agencies will not engage in a search for a theoretically least restrictive alternative that is not realistic in the practical prospective business situation faced by the parties.

When a restraint has, or is likely to have, an anticompetitive effect, the duration of that restraint can be an important factor in determining whether it is reasonably necessary to achieve the putative procompetitive efficiency. The effective duration of a restraint may depend on a number of factors, including the option of the affected party to terminate the arrangement unilaterally and the presence of contract terms (e.g., unpaid balances on minimum purchase commitments) that encourage the licensee to renew a license arrangement. Consistent with their approach to less restrictive alternative analysis generally, the Agencies will not attempt to draw fine distinctions regarding duration; rather, their focus will be on situations in which the duration clearly exceeds the period needed to achieve the procompetitive efficiency.

The evaluation of procompetitive efficiencies, of the reasonable necessity of a restraint to achieve them, and of the duration of the restraint, may depend on the market context. A restraint that may be justified by the needs of a new entrant, for example, may not have a procompetitive efficiency justification in different market circumstances. *Cf. United States v. Jerrold Electronics Corp.*, 187 F. Supp. 545 (E.D. Pa. 1960), *aff'd per curiam*, 365 U.S. 567 (1961).

4.3 Antitrust "safety zone"

Because licensing arrangements often promote innovation and enhance competition, the Agencies believe that an antitrust "safety zone" is useful in order to provide some degree of certainty and thus to encourage such activity.[29] Absent extraordinary circumstances, the Agencies will not challenge a restraint in an intellectual property licensing arrangement if (1) the restraint is not facially anticompetitive[30] and (2) the licensor and its licensees collectively account for no more than twenty percent of each relevant market significantly affected by the restraint. This "safety zone" does not apply to those transfers of intellectual property rights to which a merger analysis is applied. *See* section 5.7.

Whether a restraint falls within the safety zone will be determined by reference only to goods markets unless the analysis of goods markets alone would inadequately address the effects of the licensing arrangement on competition among technologies or in research and development.

---

[29] The antitrust "safety zone" does not apply to restraints that are not in a licensing arrangement, or to restraints that are in a licensing arrangement but are unrelated to the use of the licensed intellectual property.

[30] "Facially anticompetitive" refers to restraints that normally warrant per se treatment, as well as other restraints of a kind that would always or almost always tend to reduce output or increase prices. *See* section 3.4.

If an examination of the effects on competition among technologies or in research development is required, and if market share data are unavailable or do not accurately represent competitive significance, the following safety zone criteria will apply. Absent extraordinary circumstances, the Agencies will not challenge a restraint in an intellectual property licensing arrangement that may affect competition in a technology market if (1) the restraint is not facially anticompetitive and (2) there are four or more independently controlled technologies in addition to the technologies controlled by the parties to the licensing arrangement that may be substitutable for the licensed technology at a comparable cost to the user. Absent extraordinary circumstances, the Agencies will not challenge a restraint in an intellectual property licensing arrangement that may affect competition in an innovation market if (1) the restraint is not facially anticompetitive and (2) four or more independently controlled entities in addition to the parties to the licensing arrangement possess the required specialized assets or characteristics and the incentive to engage in research and development that is a close substitute of the research and development activities of the parties to the licensing agreement.[31]

The Agencies emphasize that licensing arrangements are not anticompetitive merely because they do not fall within the scope of the safety zone. Indeed, it is likely that the great majority of licenses falling outside the safety zone are lawful and procompetitive. The safety zone is designed to provide owners of intellectual property with a degree of certainty in those situations in which anticompetitive effects are so unlikely that the arrangements may be presumed not to be anticompetitive without an inquiry into particular industry circumstances. It is not intended to suggest that parties should conform to the safety zone or to discourage parties falling outside the safety zone from adopting restrictions in their license arrangements that are reasonably necessary to achieve an efficiency-enhancing integration of economic activity. The Agencies will analyze arrangements falling outside the safety zone based on the considerations outlined in parts 3–5.

The status of a licensing arrangement with respect to the safety zone may change over time. A determination by the Agencies that a restraint in a licensing arrangement qualifies for inclusion in the safety zone is based on the factual circumstances prevailing at the time of the conduct at issue.[32]

---

[31] This is consistent with congressional intent in enacting the National Cooperative Research Act. *See* H.R. Conf. Rpt. No. 1044, 98th Cong., 2d Sess., 10, *reprinted in* 1984 U.S.C.C.A.N. 3105, 3134–35.

[32] The conduct at issue may be the transaction giving rise to the restraint or the subsequent implementation of the restraint.

5. Application of general principles

5.0 This section illustrates the application of the general principles discussed above to particular licensing restraints and to arrangements that involve the cross-licensing, pooling, or acquisition of intellectual property. The restraints and arrangements identified are typical of those that are likely to receive antitrust scrutiny; however, they are not intended as an exhaustive list of practices that could raise competitive concerns.

5.1 Horizontal restraints

The existence of a restraint in a licensing arrangement that affects parties in a horizontal relationship (a "horizontal restraint") does not necessarily cause the arrangement to be anticompetitive. As in the case of joint ventures among horizontal competitors, licensing arrangements among such competitors may promote rather than hinder competition if they result in integrative efficiencies. Such efficiencies may arise, for example, from the realization of economies of scale and the integration of complementary research and development, production, and marketing capabilities.

Following the general principles outlined in section 3.4, horizontal restraints often will be evaluated under the rule of reason. In some circumstances, however, that analysis may be truncated; additionally, some restraints may merit per se treatment, including price fixing, allocation of markets or customers, agreements to reduce output, and certain group boycotts.

Example 9

Situation: Two of the leading manufacturers of a consumer electronic product hold patents that cover alternative circuit designs for the product. The manufacturers assign their patents to a separate corporation wholly owned by the two firms. That corporation licenses the right to use the circuit designs to other consumer product manufacturers and establishes the license royalties. None of the patents is blocking; that is, each of the patents can be used without infringing a patent owned by the other firm. The different circuit designs are substitutable in that each permits the manufacture at comparable cost to consumers of products that consumers consider to be interchangeable. One of the Agencies is analyzing the licensing arrangement.

Discussion: In this example, the manufacturers are horizontal competitors in the goods market for the consumer product and in the related technology markets. The competitive issue with regard to a joint assignment of patent rights is whether the assignment has an adverse impact on competition in technology and goods markets that is not outweighed by procompetitive efficiencies, such as benefits in the use or dissemination of the technology. Each of the patent owners has a right to exclude others from using its patent. That right does not extend, however, to the agreement to assign rights jointly. To the extent that the patent rights cover technologies that are close substitutes, the joint determination of royalties likely would result in higher royalties and higher goods prices than would result if the owners licensed or used their technologies independently. In the absence of evidence establishing efficiency-enhancing integration from the joint assignment of patent rights, the Agency may conclude that the joint marketing of competing patent rights constitutes horizontal price fixing and could be challenged as a per se unlawful horizontal restraint of trade. If the joint marketing arrangement results in an efficiency-enhancing integration, the Agency would evaluate the arrangement under the rule of reason. However, the Agency may conclude that the anticompetitive effects are sufficiently apparent, and the claimed integrative efficiencies are sufficiently weak or not reasonably related to the restraints, to warrant challenge of the arrangement without an elaborate analysis of particular industry circumstances (*see* section 3.4).

5.2 Resale price maintenance

Resale price maintenance is illegal when "commodities have passed into the channels of trade and are owned by dealers." *Dr. Miles Medical Co. v. John D. Park & Sons Co.*, 220 U.S. 373, 408 (1911). It has been held per se illegal for a licensor of an intellectual property right in a product to fix a licensee's *resale* price of that product. *United States v. Univis Lens Co.*, 316 U.S. 241 (1942); *Ethyl Gasoline Corp. v. United States*, 309 U.S. 436 (1940).[33]

[33] *But cf. United States v. General Electric Co.*, 272 U.S. 476 (1926) (holding that an owner of a product patent may condition a license to manufacture the product on the fixing of the *first* sale price

Consistent with the principles set forth in section 3.4, the Agencies will enforce the per se rule against resale price maintenance in the intellectual property context.

5.3 Tying arrangements

A "tying" or "tie-in" or "tied sale" arrangement has been defined as "an agreement by a party to sell one product . . . on the condition that the buyer also purchases a different (or tied) product, or at least agrees that he will not purchase that [tied] product from any other supplier." *Eastman Kodak Co. v. Image Technical Services, Inc.*, 112 S. Ct. 2072, 2079 (1992). Conditioning the ability of a licensee to license one or more items of intellectual property on the licensee's purchase of another item of intellectual property or a good or a service has been held in some cases to constitute illegal tying.[34] Although tying arrangements may result in anticompetitive effects, such arrangements can also result in significant efficiencies and procompetitive benefits. In the exercise of their prosecutorial discretion, the Agencies will consider both the anticompetitive effects and the efficiencies attributable to a tie-in. The Agencies would be likely to challenge a tying arrangement if: (1) the seller has market power in the tying product,[35] (2) the arrangement has an adverse effect on competition in the relevant market for the tied product, and (3) efficiency justifications for the arrangement do not outweigh the anticompetitive effects.[36] The Agencies will not presume that a patent, copyright, or trade secret necessarily confers market power upon its owner.

---

of the patented product). Subsequent lower court decisions have distinguished the *GE* decision in various contexts. *See, e.g., Royal Indus. v. St. Regis Paper Co.*, 420 F.2d 449, 452 (9th Cir. 1969) (observing that *GE* involved a restriction by a patentee who also manufactured the patented product and leaving open the question whether a nonmanufacturing patentee may fix the price of the patented product); *Newburgh Moire Co. v. Superior Moire Co.*, 237 F.2d 283, 293–94 (3rd Cir. 1956) (grant of multiple licenses each containing price restrictions does not come within the *GE* doctrine); *Cummer-Graham Co. v. Straight Side Basket Corp.*, 142 F.2d 646, 647 (5th Cir.) (owner of an intellectual property right in a process to manufacture an unpatented product may not fix the sale price of that product), *cert. denied*, 323 U.S. 726 (1944); *Barber-Colman Co. v. National Tool Co.*, 136 F.2d 339, 343–44 (6th Cir. 1943) (same).

[34] *See, e.g., United States v. Paramount Pictures, Inc.*, 334 U.S. 131, 156–58 (1948) (copyrights); *International Salt Co. v. United States*, 332 U.S. 392 (1947) (patent and related product).

[35] *Cf.* 35 U.S.C. § 271(d) (1988 & Supp. V 1993) (requirement of market power in patent misuse cases involving tying).

[36] As is true throughout these Guidelines, the factors listed are those that guide the Agencies' internal analysis in exercising their prosecutorial discretion. They are not intended to circumscribe how the Agencies will conduct the litigation of cases that they decide to bring.

Package licensing—the licensing of multiple items of intellectual property in a single license or in a group of related licenses—may be a form of tying arrangement if the licensing of one product is conditioned upon the acceptance of a license of another, separate product. Package licensing can be efficiency enhancing under some circumstances. When multiple licenses are needed to use any single item of intellectual property, for example, a package license may promote such efficiencies. If a package license constitutes a tying arrangement, the Agencies will evaluate its competitive effects under the same principles they apply to other tying arrangements.

5.4 Exclusive dealing

In the intellectual property context, exclusive dealing occurs when a license prevents the licensee from licensing, selling, distributing, or using competing technologies. Exclusive dealing arrangements are evaluated under the rule of reason. *See Tampa Electric Co. v. Nashville Coal Co.*, 365 U.S. 320 (1961) (evaluating legality of exclusive dealing under section 1 of the Sherman Act and section 3 of the Clayton Act); *Beltone Electronics Corp.*, 100 F.T.C. 68 (1982) (evaluating legality of exclusive dealing under section 5 of the Federal Trade Commission Act). In determining whether an exclusive dealing arrangement is likely to reduce competition in a relevant market, the Agencies will take into account the extent to which the arrangement (1) promotes the exploitation and development of the licensor's technology and (2) anticompetitively forecloses the exploitation and development of, or otherwise constrains competition among, competing technologies.

The likelihood that exclusive dealing may have anticompetitive effects is related, inter alia, to the degree of foreclosure in the relevant market, the duration of the exclusive dealing arrangement, and other characteristics of the input and output markets, such as concentration, difficulty of entry, and the responsiveness of supply and demand to changes in price in the relevant markets. (*See* sections 4.1.1 and 4.1.2.) If the Agencies determine that a particular exclusive dealing arrangement may have an anticompetitive effect, they will evaluate the extent to which the restraint encourages licensees to develop and market the licensed technology (or specialized applications of that technology), increases licensors' incentives to develop or refine the licensed technology, or otherwise increases competition and enhances output in a relevant market. (*See* section 4.2 and Example 8.)

5.5 Cross-licensing and pooling arrangements

Cross-licensing and pooling arrangements are agreements of two or more owners of different items of intellectual property to license one another or third parties. These arrangements may provide procompetitive benefits by integrating complementary technologies, reducing transaction costs, clearing blocking positions, and avoiding costly infringement litigation. By promoting the dissemination of technology, cross-licensing and pooling arrangements are often procompetitive.

Cross-licensing and pooling arrangements can have anticompetitive effects in certain circumstances. For example, collective price or output restraints in pooling arrangements, such as the joint marketing of pooled intellectual property rights with collective price setting or coordinated output restrictions, may be deemed unlawful if they do not contribute to an efficiency-enhancing integration of economic activity among the participants. *Compare NCAA* 468 U.S. at 114 (output restriction on college football broadcasting held unlawful because it was not reasonably related to any purported justification) *with Broadcast Music*, 441 U.S. at 23 (blanket license for music copyrights found not per se illegal because the cooperative price was necessary to the creation of a new product). When cross-licensing or pooling arrangements are mechanisms to accomplish naked price fixing or market division, they are subject to challenge under the per se rule. *See United States v. New Wrinkle, Inc.*, 342 U.S. 371 (1952) (price fixing).

Settlements involving the cross-licensing of intellectual property rights can be an efficient means to avoid litigation and, in general, courts favor such settlements. When such cross-licensing involves horizontal competitors, however, the Agencies will consider whether the effect of the settlement is to diminish competition among entities that would have been actual or likely potential competitors in a relevant market in the absence of the cross-license. In the absence of offsetting efficiencies, such settlements may be challenged as unlawful restraints of trade. *Cf. United States v. Singer Manufacturing Co.*, 374 U.S. 174 (1963) (cross-license agreement was part of broader combination to exclude competitors).

Pooling arrangements generally need not be open to all who would like to join. However, exclusion from cross-licensing and pooling arrangements among parties that collectively possess market power may, under some circumstances, harm competition. *Cf. Northwest Wholesale Stationers, Inc. v. Pacific Stationery & Printing Co.*, 472 U.S. 284 (1985) (exclusion of a competitor from a purchasing cooperative not per se unlawful absent a showing of market power). In general, exclusion from a pooling or cross-licensing arrangement among competing technologies is unlikely to have anticompetitive effects unless (1) excluded firms cannot effectively compete in the relevant market for the good incorporating the licensed technologies and (2) the pool participants collectively possess market power in the relevant market. If these circumstances exist, the Agencies will evaluate whether the arrangement's limitations on participation are reasonably related to the efficient development and exploitation of the pooled technologies and will assess the net effect of those limitations in the relevant market. *See* section 4.2.

Another possible anticompetitive effect of pooling arrangements may occur if the arrangement deters or discourages participants from engaging in research and development, thus retarding innovation. For example, a pooling arrangement that requires members to grant licenses to each other for current and future technology at minimal cost may reduce the incentives of its members to engage in research and development because members of the pool have to share their successful research and development and each of the members can free ride on the accomplishments of other pool members. *See generally United States v. Mfrs. Aircraft Ass'n, Inc.*, 1976-1 Trade Cas. (CCH) ¶ 60,810 (S.D.N.Y. 1975); *United States v. Automobile Mfrs. Ass'n*, 307 F. Supp. 617 (C.D. Cal 1969), *appeal dismissed sub nom. City of New York v. United States*, 397 U.S. 248 (1970), *modified sub nom. United States v. Motor Vehicle Mfrs. Ass'n*, 1982–83 Trade Cas. (CCH) ¶ 65,088 (C.D. Cal. 1982). However, such an arrangement can have procompetitive benefits, for example, by exploiting economies of scale and integrating complementary capabilities of the pool members, (including the clearing of blocking positions), and is likely to cause competitive problems only when the arrangement includes a large fraction of the potential research and development in an innovation market. *See* section 3.2.3 and Example 4.

Example 10

Situation: As in Example 9, two of the leading manufacturers of a consumer electronic product hold patents that cover alternative circuit designs for the product. The manufacturers assign several of their patents to a separate corporation wholly owned by the two firms. That corporation licenses the right to use the circuit designs to other consumer product manufacturers and establishes the license royalties. In this example, however, the manufacturers assign to the separate corporation only patents that are blocking. None of the patents assigned to the corporation can be used without infringing a patent owned by the other firm.

Discussion: Unlike the previous example, the joint assignment of patent rights to the wholly owned corporation in this example does not adversely affect competition in the licensed technology among entities that would have been actual or likely potential competitors in the absence of the licensing arrangement. Moreover, the licensing arrangement is likely to have procompetitive benefits in the use of the technology. Because the manufacturers' patents are blocking, the manufacturers are not in a horizontal relationship with respect to those patents. None of the patents can be used without the right to a patent owned by the other firm, so the patents are not substitutable. As in Example 9, the firms are horizontal competitors in the relevant goods market. In the absence of collateral restraints that would likely raise price or reduce output in the relevant goods market or in any other relevant antitrust market and that are not reasonably related to an efficiency-enhancing integration of economic activity, the evaluating Agency would be unlikely to challenge this arrangement.

5.6 Grantbacks

A grantback is an arrangement under which a licensee agrees to extend to the licensor of intellectual property the right to use the licensee's improvements to the licensed technology. Grantbacks can have procompetitive effects, especially if they are nonexclusive. Such arrangements provide a means for the licensee and the licensor to share risks and reward the licensor for making possible further innovation based on or informed by the licensed technology, and both promote innovation in the first place and promote the subsequent licensing of the results of the innovation. Grantbacks may adversely affect competition, however, if they substantially reduce the licensee's incentives to engage in research and development and thereby limit rivalry in innovation markets.

A non-exclusive grantback allows the licensee to practice its technology and license it to others. Such a grantback provision may be necessary to ensure that the licensor is not prevented from effectively competing because it is denied access to improvements developed with the aid of its own technology. Compared with an exclusive grantback, a non-exclusive grantback, which leaves the licensee free to license improvements technology to others, is less likely to have anticompetitive effects.

The Agencies will evaluate a grantback provision under the rule of reason, *see generally Transparent-Wrap Machine Corp. v. Stokes & Smith Co.*, 329 U.S. 637, 645–48 (1947) (grantback provision in technology license is not per se unlawful), considering its likely effects in light of the overall structure of the licensing arrangement and conditions in the relevant markets. An important factor in the Agencies' analysis of a grantback will be whether the licensor has market power in a relevant technology or innovation market. If the Agencies determine that a particular grantback provision is likely to reduce significantly licensees' incentives to invest in improving the licensed technology, the Agencies will consider the extent to which the grantback provision has offsetting procompetitive effects, such as (1) promoting dissemination of licensees' improvements to the licensed technology, (2) increasing the licensors' incentives to disseminate the licensed technology, or (3) otherwise increasing competition and output in a relevant technology or innovation market. *See* section 4.2. In addition, the Agencies will consider the extent to which grantback provisions in the relevant markets generally increase licensors' incentives to innovate in the first place.

5.7 Acquisition of intellectual property rights

Certain transfers of intellectual property rights are most appropriately analyzed by applying the principles and standards used to analyze mergers, particularly those in the 1992 Horizontal Merger Guidelines. The Agencies will apply a merger analysis to an outright sale by an intellectual property owner of all of its rights to that intellectual property and to a transaction in which a person obtains through grant, sale, or other transfer an exclusive license for intellectual property (i.e., a license that precludes all other persons, including the licensor, from using the licensed intellectual property).[37] Such transactions may be assessed under section 7 of the Clayton Act, sections 1 and 2 of the Sherman Act, and section 5 of the Federal Trade Commission Act.

Example 11

Situation: Omega develops a new, patented pharmaceutical for the treatment of a particular disease. The only drug on the market approved for the treatment of this disease is sold by Delta. Omega's patented drug has almost completed regulatory approval by the Food and Drug Administration. Omega has invested considerable sums in product development and market testing, and initial results show that Omega's drug would be a significant competitor to Delta's. However, rather than enter the market as a direct competitor of Delta, Omega licenses to Delta the right to manufacture and sell Omega's patented drug. The license agreement with Delta is nominally nonexclusive. However, Omega has rejected all requests by other firms to obtain a license to manufacture and sell Omega's patented drug, despite offers by those firms of terms that are reasonable in relation to those in Delta's license.

Discussion: Although Omega's license to Delta is nominally nonexclusive, the circumstances indicate that it is exclusive in fact because Omega has rejected all reasonable offers by other firms for licenses to manufacture and sell Omega's patented drug. The facts of this example indicate that Omega would be a likely potential competitor of Delta in the absence of the licensing arrangement, and thus they are in a horizontal relationship in the relevant goods market that includes drugs for the treatment of this particular disease. The evaluating Agency would apply a merger analysis to this transaction, since it involves an acquisition of a likely potential competitor.

---

[37] The safety zone of section 4.3 does not apply to transfers of intellectual property such as those described in this section.

6. Enforcement of invalid intellectual property rights

The Agencies may challenge the enforcement of invalid intellectual property rights as antitrust violations. Enforcement or attempted enforcement of a patent obtained by fraud on the Patent and Trademark Office or the Copyright Office may violate section 2 of the Sherman Act, if all the elements otherwise necessary to establish a section 2 charge are proved, or section 5 of the Federal Trade Commission Act. *Walker Process Equipment, Inc. v. Food Machinery & Chemical Corp.*, 382 U.S. 172 (1965) (patents); *American Cyanamid Co.*, 72 F.T.C. 623, 684–85 (1967), *aff'd sub. nom. Charles Pfizer & Co.*, 401 F.2d 574 (6th Cir. 1968), *cert. denied*, 394 U.S. 920 (1969) (patents); *Michael Anthony Jewelers, Inc. v. Peacock Jewelry, Inc.*, 795 F. Supp. 639, 647 (S.D.N.Y. 1992) (copyrights). Inequitable conduct before the Patent and Trademark Office will not be the basis of a section 2 claim unless the conduct also involves knowing and willful fraud and the other elements of a section 2 claim are present. *Argus Chemical Corp. v. Fibre Glass-Evercoat, Inc.*, 812 F.2d 1381, 1384–85 (Fed. Cir. 1987). Actual or attempted enforcement of patents obtained by inequitable conduct that falls short of fraud under some circumstances may violate section 5 of the Federal Trade Commission Act, *American Cyanamid Co., supra.* Objectively baseless litigation to enforce invalid intellectual property rights may also constitute an element of a violation of the Sherman Act. *See Professional Real Estate Investors, Inc. v. Columbia Pictures Industries, Inc.*, 113 S. Ct. 1920, 1928 (1993) (copyrights); *Handgards, Inc. v. Ethicon, Inc.*, 743 F.2d 1282, 1289 (9th Cir. 1984), *cert. denied*, 469 U.S. 1190 (1985) (patents); *Handgards, Inc. v. Ethicon, Inc.*, 601 F.2d 986, 992–96 (9th Cir. 1979), *cert. denied*, 444 U.S. 1025 (1980) (patents); *CVD, Inc. v. Raytheon Co.*, 769 F.2d 842 (1st Cir. 1985) (trade secrets), *cert. denied*, 475 U.S. 1016 (1986).

appendix B

Topical Index of Cases

I. Topical Index of Cases for Antitrust Issues in the Acquisition, Procurement, and Ownership of Intellectual Property

Table B.1

Section	Topic	Recent Cases
		Acquisition
§ 2.4	Monopolization	*Clean Conversion Techs. v. CleanTech Biofuels, Inc.*, 2012 U.S. Dist. LEXIS 117279 (S.D. Cal. 2012).
§ 2.6	Exclusivity	*United States v. United Techs. Corp. & Goodrich Corp.*, 77 Fed. Reg. 46,186 (Aug. 2, 2012).
§ 2.9	Grantbacks	*PNY Techs. v. SanDisk Corp.*, 2012 U.S. Dist. LEXIS 55965 (N.D. Cal. 2012).
		Procurement
§ 2.10	Securing Patents	*Arctic Cat, Inc. v. Polaris Indus., Inc.*, 2014 WL 532536 (D. Minn. 2014); *FTC v. Cephalon, Inc.*, 36 F. Supp. 3d 527 (E.D. Pa. 2014); *In re Lipitor Antitrust Litig.*, 2013 U.S. Dist. LEXIS 126468 (D.N.J. 2013); *Kimberly-Clark Worldwide, Inc. v. First Quality Baby Prods. LLC*, No. 14-cv-1466 (E.D. Wis. Apr. 9, 2015); *Tyco Healthcare Grp. v. Mut. Pharm. Co.*, No. 07-cv-01299 (D.N.J. 2013).
§ 2.11	Securing Copyrights and Trademarks	*S. Snow Mfg. v. SnoWizard Holdings*, 2013 U.S. Dist. LEXIS 22157 (E.D. La. 2013).

Section	Topic	Recent Cases
		Ownership
§ 2.12	Refusal to Sell or License	*Actelion Pharms., Ltd. v. Apotex Inc.*, No. 12-cv-05743 (D.N.J. filed Sept. 14, 2012); *Actelion Pharm., Ltd. v. Apotex Inc.*, 2013 U.S. Dist. LEXIS 135524 (D.N.J. Sept. 6, 2013); *Apple iPod iTunes Antitrust Litig.*, 796 F. Supp. 2d 1137 (N.D. Cal. 2011); *Bookhouse of Stuyvesant Plaza v. Amazon.com*, 2013 U.S. Dist. LEXIS 171871 (S.D.N.Y. 2013); *MiniFrame Ltd. v. Microsoft Corp.*, No. 11 Civ. 7419 (RJS), 2013 WL 1385704 (S.D.N.Y. Mar. 28, 2013); *Novell, Inc. v. Microsoft Corp.*, 731 F.3d 1064 (10th Cir. 2013); *Radio Music License Comm., Inc. v. SESAC, Inc.*, 29 F. Supp. 3d 487 (E.D. Pa. 2014).
§ 2.13	Group Boycott	*Cascades Computer Innovation v. RPX Corp.*, 2013 U.S. Dist. LEXIS 10526 (N.D. Cal. 2013); *In re Credit Default Swap Antitrust Litig.*, No. 13-md-2476, 2014 WL 4379112 (S.D.N.Y. Sept. 4, 2014); *Reg'l Multiple Listing Serv. of Minn., Inc. v. Am. Home Realty Network, Inc.*, 9 F. Supp. 3d 1032 (D. Minn. Mar. 31, 2014); *SD3, LLC v. Black & Decker, Inc.*, 2014 U.S. Dist. LEXIS 96256 (E.D. Va. 2014); *Sky Angel U.S., L.L.C. v. Nat'l Cable Satellite Corp.*, 947 F. Supp. 2d 88 (D.D.C. 2013); *TruePosition, Inc. v. Ericsson Tel. Co.*, 899 F. Supp. 2d 356 (E.D. Pa. 2012).
§ 2.14	Tying	*Oracle Am., Inc. v. Terix Computer Co.*, No. 5:13-cv-03385 (N.D. Cal. Nov. 7, 2014).

II. Topical Index of Cases for Antitrust Issues in Licensing Intellectual Property

Table B.2

Section	Topic	Recent Cases
	Licensing Restraints	
§ 3.2	Price	*SanDisk Corp. v. Kingston Tech. Co.*, 863 F. Supp. 2d 815 (D. Wis. 2012); *ZF Meritor, LLC v. Eaton Corp.*, 696 F.3d 254 (3d Cir. 2012).
§ 3.3	Output	*SanDisk Corp. v. Kingston Tech. Co.*, 863 F. Supp. 2d 815 (D. Wis. 2012); *Ohio Willow Wood Co. v. Alps S. LLC*, 2011 U.S. Dist. LEXIS 32688 (D. Ohio 2011).
§ 3.4	Customer	*Apple Inc. v. Psystar Corp.*, 658 F.3d 1150 (9th Cir. 2011); *Bowman v. Monsanto Co.*, 133 S. Ct. 1761 (2013); *Lexmark Int'l, Inc. v. Ink Tech. Printer Supplies, LLC*, 9 F. Supp. 3d 830 (S.D. Ohio 2014).
§ 3.5	Territory	*SanDisk Corp. v. Kingston Tech. Co.*, 863 F. Supp. 2d 815 (D. Wis. 2012); *PNY Techs. v. SanDisk Corp.*, 2012 U.S. Dist. LEXIS 55965 (N.D. Cal. 2012).
§ 3.6	Field of Use	*SanDisk Corp. v. Kingston Tech. Co.*, 863 F. Supp. 2d 815 (D. Wis. 2012).
§ 3.7	Exclusivity	*Am. Needle, Inc. v. New Orleans La. Saints*, 2014 WL 1364022 (N.D. Ill. 2014); *MedioStream, Inc. v. Microsoft Corp.*, 869 F. Supp. 2d 1095 (D. Cal. 2012); *Pharm. Research & Mfrs. of Am. v. FTC*, 44 F. Supp. 3d 95 (D.D.C. 2014); *Wis. Interscholastic Athletic Ass'n v. Gannett Co.*, 658 F.3d 614 (7th Cir. 2011); *ZF Meritor, LLC v. Eaton Corp.*, 696 F.3d 254 (3d Cir. 2012).

Section	Topic	Recent Cases
§ 3.8	Tying	*Apple Inc. v. Psystar Corp.*, 658 F.3d 1150 (9th Cir. 2011); *Cablevision Sys. Corp. v. Viacom Int'l Inc.*, 2014 WL 2805256 (S.D.N.Y. 2014); *Cherdak v. Vock*, 2012 U.S. Dist. LEXIS 57511 (D. Va. 2012); *Intellectual Ventures LLC et al. v. Symantec Corp.*, 2014 WL 4773954 (D. Del. 2014); *Lakeland Reg'l Med. Ctr. v. Astellas, LLC*, 2012 U.S. Dist. LEXIS 136990 (M.D. Fla. 2012); *Oracle Am., Inc. v. TERiX Computer Co.*, 2014 WL 31344 (N.D. Cal. 2014); *RealPage, Inc. v. Yardi Sys.*, 852 F. Supp. 2d 1215 (D. Cal. 2012); *Regas Christou v. Beatport, LLC*, 849 F. Supp. 2d 1055 (D. Colo. 2012); *ZF Meritor, LLC v. Eaton Corp.*, 696 F.3d 254 (3d Cir. 2012).
§ 3.9	Packaging/ Bundling	*Meredith Corp. v. SESAC LLC*, 1 F. Supp. 3d 180 (S.D.N.Y. 2014); *Radio Music License Comm., Inc. v. SESAC, Inc.*, 29 F. Supp. 3d 487 (E.D. Pa. 2014); *Synthes, Inc. v. Emerge Med., Inc.*, 2012 U.S. Dist. LEXIS 140251 (D. Pa. 2012).
§ 3.10	Royalties	*Altana Pharma v. Teva Pharm.*, 2012 U.S. Dist. LEXIS 79166 (D.N.J. 2012); *Keurig, Inc. v. Sturm Foods, Inc.*, 732 F.3d 1370 (Fed. Cir. 2013); *Kimble v. Marvel Enters. Inc.*, 727 F.3d 856 (9th Cir. 2013); *Kimble v. Marvel Enters., Inc.*, No. 13-720 (U.S. June 22, 2015); *Lexmark Int'l, Inc. v. Impression Prods., Inc.*, 785 F.3d 565 (Fed. Cir. 2015); *LifeScan Scotland, Ltd. v. Shasta Tech., LLC*, 734 F.3d 1361 (Fed. Cir. 2013); *MPEG LA, L.L.C. v GXI Int'l, LLC*, 2013 N.Y. Misc. LEXIS 2498 (N.Y. Sup. Ct. June 10, 2013); *Ninestar Tech. Co. v. ITC*, 667 F.3d 1373 (Fed. Cir. 2012); *Ohio Willow Wood Co. v. Alps S. LLC*, 2011 U.S. Dist. LEXIS 32688 (D. Ohio 2011); *PNY Techs. v. SanDisk Corp.*, 2012 U.S. Dist. LEXIS 55965 (N.D. Cal. 2012); *SanDisk Corp. v. Kingston Tech. Co.*, 863 F. Supp. 2d 815 (D. Wis. 2012); *Tessera, Inc. v. Int'l Trade Comm'n*, 646 F.3d 1357 (Fed. Cir. 2011).

Section	Topic	Recent Cases
§ 3.11	Grantbacks	
§ 3.12	Non-assertion	*Intergraph Corp. v. Intel Corp.*, 195 F.3d 1346 (Fed. Cir. 1999).
§ 3.13	No Challenge	*Indus. Eng'g & Dev., Inc. v. Static Control Components, Inc.*, 2013 U.S. Dist. LEXIS 8999 (M.D. Fla. Jan. 23, 2013); *Peparlet Co. v. Shepherd Specialty Papers, Inc.*, 2013 U.S. Dist. LEXIS 69738 (N.D. Ohio May 16, 2013); *Rates Tech., Inc. v. Speakeasy, Inc.*, 685 F.3d 163 (2d Cir. 2012).
§ 3.14	Noncompete	*Frontline Techs., Inc. v. CRS, Inc.*, 2012 U.S. Dist. LEXIS 104185 (D. Pa. 2012); *Behrend v. Comcast Corp.*, 2012 U.S. Dist. LEXIS 51889 (D. Pa. 2012).
Cross-License and Patent Pools		
§ 3.16	General	*SanDisk Corp. v. Kingston Tech. Co.*, 863 F. Supp. 2d 815 (D. Wis. 2012).

III. Topical Index of Cases for Antitrust Issues in Litigating Intellectual Property

Table B.3

Section	Topic	Recent Cases
		Procedural
§ 4.1	Jurisdiction	*Lotes Co. v. Hon Hai Precision Indus. Co.*, 753 F.3d 395 (2d Cir. 2014); *MPHJ Tech. Invs., LLC v. FTC*, 2014 WL 4724558 (W.D. Tex. 2014).
§ 4.2	Choice of Law	*Eng'g & Inspection Servs., LLC v. IntPar, LLC*, 2013 U.S. Dist. LEXIS 146849 (E.D. La. Oct. 9, 2013); *In re Lipitor Antitrust Litig.*, 2013 U.S. Dist. LEXIS 126468 (D.N.J. 2013); *IGT v. Alliance Gaming Corp.*, 702 F.3d 1338 (Fed. Cir. 2012); *Cornucopia Prods. v. Dyson, Inc.*, 2012 U.S. Dist. LEXIS 104753 (D. Ariz. 2012).
§ 4.3	Bifurcation	*Apotex Inc. v. Senju Pharm. Co.*, 921 F. Supp. 2d 308 (D. Del. 2013); *Cascades Computer Innovation v. RPX Corp.*, 2013 U.S. Dist. LEXIS 10526 (N.D. Cal. 2013); *Proctor & Gamble Co. v. CAO Grp.*, 2013 U.S. Dist. LEXIS 136675 (S.D. Ohio 2013); *Lincoln Elec. Co. v. Nat'l Standard, LLC*, 2012 U.S. Dist. LEXIS 115847 (N.D. Ohio 2012); *Otsuka Pharm. Co. v. Torrent Pharm., Inc.*, 2015 WL 3869677 (D.N.J. 2015).
§ 4.4.1	Motions to Dismiss	*Cascades Computer Innovation v. RPX Corp.*, 2013 U.S. Dist. LEXIS 10526, 2013 WL 316023 (N.D. Cal. Jan. 24, 2013); *Cherdak v Vock*, 2012 WL 1427847 (E.D. Va. Apr. 23, 2012); *Demodulation, Inc. v Applied DNA Scis., Inc.*, 2012 WL 6204172 (D.N.J. Dec. 12, 2012); *Eatoni Ergonomics, Inc. v Research In Motion Corp.*, No. 11-5328, 2012 WL 2348443 (2d Cir. June 21, 2012); *In re Nexium (Esomeprazole) Antitrust Litig.*, 42 F. Supp. 3d 231 (D. Mass. 2014); *Intellectual Ventures I LLC, et al. v. Capital One Fin. Corp., et al.*, No. 1:13-cv-00740, 2013 WL 6682981 (E.D. Va. Dec. 18, 2013); *King Drug Co. v. Cephalon, Inc.*, 2014 WL 2813312 (E.D. Pa. 2014).

Section	Topic	Recent Cases
§ 4.4.2	Failure to State a Claim	*IGT v Alliance Gaming Corp.*, 702 F.3d 1338 (Fed. Cir. 2012); *In re DDAVP Indirect Purchaser Antitrust Litig.*, 903 F. Supp. 2d 198 (S.D.N.Y. 2012).
§ 4.4.3	Lack of Antitrust Standing	*Ethypharm S.A. v. Abbott Labs.*, 707 F.3d 223 (3d Cir. 2013); *Fido's Fences, Inc. v. Radio Sys. Corp.*, 999 F. Supp. 2d 442 (E.D.N.Y. 2014); *Motorola Mobility LLC v. AU Optronics Corp.*, 775 F.3d 816 (7th Cir. 2014).
§ 4.4.4	Antitrust in ANDA Litigation (without Reverse Payment Provisions)	*In re Adderall XR Antitrust Litig.*, 754 F.3d 128 (2d Cir. 2014); *SmithKline Beecham Corp. v. Abbott Labs.*, No. C 07-5702 CW, 2014 WL 6664226 (N.D. Cal. Nov. 24, 2014).
§ 4.4.5	Antitrust and Professional Rights Organizations	*Meredith Corp. v. SESAC LLC*, 1 F. Supp. 3d 180 (S.D.N.Y. 2014); *Radio Music License Comm., Inc. v. SESAC, Inc.*, 29 F. Supp. 3d 487 (E.D. Pa. 2014); *Retractable Techs., Inc. v. Becton, Dickinson & Co.*, No. 2:08-cv-16, 2013 WL 4806905 (E.D. Tex. Sept. 9, 2013).
§ 4.4.6	Antitrust and Professional Sports Leagues	*Abraham & Veneklasen Joint Venture v. Am. Quarter Horse Ass'n*, 776 F.3d 321 (5th Cir. 2015); *Dang v. S.F. Forty Niners*, 964 F. Supp. 2d 1097 (N.D. Cal. 2013); *O'Bannon v. Nat'l Collegiate Athletic Ass'n*, 7 F. Supp. 3d 955 (N.D. Cal. 2014).
§ 4.5	Counterclaims	*Cascades Computer Innovation v. RPX Corp.*, 2013 U.S. Dist. LEXIS 10526 (N.D. Cal. 2013); *MGA Entm't v. Mattel, Inc.*, 2012 U.S. Dist. LEXIS 22055 (C.D. Cal. 2012); *Nalco Co. v. Turner Designs, Inc.*, 2014 WL 645365 (N.D. Cal. 2014); *Reg'l Multiple Listing Serv. of Minn., Inc. v. Am. Home Realty Network, Inc.*, 9 F. Supp. 3d 1032 (D. Minn. 2014).
§ 4.6	Pleading	*Evergreen Partnering Grp., Inc. v. Pactiv Corp*, 720 F.3d 33, 47 (1st Cir. 2013); *Oliver v. SD-3C LLC*, 751 F.3d 1081 (9th Cir. 2014); *Samsung Elec. Co. v. Panasonic Corp.*, 747 F.3d 1199 (9th Cir. 2014).
§ 4.7	Discovery	*In re Aspartame Antitrust Litig.*, 817 F. Supp. 2d 608 (E.D. Pa. 2011.

Section	Topic	Recent Cases
§ 4.8	Remedies	*Ace Arts, LLC v. Sony/ATV Music Publ'g, LLC*, 56 F. Supp. 3d 436 (S.D.N.Y. 2014); *FTC v. Cephalon, Inc.*, No. 2:08-cv-2141, 2015 WL 1724597 (E.D. Pa. Apr. 15, 2015); *In re Aspartame Antitrust Litig.*, 817 F. Supp. 2d 608 (E.D. Pa. 2011); *In re Corelogic, Inc.*, FTC Docket No. C-4450 (May 20, 2014); *In re Nielsen Holdings N.V. & Arbitron, Inc.*, FTC Docket No. C-4439 (Feb. 24, 2014); *O'Bannon v. NCAA*, 7 F. Supp. 3d 955 (N.D. Cal. 2014).
Enforcement		
§ 4.9	*Noerr-Pennington*	*Zenith Elecs. Corp. v. Exzec, Inc.*, 182 F.3d 1340, 1352–55 (Fed. Cir. 1999).
§ 4.10	Illegally Obtained Patents: *Walker* Process	*Adobe Sys. Inc. v Coffee Cup Partners, Inc.*, No. C11-2243, 2012 WL 3877783 (N.D. Cal. Sept. 6, 2012); *Apple, Inc. v. Motorola Mobility, Inc.*, 886 F. Supp. 2d 1061 (W.D. Wis. 2012); *AstraZeneca AB v. Glenmark Generics Ltd.*, No. CV 14-665-GMS, 2014 WL 5366050 (D. Del. Oct. 9, 2014); *Breville Pty Ltd. v. Storebound LLC*, 2013 U.S. Dist. LEXIS 58893 (N.D. Cal. 2013); *Cascades Computer Innovation v. RPX Corp.*, 2013 U.S. Dist. LEXIS 10526, 2013 WL 316023 (N.D. Cal. Jan. 24, 2013); *Clean Conversion Techs., Inc. v CleanTech Biofuels, Inc.*, No. 12-cv-239-L, 2012 WL 3585171 (S.D. Cal. Aug. 20, 2012); *In re Androgel Antitrust Litig.*, 2012 U.S. Dist. LEXIS 140259 (N.D. Ga. 2012); *In re Androgel Antitrust Litig. (No. II)*, 2014 WL 1600331 (N.D. Ga. 2014); *In re Nexium (Esomeprazole) Antitrust Litig.*, 968 F. Supp. 2d 367 (D. Mass. 2013); *In re Skelaxin (Metaxalone) Antitrust Litig.*, 2013 U.S. Dist. LEXIS 70968 (E.D. Tenn. 2013); *In re Wellbutrin XL*, 2012 U.S. Dist. LEXIS 66312 (E.D. Pa. 2012); *Person Educ., Inc. v. Allen Air Conditioning Co.*, 2014 U.S. Dist. LEXIS 70464 (S.D.N.Y. 2014); *TransWeb, LLC v. 3M Innovative Props. Co.*, 16 F. Supp. 3d 385 (D.N.J. 2014).

Section	Topic	Recent Cases
§ 4.11	Other Examples of Inequitable Conduct: *Pick-Barth* Doctrine	*FTC v. Cephalon, Inc.*, 36 F. Supp. 3d 527 (E.D. Pa. 2014); *Kimberly-Clark Worldwide Inc. v. First Quality Baby Prods. LLC*, No. 14-cv-1466, 2015 WL 1582368 (E.D. Wis. Apr. 9, 2015); *Moldex Metric, Inc. v. 3M Co.*, No. CIV. 14-1821 JNE/FLN, 2015 WL 520722 (D. Minn. Feb. 9, 2015); *RB Rubber Prods., Inc. v. Ecore Int'l, Inc.*, No. 3:11-cv-319-AC, 2012 WL 860416 (D. Or. Mar. 13, 2012); *Ring Plus, Inc. v. Cingular Wireless Corp.*, 614 F.3d 1354, 1361 (Fed. Cir. 2010); *Therasense, Inc. v. Becton, Dickinson & Co.*, 649 F.3d 1276, 1289 (Fed. Cir. 2011); *Tyco Healthcare Grp. v. Mut. Pharm.*, No. 07-cv-01299-SRC (D.N.J. 2013); *Tyco Healthcare Grp. v. Mut. Pharm.*, 762 F.3d 1338 (Fed. Cir. 2014); *WesternGeco, LLC v. Ion Geophysical Corp.*, 2012 U.S. Dist. LEXIS 21246 (S.D. Tex. 2012).
	Defenses	
§ 4.12	Patent Misuse	*Altana Pharma AG v. Teva Pharm. USA*, 2012 U.S. Dist. LEXIS 79166 (D.N.J. 2012); *Cadence Pharm. v. Paddock Labs.*, 2012 U.S. Dist. LEXIS 142585 (D. Del. 2012); *Eatoni Ergonomics, Inc. v. Research In Motion Corp.*, 826 F. Supp. 2d 705 (S.D.N.Y. 2011); *In re Lipitor Antitrust Litig.*, 2013 U.S. Dist. LEXIS 126468 (D.N.J. 2013); *In re Skelaxin Antitrust Litig.*, 2013 U.S. Dist. LEXIS 70968 (E.D. Tenn. 2013); *Intellectual Ventures I v. Capital One Fin. Corp.*, 2013 U.S. Dist. LEXIS 177836 (E.D. Va. 2013); *Masimo Corp. v. Philips Elecs. N.A. Corp. et al.*, 2015 WL 2406155 (D. Del. 2015); *Princo Corp. v. Int'l Trade Comm'n*, 616 F.3d 1318, 1329 (Fed. Cir. 2010).
§ 4.13	Copyright Misuse	*IDI Design Inc. v. A.O.D. Jewelry Co.*, 2014 WL 661355 (S.D.N.Y. 2014); *Malibu Media v. Doe*, 2014 WL 2616902 (E.D. Mich. 2014); *Oracle Am., Inc. v. Terix Computer Co.*, 2014 WL 5847532 (N.D. Cal. 2014); *Oracle Am., Inc. v. Terix Computer Co.*, 2015 WL 1886968 (N.D. Cal. 2015).
§ 4.14	Trademark Misuse	*RJ Mach. Co. v. Can. Pipeline Accessories Co.*, 2013 U.S. Dist. 186426 (W.D. Tex. 2013).

IV. Topical Index of Cases for Antitrust Issues in ANDA Litigation

Table B.4

Section	Topic	Recent Cases
§ 5.1	Reverse Payments	*FTC v. Actavis, Inc.*, 133 S. Ct. 2223 (2013); *FTC v. Watson Pharm.*, 677 F.3d 1298 (11th Cir. 2012); *FTC v. Watson Pharm.*, 2012 U.S. LEXIS 9415 (2012); *In re Aggrenox Antitrust Litig.*, No. 3:14-MD-2516 SRU, 2015 WL 1311352 (D. Conn. Mar. 23, 2015); *In re Effexor XR Antitrust Litig.*, No. CIV.A. 11-5479 PGS, 2014 WL 4988410 (D.N.J. Oct. 6, 2014); *In re K-Dur Antitrust Litig.*, 686 F.3d 197 (3d Cir. 2012); *In re Lamictal Direct Purchaser Antitrust Litig.*, 2012 U.S. Dist. LEXIS 183627 (D.N.J. 2012); *In re Lamictal Direct Purchaser Antitrust Litig.*, 18 F. Supp. 3d 560 (D.N.J. 2014); *In re Nexium (Esomeprazole) Antitrust Litig.*, 968 F. Supp. 2d 367 (D. Mass. 2013); *In re Niaspan Antitrust Litig.*, 42 F. Supp. 3d 735 (E.D. Pa. 2014); *King Drug Co. of Florence v. Cephalon, Inc.*, No. 2:06-cv-1797, 2015 WL 356913 (E.D. Pa. Jan. 28, 2015); *La. Wholesale Drug Co. v. Shire LLC*, 12 CIV. 3711 VM, 2013 WL 950833 (S.D.N.Y. Mar. 6, 2013); *In re Lipitor Antitrust Litig.*, 46 F. Supp. 3d 523 (D.N.J. 2014); *In re Loestrin 24 Fe Antitrust Litig.*, 45 F. Supp. 3d 180 (D.R.I. 2014); *In re Suboxone (Buprenorphine Hydrochloride & Naloxone) Antitrust Litig.*, 2014 WL 6792663 (E.D. Pa. 2014); *In re Wellbutrin XL Antitrust Litig.*, No. 08cv-2431 (E.D. Pa. Jan. 17, 2014) (No. 534); *Mylan Pharm. v. Warner Chilcott PLC*, 2015 WL 1736957 (E.D. Pa. 2015); *United Food & Commercial Workers Local 1776 & Participating Employers Health & Welfare Fund v. Teikoku Pharma USA, Inc.*, 2014 WL 6465235 (N.D. Cal. 2014).

V. Topical Index of Cases for Antitrust Issues for Standard Essential Patents

Table B.5

Section	Topic	Recent Cases
§ 6.1	FRAND Commitments	*Apple, Inc. v. Motorola, Inc.*, 2011 U.S. Dist. LEXIS 156969 (W.D. Wis. Oct. 13, 2011); *Ericsson Inc. v. D-Link Sys., Inc.*, 2013 U.S. Dist. LEXIS 110585 (E.D. Tex. Aug. 6, 2013); *Ericsson, Inc. v. D-Link Sys., Inc.*, 773 F.3d 1201 (Fed. Cir. 2014); *In re Innovatio IP Ventures, LLC Patent Litig.*, 886 F. Supp. 2d 888 (N.D. Ill. 2012); *Microsoft Corp. v. Motorola, Inc.*, 871 F. Supp. 2d 1089 (W.D. Wash. 2012); *Microsoft Corp. v. Motorola, Inc.*, 696 F.3d 872 (9th Cir. Wash. 2012).
§ 6.2	Duty to Disclose Obligation	*Apple Inc. v. Samsung Elecs.*, 2012 U.S. Dist. LEXIS 9932 (N.D. Cal. Jan. 27, 2012); *Barnes & Noble, Inc. v. LSI Corp.*, 2012 U.S. Dist. LEXIS 12719 (N.D. Cal. Feb. 2, 2012).
§ 6.3	Royalties	*Commonwealth Sci. & Indus. Research Org. v. Cisco Sys., Inc.*, 2014 WL 3805817 (E.D. Tex. 2014); *Ericsson, Inc. v. D-Link Sys.*, 773 F.3d 1201 (Fed. Cir. 2014); *Realtek Semiconductor Corp. v. LSI Corp.*, 2014 U.S. Dist. LEXIS 81673 (N.D. Cal. 2014).
§ 6.4	Injunctions and Exclusion Orders	*Apple Inc. v. Motorola, Inc.*, 869 F. Supp. 2d 901, 2012 WL 2376664 (N.D. Ill. June 22, 2012); *Apple, Inc. v. Motorola Mobility, Inc.*, 886 F. Supp. 2d 1061 (W.D. Wis. 2012);

appendix C

Table of Authorities

Index

NOTE: Information from footnotes is indicated by an n and note number following the page number.

M

N

S

About the ABA Section of Intellectual Property Law

From its strength within the American Bar Association, the ABA Section of Intellectual Property Law (ABA-IPL) advances the development and improvement of intellectual property laws and their fair and just administration. The Section furthers the goals of its members by sharing knowledge and balanced insight on the full spectrum of intellectual property law and practice, including patents, trademarks, copyright, industrial design, literary and artistic works, scientific works, and innovation. Providing a forum for rich perspectives and reasoned commentary, ABA-IPL serves as the ABA voice of intellectual property law within the profession, before policy makers, and with the public.